POCAHONTAS

POCAHONTAS

POCAHONTAS
The Life and the Legend

FRANCES MOSSIKER

DA CAPO PRESS

Library of Congress Cataloging in Publication Data

Mossiker, Frances.
    Pocahontas: the life and the legend   /   Frances Mossiker.
        p.   cm.
    Oiriginally published: New York: Knopf, 1976.
    Includes bibliographical references and index.
    ISBN 0-306-80699-1
    1. Pocahontas, d. 1617. 2. Powhatan women—Biography. 3. Powhatan
Indians—History. 4. Indians of North America—Virginia—First contact
with Europeans. 5. Jamestown (Va.)—History. I. Title.
E99.P85P575   1996
975.5'01'092—dc20   95-43815
[B]   CIP

*Since this page cannot legibly accommodate all
permissions and copyright acknowledgments,
they can be found following the index.*

First Da Capo Press edition 1996

This Da Capo Press paperback edition of *Pocahontas* is an unabridged
republication of the edition first published in New York in 1976.
It is reprinted by arrangement with Alfred A. Knopf, Inc.

Published by Da Capo Press
A Member of the Perseus Books Group
http://www.dacapopress.com

To the memory of my grandfather,
ALEXANDER SANGER,
and my grandmother,
FLORENCE BEEKMAN

*"In the beginning,
All America was Virginia"*

WILLIAM BYRD

Contents

Eight pages of illustrations will be found
following page 144

Acknowledgments

THE ACKNOWLEDGMENTS PAGE provides the author a welcome opportunity to thank publicly those persons who have so generously given her of their time and allowed her to draw upon their special stores of knowledge. The long list begins—and not merely for alphabetical reasons—with the name of Mrs. Benjamin P. Alsop, Jr., of Upper Shirley, Charles City, Virginia, who furnished me a state-wide *passe-partout*. Among those Virginians to whom I here express gratitude for their many courtesies are Mrs. John W. Riely, President (in 1970) of the Association for the Preservation of Virginia Antiquities; Mr. John Melville Jennings, Director of the Virginia Historical Society; Mr. Randolph W. Church, State Librarian, and Mr. Milton C. Russell, Head of Reference and Circulation Department, Virginia State Library, Richmond. I owe much to Dr. Jane Carson of the Institute of Early American History of Colonial Williamsburg and to Dr. Ben McCary of the College of William and Mary, for both their erudition and their kindness; as I do also to Mr. Paul Hudson, Museum Curator at Jamestown, and to his interpretive staff. Thanks are due, as well, to the rangers of the National Park Service who acted as my guides on numerous tours of the Colonial National Historical Park. I could have found no more knowledgeable *cicerone* at Jamestown than Mr. Park Rouse, Jr., Executive-Director of the Jamestown Foundation; I am much obliged to him for his gracious and tireless efforts to reconstruct for me the seventeenth-century scene.

In Texas, as well as in Virginia, I have amassed many debts of gratitude: to Judge Irving L. Goldberg, United States Court of Appeals for the Fifth Circuit, for his painstaking interpretation of seventeenth-century legal instruments; to the Reverend Henry C. Coke III, for his enlightening comments on seventeenth-century Anglican ritual; to Dr. Harold W. Kimmerling, for the application of modern medical knowledge in the diagnosis of Pocahontas's final illness. And I take this occasion warmly to thank Dr. William Pulte, a linguist in Southern Methodist University's Department of Anthropology, who—from out of his experience with Algonkian-speaking tribes—revived for me the sound of Pocahontas's voice and patterns of speech. Here, too, I express my profound appreciation for the psychoanalytical skills of the late Dr. Robert T. Long, brought to bear on Pocahontas as girl and woman: my delineation of her owes much to Dr. Long's rare insight into character and motivation.

At the Dallas Public Library, Ms. Phyllis Mulke and Erma McClure often worked the wonders of the Inter-Library Loan for my benefit, while librarians Linda Robinson, Lloyd Bockstruck, and Roger Carroll have all lent a helping hand in the clarification of one or another obscure point in genealogy or geography. Librarian Sue Herzog Johnson of the De Golyer Western Library at Southern Methodist University produced a number of rare items from her shelves (including a first edition of Purchas's *Pilgrimes*); while at Southern Methodist University's Fondren Library, the endeavors of the periodicals librarian, Anne Bailey, on my behalf exceeded the call of duty.

His Excellency Wiley T. Buchanan, presently United States Ambassador to Vienna, escorted me in the spring of 1970 to the offices of his friends at the head of various Washington libraries, museums, and galleries. In London, he had earlier enlisted on my behalf the good offices of the Cultural Attaché at our Embassy.

The courtesies of Dr. L. Quincy Mumford, Librarian of the Library of Congress in 1970; of Ms. Gladys Fields, Dr. Mumford's secretary, and of Mr. Robert Land, Chief of General Reference and Bibliography, contributed to the pleasure as well as to the success of my research mission there. I am grateful, too, to the staff of the Library of Congress's Local History and Genealogy Room for guidance and suggestions. At the National Portrait Gallery of the Smithsonian Institution, I have the Director, Dr. Charles Nagel, and the Research Assistant, Mr. Monroe H. Fabian, to thank for the detailed provenance of the Pocahontas portrait. In the National Anthropological Archives (Bureau of American Ethnology, Smithsonian Institution), Mrs. J. C. Scherer in the office of Dr. Margaret Balker, Department of Anthropology, helped me to locate material relative to Virginia Indians.

At the New York Public Library, Mr. Walter J. Zervas, the Administrative Assistant, made my task easier by assigning me a desk in the Wertheim Study, and I owe thanks, as well, to the staff of the Arents Collection, New York Public Library, and to Mr. Perry O'Neil, in particular, who gave me the benefit of his expertise in the exotic field of tobacco.

I am obliged to Mr. T. S. Wragg, Librarian and Keeper of the Devonshire Collections, Chatsworth Foundation, for his courtesies. At the British Museum, my work in the Reading Room, in the Print Room, and in the Manuscript Room was facilitated by the staff.

I was fortunate to have secured the services of Suzanne Naiburg Asher as a research assistant in England in 1968; thanks to her, documentation for this book was gathered at the Bodleian Library, Oxford, and the British Museum, the Victoria and Albert Museum, the Guild Hall, the Public Records Office, the Historical Manuscripts Commission, and Middlesex County Hall, London. I was fortunate, too, in having Mrs. Esther Swift, expert and meticulous as she is, to help me in preparing the final drafts of my manuscript. At the office of my publishers, Ms. Martha Kaplan has aided me in searching out, assembling, and selecting the illustrations for this volume. I have also enjoyed the assistance of Mr. Lee Goerner of that office. To have had Mr. Robert Gottlieb, president of Alfred A. Knopf, Inc., as editor for this book—as for all the others I have written—constitutes the happiest circumstance of all those recited in these acknowledgments. I rejoice in our long association.

F. M.

POCAHONTAS

POCAHONTAS

PROLOGUE

T HE FOUNDING OF JAMESTOWN by the Royal Virginia Company expedition of 1607 was England's first successful colonial effort, her first permanent settlement in the New World, and constituted her first and major claim in the Western Hemisphere as the seventeenth century opened.

If King Henry VII had literally missed the boat with Columbus (by his niggardly rejection of the explorer's proposition to sail west under the Tudor ensign), England would try to recover lost ground and retrieve lost opportunity with another Genoese, John Cabot. Her claim to the North American continent was based on Cabot's having been the first, in 1497, to touch the mainland—whereas Columbus had attained merely to the rim of the Antilles. Even after 1497, England slept on her rights, proved laggard in enforcing her claim, allowing almost a hundred years to elapse before she moved to implement it.

Elizabeth I, granddaughter of Henry VII and first Protestant Queen Regnant of England, would challenge the Papal Bull of 1493, refusing to recognize the right of the Pope to partition the Western Hemisphere between Spain and Portugal:[1] "The Queen does not acknowledge that her subjects and those of other nations may be excluded from the Indies[2] on the claim that these have been donated to the King of Spain by the Pope."[3] Queen Elizabeth would point-blank refuse to "recognize" the papal authority "to invest the King of Spain with the New World." England's repulse of the Spanish Armada in 1588 strengthened Elizabeth's hand in maintaining an open-door policy in the western world; she would nowhere recognize mere rights of "discovery": to sail past a hitherto unsighted shore was not enough; effective occupation was a prerequisite to recognition of sovereignty.[4]

France acted on the principles enunciated by England's Queen: French and English fishermen fished and fought over the North Atlantic waters; Cartier (thirty-seven years behind Cabot) laid France's claim to Canada in 1534. Holland similarly refused to "be excluded from the Indies" and also entered the competition for the New World.

By the latter half of the sixteenth century, South and Central America had been effectively occupied, had fallen incontrovertibly under Spanish and/or Portuguese dominion. Spain had, furthermore, established the first strongholds in the Antilles, although possession of these islands would be disputed for another two hundred years. The pace of international competition in North America now began to quicken. In 1565, Spain moved up from her base of power in the center to expel the French from Fort Caroline, and to found St. Augustine; Ponce de Leon, in 1513, had claimed and named "Florida"—the Spaniards' name for the entire continent.

The English name for North America would be "Virginia": the Virgin Queen honored the broad land with her name and conveyed it—all of it; almost all the Atlantic seaboard north of Spanish "Florida"—to her gallant, dashing, and mercurial favorite, Sir Walter Raleigh, by Letters Patent of 1584, entitling him "to discover search fynde out and viewe such remote heathen and barbarus landes Contries and territories not actually possessed of any Christian Prynce."

But Raleigh's colonization effort, his Roanoke Island plantation, ended in misfortune and mystery: the Roman letters C–R–O carved on a tree trunk, high on a cliff, were the only clue to the disappearance of the one hundred and seventeen men and women set ashore there in 1587.

The next setback for England's colonial aspirations came with the abandonment of the Plymouth Company's Sagadahoc Colony, planted at the mouth of the Kennebec River in Maine[5] in 1607, contemporaneously with the Virginia Company's Jamestown venture, and very similar in size and scope. The Sagadahoc Colony was abandoned after one icy winter.

Thus, all England's colonial ambitions rode with the Virginia Company's flagship, the *Susan Constant*, as she led the two smaller ships of the flotilla out of the Atlantic, past the capes, through the strait, into the Bay of Chesapeake on an April morning in 1607.

The sails of the *Mayflower* would not appear on the American horizon for another thirteen years; the Pilgrims' landing at Plymouth Rock was still more than a decade off in the unpredictable future when the Virginia Company's three vessels sailed into the unpredictable waters of the Chesapeake. And that little fleet was two full decades ahead of the first Puritan contingent, which would not arrive in Massachusetts Bay until 1630.

"It is almost certain that if there had been no Jamestown, there would have been no Plymouth" (in the opinion of Colonial historian Thomas J. Wertenbaker).

How, then, the Founding Fathers of Massachusetts contrived to steal the thunder from the Founding Fathers of Virginia is not easy to make out. Much of the larceny dates back to the vicious sectionalism of the post–Civil War period, when the Boston Brahmins wrote American history without a South. The legend of the preeminence of the Massachusetts colony began, even earlier, with the early New England chroniclers and orators, who reflected pride in the fact that theirs alone, among all the planters, had been a distinct, a purely moral purpose, a wholly religious dedication: the Puritans of New England founded "a Citty uppon a Hill." They were conscious of a worldwide audience: "the eies of all people . . . uppon us"; theirs was an Errand into the Wilderness. Nineteenth-century American literature (notably the versifying of Longfellow) enlarged on this theme, and America seized upon the identification with Puritans and Pilgrims as the most heroic of national origins. Not only was the Puritans' moral purpose loftier than the Virginians', so was their socioeconomic status: although the New Englanders were "middling" people—of middle-class origin—as were the bulk of the English settlers on this continent, they were men of some substance and of respectable station, "the best People under Heaven," compared to "the Refuse of the English Nation" dumped into Virginia. The Virginia contingent consisted of soldiers of fortune, mercenaries, vagabonds, desperados, convicts, and debtors—"the scum of people," in the words of Sir Francis Bacon, who deplored the raffish crew recruited by the Virginia Company for this colonial enterprise.[6]

Modern scholarship, in reappraising the Old Dominion, has rejected the legend of "the rollicking Cavalier" origins of the Virginia Colony. It now questions the imputation of an exclusively imperialistic, exclusively mercantilistic motivation on the part of the founders. Clearly, the Virginia Company was a joint stock company seeking profits for its Adventurers (investors) and a New World market for English commerce, but its Royal Charter of 1606 specifies with equal clarity that it was being incorporated for the glory to be achieved in the "propagating of Christian Religion to such people, as yet live in darkness." Clearly, it was a redemptive mission, an evangelical errand, a holy as well as a commercial venture—to "sowe spirituals and reape temporals," as the logic of seventeenth-century Christian imperialism was explicated by the Reverend Samuel Purchas, journalist and promoter for the Virginia Company: "All the rich endowments of Virginia . . . are wages for all this worke. . . . God in wisdome having enriched the Savage Countries, that those riches might be attractives for Christian suters."

The twentieth century tends to see the gunboat directly behind the missionary, but it would be a distortion of historical perspective to fail to recognize the validity of the religious impulse in the Elizabethan world where the American colonization movement had its inception.

For the first twenty years of the seventeenth century, the rude triangular fort and huddle of huts on the bank of the James River constituted England's sole, precarious toe-hold on the eastern rim of the vast continent, whose very extent and shape were still unguessed, unexpected.

The banks of the James River were to become the jumping-off place for the most massive migration of people in recorded history.

"No other spot in either hemisphere carries so much significance," for if the colony there had failed, "Spain and France ultimately might have divided up all of North America between them and the United States of America might never have come into being," in the opinion of one authority on Colonial America.[7]

At Jamestown, if she should succeed in establishing a base, England could begin her struggle for the conquest of the continent. The favor of Pocahontas, favorite daughter of the Powhatan tribal chief—extended to Captain John Smith, to John Rolfe, and to others in that beleaguered wilderness outpost—substantially increased the settlement's chances for survival.

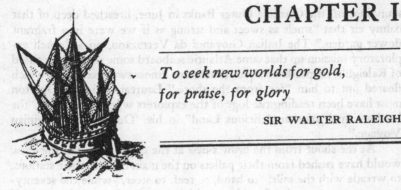

CHAPTER I

To seek new worlds for gold,
for praise, for glory

SIR WALTER RALEIGH

LANDFALL CAME ON APRIL 26, 1607.
It came at break of day, a fortunate circumstance for seventeenth-century mariners approaching an uncharted shore in cumbersome ships with unwieldy sails and rudimentary navigational instruments. And it was especially fortunate for this puny fleet of three small merchantmen mustering scarcely one hundred and sixty tons among them, so battered by storm in recent days that no one was sure of their whereabouts, and the less hardy souls aboard talked of turning back, of abandoning the voyage. But on "the six and twentieth day of Aprill, about foure a clocke in the morning, wee descried the Land of Virginia," wrote Sir George Percy, the only nobleman in that company of a hundred-odd English adventurers aboard.

Even before the first light of dawn streaked water and sky, even before the lookout in the crow's nest of the flagship *Susan Constant* could make out the low, pine-forested shore, Captain Christopher Newport, himself a redoubtable privateer, a premier commander of his time, could have sensed the loom of the land: the low-hanging clouds, the flurry and shrill of shore birds, the fragrance wafted far out to sea by offshore winds, a potpourri of bark and berry, leaf and blossom (redbud, wild plum, wild cherry, crabapple, bayberry, grape, and bog magnolia especially aromatic in a Virginia spring). That first breath of land would be especially sweet to nostrils crusty with brine after the four months and more of an Atlantic crossing. They all remarked upon it, all the early mariners and navigators coasting the sweet-smelling "new" continent: Philip Amadas and Arthur Barlowe, captaining Sir Walter Raleigh's first American expedition in 1584 and coming onto soundings off the Carolina Outer Banks in June, breathed deep of that balmy air that "smelt as sweet and strong as if we were in a fragrant flower garden." The Italian Giovanni da Verrazano, on a French exploratory mission up that same Atlantic seaboard some sixty years ahead of Raleigh's, rhapsodized about those same "most sweet savours," which floated out to him "far from the shore." Laureate Michael Drayton must have been reading the logs of the explorers when he extolled "the luscious smell of that delicious Land" in his "Ode to the Virginian Voyage."

At the shout from the crow's nest at the crack of dawn, the crew would have rushed from their pallets on the main deck to their stations, to wrestle with the sails, "to hand, to reef, to steer," while the seventy-one passengers on the flagship would have roused themselves out of uneasy sleep, out of the dark, dank, five-foot-deep hold, up onto the deck, unfastening their breeches as they jostled toward the rail to relieve their bladders over the side after the long night, to utter heartfelt hosannas, to marvel at the sight of land, the headlands of the Virginia coast looming up ahead.

Percy had probably suffered less discomfort than the others—as the eighth son of the ninth earl of Northumberland, he enjoyed a nobleman's privileges, and may well have had space in one of the Captain's two cabins—but he was no less exultant. As he wrote in his diary, "That same day, wee entered into the Bay of Chesupioc* directly, without let or hindrance. There wee landed and discovered a little way," discovering "faire meadowes and goodly tall Trees: with such Fresh-waters running through the woods, as I was almost ravished at the first sight thereof. . . ."

The first sight of the New World ravished them all, all the newcomers. Their excitement rings out across the pages of sixteenth- and seventeenth-century chronicles, the pages of Hakluyt's *Principal Voyages* and Purchas's *Pilgrimes*. Mariners and planters alike waxed lyrical about those "gallant rivers, stately harbours," those "chrystall rivers and odoriferous woods." They were wonder-struck by the bounty as well as the beauty of that virgin shore: the "goodly Woods," the game and wildfowl "in incredible abundance"—"in the world were not the like abundance," to quote Captain Amadas, coasting the Carolinas (already named "Arcadia" by a poetic Verrazano). There was

---

* The name Chesupioc, Chissapiacke, Chesapeake was first reported by Raleigh's explorers in 1584–86; the Spaniards had called it Bahía de Santa Maria. The translation of Indian place names was inconsistent and erratic, as was the orthography of seventeenth-century chronicles, logs, and maps. "At (or by) the big river" is an approximation of the Algonkian word *chesupioc*.

poetry in Amadas's log; he noted not only the treacherous reefs and shoals but also the profusion of summer grapes ("the water's edge so overgrown with grapes that the surging waves flowed over them") and the spectacle of "a flocke of Cranes, the most white," startling at the firing of a harquebus, taking wing from the water "with such a cry as if an Army of men had shouted altogether." Ralph Lane, landing on Roanoke Island with another Raleigh expedition in 1587, wrote to the geographer Richard Hakluyt: "We have discovered the main [land] to be the goodliest soil under the cope of heaven." "Beside that," he continued, "it is the goodliest and most pleasing territory of the world: for the continent is of an huge and unknown greatness. . . ." Lane's commander, Sir Richard Grenville, called it "this paradise of the world."

Columbus had thought he was speaking literally when he called it a "Terrestrial Paradise" in his "Letter to the Sovereigns," written in 1498, from what he believed to be the remote perimeter of the Garden of Eden itself. He identified the Orinoco River as the Gihon, one of the four rivers flowing out of Eden. To the orthodox Christian ear, of course, there was a tinge of heresy in such a suggestion that unredeemed man might have penetrated to even the edge of the Terrestrial Paradise. Had not the Garden gate been barred to man, after the Fall, by an Angel with a Flaming Sword?

By another ancient notion, the way to the west had been barred by Hercules, setting up his Pillars at the Strait of Gibraltar; or, according to Plato's fable, had been blocked by yet another device of the gods— "by a shoal of mud" where the Lost Continent of Atlantis had sunk and settled beneath the waves, "for which reason the sea in those parts is impassable and impenetrable."

It was not so much the fear of sailing off the edge of the world that impeded westward exploration; the theory of a spherical world had been taught as early as the sixth century. It was, rather, a sense of trespass and sin—a sense of fear and awe as well as wonder—which men felt at the approach "to the land under the western wave."[1] (The next great adventure into the unknown would not take place until the twentieth century, that into outer space, and only the landscape of the moon would bring men to marvel again as they had at the landscape of America.)

In the fifteenth century, the unknown began where the Atlantic shelf dropped off into unfathomed deeps, inaccessible to any soundings yet devised. Beyond, there stretched only a vast mystery of waters, bottomless, boundless, untracked, unmarked on the maps of medieval cartographers save for the decorative figures of blowing and broaching whales or the protean shapes of Fly-Away Islands, now here, now there; now one, now another—the Islands of Antilia, Hy-Brasil, or Buss—appearing up out of, disappearing back into, the waves, as travelers' tales caught the fancy of the map-makers or were discredited.

The *oecumene*, the inhabited world as known to medieval Europe, was tripartite—Europe itself, Asia, and Libya, representing the three parts of the world as divided among the three sons of Noah, the Japhetic, Semitic, and Hamitic. Were a fourth part of the world to exist, were it to be discovered, it would be a Dantesque "world without people," forbidden to mortal men, reserved as the abode of the souls of the blessed en route to paradise—the Isles of the Blest, the Enchanted or Happy Isles, the Hesperides, the Elysian Fields, as they had been variously known to classic antiquity. Their location, according to Homer, was on the western margin of the earth; according to Hesiod and Pindar, in the Western Ocean. The Celtic bards pointed west to Avalon as the abode of heroes—of King Arthur slumbering yet awhile before his return to Camelot. Such was Europe's recurrent fantasy, unsuppressible dream, inveterate longing for the land at the edge of the world, land of promise, land of the westering sun.

To SEE IT WITH HIS OWN EYES, on that early April morning of 1607, moved Captain John Smith—hard-bitten soldier of fortune, world-traveler that he was—to exclaim in awe and wonder, like the rest: "Heaven and earth never agreed better to frame a place for man's habitation. . . ."

Under arrest for thirteen weeks since the flotilla had watered at the Canaries in February (on vague and unsubstantiated charges of conspiracy to mutiny), Captain Smith almost missed the sight at landfall. Somehow he managed to escape confinement and make his way to the deck as the flagship rounded a point of land and entered "the verie mouth of the Bay of Chissapiacke," as he reported in his *True Relation*. "The first land we made, wee fell with Cape Henry" (sand dunes no sooner sighted than named by the expeditionaries in honor of Prince Henry, elder son and heir apparent to their monarch, James I, first Stuart king, first king of a United England and Scotland).

The one-hundred-ton *Susan Constant*, followed by the forty-ton *Godspeed* and the twenty-ton *Discovery*, dropped anchor six or eight miles beyond the point of land.

Captain Newport led the first small party ashore, to penetrate the wall of verdure that stood as sole rampart of the continent and, there, to their first encounter with the continent's inhabitants—their first moment of anthropological shock, first confrontation with a totally dissimilar culture. "At night," Sir George Percy (a member of the party) recorded in his diary,

> when wee were going aboard, there came the Savages creeping upon all foure, from the Hills, like Beares; with their Bowes in their mouthes: [who] charged us very desperately in the faces [and] hurt Captaine Gabriell Archer in both his hands, and a sayler in two places of the body very dangerous[ly]. After they had spent their Arrowes, and felt the sharpnesse of our shot, they retired into the Woods with a great noise, and so left us.

(It was Captain Newport's shot that scattered the Savages; he fired singlehanded, his other hand lost in a naval engagement on the Spanish Main.)

It is ironic that Captain Smith, who would be known to history as the first man of the Virginia contingent, was not among those to set foot that first day on Virginia soil. Still in disgrace, still under restraint aboard ship, Smith heard the news second-hand from participants in the shore excursion: "And in that place was the Box opened, wherein the Counsell for Virginia was nominated." The nominations had been made in London by the governing board of the Virginia Company, themselves appointees of King James; the list, placed in a sealed box aboard the flagship, included the names of Captain Christopher Newport, Captain Bartholomew Gosnold, Captain John Ratcliffe, Master Edward Maria Wingfield, Captain John Martin, Captain George Kendall, and Captain John Smith. These were the men selected in London to command the infant colony in Virginia.

The first name on the list, Newport's, was a name to cheer: a hero's name, along with Drake's, in the annals of the sea. He was with Drake on that daring raid into Cádiz harbor, in 1587, "to singe the beard of the King of Spain"; and on his own, in 1592, he captured the *Madre de Dios*, richest prize ever snatched by an Elizabethan privateer from the Spanish treasure fleet.

The Virginia Company had chosen well in naming Newport to the command of this expedition in 1606. It was no mean navigational feat to bring those three frail ships safely across, and across together (with no means of maintaining contact at night), through four long months in transit: from London on December 20, 1606, down the Thames, to lie at hull for almost a month of storm in the Downs, off the coast of Kent; then, on the traditional southern or tradewinds route best known to Newport: from Finistère in France to Finisterre in Spain; southwest to the Canaries; thence, in Columbus's wake, due west across the Atlantic to the West Indies, to anchor on March 24, 1607, off Dominica, in the Windward Isles. Newport's skill and confidence in bringing the three ships into the Chesapeake in 1607 suggest that he had reconnoitered those waters on previous voyages to America, perhaps en route home from the West Indies in 1605.

It was a surprise to no one, when the Box of Orders was unsealed, to find the name of Bartholomew Gosnold on the list of Council members. Captain of the forty-ton *Godspeed*, second in command to Newport, he was another old sea dog, privateer, veteran of western waters, commander of a recent (1603) voyage to the northern coast of the North American continent. Gosnold was, furthermore, one of the original promoters of the Virginia Company enterprise, "one of the first movers of this plantation," according to Captain Smith. Gosnold had spent "many yeares" soliciting financial backing and government sanction for this first colony on the Chesapeake, and was probably responsible for recruiting Smith.

All three captains of the fleet were named to the Council, although the nomination of the third was less popular: the captain of the twenty-ton *Discovery* (the least noteworthy, least stalwart of the three, the one who had lost his bearings and been ready to turn back in the storm just off the Virginia coast) was John Ratcliffe—or, rather, John Sicklemore alias Ratcliffe, traveling west under an assumed name to obscure his involvement in an Old World scandal he hoped to live down in the New, as so many after him were to do. If Ratcliffe/Sicklemore sought to shroud his past in mystery, he succeeded: the most assiduous research has failed to turn up a clue as to his origins or family connections. He must have had some navigational experience to have been placed in command of even that tiny pinnace, but his appointment to the seven-man governing board is explicable only in view of the fact that he was a substantial investor in the joint stock company, shown on the records to be inscribed for £50 (compared to Smith's paltry £9). It would be reasonable to assume that he had friends or relatives in high places, in the Stuart court at Whitehall or in the Royal Council of the Virginia Company in London.

Captain George Kendall, like Ratcliffe, must have had notable connections to have been named to the Council. Where Ratcliffe's is an enigmatic character, Kendall's is tinged with sinister undertones. Like so many others in that first century of religious schism in England, Kendall apparently paid lip service to the Anglican Church without in fact having severed his ties with the Romish. If—as was later charged—he did indeed serve His Catholic Majesty of Spain as a spy during these first crucial months of the English colonial effort, his treachery may have been due to religious rather than venal motives.

As for Captain John Martin, the next man on the list of seven, he was indisputably well born and well connected: his father, Sir Richard, was in his third term as Lord Mayor of London, and a member of the Royal Council of the Virginia Company; Martin's brother-in-law was no less a luminary than Sir Julius Caesar, Master of the Rolls and Privy Councilor, Chancellor of the Exchequer in 1606, the year the Virginia Company received its license from the monarch. In his forties, Captain Martin could point to some qualifications of his own: he had seen service under Sir Francis Drake, and won his captaincy on the sea in a day when privateering was a way of life—preying on the Spanish treasure fleet homeward bound from Central and South America.

Rank and social station alone would have similarly ensured Master Edward Maria Wingfield his place in the ruling hierarchy (the term "Master" or "Mr" was not applied below the gentry—the feudal system was being transported intact from the British Isles to the New World, although it was fated to undergo some curious sea-changes), but Wingfield had other reasons as well to expect preferment: he had served, along with his cousin Captain Gosnold, as one of the prime movers of this Chesapeake plantation, active in organizing the Virginia Company, in raising funds, in floating the stock issue. Wingfield was one of the eight petitioners to whom the monarch granted the license authorizing the Virginia Company to colonize—officially to occupy and plant the broad lands of "Virginia"[2] (which included almost the entire Atlantic seaboard of the North American continent, all save Spanish "Florida," far to the south) in the name of their sovereign, James I, King of England, of Scotland, of Ireland, of France—and now, it was to be hoped, King of Virginia. Sir Walter Raleigh's title to these lands had lapsed in consequence of his condemnation for treason in 1603 (he had been brought to trial four months after the death of his fond and indulgent patroness, Queen Elizabeth); Elizabeth's successor was free in 1606 to grant the Crown Patent to the Virginia Company petitioners, of whom Wingfield was one.

In the published list of First Planters or Ancients (as the members of the very first expeditionary force came to be designated), Wingfield's name was included with those of his fellow passengers entitled by birth or station to be categorized as "gentlemen"—the distinction between gentlemen and others was clearly drawn in that class-conscious English society. In seventeenth-century England, social concepts were based upon degree; as Raleigh expressed it in his *History of the World*: "For that infinite wisdom of God which hath distinguished His angels by degrees ... hath also ordained kings, dukes ... and other degrees among men." In that very first contingent of 1607, the "gentlemen" (elsewhere referred to as the "better sort" or "men of quality") numbered fifty or more, slightly more than half the total number of a hundred-odd. Those who did not qualify as gentlemen were classified according to crafts or trades: four carpenters, two bricklayers, a mason, a blacksmith, a barber, a "taylor," and a "sailer." An even dozen nondescripts were lumped together under the heading of "labourers" (one without so much as a last name, listed as Ould Edward). Four "boyes" (cabin-boys or grummets) are named. Going by the list published in 1612 in Smith's *Map of Virginia*, they had one drummer to keep them marching if the two surgeons aboard could keep them on their feet. There were "diverse others, to the number of 105," Smith's list concludes.

As for the seven-member Council appointed in England to govern in America, the last name on the list—although certainly not the least—was that of the redoubtable, indomitable Captain Smith. His name synonymous with that of the Virginia Colony he helped to found, he stands first and foremost among America's Founding Fathers, a role of which he was, during his lifetime, already well aware: "The most of these faire plantations," he would write (meaning New England, which he explored, mapped, and named, as well as Virginia, with which his name is usually associated), "did spring from the fruites of my adventures and discoveries."

Not only did Captain Smith lead the way onto this continent and make history here; he also wrote it. He served as major historian of England's westward adventure, his literary output as prodigious as his action—eleven travel-adventure books published between 1608 and 1631, in a typically Elizabethan flourish. In strictly literary terms, judgment on them must be qualified.[3] They are, to some extent, clumsily and awkwardly written chronicles, with not a few prize specimens of the lumbering complexity for which Virginia Woolf criticizes Elizabethan prose. Yet they are redeemed by passages which strike the reader as vivid and poignant, examples of the rich, ripe, resonant language in which Shakespeare wrote and the King James version of the Bible was composed.

The chroniclers of Plymouth and Massachusetts Bay—William Bradford, John Winthrop, Edward Johnson, Cotton Mather—crowded Smith off the pages of New England history, but his name remains indelibly imprinted on the annals of the southern colony, Virginia, England's first successful colony in North America—her first colony, for that matter, anywhere in the world, the point of origin of what would become the far-flung British Empire.

If John Smith, "President of Virginia" and "Admiral of New England," dominates the first chapter of American colonial history, there are frequent reminders that he himself penned the chapter, wielding a pen as mighty as his sword. Smith has become one of the most controversial figures in American history: a figure on a scale so heroic as to suggest the mock-heroic, a figure of fun as well as folk-hero, subject of travesty as of myth. And he came under a veritable barrage in the late nineteenth century from such anti-southern Boston Brahmins as Henry Adams and Charles Deane. When the last word is said, however, the consensus on Smith as a historian is that his work is "pretty reliable," in the main. In the main, what is more, it is eminently readable: if some passages make for hard sledding, others are compelling, lively, racy, humorous; his text is imbued with his extraordinary vitality and rugged individualism, his literary style as robustious as his life-style, as brash and self-assertive as his typically Elizabethan personality.

As to his celebrated adventures, his feats of derring-do, his travels so extensive as to put Marco Polo and Odysseus in the shade, "He alone is herald to publish and proclaim them," Thomas Fuller scathingly wrote in *The Worthies of England*. But Fuller wrote in 1662, thirty-one years after Smith's death. During Smith's lifetime, no man gainsaid him, certainly not to his face.

The swashbuckling Captain Smith, according to Stephen Vincent Benét, was a man

> *Who had been everywhere, been everything,*
> *(Or so he said) a prisoner of the Turk,*
> *(Or so he said) beggar in Muscovy,*
> *A paladin in Transylvania*
> *(Or so he said), shipwrecked in twenty seas,*
> *Lover of ladies in a dozen lands. . . .*

Benét, in his American epic poem, *Western Star*, is paraphrasing—and parodying—the mundivagant author of *The True Travels, Adventures, and Observations of Captaine John Smith, in Europe, Asia, Affrica, and America, from Anno Domini 1593 to 1629:*

> Having been a slave to the Turks, a prisoner amongst the most barbarous Salvages; . . . always in mutinies, wants and miseries; blowne up with gunpowder; prisoner among the French Pyrats . . . in the midst of wars, pestilence and *famine*, by which many an hundred thousand have died about mee, and scarce five living of them [that] went first with me to Virginia. . . .

His life had been a succession of "extreame extremities," said Anas Todkill, one of his companions in danger in the wilderness, one of the "scarce five" alive of those who had helped him to win the beachhead on the Chesapeake in 1607. John Smith had set out from England at an early age, in his fifteenth or sixteenth year, to win his spurs against the Spaniard. It was after the death of his father, sometime in 1596 or 1597 (his chronology is vague), that he crossed the Channel: "France and Netherlands had taught him to ride a Horse and use his Armes, with such rudiments of warre as his tender yeares in those martiall Schooles could attaine unto. . . ."

Careers of soldiering and privateering were among the few open in that day and time to the son of a yeoman—a freeman, freeholder, something more than a peasant or a laborer, something less than a gentleman—with only a rudimentary education and no connections. Men of mettle and little else—no rank, no property, no profession—could hope, then, to win fame and fortune only in the army or the navy.

Young John Smith departed those fields where Christian was fighting Christian to find those others where Christian was fighting Moslem; he went from Flanders toward Tartary: "He was desirous to see more of the world, and trie his fortune against the Turkes," as he said in his third-person *True Travels*. To find the Turks, he headed east through Mediterranean ports even Odysseus might have missed, to seas beyond, to the Black Sea and the Sea of Azov. And even Richard Coeur de Lion might have paled at some of the odds confronting his fellow countryman, the Lincolnshire lad, on those far-flung battlefields.

John Smith came upon the paynim beyond the Danube, and to fight him, enlisted in a battalion of the Imperial Army, under the banner of Emperor Rudolf II of Austria. The issues at stake in Transylvania were murky: centuries-old feuds between Magyar, Szekler, Vlach, and Saxon. For a mercenary like Captain Smith (he attained the rank, shortly, in the field) it was enough to know that it was the Holy Roman Empire versus the Ottoman.

The three Turks' heads emblazoned upon Smith's shield comprised a device he had won the right to wear by three victorious duels in a row, on horseback, in single combat in strict compliance with the chivalric code, against assorted Turkish challengers. The contestants entered the arena to the flourish of trumpets and hautboys, "the Ramparts all beset with fair Dames . . . who did long to see some court-like pastime." The first Turkish challenger, his visor pierced by Smith's lance, "fell dead to the ground; where alighting and unbracing his Helmet, [Smith] cut off his head." The second Turk survived Smith's lance only to succumb to his pistol, and "lost his head, as his friend before him; with his horse and Armor." The third combatant raised the hopes of Turkish sympathizers by resisting both Smith's pistol and his battle-axe, only to fall casualty to Smith's broadsword—so that "he stood not long ere he lost his head, as the rest had done."

But not even Smith's prowess could save the day for his battalion at Red Tower Pass, near the Moldavian frontier of eastern Walachia, when the Khan Ghazi Garay unleashed "near forty thousand Tatars" in a full-scale cavalry charge, "their Ensigns displaying, Drums beating, Trumpets and Hautboys sounding."

And thus, "in this bloody field, neere 30,000 lay," Smith wrote (although his battle-count, in the opinion of military historians, was often subject to inflation):

> But Smith, among the slaughtered dead bodies, and many a gasping soule, with toile and wounds lay groaning among the rest, till being found by the Pillagers hee was able to live; and perceiving [by] his armor and habit [that] his ransome might be better to them than his death, they led him prisoner with many others. . . .

In Axiopolis, a hundred miles east of Bucharest, Smith and his fellow captives "were all sold for slaves, like beasts, in a marketplace." Smith fell to the lot of one Bashaw Bagall, "who sent him forthwith . . . for Constantinople to his faire Mistresse for a slave. . . . By twentie and twentie chained by the neckes, they marched in file to this great Citie, where they were delivered to their severall Masters, and he to the young Charatza Tragabigzanda. . . ."

Whether she is to be numbered among those ladies loved by Smith "in a dozen lands" is nowhere clarified. Smith is more reticent about his amorous exploits than about his military ones. What little he tells about the young Greek girl from Trebizond, he tells cryptically: "she tooke (as it seemed) much compassion on him; but having no use for him"—there was, presumably, no place in a maiden's household for a brawny gladiator—she sent him away. Hurriedly, lest her mother sell her slave, she packed him off to her brother, who lived "in a great vast stonie Castle" in a province in Tartaria, somewhere east of the Don. "To her unkinde brother, this kinde Ladie writ so much for his [Smith's] good usage, that hee [her brother] half suspected, as much as she intended; for shee told him [Smith] he should there but sojourne to learne the language, and what it was to be a Turke, till time"—and herewith the most cryptic passage of all—"till time made her Master of her selfe."

However the reader may interpret Charatza's letter, the brother suspected the worst, and Smith bore the brunt of his suspicions: at his hands, Smith suffered "the worst of crueltie": stripped naked, head shaven, a ring of iron riveted about his neck, among "many more Christian slaves, and neere an hundred Forsados of Turkes and Moores . . . he [Smith] was slave of slaves to them all. . . .

"All the hope he had ever to be delivered from this thraldome was only the love of Tragabigzanda, who surely was ignorant of his bad usage . . . so bad, a dog could hardly have lived to endure." In desperation, Smith "beat out the Tymors [the brother's] braines with his threshing bat . . . , clothed himself in his clothes, mounted his horse, and ranne into the desert at all adventure."

Lost on those trackless steppes, he was lucky to come upon a caravan route from Astrakhan to Poland and, "upon the river Don, a garrison of the Muscovites." There he encountered another "good Lady," the Lady Callamata, wife of the Governor, who "largely supplied all his wants," including a safe-conduct to facilitate his journey west by convoy across the Dnieper into Lithuania—through "Volonia, Polonia, Hungaria, Moravia, Bohemia, Saxonie, Brunswicke, Bavaria, the Palatinate, Loraine," and so, finally, to France, which he had left three years earlier.

"Being thus satisfied with Europe and Asia . . . hee went from Gibraltar to Guta and Tangier," to the Barbary Coast. There he rejected the idea of joining in a local war among three burnoused princes, resolving instead to join an "old fox" of a naval captain on a French man-of-war, "to try some other conclusions at Sea." Those "conclusions" were frankly piratical, but they led, at long last—back home! The final page of Part One of Smith's *True Travels, Adventures, and Observations* bears no date (though it was probably 1604, the year after Queen Elizabeth's death), but the last line reads: "and then he"— Captain John Smith, a veteran of foreign wars, and probably in his twenty-fourth year—"returned into England."

How true are they, Captain Smith's *True Travels?*—there's the question! Once raised, it set off a controversy that still echoes around his name. Hero or impostor? To poke fun is a perennial temptation: the feats he describes are death-defying, his hair-breadth escapes challenge credulity. His chronology is vague; his mathematics is fanciful; his travel itinerary is difficult to trace because his spelling of place names and proper names is idiosyncratic. Many of those names had an exotic ring to his English ear; furthermore, it should be noted, irregular and inconsistent orthography was characteristic of his century. To authenticate Smith's travels and adventures is as difficult as to discredit them; attempts have been made intermittently to do either one or the other. The Smith works may continue to be mistrusted by some scholars, but they cannot be ignored in any consideration of America's beginnings. In the words of Alexander Brown, eminent turn-of-the-century historian: "When our age of reflection arrived, Smith's history was almost the only source from which we derived any knowledge of the infancy of our state . . . and it came to be regarded as standard authority on our foundation and its author as our founder." As regards Smith's wide military experience, his valor and resourcefulness, the proof lies not in his works but in his persona, his irresistible authority, his imposing presence. He took command as naturally as he took breath; he asked none of his men to go "where he would not lead them himselfe." Men followed where he led, and most of those who survived the landing on the Chesapeake were those who followed him rather than another. "The warres in Europe, Asia, and Affrica taught me how to subdue the wilde Salvages in Virginia and New-England, in America."

WHEN CAPTAIN NEWPORT opened the sealed Box of Orders on April 26, on that sandy shore off Cape Henry, and read aloud the list of councilors appointed by the Virginia Company to govern in the colony, the name of Captain John Smith would have been greeted with approval.

The approval of all save Master Wingfield and his faction. In their eyes, the admittance of a yeoman—a social inferior—to the ruling élite was a violation of the caste system: did not (in Shakespeare's phrase) "The heavens themselves, the planets, and this center / Observe degree, priority, and place"? In Wingfield's Elizabethan world, political authority was identified with social authority: Smith's very presence, exuding authority at every pore, reeking of brash self-confidence—the cut of his jib, the jut of his jaw—implied a challenge to Wingfield's birthright of precedence.

A confrontation between the two had been inevitable during the course of that grueling long voyage. It came at the Canary Islands, and any issue could have served to spark it: how many barrels of water to put aboard, how many of sack? what bait to use in what waters? whether to spit to windward or to leeward—anything or nothing!—any challenge to his own authority Wingfield would have construed as mutiny. It was, apparently, on Wingfield's charge of "concealing an intended mutiny" that Smith was placed under arrest in mid-February.

And it could only have been at the instigation of Wingfield and his faction ("such factions we had, as commonly attend such voyages") that "a paire of gallowes . . . was made" at Nevis, in the Leeward Isles, in late March, although "Capt. Smith, for whom they were intended, could not," in the Captain's own saucy phrase, "be persuaded to use them."

And it was, in all likelihood, at Wingfield's contrivance that the other six members of the Council voted to disqualify Captain Smith from service on that governing board until the issue of his guilt should be resolved. The other six councilmen, in compliance with the sealed Instructions, were sworn into service, and conducted a vote for president, electing Wingfield, who was the ranking member.

The first order of business for the newly elected President and his Council, in concert with Captain Newport, was the selection of a plantation site in accordance with Virginia Company Instructions.

Reassembling the shallop (a light, open boat primarily for river use, propelled by oar or by sail or both) that had been stowed in the flagship, Captain Newport conducted a series of exploratory trips up the James River, while the fleet waited at anchor in the Bay off Old Point Comfort. Newport chose the James because of the direction of its flow; the fact that it could be sailed toward the west raised hopes that it might point the way to the long-sought Northwest Passage, shortcut to the Orient, that will-o'-the-wisp of seventeenth-century exploration. The James did not lead to the Pacific but, even so, it was "one of the famousest Rivers that ever was found by any Christian," to quote the irrepressibly enthusiastic Percy, riding with Newport in the shallop: "It ebbes and flowes a hundred and threescore miles where ships of great burthen may harbour in safetie." And it had "many branches . . . which runne flowing through the Woods with great plentie of fish of all kindes . . . and all the grounds bespred with many sweet and delicate flowres of divers colours and kindes . . . as though it had been in any Garden or Orchard in England. . . ."

The James River, known to the original inhabitants as the Powhatan, rises in the Allegheny Mountains, flowing and winding three hundred and forty miles eastward to empty into the Bay through Hampton Roads (as it is called today)—a broad stream, broader than the Thames at its mouth; torpid, sluggish, rippling only to the rhythm of the tides, to the swoop of a gull or the leap of a fish, to the swath of a fin or the stroke of a paddle.

The plantation site favored by Captain Newport and endorsed by President Wingfield and his Council was on the banks of the James just below its confluence with the Chickahominy River; a site some forty miles upstream, inland from the open waters of the Bay, out of reach of surprise attack by prowling Spaniards; defensible, at a point where the river narrows; thus, in compliance with the chief requirements for safety prescribed by the Virginia Company in the matter of site selection for the colony. The site selected was on a low-lying, wooded peninsula, a strip of land almost rectangular, about two miles long and one wide, containing some fifteen hundred acres of high land suitable for cultivation. The peninsula was connected, at that time, to the mainland by a narrow sandbar; its erosion in ensuing centuries left Jamestown, as today, an island. The site was appealing to a mariner not only because of its defensibility but because of its deepwater landing, facilitating the loading and unloading of cargo: the *Susan Constant*, the *Godspeed*, and the *Discovery*, riding in six fathoms of water, could be moored to ancient cypresses overhanging the river. The advantages were immediately apparent; the disadvantages, the dangers lurking in the miasmal swamp, were less readily recognizable.

Captain Newport was responsible for the choice of the planting site on the James River, but the choice of the region—the Chesapeake instead of the Carolina barrier reefs upon which Raleigh's colonial hopes had foundered—had been made, sight unseen, by Richard Hakluyt, ranking geographer of an age in which geography ranked as the most popular science. "Preacher" Hakluyt (as he continued to be called long after he had forsaken the pulpit for the globe) served not only as chief propandist for the Virginia Company venture of 1607—he was one of the original six signatories to the charter petition—but as a prime mover in the westward surge of the entire English colonization movement. One of the first to collect and publish the early material relating to the New World, Hakluyt was also one of the first to perceive its immense potential. His *Principal Navigations Voyages Traffiques & Discoveries of the English Nation* stands as the classic statement of the case for English colonization. Beyond that, it has been called the prose epic of the English nation, and accounted one of the more influential books in England's history (Shakespeare was among its readers).

Although Hakluyt's selection of the Chesapeake region was predicated largely on guesswork, it was educated guesswork—as in the case of the scientists' selection of the site for the first moon landing. Hakluyt had had access to some fragmentary accounts of exploration in that area: Captain Philip Amadas, with the Portuguese Simão Fernandes as pilot, may have penetrated the waters of the Chesapeake in 1584–85 on an expedition for Sir Walter Raleigh; Bartholomew Gilbert possibly entered the Bay in 1603; Verrazano missed the strait between the capes by the merest of miles in 1524; one or more Spanish ships had almost surely sailed those waters in 1571–72; and the Roanoke Island colonists are known to have dispatched a small scouting party northward in 1585, in the direction of the Chesapeake to explore and to map.

Hakluyt's choice of the region proved fortunate: the largest bay on the Atlantic coast of the North American continent, its broad reaches promised superlative roadsteads for the maritime traffic that would one day grow up between the mother country and the "new English nation" (as Raleigh, an incorrigible optimist even on the headsman's block, envisioned it). Sadly, Hakluyt, still in his fifties but considered too old for such an adventure, was never to see with his own eyes that glistening, bounteous blue breast of the Chesapeake, billowing up out of a corsage of golden sands, dunes, beaches, spume-flecked and sown with sea-oats, saltbush, bayberry.

As for tidewater Virginia—that coastal strip extending back some one hundred miles to the western fall-line, to the Appalachian piedmont—not even Hakluyt could have foreseen such a geographical curiosity: a land in thrall to the sea, subject to the ebb and flow of the tide through the estuaries, deep into the interior; five of the rivers—the James, the York, the Piankatank, the Rappahannock, and the Potomac—spread out like the five fingers of a giant hand, thrusting into the land and dividing it into verdant strips and peninsulas. Tidewater Virginia was environed, crossed, streaked, laced, and ribboned by water, which was as vital an element in its composition as earth: a labyrinth of estuaries, streams, and swamps; a low, flat, fertile land, pine- and cypress-forested, alive with game; a reservoir of salt water and fresh, with the bounty of seafare peculiar to such a combination.

Of the several peninsulas formed by Virginia's major estuaries, the one lying between the James River and the York is referred to as The Peninsula (sometimes as The Cradle of the Republic), an eighty-mile-long tongue of land reaching from Old Point Comfort to Richmond. It was here that the Council decided to plant the colony, and to name it James Town or James Fort, in honor, like the river, of their King.

On May 14, the square-rigged linen-flax sails furled and secured, the three ships were moored to trees overhanging the bank, and the unloading began: the bare necessities of provisioning and equipment for the settlement were set ashore.

Seamen and settlers alike must have rushed to disembark, their longing for *terra firma* unassuaged by an occasional brief excursion from ship to shore and back to ship again; they were eager to feel solid ground instead of a heaving deck beneath their feet, to expel the reek of bilge-water from their lungs and to breathe in pine-fresh air instead, to stretch themselves, to stand straight, stand alone, after the long months penned up together in those dark, cramped shipboard quarters. They could congratulate themselves on having survived an Atlantic crossing: formal thanksgiving services had been conducted by their gentle chaplain, Robert Hunt, on April 29, at Cape Henry, where a commemorative cross had been erected. These mariners and adventurers constituted a rare breed of men, found in every generation—the first to go up in the flying machine or down in the submarine, the first to rocket into outer space.

After the meager shipboard diet of hardtack, corned meat, and weevily gruel en route from England, no wonder Sir George Percy exclaimed in delight at the bounty of the Chesapeake, at the great variety as well as plenty of fish and shellfish, at "the good store of Mussels and Oysters, which lay on the ground as thicke as stones . . . and large and delicate in taste." Not to mention the sturgeon—since "all the world cannot be compared to it," or the "Turkie nests and many Egges," "the Strawberries, Rasberries, Mulberries and Fruites unknown." No wonder Percy called it "this Paradise."

And Captain Smith—still denied his seat on the Council, but finally free of physical restraint—echoed Percy's elation: "such pleasant plaines, hills and fertile valleyes, one prettily crossing another, and watered so conveniently with their sweete brookes and christall springs, as if art itselfe had devised them."

"The fourteenth day [of May], we landed all our men," according to Percy's diary, the only detailed account of those first weeks ashore, "which were set to work about the fortification, and others some to watch and ward as it was convenient."

"Now falleth every man to worke"—even the gentlemen, as one of them, Thomas Studley, reported in *The Proceedings of the English Colony in Virginia*—"the Councell contrive the Fort, the rest cut down trees to make place to pitch their Tents; some provide clapbord to relade the ships; some make gardens, some nets, &c." There was a rush to sow the seeds of English wheat, oats, and barley in a spring season already far advanced. The fort contrived by the Council was to be triangular in shape, covering approximately an acre of ground, and fenced against the still unknown dangers of the wilderness surrounding them.

The red men, the principal danger of the wilderness, had allowed themselves to be seen infrequently after that initial brush with the landing party near Cape Henry on April 26, the day of landfall. Percy, as member of another small reconnoitering party on the twenty-seventh, expressed disappointment that "We could not see a Savage in all that march." During the next few days, discovering farther up the Bay in the shallop, they came upon signs of human life: "A Cannow . . . made out of a whole tree . . . five and fortie feet long by the Rule"; then, still deeper in the woods, "great smoakes of fire. . . . But all this march we could neither see Savage nor Towne." Still, "the Savages had been there, burning down the grasse; as wee thought either to make their plantation there, or else to give signes to bring their forces together, and to give us battell."

Finally, on the thirtieth day of the month, at the point they had named Point Comfort, they saw "five Savages running on the shoare."

Captain Newport, ordering the shallop to be rowed to the shore, called to them "in signe of friendship" (signs he had learned in previous encounters with the aborigines of the Western Hemisphere). At Newport's "signe"—hand on heart, a universal symbol of goodwill and truth—they "laid down their Bowes and Arrowes," and beckoned the English to their town, Kecoughtan. There, "we were entertained by them very kindly." And very ceremoniously: a feast was spread, a pipe smoked, a dance performed. "On the fourth day of May we came to the King or Werowance [an Algonkian word the English had learned from Raleigh's Roanoke Island adventurers] of Paspahe [Paspahegh]: where they entertained us with much welcome." As did the Rappahannock, who entertained the visitors from across the sea "in good humanitie." Up and down the James, the two ritual shouts—the protocol of welcome among the Algonkian tribes of Virginia—rang out more often than not at the approach of the English oarsmen.

Up and down both seaboards, the Atlantic and the Pacific, men from across the sea were in the first instance greeted cordially, welcomed by the native inhabitants: "North American natives were usually friendly to the first Europeans they encountered, and hostile only after being abused or cheated," in the judgment of Samuel Eliot Morison.

On the West Coast in his voyage of 1579–80, Sir Francis Drake blushed at being hailed as a god by "people of a tractable free and loving nature, without guile or treachery," at being offered tribute—baskets "filled with an herb they called Tabah" (tobacco).

On the East Coast, far to the north in Newfoundland, in 1501, Gaspar Corte-Real had only praise for the Beothuks, for their "manners and gestures most gentle." (Who could have dreamed those gentle Beothuks would soon be exterminated, hunted down like wild beasts by the French and English?) At the Rock of Quebec, in 1535, the Hurons flocked to the banks of the St. Lawrence to greet Jacques Cartier; while the chiefs made orations, the women danced and sang, wading knee-deep into the river to serenade the longboat, their song of welcome carrying miles downstream to the flagship. The Italian Verrazano, on a French exploratory mission along the southerly coasts of the Atlantic seaboard in 1524, met with "divers signs of friendship" from "very courteous and gentle" red men. Farther north, in New York Bay, at the Narrows since renamed in Verrazano's honor, "the people . . . clad with feathers of fowls of divers colors . . . came toward us very cheerfully, making great shouts of admiration, showing us where we might come to land most safely with our boat." The Wampanoags of Massachusetts were hospitable, helpful, pleasant, too (Verrazano's judgment was to be corroborated a century later by such prominent

New England chroniclers as Roger Williams, William Wood, Thomas Morton, and Daniel Gookin). The Abnaki were the exception: howling, jeering, obscene, "exhibiting their backsides and laughing immoderately," giving Maine a bad name on Verrazano's brother's map—*Terra Onde di Mala Gente*, the Land of Bad People.

Elsewhere, initial contacts were idyllic: in "the country Wingandacoa, now named Virginia by Her Majesty," a smiling king made "signs of joy and welcome" to Amadas and Barlowe, captains of Raleigh's 1584 expedition, when they disembarked upon his shore (somewhere, probably, along the coastline of present-day Georgia). The signs made by the king, "striking his own head and breast and then ours," were meant to "show that we were all brothers, all made of the same flesh." Barlowe declared,

> We have never in the world so far encountered a more kind and loving people. . . . We were entertained with kindness and friendship and were given everything they could provide. We found these people gentle, loving, and faithful, lacking all guile and trickery. It was as if they lived in a golden age of their own.

And Thomas Hariot, in his 1585 encounter with the tribes of the North Carolina barrier reefs, was similarly impressed: he could not remember having "ever seen a better or gentler folk than these. . . ."

But to begin at the beginning is to begin with Columbus: the reception accorded him—the first white man ever seen by the red—was friendly. The pleasant island that the *Santa Maria* came upon in the warm, blue Caribbean Sea (probably San Salvador), "full of green trees and abounding in springs," was "inhabited by a multitude of people" (though not such a multitude that they could not, shortly, be exterminated, all the Bahamas all too soon depopulated by the Spaniards)

> who hastened to the shore, astounded and marveling at the sight of the ships. . . . the Admiral perceiving they were a gentle, peaceful, and very simple people, gave them little red caps and glass beads which they hung about their necks. . . .

Even so, first blood was drawn there, in the Bahamas, in 1492. For "when the Christians showed them a naked sword, they foolishly grasped it by the blade and cut themselves." Only a nick. Only skin deep, but the wound was mortal: the native inhabitants were to be exsanguinated upon that cold steel—by the technological superiority of the invader (the Spaniards were responsible, it is estimated, for at least six million deaths in the Caribbean).

AT JAMESTOWN, just over a century later, President Wingfield avoided any show of weaponry; he would "admit no exercise at armes, or fortification, but the boughs of trees cast together in the forme of a halfe moone." He came in for criticism (from Thomas Studley, among others) but he was only following the Instructions of the Royal Council in London, "not to offend the Naturals, if you can eschew it."

The Council in Virginia could not have guessed that they had offended the "Naturals" by the very choice of the site for their plantation: they had trespassed by locating their colony on an ancient hunting ground of the Paspahegh tribe. Though it appeared unoccupied ground to Captain Smith—"where now is Jamestown, then a thick grove of trees"—it was, in fact, a second growth, and recent archeological work has established the fact that the tongue of land on which the English settlement was located had been, within the previous century, an Indian campground, probably Paspahegh. (Relocating a village and its encompassing fields—to let the land lie fallow—was a common practice, the sole method of land rejuvenation known to primitive cultivators of the soil.) In spite of tribal rivalries and conflict, one tribe's territorial rights were respected by the others in the region; a tribe identified itself with a specific area characterized by sacred landmarks and placenames to which its rituals and mythology related. In a sense, the land was an integral part of the tribe's religion: abounding in beauty and tradition as well as in game and fish, it provided sustenance for soul as well as body. (It was in this sense that the Black Hills were the religion of the Sioux: the loss of the land in 1875, at the time of the gold rush—in flagrant violation of the treaty of 1851 which had guaranteed them its possession in perpetuity—was not simply a material calamity for the tribe, but a spiritual one as well.)

"The first night of our landing, about midnight," Sir George Percy noted in his diary, "there came some Savages sayling close to our quarter. Presently there was an alarum given; upon that, the Savages ran away, and we [were] not troubled any more by them that night"—although those "Savages" doubtless paddled their canoes swiftly back to the Werowance of Paspahegh to report developments on the spit of land in the James where the three sailing ships were moored.

The newcomers had been under constant surveillance since their arrival. "The great smoakes of fire" seen by Percy in the woods were very probably signals, as he suspected, to other lookouts across the river, across the Bay, up and down the coastline from Point Comfort, to the Warrasqueocs and Nansemonds to the south, to the Kecoughtans and Chiskiacks to the north, to the Accomacs on the Eastern Shore. Drums were used as well as smoke signals: the drums which could be heard for great distances, especially along the water, would have beat out a prompt alarm.

A report on the three white-winged ships and the white-skinned, armored men aboard would have been on its way within hours after the first sail breached the strait, to the Supreme Chieftain of the region's tribes, at his principal residence, far up the Pamunkey.

"Watchful he is over us, and keeps good espiall upon our proceedings," as colonist William Strachey would later report: "Concerning which he hath his Sentinells, that at what tyme soever any of our boates, pinaces or shippes, come in, fall down, or make up the River, give the Alarum, and take yt quickly the one from the other"—on foot along the narrow, tortuous woodland trails, and so, finally, to the Pamunkey River; "the Alarum" given by the sentinels, it was taken "quickly the one from the other; until yt reach and come even to the Court, or hunting howse, wheresoever he, and . . . his Councellors, and Priests, are."* The "he" to whom Strachey refers being the great Powhatan, chief of chiefs, werowance of werowances, holding sway over a confederacy of thirty or more tidewater tribes, making his headquarters on the north bank of the Pamunkey River, at Werowocómoco. If it was not, properly speaking, a "Court"—as Strachey, with his Old World monarchical concepts, termed it—then it was Powhatan's stronghold, his seat of government, his palace, his sanctuary, his ossuary, his treasure-house.

* William Strachey, *Historie of Travell into Virginia Britania*, p. 58.

CHAPTER II

That unripe side of earth,
that heavy clime
That gives us man up now,
like Adam's time
Before he ate. . . .

JOHN DONNE

THE SOVEREIGNTY of the Supreme Chieftain Powhatan extended over virtually all tidewater Virginia: the entire coastal belt stretching one hundred miles inland to the fall-line on the west, and including the peninsula across the strait, the Eastern Shore—an area approximately one-fifth of the present-day state. The Powhatan Confederacy included most of the Algonkian-speaking tribes in the tidewater country; hostile Siouan and Iroquoian tribes occupied the other four-fifths of what is now the state.

The Algonkian language family, to which the Powhatan tribes of Virginia belonged, was one of the largest and most widespread on the North American continent: Algonkian dialects were to be heard all the way across the continent, from Labrador to beyond Hudson Bay, in the Great Lakes region, in the Mississippi Valley.[1] Not that a common language was indicative of a common cultural level: Algonkian was the tongue of primitive nomadic hunting bands in the subarctic, devoid of all but the most rudimentary societal organization; Algonkian was the tongue, as well, of culturally advanced corn-growers in the south, along the north and central Atlantic seaboard, agricultural societies boasting fairly complex and sophisticated political structures.

Algonkian was one of the five major linguistic stocks of this continent,[2] one as different from the other as English from Bantu, Hebrew from Chinese. These five major stocks are thought to represent five major waves of migration—each of the five peoples with a different language, different origins, different background—that came to the Americas from different regions of Asia tens of thousands of years ago (archeologists make educated guesses ranging anywhere from twelve or fifteen thousand to thirty thousand years ago), sometime toward the end of the Ice Age. At that time the Narrows (a mere fifty-six miles) between Siberia and Alaska were spanned by a land bridge which had come into existence as the sea levels fell, as the receding waters of the glacial age exposed the bed of the shallow Bering Strait.* Having crossed from one continent to the other, these groups of hunters of Mongoloid stock dispersed south and east, following the big-game herds along the ice-free valleys which served as avenues across and down the North American continent. Some settled there; others continued through Central America and on to South America; on and on, until land's end was reached at Tierra del Fuego.

This theory of the peopling of the Western Hemisphere is the consensus of twentieth-century science. As late as the third quarter of the twentieth century, no evidence has come to light to refute it; to date, archeological research in the Americas has turned up no traces of a pre–*Homo sapiens* type of man, such as have been discovered in Europe, Asia, and Africa—a fact leading to the conclusion that the man who settled this hemisphere must have arrived already well along the long evolutionary road, already equipped to settle new continents. The First Act was evidently not played out here.

Columbus's Renaissance world had no such scientific consensus to explain the presence of man in a region where man had not been thought to exist—a fourth quarter of a world thought, until that time, to be tripartite.

It was the Passage to India that Columbus had sailed to seek; it was the East Indies he thought he sighted in that blue Bahaman sea on October 12, 1492. Once Columbus had determined that the isles he found were not off the coast of Asia—neither Cathay nor Cipango—then it followed that the inhabitants were not "Indians," after all, though the misnomer stuck.

But if not "Indians," what were they? It was the question every troubled European from Columbus on was to ask himself at sight of those red men of the New-Found Land. If not descendants of Noah

---

* This theory does not preclude the possibility that when the land bridge disappeared at the close of the Ice Age, some 10,000 years ago, other migrants from Asia came to this continent by boat across the open waters of the narrow Bering Strait, as the Eskimo-Aleuts are believed to have done.

(and they could not be, since Noah had only three sons, whose descendants were already accounted for—in Europe, Libya, and Asia, according to Judaeo-Christian cosmology and doctrine), they could not count their descent from Adam; in which case, they could not be accounted part of the Judaeo-Christian creation scheme. In that case, did they have souls, were they members of the human race? (It was the point upon which the issue of slavery depended: if the red men were subhuman, beasts of the forest, they were subject to enslavement like any other beast of burden. The debate as to whether the Indians had souls continued into the sixteenth century.) Even as the Church at Rome debated the point (Pope Paul III finding at long last in the affirmative[8]), philosophers pondered the question Columbus had posed when he first set foot on San Salvador: "What manner of people" might these redskins be?—Did they have their origin in the Lost Continent of Atlantis or Mu? Did they belong to one of the ten Lost Tribes of Israel? So the Puritans contended; so do the Mormons, to this day. Might they be "moone children" gone "amisse"—lunar changelings? Such was the theory proposed by Francis Godwin in his mid-seventeenth-century science-fiction story, *The Man in the Moone.* *

To these questions, few answers were forthcoming.

The times prior to the arrival of Columbus in America belong, for the most part, to prehistory—aeons of time without a written record, vast regions of land-space with scarce a monument. The two huge continents yield few clues to archeological research. In South America, the ruins of Inca and pre-Inca civilization long lay inaccessible in the Andes. It is in Central America and Mexico where most of the evidence available is to be found: the pyramids of Teotihuacán, the ziggurats of Yucatán and Guatemala, the rare Mayan codices to survive the Spanish invaders' torch, though without a Rosetta Stone to illuminate them.

Elsewhere, not so much as a menhir standing, and the minimal archeological rubble: prehistory guards its secrets well. Whereas it has been established that man was present in the northeastern area of North America as long as ten thousand years ago, there remain only his spearpoints and his grinding-stones among the bones of the game he hunted to attest his presence, and only new radiocarbon and Rosholt

---

* By Godwin's theory, the people of the moon exchange their wayward children for earthlings, sending their own who "doe amisse" to "a certaine high hill in the North of America, whose people I can easily beleeve to be wholly descended of them, partly in regard of their colour, partly also in regard of the continuall use of Tobacco which Lunars use exceeding much. . . ." (Francis Godwin, *The Man in the Moone: A Story of Space Travel* [Hereford, *The Hereford Times*], 1959).

dating techniques to enable the archeologist to attribute the artifact to the proper period.

A number of prehistoric cultures flowered in the Ohio and Mississippi valleys—mound-building cultures, characterized by a cult of the dead, an elaborate funeral ritual, and funerary arts. The influence of these cultural centers made itself felt all along a well-established trade network that extended into the Great Lakes region and up and down the Atlantic coastline, including the Northeast Woodlands. Here, across the northern forest zone from Minnesota and the Great Lakes to the St. Lawrence Valley and New England, a series of interrelated cultures developed, and a culture pattern was set to serve the prehistoric ancestors of historic tribes, the tribes that would be known to history as Siouan, Iroquoian, and Algonkian. The cultural pattern common to all the historic tribes throughout this region has been designated by anthropologists as the "Northeastern Woodlands" type.[4]

Tradition had it that numbers of Algonkian-speaking peoples—bands of primitive nomadic hunters—had changed their habitat from the northernmost extremity of the Northeast Woodlands area to the Chesapeake Bay area, moving south several centuries before the English landing there in 1607—sometime about the fourteenth century. Thus said, at least, a Powhatan tribal tradition current in the early seventeenth century; archeological proof has yet to be produced in substantiation of the legend.

Moving south, these peoples had exchanged a rigorous subarctic environment for a tidewater land of waters teeming with fish, shellfish overflowing onto the beaches into the very hands of the gatherer, and forests filled with game, abounding in wild fruits, berries, nuts. The fertile Virginia soil yielded four yearly corn harvests; fields were planted near hunting and fishing grounds. The struggle for survival no longer absorbed the major life force of the people; the Algonkian-speaking newcomers acquired new skills, exercised new talents, devised well-ordered and impressively complex political systems to accommodate and coordinate the constantly increasing population, revised religious, social, and political hierarchies, strengthened central authority, established chiefdoms—and in the late sixteenth century, formed a confederacy, a political phenomenon exclusive to the Atlantic seaboard, in evidence from Maine to Virginia.

THESE WERE THE POWHATAN TRIBES of Virginia, and this was the cultural stage they had attained at the time of their first encounter with the white invader. When the English landed on the banks of the James in

1607, the Algonkian tribes of the Chesapeake Bay region were still in the process of consolidating their confederacy.

The confederacy had been the creation—and had taken the name—of its Supreme Chieftain, Powhatan, who had adopted the name of his natal tribe.

Powhatan had inherited sovereignty over a nucleus of six cognate tribes and territories within a fifty-mile radius of present-day Richmond; the Powhatan, Arrohatoc, Appomatoc, Youghtanund, Mattaponi, and Pamunkey tribes, most taking their names from the rivers on whose banks they dwelt, composed an already unified intertribal organization with strong social ties and a communality of culture. The rest of the tidewater Algonkian tribes—two dozen or more—had been brought under Powhatan's dominion somewhere around the turn of the century either by force of arms or by strategic maneuver. John Smith's *True Relation* lists twenty-eight tribes in the Powhatan confederation, while his map of 1612 shows thirty-six "kings' houses" or tribal capitals in the Powhatan sphere of influence, along with one hundred and sixty-one villages, large and small, whose chiefs and subchiefs, local and regional werowances, all rendered homage and paid tribute to Powhatan, looking to him for the maintenance of peace within the confederacy, and for defense against the alien Sioux and Iroquois who surrounded and occasionally raided the tidewater territory of the Algonkians.

The Powhatan league of tribes lacked the power and elaborate political structure of its contemporary, the Iroquois Confederacy; it lacked the idealistic concepts, the primitive democratic elements, the elements of representative government apparent in the latter—concepts and elements which may have exerted an influence on the democratic political theory later to be developed in the Colonies.* But Thomas Jefferson was justified in applying the term "confederacy" to the Powhatan bloc: it was a well-structured political organization developed for the purpose of peace-keeping and trade, without undue interference in the domestic autonomy of the member tribes. Not that Powhatan's control was absolute and unchallenged at the turn of the century: the tribes at the periphery of the empire, those farthest removed from central authority, most frequently and most successfully defied it; some few large and powerful tribes, closer to the base of power, might occasionally insist on pursuing an independent policy, as would happen in reaction to the English invasion crisis. Insubordinate tribes were

---

* Frederick Jackson Turner's famous phrase "Democracy came out of the forest" could have alluded to the Iroquois, if not the Powhatan, Confederacy.

disciplined—either relocated in areas where closer surveillance could be exerted over them, or subjected to the rule of one of Powhatan's trusty allies or kinsmen. His three brothers (Opitchapan, Kecatough, and Opechancanough) were in command of the heavily populated Pamunkey River region; two of Powhatan's sons served him as tribal chieftains, Parahunt (or Tanx-Powhatan, as the English called him) over the Powhatans, Pochins over the Kecoughtans.

Powhatan was in the process of extending and consolidating his empire precisely when the English burst upon the scene. Given time, he might have succeeded in expelling hostile Siouan tribes of the Piedmont, in extending the confederacy's frontiers north of the Potomac or south of the Nottoway.

It was overall a time of expansion, of florescence, for the Northeast Woodlands cultures. The position of the Virginia Algonkians in the early seventeenth century was distinctly advantageous: in the security provided them by the confederation, enjoying the natural bounty of the Chesapeake, and practicing a few provident techniques to preserve and store that bounty out of season, they could further develop their social institutions and refine their culture. By aboriginal standards, the population of the confederacy was large: eighty-five hundred to nine thousand outnumbering all the rest of the Virginia Indian tribes combined; the tidewater Algonkians, settled and well housed in secure villages surrounded by cultivated fields, could support a denser population than could the seminomadic hunting-and-gathering tribes in the other parts of Virginia.

"Primitive" is a misleading adjective for a society as sophisticated and complex as that of the Powhatans, with its well-defined class distinctions and social controls, with its occupational specializations and orderly secular hierarchy of command. The distribution of supplies through exchange as practiced by the tribes of the confederacy was an economic concept that had its parallel in European society. The notable artifacts that survive give proof that there was a religious and aesthetic motivation as well as a utilitarian purpose in the mind of the maker.

From James Fort on the James River to Werowocómoco on the Pamunkey was only fourteen or fifteen miles as the crow flies, but it was farther for the runner on the tortuous forest trails or for the boatman along the circuitous waterways—six or seven hours on foot or by canoe. As soon as Powhatan received word of white men on his shores, he would have summoned his counselors to join him in a conference—to consult the omens, to confront the crisis, and to consider the options open to them in dealing with it.

The European white man was not a totally unknown quantity to the Indians around Chesapeake Bay. They had already known him, either by direct contact or by hearsay, for something like a hundred years. Intertribal trade was the conduit for news—north and south, up and down the coast, as well as east and west, as far west as the Great Lakes; exchange of news and cultural ideas accompanied the exchange of goods, for generations. (The most highly prized ornaments and utensils of the Virginia Indians were of copper, as the English observed in the early 1600's; the metal must have been imported from the Lake Superior region, obtained in trade for coastal pearls and shells, which have turned up in inland archaeological excavations.)

Word had undoubtedly been passed up from the Gulf Coast, after 1520, when the Spaniards began their slave raids there to rebuild the labor forces of their West Indies plantations, to replace the native Caribbean islanders who were being so rapidly exterminated.[5] The kidnapping started in 1496, when Columbus seized thirty redskinned, paint-daubed, befeathered creatures from Hispaniola for shipment back to Granada, to titillate the Court of Ferdinand and Isabella.

The Virginia Indians would surely have heard, in 1524, from their Algonkian-speaking neighbors immediately to the south, on the Carolina Banks, that a great ship from beyond the seas had appeared inside the barrier reef. The ship was *La Dauphine*, with Verrazano in command. Although he was courteously received, his French crew reciprocated by snatching a child from its mother's arms—not to mention "a young woman which was very beautiful and of tall stature" whom they tried unsuccessfully to abduct ("could not possibly, for the great outcries that she made, bring her to the sea"). The early French and English voyagers did not go in for professional slaving as did the Portuguese; they kidnapped merely to collect interesting specimens of the exotic fauna of this newfound land—live souvenirs of their travels, living proof of their discoveries.

There is evidence, but no conclusive proof, that the Indians of the Chesapeake area had direct contact with European white men in 1570 or 1571, when a Spanish Jesuit mission was founded on the York River. Its destruction by the Indians is said to have been avenged in 1572 by a punitive expedition sent up from a Spanish base in Florida.

After the Spaniards' depredations along the southern and central Atlantic coast, the natives could have formed no favorable impression of the white man. Sir Richard Grenville, leading the Raleigh expedition to the Carolina Banks in 1584–85, did nothing to ameliorate that impression when, in retaliation for a theft, he set fire to a Secotan village on the Pamlico River where he had admittedly been "well entertained": "At Aquascagoc the Indians stole a silver Cup, wherefore we burnt the

Towne and spoyled their corn"—the first English atrocity on that shore. Thomas Hariot, the brilliant polymath-poet-magus delegated by his pupil-patron-friend Sir Walter Raleigh to sail as surveyor and historian of the expedition, deplored his companions' overreaction: "Some of our company . . . shewed themselves too furious . . . upon causes that on our part might have bin borne with more mildenesse."

Powhatan had doubtless been notified by the Secotan tribe of the white man's presence in the vicinity, as a common danger—the Pamlico River area is less than one hundred fifty miles south of the Chesapeake. It is even conceivable that Powhatan later cooperated with those Algonkian-speaking neighbor tribes in the attack on Raleigh's Roanoke Island Colony, in the massacre or abduction of the hundred-odd Englishmen and women who had settled there in 1587. (Another possibility, suggested by historian David Beers Quinn, is that the English colonists left at Roanoke by Governor White in 1587 departed that island shortly thereafter and made their way north to the Chesapeake region, where they were massacred by Powhatan Confederacy forces shortly after the turn of the century.)

IN APRIL OF 1607, the white men appeared upon Powhatan's own shores—the shores of the Chesapeake, the banks of his own river—and, in concert with his priests and counselors, he faced a crucial decision on the policy and strategy to be adopted in the face of the invasion. There was resort to ritual: ritual paint and feathers were applied, ritual robes donned, sacred relics displayed, pipes passed, drums beaten, dances executed, incantations and supplications performed; auguries were interpreted, orations declaimed by sages and elders.

But the memory of a dread and ancient prophecy haunted them all, a prophecy recorded by the colonist-adventurer William Strachey when he reached Virginia in 1610:

> There be at this tyme certayne Prophesies afoote amongst the people enhabiting about us . . . which his [Powhatan's] priests contynually put him in feare of. . . . How that from the Cheasapeak Bay a Nation should arise, which should dissolve and give end to his Empier, for which not many years synce (perplex't with this divelish Oracle . . .) he destroyed and put to sword, all such who might lye under any doubtfull construccion of the said prophesie, as all the Inhabitants, the weroance and his Subjects of that province and so remayne all the Chessiopeains at this daie, and for this cause extinct.

The Powhatans, according to Strachey, had exterminated the Chesapeake tribe, but fate could not so easily be forestalled, and "a second Prophesy" foretold

> that twice they should give overthrowe and dishearten the Attempters, and such Straungers as should envade their Territoryes, or laboure to settell a plantation amongest them, but the third tyme they themselves should fall into their Subjection and under their Conquest.

If the Powhatans had twice successfully repulsed aggressors from the east, from the direction of the Bay—if they had, in recent years, wiped out the Chesapeake tribe and, in 1570 or 1571, the Spanish Jesuit mission on the York—then must they now construe the appearance of the English from out the Bay in 1607 as the fatal third time of the prophecy? Were these the strangers fated to accomplish the downfall and subjection of the Powhatans? (A similar prophecy of impending doom current in Mexico prior to the arrival of Cortez, in 1518, may have been responsible for the paralysis that gripped the Aztecs and explained their otherwise inexplicable lack of resistance—the inexorability of fate being a kind of self-justification for failure to resist.)

Whether any such paralysis or despair affected the Powhatans or whether it was simply that unanimity eluded them in their council, no full-scale attack was mounted by the confederacy against the invaders. At that juncture, the English—in the process of unloading and with their fortifications incomplete—were most vulnerable; they could have least successfully withstood an assault by the combined forces of the thirty-odd tribes of the confederacy. The Englishmen's superiority in weaponry would have been offset by the Powhatans' superiority in numbers—two to three thousand Indian warriors against no more than one hundred forty Englishmen, including the ships' crews.

But the policy adopted by Powhatan and his council was apparently to wait and see. It was the purpose of the newcomers that perplexed the native Indians. If the white men had come to fish, as the French, English, and Portuguese had been fishing the North Atlantic seaboard for some hundred years, their catch would not be begrudged them. If they had come to trade, they would be welcome: their armor, breastplates, and helmets glittered in the sun, so they might be bringing scarce metals highly prized by the Indians for tools and ornaments; they might be bringing powerful new weapons which the Powhatans could turn against their traditional enemies with devastating effect—as, for example, the "thundersticks" with which the English had repelled their attackers at Cape Henry. If it was a matter of trade, the Powhatans would negotiate with them, would offer pearls and shells, deerskins and beaver pelts in exchange for novelties from overseas. But if the strangers had come to settle, rather than to fish or to trade, their presence might constitute a peril. The report that the newcomers had been seen planting seeds suggested that more than a brief sojourn was intended; there was need for clarification. So long as they were not allowed to gain ascendancy, they might prove useful allies against the Powhatans' traditional enemies. A close watch was ordered to be kept over the intruders' every move; a relay of messengers ensured prompt delivery of reports to Chief Powhatan at Werowocómoco.

The intertribal confederation in the tidewater was, at that point, clearly gaining in strength, despite divisive reaction by several powerful and independent member-tribes. The Powhatan Confederacy may have enjoyed a sense of false security in the knowledge that the invaders— despite their technological advantages—were vastly outnumbered. They may have put reliance, too, on the fact that previous European settlements on their shore had been short-lived, on the fact that the Europeans appeared unable to survive in an environment which the native inhabitants exploited efficiently.

Apparently there was, from the beginning, a difference of opinion among the tribes of the confederacy as to how to deal with the situation. This difference of opinion was reflected in the uncertainties of red-white relations over the first few years of contact—the resultant inconsistency of policy was interpreted by the Europeans as native "treachery." (The English seemed equally unreliable to the Indians.)

In May, the chieftain of the Appomatocs made clear to Percy his displeasure at the English presence: "with his Arrow readie in his Bow in one hand, and taking a Pipe of Tobacco in the other . . . demanded of us of our being there, willing us to bee gone." Percy heard the mutter of discontent from Powhatan tribesmen, too: they "murmured at our planting in the Countrie," although as Percy noted, their werowance (Powhatan's son Parahunt) defended the Englishmen's right to be there; he

> made answere againe very wisely of a Savage, Why should you bee offended with them, as long as they hurt you not, nor take any thing away by force. They take but a little waste ground, which doth you nor any of us any good.

The chieftains of the many tribes of the confederacy all looked to Powhatan for a decision, but the Supreme Chieftain would bide his time and reserve his judgment. A close surveillance was to be maintained over the intruders, and Powhatan would watch and wait: watch developments and wait for a sign, an omen, a dream, a vision—as much or more reliance placed upon inspiration and the supernatural as upon logic.

Powhatan was a man "of such subtile understanding and politique carriage" as to impress all who came into his presence, including Strachey, who wrote in his *Historie of Travell into Virginia Britania*: "And sure yt is to be wondered at, how such a barbarous and uncivil Prynce, should take unto him . . . adorned and set forth with no greater outward ornament"—naked, save for his paint and ornaments and breechclout—"a forme and ostentacion of such Majestie as he expresseth, which oftentimes strykes awe and sufficient wonder unto our people, presenting themselves before him." (His air of striking majesty, Strachey reasoned, could be attributed only to the aura of Divine Right with which even a savage monarch was invested.) If the English were awed by Powhatan's presence, no wonder his own people groveled: "It is straung to see with what great feare and adoration all these people doe obey this Powhatan, for at his feet they present whatsoever he Commaundeth, and at the least frowne of his brow, the greatest will tremble. . . ."

In principle, each tribe in the confederacy adhered to its traditional boundaries, guaranteed inviolable by the Supreme Chieftain: "Every Weroance knowes his own Meeres," or boundaries, as Strachey continued, knows his own "lymitts to fish fowle or hunt in. . . . But they hold all of their great Weroance Powhatan unto whome they paie 8 parts of 10 tribute of all Commodities which their Country yieldeth." Powhatan's treasure-house was filled to the brim, ran over with corn, beans, skins, pelts, copper, beads, pearls, shell, turkeys, and other wild game; the tribute symbolized the werowances' submission to Powhatan, their obligation to furnish warriors at his demand. Strachey could not have failed to be struck by the parallel with the European feudal system: all the minor chiefs (or vassals) acknowledging their allegiance to the Supreme Chieftain (or suzerain) under whom they held their chiefdoms (or fiefs) and to whom they rendered homage, tribute, service.

Supreme Chieftain Powhatan was the law-giver, the law-enforcer, the embodiment of the law:

Nor have they positive lawes, only the lawe whereby he ruleth is custome; yet when he pleaseth his will is lawe, and must be obeyed, not only as a king, but half as a god, his People esteeme him so. . . .

Strachey describes Powhatan as he saw him in 1610:

He is a goodly old man, not yet schrincking though well beaten with many cold and stormy wynters. . . . He is supposed to be a little lesse than 80 yeares old.* . . . Of a tall stature and cleane lymbes, of a sad aspect, rownd fat visage'd with gray haires, but playne and thin hanging upon his broad showlders, some few haires upon his Chynne, and so on his upper lippe. He hath bene a strong and able salvadge, synowie, active, and of a daring spiritt, vigilant, ambitious, subtile to enlarge his dominions. . . . The greatnes and bowndes of whose Empire by reason of his Powerfulnes, and ambition in his youth, hath lardger lymittes than ever had any of his Predicissors in former tymes. . . . Cruell he hath bene and quarrellous, as well with his owne Wero-ances for triffles, and that to stryke terrour and awe into them of his power and condicion, as also with his neighbours in his younger dayes, though now delighted in security, and pleasure, and therefore standes upon reasonable condicions of peace, with all the great and absolute Weroances about him, and is likewise more quietly setteled amongest his owne.

"In all his ancient Inheritaunces"—the six cognate tribal areas which he had inherited according to the traditional matrilineal tribal succession—

he hath howses built after their manner, and at every howse provision for his entertaynement . . . : about his person ordinarily attendeth a guard of 40 or 50 of the tallest men his Country doe affourd. . . .

According to the order and custome of sensuall Hethenisme in the Allowance of Poligamy, he may have as many women as he will, and hath (as is supposed) many more than one hundred, All which he doth not keepe, yet as the Turke in one Saraglia or howse but hath an appointed number, which reside still in every their severall places, amongest whome when he lyeth on his bedd, one sitteth at his head, and another at his feet, but when he sitteth at meat, or in presenting himself to any Straungers, one sitteth on his right hand, and another on his leaft. . . . when he dyneth or suppeth, one of his women before and after meat, bringeth him water in a wooden platter, to wash his handes, another wayting with a bunch of feathers to wipe them instead of a towell.

* Captain Smith estimated Powhatan's age at sixty.

Of his women there are said to be about some dozen at this present, in whose Company he takes more delight then in the rest being for the most parte very young women, and these Commonly remove with him from howse to howse, either in his tyme of hunting, or visitation of his severall howses. . . . The names of the women I have not thought altogether amisse to set downe . . . and as they stood formost in his Kings affection, for they observe certayne degrees of greatnes, according to the neerenes they stand in their Princes love, and amourous entertaynment. . . .

Winganuske.*	Attossocomiske.	Ortoughnoiske.
Ashetoiske.	Ponnoiske.	Oweroughwough.
Amopotoiske.	Appomosiscut.	Ottermiske.
Ottopomtacke.	Appimmonoiske.	Memeoughquiske.

Henry Spelman, a semiliterate young reprobate from a distinguished family, who spent many months in captivity among the Powhatans in 1609–10, elaborates on the marital customs of their chieftains:

When yᵉ Kinge of yᵉ cuntry will have any wives he acquaintes his cheef men with his purpose, who sends . . . into all partes of yᵉ cuntry for yᵉ fayrest and cumliest mayds out of which yᵉ Kinge taketh his choyse given to ther parents what he pleaseth. If any of yᵉ King's wives have onc[e] a child by him, he [never lieth with hir more] keepes hir no longer but puts hir from him givinge hir suffitient Copper and beads to mantayne hir and the child while it is younge and then [it] is taken from hir and mantayned by yᵉ King[s charge], it now beinge lawfull for hir beinge thus put away to marry with any other.

"As he is weary of his women," Strachey reports,

he bestowes them on those that best deserve them at his handes. . . . The reason why each chief Patron of a famely especially Weroances are desirous and (indeed) strive for many wives,† is because they would have many Children, who may if chaunce be fight for them, when they are old, as also then feed and maynetayne

* The name of Winganuske, Powhatan's leading lady, translates as Lovely Woman.
† "Kings have as many women as they will," John Smith tells us, "his Subjects two, and most but one."

them. . . . They often reported unto us that Powhatan had then lyving twenty sonnes and ten daughters. . . .

Of these ten daughters, the Supreme Chieftain showed marked favor to one. The name of this signally favored daughter of Powhatan was Pocahontas.

Or, rather, Pocahontas was one of her names—her nickname, her public name, the name by which she was known outside the tribe. Her real name—her secret or proper name—was Matoaka or Matowaka (a word found also spelled Matoka, Matoaks, or Matoax). The Powhatans regarded a person's clan name as magic, a part of his essence (as do the Navajos, to this day); this secret name—given at birth, derived from totems, and dependent on esoteric knowledge—was a sacred name known only to the immediate family or the clan, never used in everyday life, lest some of the supernatural elements inherent in the name be diminished, profaned by common usage. ("Her real name," according to William Stith's reliable eighteenth-century chronicle, "it seems was *Matoax* which the Indians carefully concealed from the English and changed it to Pocahontas, out of a superstitous fear, lest they, by the Knowledge of her true name, should be enabled to do her some hurt.") Thus, a public name was provided for every member of the tribe, usually descriptive of some habit or trait connected with the child's social personality. The name *Pocahontas* or *Pocahantes* (for *Pokahantesu*) derives from an adjective meaning "playful, sportive, frolicsome, mischievous, frisky."

"Both men and women and Children have their severall names at first" (as William Strachey discovered in 1610),

according to the severall humour of their parents and for the men-children at first, when they are young their mothers give them a name, calling them by some affectionate Title, or perhappes observing their promising inclynation give yt accordingly, and so the great king *Powhatan*, called a young daughter of his, whome he loved well Pochahuntas, which may signifie Little-wanton, howbeit she was rightly called Amonute. . . .[6]

"After the mother is delivered of hir child," Spelman observes in his *Relation of Virginea*, in a passage so obscure as almost to require translation, "with in som feaw dayes after the kinsfolke and neyburs beinge intreated ther unto, cums unto y⁵ house: wher beinge assembled the father, takes the child in his armes: and declares that his name shall be, as he then calls him, so his name is, which dunn, y⁵ rest of y⁵ day is spent in feastinge and dauncinge." In the case of a child of the Supreme Chieftain, the celebration would have been on a lavish, right royal scale—Powhatan taking the girl child in his arms, declaring her clan name to be Matoaka, and her nickname Pocahontas.

If Spelman was well informed, if he had correctly understood his informant (there was not only a language barrier to overcome in communication, there was a vast cultural gap) and it was true that a werowance's wife was dismissed from his household after the birth of a first child and that the child was returned to its father's charge as soon as it could be separated from its mother, then Pocahontas would have been returned to Powhatan's charge as soon as she had been weaned, probably at the age of at least three or four.[7] Pocahontas's mother is not named or mentioned by any contemporary witness. It would appear that she had, indeed, been dismissed from Powhatan's entourage at the time of her daughter's birth. It is possible that she was bestowed in marriage by Powhatan—in token of his esteem—upon some petty werowance or war-party leader.

It is no more possible to specify the date of Pocahontas's birth than to identify her mother. She was, in 1607, an adolescent or on the threshold of adolescence, somewhere between the ages of ten and fourteen, with the bulk of contemporary evidence pointing to the latter. The age of twelve was generally considered by the Indians to be the age of maturity, the age at which responsibility was expected. Those who saw Pocahontas and attempted to estimate her age could base their estimate only on her appearance, her apparel, and the degree of responsibility with which she functioned in her society.

The English learned that maidens could be distinguished from matrons by their hair styles: "The Maids you shall alwayes see the forepart of their head and sides shaven close," as Percy observed in his diary, "which they tie in a pleate [plait] hanging downe to their hips. The married women weares [sic] their haire all of a length, and [it] is tied of that fashion that the Maids are."

Not only their hair styles but their costumes differed: John White, the gifted artist who accompanied Thomas Hariot on the Raleigh expedition of 1584–85, painted the charming portrait of a little girl belonging to one of the Algonkian tribes on the Carolina barrier reefs, daughter of "A Noblewoman of Pomeiock," a town "about twenty miles from Roanoke . . . close to the sea," by Hariot's accompanying description. The little girl of John White's watercolor was therefore a close neighbor of Pocahontas's, the product of a similar culture, and like Pocahontas, a werowance's daughter. Thus her portrait is the next best thing to a portrait of Pocahontas at an early age: "These little girls of seven or eight years," according to Hariot's caption, "wear girdles of skin, padded with moss, which pass between their legs." Nothing else. (The little boys went entirely naked until the age of ten or twelve, at which time they donned the regular male attire, the breechclout of skin between their thighs, barely covering their "privities," as Strachey put it.) As the girls approached puberty, at the age of eleven or twelve, the single, narrow, moss-padded skin strap was exchanged for a short leather apron of dressed skin.

The young girls, after undergoing the rites of puberty, graduated to women's dress: a buckskin skirt attached at the waist and reaching down, in front, to a point just above the knees; the "hynder parts" undraped, bare. This skirt was usually made of finely dressed deerskin ("in winter dressed with the haire, but in the Sommer without"), fringed at the drape about the waist and again at the drape above the knees. According to Strachey, some of "the better sort of women"—such as a Princess Pocahontas—

> cover them (for the most parte) all over with skyn mantells, fynely drest, shagged and frindged at the skirt, carved and coulored, with some pretty worke or the proportion of beasts, fowle, tortoyses, or other such like Imagery as shall best please or expresse the fancie of the wearer. . . . Some use mantells, made both of Turkey feathers and other fowle so pretely wrought and woven with threeds that nothing could be discerned but the feathers, which were exceeding warme and very handsome.

But mostly they were bare. In John White's watercolors, the wives of the Carolina werowances are naked above the fringed waist drape of their buckskin mini-skirts: bare-breasted save for the multiple strands of pearls or shell beads draped about their necks, and "their hands upon their shoulders, thus covering their breasts" (a sign of what Hariot took to be "maidenly modesty," although he was the only one so to identify it).[8] Their breasts were "remarkable," to quote Robert Beverley in his panegyric on the Virginia Indian women, in his observation of the few who survived at the dawn of the eighteenth century; their "small round . . . Breasts so firm, that they are hardly ever observ'd to hang down even in old Women."[9]

"Their women are generally Beautiful," Beverley continued, "possessing an uncommon delicacy of Shape and Features." He agreed with Strachey, who had found the Powhatan women endowed with "handsome lymbes, slender armes, and pretty handes."[10] Beverley's brother-in-law, Colonel William Byrd II (first native-born member of that distinguished Virginia line), like Beverley a connoisseur of female flesh, admitted to a sneaking admiration for the Virginia Indian women: one he saw at Nottoway Towne, early in the eighteenth century, on his way to settle Virginia's boundary line dispute with North Carolina, had such a "fine Shape and regular Features" as to make her "appear like a Statue in Bronze done by a masterly hand."[11]

And to quote Beverley again (writing a century after Strachey): "The Indians are of the middling and largest stature of the English"— taller, actually, than all but the tallest Englishmen, an average of six feet, according to a 1940 study of skeletal parts found at an Indian ossuary on the York River, near West Point.

> They are straight and well proportion'd, having the cleanest and most exact Limbs in the World: They are so perfect in their outward frame, that I never heard of one single Indian, that was either dwarfish, crooked, bandy-legg'd or otherwise mis-shapen. But if they have any such practice among them, as the Romans had, of exposing such Children till they dyed, as were weak and mis-shapen at their Birth, they are very shy of confessing it, and I could never yet learn that they had.

There was, nonetheless, among the Indians, a decided emphasis (not unlike our own) on standards of physical excellence, a pre-occupation with physique: among the West Coast tribes, such as the Makah of northern Washington, the maiden's puberty ritual entailed her sitting in a corner of her dwelling for the four days of her isolation, with her back against the wall to make it straight, her knees against her abdomen to make it flat. Pocahontas, like the other maidens of her tribe, would have been impressed with the importance of a good carriage, been trained to hold herself erect—shoulders back, stomach muscles taut; contemporary comment on her great dignity and her imposing mien is, perhaps in part, a tribute to her noble bearing.

Pocahontas, if she was twelve or thirteen years old in 1607, had probably already undergone the tribal puberty ceremonies.

Information about the puberty rites of the Powhatans, as of all East Coast tribes, is scanty for the reason that the tribes east of the Mississippi were the first to be exterminated or to suffer cultural dis-integration. They were subject to no truly scientific anthropological study such as has been made in this century among surviving tribes west of the Rockies—tribes whose cultural patterns are still intact, or almost so. It is possible that the seventeenth-century explorers and early settlers—the only witnesses and reporters of the East Coast aboriginal cultures—were unable to recognize or distinguish the puberty ritual among other more elaborate ceremonials. These firstcomers were, from the modern anthropological-ethnological point of view, untrained as observers, inept as investigators. Ethnocentric rather than objective, they were guilty of gross cultural misunderstandings and misinterpretations.

William Strachey, in his *Historie of Travell into Virginia Britania*, is the only contemporary witness to touch on the periodic segregation of Powhatan women:

> The women are themselves so modest, as in the tyme of their sicknes, they have great care to be seene abroad, at what time they goe apart, and keepe from the men in a severall roome, which they have for themselves as a kynd of Gynaeceum. . . .

Strachey misunderstood and misinterpreted what he had observed; lacking any background knowledge of "primitive" cultures, he could not have known that female segregation at this period, as at puberty, did not stem from female modesty, but rather from an ancient, worldwide taboo or fear-avoidance concerning the life-giving, female reproductive power, which was held to be a form of magic inimical to the male.

It is assumed by twentieth-century anthropologists that there prevailed, originally, among the tribes of the East Coast, much of the same ritual associated with the segregation of maidens as was later found to prevail among tribes in the West. Traditionally, among the western and northern tribes, the adolescent girl was secluded—for a period ranging from an average of four days to as long as a month—in a specially constructed isolation hut made of grass, bark, or hides, or in a corner of her family dwelling. Fasting was a part of the ritual (as in the case of the adolescent boy): the girl was further enjoined, however, to avoid all forms of contact, to keep her face turned from the sun and from the fire. Lest her lips contaminate the sacred element of water, she drank through a tube; and lest the supernatural power active within her at this period imperil her own body, a scratching stick of shell or wood was used by her to scratch her head, the most vital bodily member. During her seclusion, clan songs were sung by relays of dancer-singers, and toward the close of the period of isolation, instruction was given to the girl by the clan leader himself—another similarity to the initiation ritual of the boys—instruction in tribal genesis myths, in tribal standards of conduct and etiquette, with special emphasis on the desirable female attributes of peacefulness, courtesy, and good-housewifery. Among the

Sioux, the four cardinal female virtues to be inculcated in the adolescent girl are noted as fortitude, generosity, truthfulness, and child-bearing. The puberty ceremonial can also be a celebration of female virtues, as with the Apache, where it is an occasion of happiness and blessing for the entire tribe, for feasting and dancing, with the maiden scattering pollen upon all, especially upon the children.

If Pocahontas was brought up motherless, she was brought up, nevertheless, a privileged person in the household of the supreme werowance of the Powhatan Confederacy. If she missed the normally close and tender relation between Indian mother and daughter, still she would surely have been tended and pampered by her father's numerous current wives. And she, as they, would have been spared the travail, the drudgery that was the lot of the other women of the tribe. In the werowance's household, there were attendants to perform the rigorous, never-ending domestic chores: the gathering, the preparation, and the storage of food; the cultivation of the fields, the collection of wood and hauling of water; the making of household apparatus and of wearing apparel, the tanning of hides, the stitching of garments with awl and deer sinew; the upkeep and repair of wigwams, the erection of temporary shelters for use by the huntsmen on game drives away from the settlements.

Pocahontas's would have been an active, lively, a free and unconfined, an idyllic childhood. There were the countless "chrystall rivers," streams, creeks, and bays of her tidewater Virginia to wade and splash in, to bathe and swim in. Across the entire continent, as colonists and settlers moved west, they saw—wherever there was water—the Indians disporting themselves in it. They swam like fish, tackling the fish in their own element, as Robert Beverley, writing in the early eighteenth century, would describe the sport of sturgeon-wrestling in the Virginia estuaries:

> The Indian way of Catching Sturgeon, when they came into the narrow part of the Rivers, was by a Man's clapping a Noose over their Tail, and by keeping fast his hold. Thus a Fish finding it self intangled, wou'd flounce, and often pull him under Water, and then that Man was counted a *Cockarouse*, or brave Fellow, that wou'd not let go; till with Swimming, Wading, and Diving, he had tired the Sturgeon, and brought it ashore.[12]

A "brave Fellow" could count on an admiring audience among the women: "They love to walk in the fields and along the rivers," Thomas Hariot wrote of the North Carolina Indian women, "watching the deer-hunting and the fishing." If Pocahontas was the tomboy her name implies, she would not have been content with watching; she would have joined in the rough-and-tumble water sports—diving for mussels, ducking for terrapin, wading the shallows, gigging frogs and smaller fish, as the boys did. "Before the Arrival of the English there, the Indians had Fish in such vast Plenty," as Beverley wrote in 1705, "that the Boys and Girls wou'd take a pointed Stick, and strike the lesser sort, as they Swam upon the Flats." Pocahontas would have learned to swim at a very early age. The men, women, and children of the Powhatan tribe made a ritual of ablutions in the river at sunrise and sunset[13]—the children too young to swim were borne into the water on their mothers' shoulders.

Water sports of every kind were popular with the Atlantic seaboard Indians: "It is a pleasure to see these people wading and sailing in their shallow rivers," Hariot wrote in 1585 in the Carolinas. And he found "the way they build their boats . . . very wonderful . . . as good as ours" (despite the lack of metal tools) and "seaworthy enough to take them fishing or sailing wherever they want to go." Tree trunks— some, for war-canoes, as long as forty or fifty feet—were felled by building a fire at their base; firebrands and scraping tools were then used to hollow out the trunk. (The more familiar luted birchbark canoe was not in use by the Virginia Indians.) Among the tribes who used canoes, as the Powhatans, the women were expert with pole and paddle. In a small canoe, young Pocahontas and her companions would have explored the myriad beautiful waterways of the tidewater, pulling in at golden beaches on the Bay to run and frolic, stopping to refresh themselves at the villages of friendly confederation tribesmen across the coastal belt.

On foot, Pocahontas could have explored—she and her companions, in single file and silent—the pine-carpeted narrow trails, seldom more than twenty inches wide, that traversed the seemingly impenetrable forests; trails made originally by the animals, taken up and traveled by the Indians on intertribal trading missions or on the warpath (trails to be discovered and followed by the first white explorers, settlers, and traders; trails eventually to become the wagon-trails, in some cases, the turnpikes or railway roadbeds of nineteenth- and twentieth-century America[14]).

With all the great, green Virginia forests for a playground—no enemies to fear, no dangerous animals save the bear—the Powhatan children ran free. It was not entirely poetic license, Vachel Lindsay's description of "Our Mother Pocahontas": "the maid / Who laughed among the winds and played" and "Birdlike/In the grape-vine swung." Those vines grew "thick as a man's thigh," as Percy commented, in the primeval forests of her homeland. (Lindsay may have seen Alfred Jacob Miller's portrait of another such frolicsome Indian maiden in that very pose—a Shoshone girl painted by Miller, in the Rockies, in the 1830s—swinging on a tree branch, bare to the waist, her long dark hair streaming in the breeze like the fringe of her buckskin skirt.)

Roaming the virgin Virginia forests to gather wild fruits and nuts and berries would have seemed no chore to a child such as Pocahontas: the berries grew in the fire-swept clearings—"fine and beautiful Strawberries foure times bigger and better than ours in England," as Percy conceded; and not only strawberries, but raspberries and mulberries, and other fruits unknown to England. The indigenous fruits were relished by planter-horticulturist Robert Beverley, a century later: "Cherries, Plums, Persimmons. . . . Cherries natural to the Country, and growing wild in the Woods . . . in Bunches like Grapes." Pocahontas and the other young girls could have filled their baskets with "several Sorts of good Nuts," listed by Beverley as growing wild in the Virginia woods: "viz. Chestnuts, Chinkapins, Hasel-nuts, Hickories, Walnuts, &c."

The baskets woven by the Powhatan women were of various kinds and sizes, made of corn husk, the bark of trees, wicker, native hemp, or silk grass. Beverley's *History and Present State of Virginia* (published in 1705, the first history of the colony written by a native Virginian) includes the sketch of an Indian woman weaving: she sits beneath the branch of a tree upon which she has tied her work, eyes and arms upraised, weaving her basket from below, as it hangs in midair, the open end down. The early settlers referred to the Powhatan baskets as "painted," but a Swiss traveler in Virginia in 1702 describes figures woven into the baskets, "all kinds of animals, flowers, and other strange things very beautifully."

The little girls—Pocahontas presumably among them, in her day—gathered about the basketmaker, under the tree, looking up, asking questions, teasing to be allowed to select a color or to weave a strand, learning the craft as they watched. Just so, they would have learned the craft of beadwork by watching a skilled practitioner, the beginners working out their first patterns on dolls' clothes: a single stripe of contrasting color down the middle of a chain, to begin with; the next step, a simple diagonal or zigzag pattern in two colors.

Most of the beads were made of shells, and the shells were there, in a plenitude, for the gathering—all along the riverbanks, on the shores of the Bay, in the shallows. The children raced and darted, waded and splashed to gather them: young Pocahontas and her friends would have vied with one another to fill their baskets with the choicest specimens: the small marine snails (the spiral Marginella shells) were used not only as beads for trimming deerskin garments such as mantles, moccasins, shirts, and pouches, but also as a form of currency, known as *rawrenoke* in the Algonkian (with *roanoke* being the Anglicized form of the word).[15] The larger spiral univalves—the gastropods, mollusks, conches—were other sought-after prizes to be found along the dunes and estuaries; from their yield of columella, larger oval and circular beads—called *peak*—were fashioned into ornaments, strung on thin cord and wrapped several times around the neck or wrist.

Porcupine-quill ornamentation was another ancient North American art: the Powhatan women, skilled at that elaborate and intricate form of embroidery on soft tanned leather or birchbark, would inevitably have attracted their circle of eager young apprentices. Young girls like Pocahontas would have helped to sort and grade the four different sizes of quills as they were plucked—or even to assist with the plucking. The largest and coarsest quills from the tail were used in broad masses of embroidery: for fringes, for club handles, for pipe stems; a smaller and finer quill came from the back of the animal; a quill smaller and finer still, from the neck; the smallest and finest, from the belly, were used for the most intricate and most exquisite designs.

The cosmetic arts were, of course, the most fascinating to the girls: they learned the painstaking and painful process of "pouncing," or tattooing, by watching their mothers embellish themselves: "The women have their armes, breasts, thighes, showlders and faces, cunningly imbroydered with divers workes," Strachey tells us,

> for pouncing and searing their skyns with a kynd of Instrument heated in the fire, they figure therein flowers and fruicts of sondry lively kyndes, as also Snakes, Serpents, Efts, etc. and this they doe by dropping upon the seared flesh, sondry Colours, which rub'd into the stampe will never be taken away agayne because yt will not only be dryed into the flesh, but grow therein.

John White has left us sketches of the elaborate and beautiful geometric tattoo patterns preferred by the Carolina Algonkian women. Though there exists no such pictorial record of the Virginia Algonkians at work and at play, White's watercolors of their immediate Algonkian neighbors to the south may be considered, once again, the next best thing.[16]

The question of whether Pocahontas was tattooed, like the rest of the women of her tribe, remains unanswered: no contemporary reporter made specific mention; the one authentic portrait of Pocahontas —the only portrait painted from life, a bust portrait—reveals no tattoo marks, although it must be noted that she is portrayed in English court-dress, long-sleeved, ruffed at neck and wrist, only her face and one hand exposed. It may be that tattooing among the Powhatans was not practiced until later in life, and that Pocahontas had left the tribe before that age was reached. And yet, among most tribes, tattooing was done at the time of puberty.

Pocahontas's youth would have been exuberant, uninhibited, carefree, and unconfined. The Indians' was a culture for the young. Permissiveness is an enduring Indian parental trait: punishment is rare, with as little discipline exercised as in the most extreme "progressive" educational practice. Indian mothers are indulgent with their children; the mother-daughter relationship is especially close, characterized traditionally by great tenderness and patience on the part of the mothers, who enjoy their daughters' company and their games. "They are very often accompanied by their young daughters," Hariot noted in 1585 of the women in the Carolina coastal area; that companionship is as close today, according to researchers in western tribal customs. No matter how arduous their daily chores, the Indian women found time to frolic with the children, to prepare pleasant surprises for them. The spring's first taste of maple sugar went to the children: as soon as the sap had been gathered from the trees and boiled in the large earthenware vats, as soon as the sugar began to form under their wooden paddles, the women would interrupt their work to provide the children with a treat: sweet dollops spooned up and tossed out upon the snow to harden into candy; in some tribes, the liquid maple sugar was poured into a duck-bill to be shaped into a lollipop for the youngster's daylong delight.

Indian mothers were ingenious at devising games for their children's amusement: they showed the little girls how to string cranberries on nettle fiber for necklaces, how to make miniature snowshoes out of pine-needles—a lesson in the very patterns the girl would later use in netting snowshoes for her family.

The Indian women not only made a game of teaching their little girls domestic tasks, they joined with them in athletic games, as well: in the game of football, for example, a sport popular with both sexes among the Powhatans, as Henry Spelman observed during his days of captivity among those tribes: "They use beside football play, which women and young boyes doe much play at. . . . They make their Gooles [goals] as ours only they never fight nor pull one another doune. . . ." Only the foot was allowed to be used to move the ball toward the goal, requiring speed and dexterity.

Indulgent Indian mothers made dolls for their little daughters, ingenious if crude concoctions of clay, wood, leather—some ancient specimens are still extant. John White's artist's eye was caught by a seven- or eight-year-old Carolina child (the little girl pictured wearing the moss-padded breechclout) skipping along beside her mother on the riverbank, proudly holding out her new doll to show the artist.* Hariot's caption for that sketch reads, "When we gave them the puppets and the dolls that we had brought from England, they were highly delighted." The gift of such an elaborate "puppet"—dressed, according to White's portrait, in Elizabethan court costume—must have made that wero-wance's daughter the envy of the entire younger set of her town of Pomeiock.

Indian mothers played with their small daughters much as they had with their dolls, dandling, fondling, adorning the little girls, ar-ranging their hair, oiling it, trimming it—or, rather, grating it off be-tween two sharp-edged shells—to the desired length, dressing it with feathers, leaves, or flowers.

Indian mothers had a great store of myth and legend upon which to draw for their story-telling: tales of sacred totem animals—comic and adventurous animal stories—were handed down from generation to generation, as were solemn tales of creation and of culture heroes. Mothers taught their children incantations by which to call up the spirit of the forest or the spirit of the stream, taught them magic verses and spells, a charm to summon butterflies.

The mood of Indian women has always been high-spirited, sportive, disposed to merriment; their humor, inclined to ribaldry. They are, traditionally, gregarious; coming together to sit in the sun at the wig-wam door or in the shade of a tree to perform common tasks in the company of relatives, friends, neighbors: to shell beans, to pound corn for meal, to shape pottery, to weave the reed mats used as roofing for the wigwams or longhouses—a variety of domestic tasks performed, pref-erably, in company, to the shrill obbligato of laughter, chatter, gossip.

GREGARIOUSNESS AND SPORTIVENESS may have been a characteristic of Indian women in certain social situations, but the character of the American aborigine has been marked, from the earliest records through the latest, with a disposition to aloofness, withdrawal, reticence, secre-tiveness, impenetrability.

The Indian has been noted to turn to solitude and silence for the invocation of a secret, mystic, inviolate self, for an identification with the spiritual essence of the universe (the spiritual force linking all human beings to all other living things, the force pervading all mankind

* See first picture in the group of photographs following page 144.

and all nature, animate and inanimate: the force referred to as *wakan* by the Sioux; as *oranda* by the Iroquois; as *manitou* in the Algonkian tongue).

In tribes all across the land, from the East Coast to the West, one rite of adolescence was the Vision Quest: young boys—and sometimes young girls, as among the Algonkian tribes and the Salish—sought contact with the supernatural, with their especial spiritual guides or guardians, by means of solitary fasts and vigils in the wilderness; the symbol, the song, the directive, the token of that contact with the supernatural became a lifelong inspiration, a lifelong motivating force in the boy's or girl's existence; an esoteric, religious secret, a sacred and inalienable personal treasure.

The attitude of the Indian toward silence and solitude and secretiveness is distinctive: the stillness within is not something to be dreaded, but, rather, to be sought and induced as a reservoir of spiritual strength. Pocahontas, like other Indian children, would have been taught to cultivate that inner stillness—trained to sit quietly beside a mother or a sister who was sitting quietly. "Training began with children who were taught to sit still and enjoy it," in the words of the Lakota Indian chief, Standing Bear. "They were taught to use their organs of smell, to look when there was apparently nothing to see, and to listen intently when all seemingly was quiet. A child that cannot sit still is a half-developed child."[17]

The Lakota chief put great emphasis on the child's training in manners. Pocahontas, as the daughter of the Powhatan chief, would inevitably have been brought up to represent the best of her people's social etiquette: "Excessive manners were put down as insincere, and the constant talker was considered rude and thoughtless. Conversation was never begun at once, nor in a hurried manner. No one was quick with a question, no matter how important, and no one was pressed for an answer. A pause giving time for thought was the truly courteous way of beginning and conducting a conversation." Among the Papago, the tone of voice was important: "My father went on talking to me in a low voice," a Papago woman told anthropologist Ruth Underhill recently. "That is how our people always talk to their children, so low and quiet, the child thinks he is dreaming. But he never forgets."[18]

As close as were Pocahontas and her father, Powhatan, throughout her childhood, she would in all probability (like the Papago woman) have cherished the memory of his voice "low and quiet" in her ear, his endearments and his precepts—those who quote Powhatan verbatim reveal him as highly articulate, as eloquent, with a sentimental, a poetic, as well as a philosophical turn of mind. The extraordinary closeness between father and daughter was attested to by almost every reporter of the period: those who saw Powhatan saw Pocahontas at his side, in his longhouse, at his hearth, in his retinue.

Thus she would have been among the first, on April 26, to have heard the news of the startling apparition—the English flotilla gliding white-winged into the Bay of the Chesapeake, news of the white men's landing in Powhatan territory. She would have heard the reports brought to Powhatan in the ensuing days and weeks, by relays of Indian messengers, from the small triangular fort being laid out on the narrow, dry-land peninsula tenuously connected to the bank of the River James, fifteen miles to the southeast of Powhatan's seat, Werowocómoco, on the Pamunkey.

Her curiosity aroused, like that of the others, it is reasonable to assume that Pocahontas made her way, like the others, from Werowo-cómoco, through the forest or along the waterways—a six- or seven-hour journey on foot or by canoe from the Pamunkey to the James—to see for herself the strangers in all their strangeness: the color of their skin, their glittering cuirasses, their earth-shaking cannon, their three great, flag-decked sailing vessels.

CHAPTER III

*I always consider the settlement of
America with reverence and wonder.*

JOHN ADAMS

WERE THEY BIRDS, as first reported, the three great white-winged vessels from over the horizon? If so, their wings were folded, now; pinioned, held fast by ropes tied around the trunks of the towering trees at the water's edge. If they were not birds, were they whales?* Were they floating islands? Were they gods?

To the Powhatan tribesmen converging on the James, they were a sight to behold: the three ships from beyond the seas, pennants—the red cross of St. George on a white ground—fluttering at the mastheads; the topsides of the ships gaily painted; the royal arms—strange beasts, the unicorn and the lion—carved and gilded across the flat broad back of the lofty sterncastle; the coats of arms of the two armigerous gentlemen aboard (Sir George Percy and President Wingfield) painted upon the waistcloth—the long canvas strip fitted and lashed onto the sides of the ship to keep out water in a high sea, or to repel boarding attempts in case of attack by another vessel. The mariners' costumes—bright red and blue shirts, caps, long trousers or "trews"—added further color accents as the men scurried about the decks, clambered up and down the rope ladders, into the rigging.

Neither the sailors from their vantage point high in the rigging nor the soldiers on sentry duty at the fort could spot any movement in the shadowy depths of the forest or among the high reeds in the marshes surrounding the fort. Nothing stirred within their range of vision; but they were under constant surveillance, they were the cynosure of curious and, often, hostile eyes.

* Throughout medieval times, Europe clung to the belief that seagoing ships should be shaped like whales.

Tribesmen of the Powhatan Confederacy—from all over the tide-water, in all likelihood—would have made their way to the spit of land in the James River just below the mouth of the Chickahominy, where the *Susan Constant*, the *Godspeed*, and the *Discovery* were moored in six fathoms of water: tribesmen from villages up and down the James and from the tributary Chickahominy would have come; tribesmen from villages farther removed, as from Pocahontas's home on the banks of the Pamunkey, as from the York River area and the Piankatank, from as far away as the Mattaponi and the Rappahannock rivers—even, perhaps, from as far away as the south bank of the Potomac. Not that those whom they had come to see were aware of the convocation. Experts at tracking, at concealment, even camouflage (for deer-stalking, they wrapped themselves in deerskins and attached antlers to their heads), the Indians reconnoitered the site of the English landing, peering out from the rippling marsh grass, from behind tree trunks, from out of leafy branches—unseen by those over whom they kept watch.

The reward of patience—waiting silent, motionless, tireless—was the sight of one or more of the white men emerging from a gate in the palisade—only to find that white was not the word for them, after all: nowise so white as the snow or the snowy heron, neither so white as the ermine, although their faces were certainly pale in comparison with the ruddy hue of the people indigenous to the continent.

Only their pale faces were visible, their bodies being entirely concealed under the bulky armor, the long hose, the knee breeches and doublets, behind the flaring collar or ruff; and even their faces were shrouded by beards and mustaches. The Indians affected no such hirsute facial adornments; their scanty facial hair was plucked out by means of clamshell tweezers in the hands of the women who served as barbers to the tribe. (Not that lack of facial and body hair denoted lack of virility, as was a popular misconception of European natural historians in the eighteenth century.*) The growth of hair on the heads of Indian males was luxuriant; the scalp lock on the left side was allowed to grow long and thick, hanging down to the shoulder or tied up in a knot, decorated, variously, with a bird-wing, with feathers, or with shells; the hair on the right side was shaven close to prevent its becoming entangled in the bowstring.

* The Indian was pictured, in the eighteenth century, either as a sexual fiend and rapist or as deficient in sexual prowess. Thomas Jefferson, in his *Notes on the State of Virginia*, felt obliged to refute George Louis Buffon's conception of the Indian male as practically hairless and sexually weak. Another French natural historian of that era furnished his book with an illustration of an Indian male not only hairless but with milk in his breast.

The white men emerged, from time to time, from behind the picket fence, to relieve themselves, to fetch water, to tend their plantings, to cut and gather logs for their construction work, and to prepare clapboard (the sole exportable commodity thus far discovered) as cargo for the return voyage of the ships. The flash of the metal axe-blade and the speed with which it felled and split the timber impressed the Indians, who possessed only fire-brands and scraping-tools for such work.

The Indians keeping watch on the activities at James Fort could see the encampment taking form, ultimately a triangle in shape, enclosing approximately one acre: its base on the river side four hundred feet in length, each of the two other sides three hundred feet long; a main gate was to be located at the center of the long south or river side, with three other openings provided, one at each corner of the triangle. Such was the layout recommended by the seven councilors ("The Councell contrive the Fort," in Smith's words). But President Wingfield, ever mindful of the Virginia Company's instructions to exercise the greatest tact in dealing with the natives, confined the defensive measures to the erection of a frail "bulwarke" composed, as Smith noted scornfully, only of "the boughs of trees cast together in the forme of a halfe moone."

Behind that flimsy barricade, some few rude huts or booths could be seen under construction, and some few tents being pitched, all aligned around an open, central yard; one or more storehouses were going up, as were a number of makeshift shacks for use by President Wingfield and the councilors and for such of the fifty-odd gentlemen of the expedition who could afford to hire and pay carpenters for their efforts, or who were willing to exert efforts of their own to provide themselves with shelter. A hole in the ground had to serve for the man who could afford no better; he crawled in and pulled canvas or boughs over his head as protection from the elements. The major effort of the colonists, under the direction of their chaplain Robert Hunt, went into the construction of the church: "Wee did hang an awning (which is an old saile) to three or foure trees to shadow us from the Sunne," as Captain Smith remembered.

Our walls were rales of wood, our seats unhewed trees till we cut plankes, our Pulpit a bar of wood nailed to two neighboring trees. In foule weather we shifted into an old rotten tent; for we had few better. . . . The best of our houses of the like curiosity; but the most part farre worse workmanship, that could neither well defend from wind nor raine. . . .

The only Indians who showed themselves during that week in May were the Paspaheghs: one hundred strong, armed with bows and arrows, the braves approached the fort openly, bearing "a Fat Deare as a gift." Their chieftain indicated his willingness to give the newcomers as much land as they needed (or so Percy understood it), but may have suffered disappointment that his generosity was neither recognized nor rewarded by the English, who were unaware that they were trespassing on an ancient Paspahegh hunting preserve.

The parley ended abruptly in hostility at the attempted theft of a hatchet. The Indian may merely have wanted to take the curious instrument into his hand to examine it, but if it was another example of Indian thievishness, it was likewise another example of the English tendency to overreact to petty larceny. When the English reached for their muskets and their swords, the Werowance of the Paspaheghs "went suddenly away with all his company, in great anger," threatening revenge, according to the report of the incident in Percy's diary.

Sometime in mid-May, Captain John Smith shuffled off the restraint—perhaps even the irons—under which he had chafed for so many months, so many nautical miles, ever since his confrontation with Master Wingfield in the Canary Islands in February. He was set free just in time to join the small party of gentlemen chosen by Captain Newport to accompany him, on May 21, on an exploratory mission up the James. (It was a mission that would not lack for recorders; records were kept by three of the five gentlemen aboard: by Smith with his account in the *Generall Historie*, by Percy with his diary, and by Captain Gabriel Archer with his *Relatyon of the Discovery of Our River*, the official record presented to the Virginia Company by Captain Newport upon his return to England later in the year.)

Captain Newport, the five "Gentlemen," a crew of four "Maryners" and fourteen "Saylours" set off in the shallop, in compliance with Virginia Company directives, "to discover the River" to its head, in the hope of finding either the Northwest Passage or deposits of precious metals, treasures of gold and silver such as the Spaniards and Portuguese had come upon in Mexico and Peru. The third major objective of the Virginia Company venture was to discover some trace of Raleigh's lost colony, to track down any possible survivors of whatever disaster had befallen them at Roanoke Island.

Sailing and rowing upstream, the passengers in the shallop with Newport could watch the river wilderness unfold before their eyes: native villages dotted the banks, located on high ground for security against flood, surrounded by broad acres under cultivation (anywhere from twenty acres to two hundred), fields cleared by fire (by the native slash-and-burn technique[1]) to make a veritable "Garden of Tobacco and other fruits and herbes," as Sir George Percy saw and described it.

Once past the hostile Paspahegh territory, the expeditionary force was "entertayned with much Courtesye in every place" (according to Gabriel Archer's account); greeted "with many signes of love" (according to Smith's): "the people in all places kindely intreating us, daunsing and feasting us. . . ." When Captain Newport reciprocated with gifts of trade-goods ("Bels, pinnes, Needles, beades, or Glasses"), "his liberallitie made them follow us from place to place"—canoe-loads of naked, painted, whooping red men paddling swiftly from the shore to overtake the shallop, circling her, shooting ahead, riding in her wake. While hundreds of people lined the banks to watch the passage of the shallop, their arms outstretched in offer of hospitality: "The people on either syde of the Ryver stand in Clusters all along; still proferring us victualls": "basketes full of Dryed oysters," "a Deare roasted," "round balls or Cakes" (maize-cakes specially baked by the women for the occasion). Ashore, reed welcome-mats were ceremonially spread for the honored guests: the supreme gift of tobacco was offered, long-stemmed clay pipes were passed—to which "friendly wellcome," Captain Archer and the rest soon learned to make the traditional response of "two greate Showtes," and to speak the traditional "words of kyndnes, *Wingapoh*."

Friendly werowances of the Arrohatoc and Powhatan tribes provided guides, and mapped the course of the river for the explorers (though the Indians might use their toes to trace their maps in the sand, their sense of direction and memory for landmarks were remarkable; provided with pens and paper, they would prove excellent cartographers).

At the falls (near present-day Richmond), the river proved "impassable for boates any further," Captain Gabriel Archer reported, and the company turned back, discouraged from further exploration afoot by young Tanx-Powhatan—werowance of the village of Powhatan, from which the tribal name derived, and of the small tribe resident there—his strategy, evidently, to try to prevent a meeting and possible alliance between the English and the Monacans, a tribe of Siouan stock who occupied the region from the fall-line west to the Blue Ridge Mountains, foes of the Powhatans and frequent raiders.

Captain Newport mistook Tanx-Powhatan—Little Powhatan—for his father, Great Powhatan, the Supreme Chieftain of the Powhatan Confederacy, whose name and fame had, by this time, reached the ears of the English. To the son's delight, the Englishmen loaded him down with trade-goods and favor intended for the father.

Farther downstream, the English encountered another werowance, Opechancanough, ruler of the Pamunkey tribe, but failed to recognize him as the Supreme Chieftain's younger brother—one of three brothers —second in line to the supreme chieftaincy. (In accordance with Powhatan tribal tradition, the succession was matrilineal: hereditary leadership fell first to surviving male siblings, then to female siblings and to their offspring, beginning with the eldest sibling.) Although it should have been immediately evident that Opechancanough was of lofty rank, Captain Archer snorted with indignation at such arrogance in a naked heathen: "This kyng . . . so set his Countenance stryving to be stately, as to our seeming he became a foole." Opechancanough's tribal capital was on the Pamunkey River above Werowocómoco; he had come south to the region of the James to assess the situation in the wake of the English landings; to report on it, presumably, to his brother, Powhatan.

No intertribal solidarity had apparently, at that point, been achieved, no overall policy or strategy yet adopted for dealing with the newcomers. "Signes of love," the English discovered, were not universal; all was not dancing and feasting up and down the river. While the Powhatans, the Pamunkeys, and the Arrohatocs had all shown themselves cordial to the English, the Paspaheghs had been downright hostile; the Weanocs, surly. The werowance of the Appomatocs had willed them to be gone, but his sister, the weroansqua, had offered them the "accustomed Cakes, Tobacco and wellcome." She held sway—if only over a village—with "as greate authority" as her brother, and with even "more majesty," in the opinion of Captain Archer: holding court under a mulberry tree, surrounded by her attendants, she was an imposing sight: "a fatt lustie manly woman," with "much Copper about her neck, a Crownet of Copper upon her hed"; with "long black haire, which hanged loose down her back to her myddle, which only part was Covered with a Deares skyn, and ells all naked." (The title *weroansqua* was composed of the Algonkian word *weroans* [chieftain] in combination with the word *squa* [woman]. Hereditary leadership occasionally devolved upon women, as in the case of this queen of the Appomatocs, who held her rank by virtue of some obscure genealogical reckoning.)

A series of disturbing incidents marred relations between reds and whites: there were contretemps, challenges and retractions, flashes of animosity, huffs of anger, misunderstandings giving rise to mistrust.

The Europeans' judgment of the Indians was that they were thievish, childishly curious (especially concerning the novel metal tools and weapons), childishly volatile in temperament; now kind, now cruel;

"inconstant in everything," in John Smith's judgment; "craftie, timerous, quicke of apprehension, and very ingenious," in Strachey's judgment: "Some are of a disposition fearful, some bold, most cautelous, all Savage. They are soone moved to anger, and so malicious, that they seldom forget an injury. . . ."

When the disappearance of a knife and two bullet-bags was protested by the English party, Tanx-Powhatan located and restored the missing objects to Captain Newport, who "made knowne unto them the Custome of England to be Death for such offense"—the death penalty for larceny was not to be expunged from English statute-books until 1861. (The concept of the sacredness of private property, basic to the Anglo-Saxon ethic, remains to this day alien to the Indian. Originally, most tribal lands were held communally; and it continues to be a point of honor among Indians to share their personal possessions with those less fortunate, generosity ranking as a cardinal virtue—well above industry—in the Indian moral scheme.)

If the white men took offense at the theft of a knife or a cup, the Indians were offended when the white men insolently pre-empted land owned and occupied, for generations, by the native inhabitants. When the English erected a cross—bearing the inscription JACOBUS REX, 1607—to stake their claim to an island at the head of the river, the local residents expressed displeasure, and were only slightly mollified by Captain Newport's glib explanation of the Christian symbol: that "the two Armes of the Crosse signified king Powatah and himselfe, the fastening of it in the myddest was their united Leaug. . . ."

It proved, furthermore, a mistake on the part of the English to have plied Powhatan's son with "beere, Aquavite, and Sack": he did not thank them, next day, for the "hott Drynckes" which he thought had "caused his greefe."

The sound of a musket shot was shattering to the eardrums of men accustomed to the silence of the forest fastnesses; it terrified them, and embarrassed them for the terror they had been betrayed into showing— one Indian riding in the shallop with the English "leapt over boorde" at the crackle of a musket, "at the wonder thereof." Captain Newport hastened to assure young Tanx-Powhatan "that wee never use this thunder but against our enemyes." But not even such an assurance, not even the gift of a red waistcoat could fully restore confidence.

When, suddenly and abruptly, on the way downstream just above Jamestown, a hitherto faithful Arrohatoc guide abandoned the party of Englishmen, refusing to accompany them further, and offering the lamest of excuses for his departure, Captain Newport smelled a rat. "So our Captayne made all haste home" (according to Archer's *Relatyon*):

"as fearing some disastrous happ at our forte. Which fell out as we expected, thus."

"Thus," on May 26, one day before the Newport party returned to James Fort, a party of two hundred Paspahegh warriors attacked (two hundred attackers by Captain Archer's account; four hundred by Captain Smith's), and might have overwhelmed the defenders (whose muskets were not at the ready) had not the ships' ordnance saved the day, repelling the furious onslaught. It was a close call, as Archer called it: "They came up allmost into the ffort, shot through the tents, appeared in this Skirmishe (which indured hott about an hower) a very valiant people." English casualties were numerous: one of the four ship's boys was killed outright; eleven men (including four councilors) were wounded, one mortally. President Wingfield was lucky: had one arrow "shott cleane through his bearde, yet scaped hurte. . . ."

Plucking the stone-tipped reed shaft out of his whiskers, the president was, at last, sufficiently aroused to defy the Virginia Company injunction "not to offend the Naturals"; to proceed, at last, with the palisading of the fort, a high stake fence around all three sides, with "three Bulwarkes, [one] at every corner . . . and foure or five pieces of Artillerie mounted in them; [thus] we had made ourselves sufficiently strong for these Savages," as Sir George Percy recalled the harrowing events of that last week of May and first three weeks of June.

It was high time to fortify, in the opinion of Captain John Smith and his partisans, whose numbers were multiplying, while Wingfield's dwindled.

Not that the "Naturals" gave up on their raids, their ambushes, their surprise attacks, but now they stayed beyond the range of musket fire. When they came, they "came lurking in the thickets and long grasse," and it was woe to stragglers:

> . . . and a Gentleman one Eustace Clovell unarmed stragling without the ffort, shot. 6. Arrowes into him, wherwith he came runinge into the ffort, crying Arme Arme, these stycking still: He lyved. 8. Dayes, and Dyed. The Salvages stayed not, but run away.

So wrote Captain Archer, another critic of the president's policies and strategies, another competitor in the power struggle for control of the colony. The guerrilla warfare unnerved the Europeans, brought up as they had been in the chivalric code of medieval combat, a rite of battle as precisely choreographed as a ballet. Captain Archer complained bitterly of a sneak attack perpetrated, at "breake of day" on "a man of ours going out to doe naturall necessity"; three redskins skulking in the high grass under the bulwarks let their arrows fly, "shott him in the head, and through the Clothes in two places but missed the skynne. . . ."

The suggestion "to Cutt Downe the long weedes round about our ffort" in which the Indian attackers concealed themselves had to come from an Indian, the friendly Arrohatoc who had guided the Newport party up the James in May, and who had now rejoined them at the fort. If the idea had ever occurred to President Wingfield, he had not taken action on it. More and more, Wingfield's competence as a commander had come into question in the community.

Captain Smith, on the other hand, despite his lowly social origins, had risen steadily in the esteem of the company at Jamestown: resourceful as well as intrepid, he had given a splendid account of himself on the trip upriver, shown himself a good man to have in one's boat, on one's side. He possessed an adventuring genius: he showed initiative in confrontation with the unexpected; he met a crisis coolly. He succeeded better than any other man in the expedition in dealing with the Indians, as good an Indian-trader as an Indian-fighter.

It was high time, the Jamestown colonists decided, for Smith to take his rightful place on the Council; a petition was drawn up—a "Gentleman's Petityon," Archer called it—for presentation to the president and the councilors at the June 10 meeting of the Council. Captain Newport, on the eve of departure for England, brought all his persuasive powers to bear to effect that action and to reconcile the several factions, embittered over this as over other issues. Newport reminded the members of the Council "of their dutyes to his Majestie and the Collonye" and to their president, as their president himself duly noted in recording Newport's speech in his (Wingfield's) *Discourse of Virginia* (an exercise in self-justification but, nonetheless, another valuable contemporary account of the events of the crucial early months at Jamestown).

As to Smith, "so wel he demeaned himselfe in this busines" (in Smith's third-person account of these same events),

> as all the company did see his innocencie, and his adversaries malice. . . . Many were the mischiefes that daily sprong from their ignorant (yet ambitious) spirits; but the good doctrine and exhortation of our preacher Maister Hunt reconciled them, and caused Captain Smith to be admitted of the Councell.

(Smith had the highest praise for the Reverend Hunt: "an honest, religious, and couragious Divine; during whose life our factions were oft qualified.")

"The next day all receaved the Communion," as the text of Smith's second published work, *Map of Virginia*, continues; "the day following the Salvages voluntarily desired peace" (the friendly Arrohatoc guide insisting that his "king" along with the "kings" of Pamunkey and other friendly tribes would align themselves with the English against their enemies or would serve as peacemakers between the English and the hostile tribes), "and Captain Newport returned for England with newes; leaving in Virginia, 100."

The one hundred colonists left stranded in that alien land must have huddled forlorn at the water's edge to watch the *Susan Constant* and the *Godspeed* depart. The sailors slipped the knots, loosened the ropes whereby the bows were moored to the trees overhanging the riverbank, swung the bows round with the ebbing tide, unfurled the sails to catch the breeze, and, happy to be homeward bound, waved and shouted jubilant farewells. With the disappearance of the last white sail downriver, the handful of men left standing on that desolate shore were struck with the full realization of their isolation, their abandonment: the last link with home severed, they were totally cut off from the Old World, the known world, marooned in the New, the unknown—in "Terra Incognita," to use Smith's own term. The land where they stood had been named "Virginia" but, as Smith wrote, no man "understandeth or knowes what Virginia is." They were all standing at the very "edges of those large dominions, which doe stretch themselves into the Maine, God doth know how many thousand miles." God only knew where they were!—whether it was an island (as Sir Humphrey Gilbert had suspected), an isthmus (as Verrazano had taken the Carolina Outer Banks to be), a continent (as Smith surmised).

Wherever they were, those hundred Virginia Company adventurers, they were surrounded by an alien host of unknown number and disposition: some hostile, some friendly, although not consistently so, and the one not easily distinguishable from the other by the Englishmen; a strange people, infrequently visible, still more infrequently comprehensible to the English; savages "whom we neither knew nor understood," in John Smith's view, after years spent among them.

"Being thus left to our fortunes," Smith continues grimly in *A Map of Virginia*, "it fortuned that, within tenne daies, scarce ten amongst us coulde either goe, or well stand; such extreame weakness and sicknes oppressed us." Even stalwart Captain Smith fell ill along with the president and several Council members: Captains Ratcliffe, Martin, and Gosnold, all stricken.

Of these four, Gosnold alone succumbed; with "all the Ordnance in the Fort shot off" to mark his passing, and mourned by his cousin,

President Wingfield, not only as an ally but as a "worthy and religious gentleman," "upon whose lief stood a great part of the good succes and fortune of our government and Collony."

From the time of Gosnold's death, President Wingfield could foresee his own deposition: "so much differed the President and the other Councillors in managing the Government of the Collonye."

"Our men were destroyed with cruell diseases," Percy lamented, "such as Swellings, Flixes, Burning Fevers, and by warres; and some departed suddenly: but for the most part, they died of meere famine. . . ." "Whilest the ships staied," Captain Smith explains,

> our allowance was somewhat bettered by a daily proportion of bisket which the sailers would pilfer to sell, give, or exchange with us, for mony, saxefras,[2] furres, or love. But when they departed, there remained neither taverne, beere-house, nor place of relefe but the common kettell. Had we been as free from all sinnes as gluttony and drunkenness, we might have bin canonized for Saints. . . .

The content of the "common kettell" was

> halfe a pinte of wheat, and as much barly, boyled with water, for a man a day; and this having fryed some 26 weeks in the ships hold, contained as many wormes as graines. . . .

As for the water, it came "cold" from "the River," as Percy notes, "which was, at a floud, verie salt; at a low tide, full of slime and filth: which was the destruction of many of our men"—probably by typhoid and dysentery. The Jamestown site had been chosen because of its defensibility, but it was a swampy lowland, miasmal and malarial. Smith complained, too, of "the extremity of the heate" which "had so weakened us."

Percy's Roll Call of Death began in August:

> The sixt of August, there died John Asbie, of the bloudie Flixe.
> The ninth day, died George Flowre, of the swelling.
> The tenth day, died William Bruster Gentleman, of a wound given by the Savages, and was buried the eleventh day.
> The fourteenth day, Ierome Alikock, Ancient, died of a wound.
> The same day, Francis Midwinter [died, and] Edward Moris Corporall died suddenly.

The fifteenth day, their died Edward Browne and Stephen
Galthorpe.

The sixteenth day, their died Thomas Gower Gentleman.

The seventeenth day, their died Thomas Mounslic.

The eighteenth day, there died Robert Pennington, and John
Martine Gentlemen [the last named, the son of Captain
Martin, the councilor].

The nineteenth day, died Drue Piggase Gentleman.[3]

On the twenty-second, Captain Gosnold's death is noted in Percy's
diary, and then four more deaths between August 22 and 28. On the
twenty-eighth, Percy's record shows the death of Thomas Studley,
"Cape Merchant" (Supply Officer), to whose post Captain Smith was
appointed to succeed—an acknowledgment of his leadership capabilities.

In September, the death toll mounted: one death noted by Percy on
the fourth, another on the fifth. "There were never Englishmen left
in a forreigne Countrey in such miserie as wee were in this new discovered Virginia," Percy lamented.

Wee watched every three nights, lying on the bare cold ground,
what weather soever came; [and] warded all the next day;
which brought our men to bee most feeble wretches. . . . Thus we
lived for the space of five months [August 1607–January 1608]
in this miserable distresse, not having five able men to man our
Bulwarkes upon any occasion. If it had not pleased God to have
put a terrour in the Savages hearts, we had all perished by those
vild and cruell Pagans, being in that weake estate as we were;
our men night and day groaning in every corner of the Fort most
pittiful to heare. If there were any conscience in men, it would
make their harts to bleed to heare the pitifull murmurings and
out-cries of our sick men without reliefe, every night and day,
for the space of six weeks [August 8–September 19, 1607?];
some departing out of the World, many times three or foure in
a night; in the morning, their bodies being trailed out of their
Cabines like Dogges, to be buried. . . .

The burials were performed in secret, the graves dug in the dark of
night, in accordance with Virginia Company Instructions: "Do not
advertize the killing of any of your men, that the country people
may know it."

"From May to September," Smith recalled, "those that escaped lived upon Sturgion and sea-Crabs. . . . 50 in this time we buried"—fifty, that is, out of a hundred, a frightful casualty rate established by the Jamestown expedition in the fourth month after landfall. (And the number of survivors would shrink still further before the year was out.)

The fact was that Wingfield was about to be deposed: when he refused to grant demands for an increase in the daily rations from the common store, he was accused of having diverted it to his own personal use.[4]

What the attacks of hostile Indians, privation, and disease could not accomplish in bringing about the destruction of the colony, internecine strife and dissension wrought. With Gosnold and Newport gone, the Council erupted in conflict and contention, the four remaining members openly defiant of Wingfield's authority. Wingfield hoped that the arrest of Councilman Captain Kendall might put an end to the "mortall hatred and intestine garboile," since Kendall (in Wingfield's opinion) "did practize to sowe discord between the President and the Councell."

But the tide of opinion was running against the president, and could not be stemmed; his fatal combination of arrogance and ineptitude had antagonized Council members and colonists alike: "Captaine Wingfield having ordred the affaires in such sort that he was generally hated of all," by Captain Smith's summary. Captain Martin held Wingfield to blame for the death of his son on August 18, claiming that the president "hath starved my sonne, and denyed him a spooneful of beere. . . ."

As for Smith and Wingfield, there had been bad blood between them from the day they had boarded ship in London, their original mutual antipathy exacerbated by the confrontation at the Canary Islands which had resulted in Smith's arrest. They had recently had it out over Gosnold's deathbed: Wingfield called Smith a liar for having "spred a rumor in the Collony that I did feast myself and my servantes out of the comon stoare" and accused Smith "to his face" of having "begged in Ireland like a rogue, without a lycence. To such I would not my name should be a Companyon" were the aristocrat's final, haughty words to the yeoman. (Wingfield's charge is unsubstantiated; there is no evidence anywhere to show that Smith had ever set foot in Ireland, certainly not by his own extensive travel itinerary.)

Wingfield's enemies were closing in on him: he had managed to alienate even the surgeon, Wooton, and the gentle, forbearing chaplain, Robert Hunt. Wingfield claims that he was unfairly charged with being an atheist on the ground that his sea-chest did not include a Bible. There is greater likelihood that his Catholic family connections gave rise to the rumor of his pro-Spanish sympathies. It was, however, the growing suspicion that the president and some of his henchmen were about to seize the pinnace and make off in her for Newfoundland that brought him down. "The Presidents projects to escape these miseries in our Pinnes by flight . . . so moved our dead spirits, as we deposed him."

On September 10, Captains Smith, Ratcliffe, and Martin, three of the four remaining Council members, joined their signatures on a warrant for the deposition of the president, for his removal from the presidency and from the Council, and for his arrest and confinement aboard the pinnace *Discovery*. Wingfield denounced Smith, Ratcliffe, and Martin as the "Triumvirate," accusing them of illegal seizure of power—although, technically, they had followed a deposition procedure provided in the Virginia Company Articles for just such an emergency.

Out of the murk of the ensuing power struggle, Captain Ratcliffe emerged the winner, nominated by a convalescent Captain Smith and a chronically ailing Captain Martin (the other two of the three remaining Council members) to succeed Wingfield in the presidency. But no matter how influential Ratcliffe's connections in England, no matter how substantial his holdings in the Virginia Company, he proved an unhappy choice for the presidency, accomplishing little to alleviate the colony's distress, showing little ability for dealing with the men under his command.

"Notwithstanding our misery," Smith observed in his *True Relation*, "the company . . . little ceased their mallice, grudging, and muttering." The muttering concerned the harshness of the discipline, or so Wingfield's rancorous version suggests: "Wear [were] this whipping, lawing, beating, and hanging, in Virginia, knowne in England, I fear it would drive many well affected myndes from this honourable action of Virginia."

Men muttered against Captain Martin, too. With only three men left on the Council to take command in this desperate situation, Martin was a perennial invalid.

No wonder so little was accomplished in and around the encampment. No wonder, as Smith saw it, that

> as yet we had no houses to cover us, our tents were rotten, and our Cabbins worse than nought. . . . Most of our chiefest men either sicke or discontented, the rest being in such dispaire, as they would rather starve and rot with idlenes, then be perswaded to do any thing for their owne reliefe. . . .

No wonder men turned to Captain Smith for leadership. Smith was— if he had to say so himself, in his third-person narrative—the only effective member of the ruling hierarchy:

> The new President, and Martin, being little beloved, of weake judgment in dangers and lesse industry in peace, committed the managing of all things abroad to captaine Smith; who, by his owne example, good words, and faire promises, set some to mow, others to binde thatch; some to build houses, others to thatch them; himselfe alwaies bearing the greatest taske for his own share; so that, in short time, he provided most of them lodgings. . . .

The time was ripe for Smith's advancement: he had, by that time, not only been exonerated of the charges of "conspiracy to mutiny," he had been awarded two hundred pounds in damages by the jury that had found Wingfield guilty of the libel.

Then it was, in November, 1608, when Jamestown found itself down to a handful of survivors ("with but fortie in all to keepe possession of this large Country," by Smith's reckoning) and, furthermore, in "a desperate extreamity" ("all our provision spent, the Sturgeon gone, all helps abandoned, each houre expecting the fury of the Salvages. . . ."), then it was "when God . . . so changed the harts of the Salvages, that they brought such plenty of their fruits and provision, as no man wanted." It is not to deny God's hand in the occasion to recall that Indian relief came just as their autumn corn crop ripened. Earlier, in midsummer, in refusing the colonists' request for corn, one of the chieftains had explained to Wingfield that the old crop was exhausted, and the new "not at full groath by a foote; that as soone as any was ripe, he would bring it; which promise he truly performed" (though earning little credit for it). In the view of the early settlers, Virginians and New Englanders alike, it was never the savage heart that relented toward the invader; it was the work of Divine Providence; any generosity or mercy exhibited by the red man was attributable solely to the Almighty. "God, the absolute disposer of all heartes," as Smith expounds seventeenth-century Christian logic, "altered their conceits, for now they were no lesse desirous of our commodities then we of their Corne. . . ."

Even so, within a few weeks' time, Smith could see "the Salvages superfluity beginne to decrease" in the immediate vicinity of Jamestown and along the lower reaches of the James where he traveled to barter for the crop, and it became clear that the trade area would have to be extended in other directions, among tribes with richer stockpiles of provision.

Smith was obviously the man to head the project: not only was he the official supply officer of the colony, he was conceded to be, far and away, the best Indian-trader: shrewd and ingenious, he had won the respect of the Indians, who found him tough but fair, even-handed; a man of his word, whether the word was a threat or a promise. His Algonkian vocabulary, although limited, far exceeded that of any of his compatriots. (There is a strong possibility that he had acquired it in study with Thomas Hariot or in conversation with the five Algonkian-speaking Indians kidnapped in 1605 from the northern Atlantic coast by Captain Weymouth and brought by him to England, where Smith, enterprising as he was, may have sought them out for practice in conversation.)

In November, "and with much adoe, it was concluded," again according to Captain Smith, "that the pinnace and the barge should goe towards Powhatan"—towards Powhatan, for the reason that, by now, the English had realized that it was with him they would have to deal, with the Great Powhatan, the Supreme Chieftain of the tidewater confederacy, whom they had not yet encountered. They had realized, too, that he would not come to them and that they, therefore, would have to "goe towards" him, seek him out at his residence of Werowocómoco on the banks of the Pamunkey.

When "Lotts were cast who should go . . . the chance was mine," Smith explains, although enigmatically, he fails to reveal whether he was the winner or the loser of that roll of the dice or that toss of the coin.

Smith and a group of fifteen (including "Gentlemen," "Maryners," and "Labourers"), nine aboard the barge, seven aboard the pinnace, set off on the flood tide, entered the Chickahominy River at its mouth, some six miles above Jamestown, and headed upriver—a voyage "as well for discoverie as trading," as Smith reminds us: no opportunity was lost to map this trackless, hitherto unexplored region. Another purpose of the voyage was the search for the glister of gold that had dazzled the Spanish in Mexico and Peru. And—who could tell?—it might just be the shallow, tortuous, densely wooded Chickahominy that had its source in a lake; and if so, as the Virginia Company Instructions suggested, then "the passage to the other sea [the Pacific] will be more easy." Something was needed, some discovery "of worth to encourage our adventurers in England."

The Chickahominies, while acknowledging membership in the loosely knit confederacy, constituted so large and powerful a tribe as to be semi-autonomous; their council of elders was apparently free to make policy decisions independently of Powhatan—such as whether to enter into peaceful trade with the white strangers presently poling and rowing up their waterways. "With many signes of great kindness" from the Chickahominies ("at each place, kindly used," according to Smith's account), with trade brisk—the riverbanks lined with natives proferring great baskets of bread, corn, game, fish, in exchange for "copper and hatchets," beads and bells—the ships were soon laden to the gunwales with provisions to relieve the shortage at Jamestown.

There, upon his return to the fort, Smith found all in turmoil: "al thinges at randome in the absence of Smith," according to Smith. Whether it was President Ratcliffe and Recorder Gabriel Archer, or ex-President Wingfield and ex-Councilman Kendall who were hatching a plot to abandon the colony, abscond with the pinnace to Newfoundland or New England (accounts differ)—whoever the miscreants may have been, their "project was curbed and suppressed by Smith" upon his return from that first trip up the Chickahominy.

"Disgustfull brawles" continued to disrupt the community, and Smith deplored them. President Ratcliffe had lost whatever authority he may originally have had over the men in his command: when he reprimanded the blacksmith, the latter threatened to strike the president, and was tried for mutiny, condemned by a jury to be hanged. Halfway up the ladder, the blacksmith managed to extricate his own head from the noose by implicating Captain Kendall in a Spanish spy plot.

Kendall, after trial and under sentence of death, challenged the authority of President Ratcliffe to order his execution, on the ground that Ratcliffe was not Ratcliffe, at all, but Sicklemore, an imposter—the scandal he had hoped to leave behind in the Old World had followed him to the New. Councilor Martin had to drag himself off his sickbed to issue the command for execution (not that the rope intended for the blacksmith could be used for the captain; in that seventeenth-century world of privilege, it was a gentleman's prerogative to demand the services of a firing squad).

These crises once past and the common store replenished, Captain Smith was free to go back up the Chickahominy "to finish this discovery." Indeed, he had been the butt of criticism from his fellow Council members (increasingly suspicious and jealous of Smith's growing popularity and influence in the camp) for his failure to achieve two other vital goals of the mission assigned him: to find the source of the Chickahominy—and to find Powhatan.

Choosing the barge (for its shallow draft) and nine men to accompany him on it, in early December, Captain Smith headed back upstream "towards Powhatan"—and toward Pocahontas, toward his encounter with the Supreme Chieftain and the Chieftain's daughter, an encounter resulting in an incident as controversial as any in recorded history, and one of which Smith, himself, the protagonist, was the sole literate witness, the sole recorder.

Whether we believe or disbelieve Smith's report of what happened at Werowocómoco in the last weeks of the year 1607 and the first weeks of 1608, depends on our judgment of his veracity. From his time to ours, it has been Smith's credibility that is at issue. It is Smith's story, Smith's alone, with no other eyewitness to corroborate or contradict, a story told in one interminably long, rambling, disjointed sentence, a story with undertones of miscegenation and overtones of racial reconciliation, a story to stir and hold the imagination, to nag at the collective unconscious. Smith's story, as he tells it, is a compelling story fraught with symbolism, with all the makings of a myth—if, if, if— if it really happened as he told it.

The chances are that it did.

CHAPTER IV

Captain John Smith
Didn't belong to the B'nai B'rith,
He was a full-blooded Briton,
The same as Boadicea and Bulwer-Lytton,
But his problem and theirs were not quite the same,
Because they didn't have to go around assuring everybody that
was their real name,
And finally he said, This business of everybody raising their eye-
brows when I register at an inn is getting very boring,
So I guess I'll go exploring,
So he went and explored the River James,
Where they weren't as particular then as they are now about
names,
And he went for a walk in the forest,
And the Indians caught him and my goodness wasn't he
embarrassed!
Yes, his heart turned to plasticene
Because he certainly was the center of a nasty scene,
And he was too Early-American to write for advice from
Emily Post,
So he prepared to give up the ghost,
And he prayed a prayer but I don't know whether it was a silent
one or a vocal one,
Because the Indians were going to dash his brains out and they
weren't going to give him an anaesthetic, not even
a local one . . .

OGDEN NASH,
"Captain John Smith," 1939

BYPASSING ALL THE TOWNS at which he had recently traded, Captain Smith proceeded, sometime by sail, sometime by oar, forty miles upriver to Apokant, last of the Chickahominy settlements.

Beyond Apokant, the going became difficult; at one spot, a giant tree fallen athwart the waterway had to be cut "insunder" to clear a passage for the barge. "Heere the river became narrower, 8, 9 or 10. foote at a high water, and 6. or 7. at a lowe: the streame exceeding swift. . . ." For these reasons, "we resolved," as Smith explained, "to hier a Canow, and returne with the barge to Apocant, there to leave the barge secure and put ourselves upon the adventure; the country onely a vast and wilde wildernes. . . ."

Leaving seven men aboard the barge ("in a broad bay out of danger of shot") with orders not to venture ashore until his return, and taking only two men with him—Jehu Robinson, identified on the ships' register as a gentleman, and Thomas Emery, a carpenter—Smith hired a canoe with two Chickahominies as guides, using the pretext of "fowling" to explain his exploration of the upper reaches of the river.[1]

"Twentie myles in the desert," when the channel grew so "combred with trees" as to become impassable even by canoe, Smith set off on foot with one of the two Indian guides, leaving the other with Robinson and Emery beside the riverbank, with instructions to keep "their matches light"—their matchlocks at the ready—and to fire a warning shot "at the first sight of any Indian."

"But within a quarter of an houre," Smith "heard a loud cry, and a hollowing of Indians"—though not a warning shot.

Concluding that Robinson and Emery had been taken by surprise, and suspecting the two Indian guides of having betrayed them all, Smith "seazed" the one accompanying him ("whome hee bounde to his arme and used as his buckler"), leaving himself one hand free with which to cock his "french pistoll."

And not a moment too soon: at that very instant a flight of arrows whizzed through the air, one of them striking him "on the right thigh; but without harme"; many others "stucke in his cloathes but no great hurt," evidently blunted on his carapace of armor.

"Beset by 200" yet undaunted, Smith managed somehow, for some time, to hold off the entire Pamunkey hunting-party. (Two he picked off with his pistol, reducing the odds, though not substantially.)

"Retiring" (the word "retreating" does not exist in Smith's vocabulary) toward the riverbank where he had left his two English companions, and walking backward so as to keep an eye on his foes,

Smith stumbled and "slipped up to the middle in an oasie creeke and his Salvage with him." Asprawl in the "bogmire," Smith had no choice but to surrender his arms to his enemies and "to trie their mercies."

No mercy had been shown to Gentleman Jehu Robinson, whom Smith saw lying close to the canoe at the riverbank, a human pin-cushion "with 20 to 30 arrowes in him." Emery, the carpenter, Smith "saw not," nor was he ever to be seen again.

Six of the seven Englishmen Smith had left aboard the barge were presumably heading back to Jamestown. The seventh, George Cassen (a "Labourer"), had been ambushed ashore, as Smith learned from his captors, cruelly tortured (to make him reveal the size and whereabouts of the English party), finally slain.

Smith's life was spared due to an Indian protocol of war whereby war-party leaders, chieftains, and werowances were entitled, upon capture, to certain formalities prior to execution. Smith's rank and station would have to be verified by the Pamunkey chieftain, Opech-ancanough (Powhatan's brother), to whom Captain Smith was pres-ently delivered by his captors. Opechancanough and Smith had met during the summer, in the course of the James River expedition led by Captain Newport. Smith remembered Opechancanough's imposing presence and profound dignity, and Opechancanough remembered Smith as a member of the English high command.

Surrounded by bowmen with their arrows nocked, Smith lost no opportunity to impress his captors not only with his military status but with his magic. (Smith may have known that Hariot had awed his savage audience by a demonstration of his mariners' instruments.[2]) Smith forthwith produced his

> round Ivory double compass Dyall. Much they marvailed at the playing of the Fly and Needle, which they could see so plainely, and yet not touch it, because of the glasse that covered them. But when he demonstrated by that Globe-like Jewell, the round-ness of the earth, and skies, the spheare of the Sunne, Moone, and Starres, and how the Sunne did chase the night round about the world continually; the greatnesse of the Land and Sea, the diversitie of Nations, varietie of complexions, and how we were to them *Antipodes*, and many other such like matters, they all stood as amazed with admiration.

Though not for long: "inconstant as a weather vane," within the hour, their mood had turned menacing again, and "they tyed him to a tree," arrows nocked to their bowstrings, ready to shoot.

Only at a sign from Opechancanough did the braves lower their

six-foot bows and form a procession, "the King in their middest" and
Smith directly behind him, guarded by a squad of twelve warriors, six
on each side, plus "three great Salvages, holding him fast by each
arme." Thus, "in a triumphant manner," did they lead him toward their
temporary hunting camp ("onely thirtie or fortie hunting houses made
of Mats, which they remove as they please, as we our tents," Smith
wrote, explaining further that "These their women beare after them,
with Corne, Acornes, Morters, and all bag and baggage they use").

There, the warriors broke ranks, burst into frenzied song and
dance, "cast themselves in a ring" around Smith and Opechancanough,

> singing and yelling out such hellish notes and screeches; being
> strangely painted, every one his quiver of Arrowes, and at his
> backe a club; on his arme a Fox or an Otters skinne . . . their
> heads and shoulders painted red . . . which Scarlet-like colour
> made an exceeding handsome shew. . . .

The dances over, Smith was "conducted to a long house" with
"thirtie or fortie tall fellowes" to guard him, and "all the women and
children staring to behold him."

There, "he was after their manner kindly feasted," although the
feast had ominous overtones: "more bread and venison was brought him
then would have served twentie men" and yet "not one of them would
eate a bit with him . . . which made him thinke they would fat him to
eat him." (The fear of cannibalism among North American Indian
tribes had not yet been eradicated from the English mind.[3]) "I thinke
his stomacke at that time was not very good," Smith concluded
wryly.

But he may have become less queasy as the days went by without
incident, and he was "well used," provided with heavy robes to protect
him from the December frosts; his "gowne, points and garters," along
with his compass and writing tablet, were restored to him.

Later in the month, the Pamunkey chief led his English captive
on a cross-country tour: up to the headwaters of the Pamunkey and
down again, overland to the Piankatank River, to the Mattaponi, the
Rappahannock, the Potomac. It could only have been to consult, to
powwow with the other tribes of the confederacy, to let them see and
hear for themselves this specimen of the foreign host, and make a
judgment.

One of Opechancanough's objectives was to give the tribesmen a
chance to identify Smith as the white sea-captain who had cruised the
Chesapeake in recent years, reciprocating tidewater hospitality with
murder and kidnap. Smith could thank his lucky stars that he was a

man of decidedly short stature; the other European, the vicious raider, while bearded like Smith, had been conspicuous for his height.

"Over all those rivers, and backe again by divers other severall Nations to the Kings habitation at Pamaunkee," or, rather, at Menapacant, a major village of the Pamunkey tribe, a settlement of "an hundred houses, and many large plaines." ("A pleasanter seat," as Smith could see despite his sad predicament, "cannot be imagined.")

There, at Menapacant, on the Pamunkey River just above present-day West Point, Smith witnessed the "most strange and fearful Coniurations"—"the meaning whereof they told him, was to know if he intended them well or no."

In an elaborate three-day ceremonial, "a great fire was made in a long house" (some houses were as much as "fourescore or an hundred foote in length"). The "chiefe Priest," "all painted over with coale, mingled with oyle," with "a Coronet of feathers" on his head (a hairdress of snake and weasel skins, the tails tied in tassels)—"a great grim fellow with a hellish voyce and a rattle in his hand." "With most strange gestures and passions he began his invocation." In his train, six "more such like devils" ("painted halfe black, halfe red," "with red eyes, and white stroakes over their blacke faces") danced, sang, orated, and assisted the chief priest in arranging concentric circles about the fire: the first of cornmeal, the next of grains of corn, the last of "little stickes": "the circle of meale signified their Country, the circles of corne the bounds of the Sea, and the stickes his Country. They imagined the world to be flat and round, like a trencher; and they in the middest."

Whatever the augury was, however the priests interpreted it—whether the white man was seen by them to come in peace or war, whether to fish and trade or to wrest the land away from the rightful owners—Smith, if he knew, offers no clue.

Whether or not the invaders should be driven back into the sea whence they had come must have been a point of contention, from the beginning, between Opechancanough and his brother Powhatan. In view of Opechancanough's record of unwavering opposition to the white incursion, it is reasonable to assume that the contest of wills between him and Powhatan—as to what course of action to take vis-à-vis the intruders—began the day of the English landing on the James. And the question of executing Captain Smith and proceeding to the annihilation of James Fort may have been the focus of discussion between the two brother-chieftains throughout the last weeks of the year of 1607.

Circumstances point to Opechancanough as the proponent of

swift and relentless action against the invading forces, and to Powhatan as still irresolute, still uncertain, still vacillating between the two options open to him: to exterminate the invaders or to enter into an alliance with them—and leaning toward the latter by reason of the economic and military advantages to be derived from such an alliance. It is conceivable, too, that his will and courage to resist had been eroded by the ancient prophecy of impending doom at the hands of a foe from the east.

There can be little doubt that Opechancanough, throughout the weeks following Smith's capture, maintained constant contact with his brother, reporting to the Supreme Chieftain at every move, receiving his instructions from Werowocómoco and following them, no matter how reluctantly. The Werowance of Pamunkey would have reported to Powhatan on opinion throughout the confederacy, as he sampled it in the course of his journey with Smith in tow. Opechancanough would have reported as well on the words of advice and words of warning spoken to him along his way by the werowances, the elders and sages of the various tribes of the confederacy, reported on dreams and omens, signs and portents experienced by medicine-men and priests across the tidewater. (In Smith's opinion, the final decision as to peace or war would have been made by the priests: "When they intend any warres, the Werowances usually have the advice of their Priests and Conjurers, and their Allies and ancient friends; but chiefly the Priestes determine the resolution. . . .")

In the first week of January, 1608, an order came from Powhatan to bring the English captive to him at Werowocómoco. By then, he had apparently at last come to a decision with regard to Smith—and perhaps the entire English contingent at Jamestown—and was ready to deal with the white man, face to face.

"At last they brought him," Smith wrote, "to Werowocómoco, where was Powhatan, their Emperor."[4]

Werowocómoco (usually translated from the Algonkian as "rich [or royal] Court") came into view from the river,[5] built on a rise above the bank, as was the custom in the tidewater to afford both protection from flood and a pleasant prospect. The Pamunkey widened, at that point, forming a bay with three tributary creeks. As the main seat of government of the "Emperor" of the confederacy, Werowocómoco was one of the largest towns in the area: a hundred or more houses set among some two hundred cultivated acres, flourishing fields of corn and beans, well-tended gardens of tobacco, pumpkins, gourds, and sunflowers. The royal compound, containing the houses of the king, his family, counselors, and priests, was palisaded, enclosed by a heavy stockade, probably circular, constructed of ten- or twelve-foot-high poles set close together in the ground, with only one narrow aperture for entrance.

The Virginia longhouse (or wigwam, to use the generic Algonkian word denoting a lodge or dwelling) reminded Smith of an English garden-bower, a vine-clad trellised rustic retreat—"arbour-like" is the word he chose to describe it.[6] The longhouse (in no way resembling the conical skin teepee of the Plains Indian) was built on an arched framework of slender, upright green poles, the thickest ends implanted in the ground, two or three feet apart; the upper ends arched to meet across the top, and were firmly fastened together with strips of bark or fibrous roots. This arched framework was thatched with reed or rush mats, the sides sheathed with strips of bark which could be rolled up on fine days to admit air and sun and breeze. The doors at each end were likewise hung with mats which could be raised or lowered, depending on the weather. A small hole or slit in the center of the roof thatch provided partial escape for the smoke rising from the longhouse's central hearth.

Some of the smaller dwellings were oval or circular ("the beehive" form), but the larger structures were oblong or rectangular with barrel roofs (similar to a Quonset hut), some twelve to sixteen yards in length, the length usually double the width, and containing, usually, a single area accommodating six to twenty persons. A very large house, such a one as Powhatan's, might extend fifty or sixty yards in length, and be partitioned into several inner chambers, with several hearths, several smoke-holes.

In such a longhouse as this, Smith came face to face with Powhatan.

Within, great fires blazed, throwing off great warmth. Pine-cones crackling among the logs, and tobacco glowing in long-stemmed clay pipes, scented the air, as did the sweet grass mats and pine bark, the bundles of rawhide, the strings of smoked and salted fish, the stores of tallow, and the rancid bear oil glistening on the Indians' skin in the sultry atmosphere.

A stranger such as Smith had to rub his eyes, smarting in the clouds of acrid smoke, adjust them to the gloom of the windowless wigwam. Still, he could sense the presence of a great throng in the shadows, could feel their eyes upon him, fixed in a malevolent glare: "Here more than two hundred of those grim Courtiers stood wondering at him, as he had beene a monster."

Short, stocky, bearded, his metal breastplate and thigh-plates glinting in the firelight, he stood his ground under that hostile scrutiny "till Powhatan and his trayne had put themselves in their greatest braveries," until the supreme Werowance and his entourage had solemnly taken their places:

> Before a fire upon a seat like a bedsted[7] . . . richly hung with manie Chaynes of great Pearles about his necke . . . he sat covered with a great robe, made of *Rarowcun* [raccoon] skinnes, and all the tayles hanging by. At [his] heade sat a woman, at his feete another; on each side sitting uppon a Matte uppon the ground, were raunged his chiefe men on each side the fire, tenne in a ranke, and behind them as many yong women . . . with all their heads and shoulders painted red: many of their heads bedecked with the white downe of Birds; but every one with something: and a great chayne of white beads about their necks . . . and [Powhatan] with such a grave and Majesticall countenance, as drave me into admiration to see such state in a naked Salvage.

Captain Smith had come into the presence. It was a presence that made itself felt. Not even the most supercilious Englishman could deny the imposing majesty in which the "naked Salvage" was clothed: "Such a Majestie as I cannot expresse," wrote Smith, "nor yet have often seene, either in Pagan or Christian."

There was every evidence of Powhatan's self-consciousness of his supremacy: the power of life or death held by him over the multitude of his subjects; his word was the law for the thousands within his domain. A stranger to the European feudal concept of the Divine Right of Kings, Powhatan no less confidently affirmed—and his people accepted—his right to rule over the dominions to which he was rightful heir. Tribal tradition had given religio-political sanction to his succession.

"He is of parsonage a tall well proportioned man, with a sower looke," as Smith could finally make out in the smoky obscurity of Powhatan's great house, "his head somewhat gray, his beard so thinne that it seemeth none at al. His age neare 60; of a very able and hardy body to endure any labour. . . . This proude salvage, having his finest women, and the principall of his chiefe men assembled, sate in rankes as before is expressed: himself as upon a Throne at the upper ende of the house. . . ."

"At his [Smith's] entrance before the King, all the people gave a great shout"—the shout of greeting, the salute or hail, traditional among the Powhatans—"I being the first Christian this proud King and his grim attendants ever saw. . . ."

A woman came forward, "a comely young savage": "The Queene

of Appomatuck was appointed to bring him water to wash his hands."
(If Smith recognized her as the "fatt lustie manly woman,"* the weroansqua who had received Newport's party on the upper James in May,
he may have thought better of showing recognition, now, when she
showed none.) Her task accomplished, another woman approached:
"Another brought him a bunch of feathers, in stead of a Towell to
dry them"—the customary prelude to the feast, among the Powhatans.

And "having feasted him after their best barbarous manner they
could, a long consultation was held. . . ."

It was a powwow for which they had gathered from the farthest
confines of the confederacy—werowances, elders, sages, priests, and
shamans—to advise together, to consult omens and auguries. Opechancanough was, to the end of his days, a proponent of all-out war
against the invaders; it would have been in character for him, at that
point, to have pressed for the death of this invader in their hands, and
he commanded a large following.

When all had had their turn at speaking, and the assembly fell
silent, one clear, shrill, high-pitched voice rang out—a girl's voice raised
in entreaty.

But Powhatan had heard them all, and had reached his own conclusions:

> The conclusion was, two great stones were brought before
> Powhatan: then as many as could layd hands on him [Smith],
> dragged him to them, and thereon laid his head, and being ready
> with their clubs, to beate oute out his braines. . . .

The massive wooden clubs (studded with jagged rock and sharp fangs
of bear or wolf) upraised, brandished over his head, Captain Smith
could not but have believed the end had come, and waited for the blows
that would crack his skull and bring oblivion.

His head pressed down upon the altar stones—as upon a headsman's
block—he could not have seen the figure that suddenly detached itself
from Powhatan's entourage, from Powhatan's side, and raced from the
upper end of the house toward the spot where Smith lay in the clutch
of the executioners. He may have heard the sound of light and rapid
footfalls on the sod floor and a girl's voice—high and clear and shrill, the
same voice raised earlier in entreaty—coming closer and closer to his
ear. Next came the shock of a body hurtling against his, across his,

---

* This latter description is Gabriel Archer's, who apparently did not find the weroansqua as attractive as Smith did.

upon his, a slight weight upon his back, small arms encircling his shoulders, small hands gripping his head, a dark head laid upon his; black hair—sleek, shining "like a Raven's wing"—streaming across his face.

The fleeting form, the racing feet, the high-pitched voice entreating, were Pocahontas's. It was "Pocahontas, the Kings dearest daughter, when no intreaty could prevaile, got his head in her armes, and laid her owne upon his to save him from death"—her body interposed between his and death, an immolation, an intimate if chaste embrace, performed on her part with all the candor of a bride.

The effect was electrifying. The tension that gripped the assembly snapped, and there was, briefly, pandemonium. Their mood changed instantly, in response to the sign from their emperor-priest. At his commutation of sentence, bloodthirsty anticipation was not slaked by blood but transmuted by grace.

"Whereat the Emperour was contented he [Smith] should live to make him hatchets, and her [Pocahontas] bells, beads, and copper. . . ." The grim scene of death—if that is what it was—was transformed by a word from the Emperor into one of redemption, reconciliation, rejoicing. Even humor, for there is surely a note of humor detectible in the proposition that the brash, burly, bearded legionary should hang up his arms to sit at the feet of Pocahontas, stringing beads and bells, concocting baubles for her adornment.

The first question to perplex the narrative (brief as is the text, thirty-odd lines in all, one interminable sentence*) is whether it was actually death that Smith was facing or only a simulation of death. In all probability, the latter: such is the consensus of twentieth-century anthropology after decades of research on the cultural patterns of North American Indians; that is to say, that the ceremony—the mock-execution—described by Smith is typical of an aboriginal adoption-initiation ritual. Adoption was prevalent among the Northeast Woodlands tribes in the seventeenth and eighteenth centuries—so prevalent, for example, in the late 1700s, in the aftermath of the beaver wars and the Colonial Wars, that the population of some Iroquois villages was composed predominantly of adopted war-captives. Although the Powhatan Confederacy was not a quasi-matriarchy like the league of the Iroquois, still the women of both societies were entitled to make disposition of captured enemy warriors; theirs was the right and responsibility to adopt these captives or to consign them to death (not to omit mention of the right and responsibility of officiating at the torture ritual that preceded death). Adoption was intended to serve as compensation

* See Appendices A and B for Smith's two narratives of the event.

for a war casualty. Traditionally, it was the woman who had lost a kinsman who might claim the life of a captive of another tribe to take the place of the member of her family lost in battle, although the right of adoption was often accorded to the men of the tribe, as well. A kinsman lost in war was avenged only when a warrior of another tribe was killed, or captured and adopted. The captive who was adopted was initiated into the tribe of which he was henceforward to be a member; the adoption rite was followed by the initiation rite. Symbolism of death has been and continues to be a feature of the initiation rite among a number of primitive societies steeled to endure the anguish of simulated death as a preparation for the anguish of death itself. In some tribes, the candidate for initiation is laid in a freshly dug grave or lies motionless under branches, in simulation of a corpse; initiation serves as an ultimate test, an ordeal to try the mettle of a man. (Initiation has its place among peoples less primitive, as well: mystical death and regeneration are believed to have played a part in the Eleusinian Mysteries.)

The fact that Smith so accurately described the extraordinary and complicated ritual of an alien culture, one with which he could not have been familiar, is construed in some quarters as a validation of Smith's veracity. In other words, it seems unlikely that he could have fabricated an episode illustrative of folkways of which he was ignorant.

On the other hand, in other quarters, those who question Smith's veracity point out that he need not have invented the episode, but could have borrowed it intact from a travel book by Richard Hakluyt published in London in 1609 (the year of Smith's return from Virginia). Hakluyt translated the account of Juan Ortiz, a Spanish soldier captured by the Hirrigua Indians of Florida in 1529, snatched from the flames by Ulalah, daughter of Chief Ucita. Another hair-breadth escape, another white European rescued by another Indian princess: read Pocahontas for Ulalah, Powhatan for Ucita, Smith for Ortiz, the stake for the altar-stone!

But the prototype of the story predates Hakluyt, one of the oldest stories known to man; a story not only archetypal but universal, a part of folklore. The story line is simple, direct; the plot, elementary: the hero (adventurer, explorer, sailor, soldier, crusader) falling into the clutches of a foreign despot (emperor, sultan, giant, demon, sorcerer), rescued in the nick of time by the despot's daughter, enamored of her father's captive. Ethnologists date the legend back to the cave, to the ancient custom of marriage by capture or by purchase, inevitably pitting the lover against the father. To Hate the Alien Father and Love the Alien Daughter is another way to say it, to be illustrated by such classic examples as Medea and her feral father, King Aetis; as Ariadne and hers, King Minos of Crete; while such literary examples as Shylock and Portia, as Ivanhoe's Rebecca and her father, Isaac of York, come to mind.

Medieval scholars referred to the genre as The Enamored Moslem Princess story: here, instead of a shipwrecked Greek hero, it is a Christian knight, a crusader, captured by a sultan whose daughter renounces her nationality and faith to rescue the prisoner and flee with him. To attest the universality of the theme, Andrew Lang's *Custom and Myth* lists prototypes of the rescue story, "ranging from Finland to Japan, from Samoa to Madagascar, from Greece to India."

If Captain John Smith's updated, New World version of the archetypal, universal legend was factual, if he actually experienced that ultimate ordeal of symbolic death/symbolic deliverance as part of a not uncommon North American initiation/adoption ritual, as is reported by him in his *Generall Historie of Virginia, New England, and the Summer Isles*, published in London in 1624, then why in the world did he wait sixteen years to make it public?

He claims that he made known the story earlier in a letter written in 1616 to the Stuart Court, to his sovereign Queen Anne, consort of King James: a formal petition addressed to that "most high and vertuous Princesse," requesting that royal grace and favor be extended to the Princess Pocahontas to reciprocate the grace and favor shown to Captain Smith and the English colony by the Indian princess and her emperor-father. The Court of Whitehall owed the Powhatan princess, Smith pointed out, a debt of gratitude: if the English colony in America survived, it would be thanks to Pocahontas: "seeing this Kingdome [England] may rightly have a Kingdome [America] by her meanes." Pocahontas, in saving Smith's life and extending him her favor, had extended her favor to the colony and saved it, along with him. The much-discussed rescue story, as Smith claims to have told it in 1616 to Queen Anne, was even briefer than the brief 1624 account : "After some six weeks fatting amongst those Salvage Courtiers, at the minute of my execution, she hazarded the beating out of her owne braines to save mine."[8]

Whether or not Captain Smith related his story to the Queen by letter in 1616, that hair-raising tale never came to the attention of the general public until 1624, when it was first published in that ponderous tome, the *Generall Historie*. It remains difficult to grasp that no reference to that supremely climactic encounter with Pocahontas at the altar-stone is to be found in Smith's first published volume, bearing the date of 1608, his *True Relation of Such Occurrences and Accidents of Note As Hath Hapned in Virginia Since the First Planting of That*

Colony. What occurrence or accident of note could have been more noteworthy than that execution scene and last-minute rescue?

Very little is known of the circumstances concerning the editing of Smith's manuscript or its publication: the work was evidently compiled in London from the rough notes of an unpaginated report sent back by Smith from Jamestown, by courtesy of a returning ship's captain, in June of 1608, addressed to a friend (or possibly to an editor, if in the hope of publication). Captain Smith is not even named as author in the first printing; not until the title page was twice corrected and twice reset was he to have the satisfaction of seeing the volume ascribed to him.[9]

The London editor of the *True Relation*, whoever he was (identifying himself only by the initials "I.H." and blaming the "rashnesse" of the printers for the error in attribution of authorship), warns the Courteous Reader, in the preface, that something less than the full story is being told, that certain material has been censored or suppressed, that "somewhat more was by him [Smith] written, which being as I thought fit to be private, I would not adventure to make it publicke."

If it was the rescue scene which had been deleted, one puzzles over the motivation: what was there "fit to be private" about it? Was it the hint of sex and race, the bugaboo of miscegenation, which both Smith and his editor feared might offend English moral attitudes and thus prove damaging to Smith's reputation or injurious to his ambitions in the colonial enterprise? The English fancied themselves as morally superior to the Latins, and disdained the Spaniards for their promiscuity in cohabiting with natives in Mexico and the Caribbean. Thomas Hariot, in his published work of 1588 and 1590, had made a point, as Smith well knew, of the total sexual continence practiced by the Raleigh expedition of 1585–86.

One possibility is that Virginia Company promoters blue-penciled the controversial execution scene for fear that such a harrowing example of aboriginal savagery might frighten off prospective investors and colonists at the very hour when these were being most urgently recruited. But this theory, propounded by generations of Smith apologists, is weakened by the fact that other, equally horrific examples of savagery (such as the murders of Robinson and Cassen, Smith's two unfortunate companions on the Chickahominy) were not censored or suppressed, but recounted and printed in gory detail, in that very same 1608 edition of *A True Relation.*

Smith's detractors, on the other hand, theorize that Smith did not report the execution-rescue scene in 1608 because he had not yet invented it, that it was a later product of Smith's imagination, to be advanced only in 1624, when Pocahontas and Powhatan were no longer around to dispute it. But this argument falters, too, on the ground that even if the chief protagonists were gone from the scene by then, there were numerous others still alive and still articulate in 1624. There were in London, at that date, several survivors of the pioneer days in Jamestown, who had known Smith, Pocahontas, and Powhatan and their relations to one another, who could have challenged Smith's published story, but did not do so. There was diarist Sir George Percy, for one, who took issue in print, in 1625, with some of the facts published the previous year in Smith's *Generall Historie*—but not with the salient fact, the most conspicuous, most talked-about adventure in the entire bulky volume. Others who might have contradicted Smith's story and did not were Ralph Hamor, Captain Argall, David Wiffin, and Michael and William Phettiplace, to name at least five veterans known to have been back in London at that date. Smith's account of his rescue at the hands of Pocahontas stood unrefuted, in 1624, by Percy or by any other of the several First Planters and veterans of the First or Second Supply known to have returned from Virginia to London at that time.

The Smith saga was taken on faith throughout the seventeenth and eighteenth centuries; it remained for nineteenth-century historians to shoot it full of holes. It remained, more specifically, for Henry Adams to demolish the canon so dear to the South, less out of any genuine conviction than out of spite, an anti-Southern bias in a post–Civil War period marked by vicious sectionalism. To Adams, it was a mere exercise in iconoclasm: "The Virginia aristocracy," he gloated, "will be utterly gravelled by it." It was "a literary toy," Adams's first published article (1867), for which he had chosen as subject a figure so towering that the crash of its downfall—if he could bring it down!—would be audible nationwide. In fact, as he admitted many years later, the subject's publicity value was itself an additional incentive for this effort to explode the Pocahontas myth: "No other stone that could be thrown by a beginner," he wrote in his *Education of Henry Adams*, "would attract as much attention, and probably break as much glass."[10]

Beginning in 1867 with Adams's potshot, the question of Smith's credibility as a historian has been hashed and thrashed out in an endless stream of print, producing no definitive answer. Less controversial is the fact that Smith explored and mapped not only the shores of the Chesapeake but those of New England, the only significant seventeenth-century colonist to record the exploratory missions and early colonial efforts in both regions. The egocentricity, the bravura of Smith's personal adventures may be, in the long run, beside the point. "Smith's history," as Alexander Brown concedes in the preface of his *First Re-*

public in America, "was almost the only source from which we derive our knowledge"; furthermore, as he reminds us, "the history of any nation begins with myth." Even if we concede him "a liar's gorgeousness" (as does Stephen Vincent Benét), Smith had the virtues of his defects, and his was the gorgeous feat of having kept that hard-pressed Jamestown colony alive throughout the cruel winter of 1607–8, and having done it almost single-handed—his own stupendous instinct for survival extended to include the dwindling company under his command ("but fortie in all to keepe possession of this large country").

Beyond Smith's own word—his braggart's word, if you like—for that controversial execution-rescue episode, there is evidence that a very special and enduring relationship was established between him and Pocahontas at Werowocómoco in January of 1608, evidence that supports belief in the adoption theory, belief that there transpired—much as Smith described it—a traditional Powhatan tribal sacrament in which he, unconsciously, and she, consciously, played out ritual roles.

From that date forward, as will be shown, Pocahontas's actions, the high emotional pitch of her attitude toward Smith, and her constant concern for his safety make clear that she had made a commitment at the altar, that she had assumed a responsibility for Smith—and by extension for his people; that she stood as Smith's tribal sponsor, guarantor, intermediary between him and her people, between him and her father. And eventually, before it was all over, as will also be shown, she would reproach Smith for his failure to fulfill an obligation he in turn owed her and her people—although he apparently had never understood, never recognized it as such.

It remains a question whether Pocahontas, in exercising her right to claim and spare the life of a captive of the tribe, acted spontaneously on her own initiative or at the behest of her father Powhatan. In any event, the fact remains that no other sponsor of adoption would have been so well calculated as she to win over the opposition. Her uncle Opechancanough and the militants of the confederacy, who opposed any show of mercy to the captive Englishman or to the other hapless Englishmen at James Fort, would have found it difficult to counter the sponsorship of Pocahontas. She was a paragon, privileged and indulged, not only her chieftain-father's favorite child, his "great Dearling," "his dearest jewell and daughter," not only "his child which he most esteemed" but "the very Nomparell of his kingdome," who "for feature, countenance and proportion, much exceedeth any of the rest of his people," as is repeated by Captain Smith, by William Strachey, by Ralph Hamor, by almost every contemporary writer who witnessed her superiority in rank and merit.

Why, then, did Smith, in his *True Relation* of 1608, make no mention of meeting—or even seeing!—the Princess Pocahontas at Werowocómoco in early January of that year, much less any mention of being rescued by her? Indeed, in the 1608 version, there was no need for rescue since there was no threat of execution. In the 1608 version, Powhatan was all geniality when Captain Smith was led captive into his presence: "Hee kindly welcomed me with good wordes, and great Platters of sundrie Victuals, assuring mee his friendship, and my libertie within foure days." He marveled at Smith's ivory compass with its magic needle oscillating under glass, at Smith's discourse on cosmology: "the roundnesse of the earth, the course of the sunne, moone, starres and planets."

But what Powhatan really wanted to learn from Captain Smith was the purpose of the white men's presence on his shores, whether it was temporary or permanent, whether they came as traders or invaders: "Hee asked mee," Smith said, "the cause of our comming." The Virginia Company had warned explicitly not to allow the Naturals to perceive that "you mean to plant among them," not to reveal that the true purpose of their coming was colonization—the seizure of land occupied, hunted, and cultivated by the indigenes for centuries. Smith could perceive that the admission of the intent "to plant"—to settle and to dispossess—must constitute a *casus belli* on any continent. He spun a tale out of whole cloth designed to lull Powhatan's suspicions: a tale about a storm at sea, a disastrous naval engagement with the Spaniards, the need to take refuge ashore to tend men's wounds and mend a leaky hull, to await the return of Captain Newport with relief from overseas.

Powhatan was not so easily taken in; he was "a politick salvage," by Smith's own appraisal: "He demaunded why we went further with our Boate." Why the voyage up the Chickahominy?

Smith was ready with that answer, too: it was the Northwest Passage of which they had gone in search, "the backe Sea," the Pacific, the shortcut to the Orient.

There followed an exchange of superbities: Powhatan regaled Smith with an inventory of his "great and spacious Dominions"; Smith reciprocated with a list of "the territories of Europe, which was subject to our great King."

Powhatan could see the advantages of securing the Englishmen, with their superior weaponry and technology, as allies, even as members of the confederacy, and proposed a transfer of allegiance—Smith and his company should leave the settlement on the James and come "to live with him upon his River, a Countrie called Capa Howasicke. Hee promised to give me Corne, Venison, or what I wanted to feede us: Hatchets and Copper wee should make him, and none should disturbe us."

"This request I promised to performe," Smith wrote,

and thus, having with all the kindnes hee could devise, sought to content me, hee sent me home, with 4 men: one that usually carried my Gowne and Knapsacke after me, two other loded with bread, and one to accompanie me.

Thus, the brief 1608 version of Smith's capture, his interview with Powhatan, his prompt release and return to Jamestown. No mention of Pocahontas, no mention of an execution or a rescue.

In the *Generall Historie* account of 1624, the ceremonial at the altar stone is followed by another, two days later—probably the adoption ceremony. It took place in a great house in the woods whither Smith was led,

there upon a mat by the fire left to be alone. . . . Not long after from behinde a mat that divided the house, was made the most dolefullest noyse he ever heard; then Powhatan more like a devill then a man, with some two hundred more as blacke as himselfe, came unto him and told him now they were friends, and presently he should goe to James towne, to send him two great gunnes, and a gryndstone, for which he would give him the Country of Capahowosick, and for ever esteeme him as his son Nantaquoud.

The gift of land in the heart of the confederacy, the allusion to the father-son relation, should have made clear to Smith that he had become a member of the tribe by adoption. Powhatan would later make it clearer still, proclaiming Smith "a *werowanes* of Powhatan and that all his subjects should so esteeme us, and no man account us strangers . . . but Powhatans, and the corne, woemen and Country should be to us as to his owne people."

Smith saw Pocahontas's hand in his release; she had saved his life, "and not onely that, but so prevailed with her father, that I was safely conducted to James towne."

So to James towne with 12 guides[11] Powhatan sent him. That night they quartered in the woods, he still expecting (as he had done all this long time of his imprisonment) every houre to be put to one death or other: for all their feasting. But almightie God (by his divine providence) had mollified the hearts of those sterne Barbarians with compassion. The next morning betimes they came to the Fort. . . .[12]

Once safely back on the ramparts, Smith could well afford to offer his guides the "two great gunnes, and a gryndstone" specified by Powhatan and promised by Smith as ransom payment: the two small cannon weighed three or four thousand pounds apiece. No wonder the Indians "found them somewhat too heavie" to haul back to Werowocómoco, as Smith sardonically commented. Instead, he treated them to a demonstration-firing, using a load of stones and aiming at "the boughs of a great tree loaded with Isickles." As a result, "the yce and branches came so tumbling downe, that the poore Salvages ran away halfe dead with feare." It took Smith some time to induce them to come back: "But at last we regained some conference with them, and gave them such toyes; and sent to Powhatan, his women, and children such presents, and gave them in generall full content" (although it is difficult to believe that Powhatan would have been contented with "such toyes" as a substitute for the armament and implement solemnly agreed upon).

Back at Jamestown, perils were in store for Smith as grave as those he had just escaped at Werowocómoco: "Now in James Towne," he wrote, "they were all in combustion, the strongest preparing once more to run away with the Pinnace" (an attempt frustrated by Smith at "the hazzard of his life"). "Some no better then they should be" (Captain Gabriel Archer, for example, who had wangled an illegal appointment to the Council during Smith's absence) "had plotted with the President to have him [Smith] put to death by the Leviticall law" —"an eye for an eye, a tooth for a tooth"; Smith's life to be claimed as forfeit for the lives of Robinson, Emery, and Cassen, "pretending the fault was his that had led them to their ends."

Only the arrival from England of Captain Newport, bringing the *Susan Constant* back to Jamestown on the evening tide, saved Captain Smith (and ex-President Wingfield, as well) from that kangaroo court and imminent execution. "But it pleased god to send Captain Newport unto us the same eevening, to our unspeakable comfortes," according to Wingfield's *Discourse of Virginia*, "whose arryvall saved Master Smyths leif and mine."

Beyond establishing the dates for his departure and return (the only one to do so), Wingfield's *Discourse* has few lines to spare for Smith's wilderness excursion: "The 10th of December, Master Smyth went up the Ryver of the Chechohomynies to trade for corne. . . ." Wingfield gave only the barest facts concerning Smith's capture, his cross-country trek with Opechancanough, his interview with Powhatan: "At last, he [Opechancanough] brought him [Smith] to the great Powatan (of whome before wee had no knowledg) who sent him home to our Towne the viijth of January." Not a word from Wingfield about an execution or a rescue. Not a word about Pocahontas.

Neither official Recorder Gabriel Archer nor diarist Sir George Percy had been invited to accompany Captain Smith on his journey into the heart of the Powhatan Confederacy in December–January, 1607-8; neither made any reference whatsoever to Smith's journey. But, then, Percy's last diary entry is dated September 19, 1607, and Archer's *Relatyon of the Discovery of Our River* dealt only with the period May 22–June 22, 1607, the dates of the exploratory mission up the James River.

Not only Smith and Wingfield but the colony itself might be said to have been saved when the *Susan Constant* arrived with her complement of between eighty and a hundred new colonists, come to reinforce the pitiful few remaining out of the original hundred. The First Supply (as this contingent of 1608 was to be known in history) consisted of thirty-three gentlemen, twenty-one laborers, four "Taylers," one surgeon and two apothecaries, a gunsmith and a goldsmith, a cooper, a blacksmith, a tobacco-pipe maker, two refiners, a perfumer and a jeweller (only the last two seem superfluous; the goldsmith and the refiners would serve a useful purpose, should the search for precious metals prove successful).

In addition to the "neare a hundred men" (by Smith's estimate) aboard the *Susan Constant*, she had sailed "well furnished with all things could be imagined necessary for both them [the newcomers] and for us": supplies of all kinds, agricultural equipment as well as armament, foodstuff, clothing, ornament, trade-goods.

But no sooner had the hundred-ton ship been unloaded than a fire devastated the settlement—a tinder-box with its reed thatch—leaving old settlers and new to shiver "in that extreame frost," bereft of shelter and supply.[18] "Many of our old men [original planters] became diseased, and many of our new for want of lodging perished."

The course of the colony, like the life of Captain Smith, went from "extreame extremitie" to extremity still more extreme. Now again, in the second week of January, 1608, the fate of the colony—the fate of the English colonization movement in America—hung in the balance. There had been talk of abandoning the settlement before Smith's return from Werowocómoco; the topic must have been revived in the wake of the fire.

In straits so dire that the colony's survival was in question, help came from Captain Smith's new-found native friends and foster family.

Pocahontas, who had stood sponsor for Smith at the altar stone, now led troops of Powhatan tribesmen out of the forest, up to the gate of the triangular palisaded fort at Jamestown to deliver life-saving gifts of game and wildfowl to Smith for the sick and starving—great carcasses of deer and braces of turkey lashed to poles balanced on the red men's shoulders, large reed baskets of cornbread on their arms.

"Yet it pleased God," as Smith explained in a brief communiqué addressed to "His Majesties Commissioners," "to make their great Kings daughter the means to returne me safe to James towne, and releeve our wants."

Throughout January and February, throughout that grim winter, emissaries from Pocahontas and Powhatan came often, as often as "every other day," and "brought such plentie of bread, fish, turkies, squirrels, deare and other wild beasts" as preserved the colony from starvation. The Salvages "every other day repaired, with such provisions that sufficiently did serve them from hand to mouth." "Presents from their Kings, or Pocahontas" were delivered to Smith, again and again, at Jamestown. "The Emperour Powhatan, each weeke once or twice, sent me presents of Deare, bread, Raugroughcuns [raccoon]," Smith stated.

"Such was the weaknesse of this poore Commonwealth" (as Smith would tell Queen Anne in his letter of 1616) "as had the Salvages not fed us, we directly had starved. And this reliefe, most gracious Queene, was commonly brought us by this Lady Pocahontas." "Notwithstanding all these passages," he continued in the next paragraph,

> when inconstant Fortune turned our peace to warre [when hostilities broke out again] this tender Virgin would still not spare to dare to visit us, and by her our iarres [jarres, discords, dissensions] have oft been appeased, and our wants still supplyed; were it the policie of her father thus to imploy her, or the ordinance of God thus to make her his instrument, or her extraordinarie affection to our Nation, I know not. . . .

As early as the mid-eighteenth century, the tendency was to interpret Pocahontas's emotion vis-à-vis Smith as love—nay, even "*passion*," in the view of the anonymous author of a piece appearing in the *London Magazine* in 1755, under the title "A Short Account of the British Plantations in America." "Pocahontas easily prevailed with her father and her countrymen," it says,

> to allow her to indulge her passion for the captain, by often visiting the fort, and always accompanying her visits with a fresh supply of provisions; therefore it may justly be said, that the

success of our first settlement in America, was chiefly owing to the love this young girl had conceived for Capt. Smith, and consequently in this instance, as well as in many others,

Love does all that's great below!

Whether acting on her own impulse (out of her own compassion or affection), at her father's direction, or as the instrument of God, Pocahontas was clearly the agent of deliverance—Smith's savior and, by extension, the savior of the colony.

For the rest, Smith took it all as a personal tribute: the Indians' manifestations of goodwill and benevolence he took as compliments to his own personal influence, the good impression he had made on his captors, on the Supreme Chieftain, and on his beloved daughter Pocahontas. ("So he had inchanted these poore soules being their prisoner," he wrote unblushingly. Or again: "Such acquaintance I had amongst the Indians, and such confidence they had in me, as neare the Fort they would not come till I came to them." As might have been expected, "The President and Council much envied his estimation amongst the Salvages. . . .")

As for the Lady Pocahontas and what she was to him, Smith steadfastly sidestepped any explanation of the relation—one to excite gratitude and wonder, yet perhaps best glossed over, lest some suggestion of erotic dalliance be inferred. In the light of the strong Puritan ethic pervading England in that era, the strong Puritan faction evident in the Virginia Company's high councils, it is easy to understand why Smith should have carefully avoided any hint of interracial sex in his *True Relation* of 1608, at a time when he still cherished hope of advancement within the company.

Still another risk was involved, in 1608, in any exposé of fraternization with the heathen: there might be mass desertions from that pest-ridden, famine-stricken encampment on the James if the word got out that an English defector could expect to find a warm welcome and a "comely and personable" young squaw awaiting him in a well-provisioned, well-heated Powhatan wigwam. ("Comely and personable" are adjectives used by Ralph Hamor to describe the young women he saw in Powhatan's longhouse in 1610.)

Captain John Smith would be neither the first nor the last white Christian European to live out male sexual fantasies in the wildwood of the New World. All the European invaders of the two Americas—English as well as Italian, Spanish, Portuguese, and French—interpreted the ready compliance of the Indian women not as an indication of a sexually permissive society but as a personal compliment, a tribute to their own irresistible masculine attractions, and the attraction primarily of the white race—the white skin—for the red. "The whiteness of his flesh," as the Florentine Verrazano reported to the French king, was a marvel to the redskins of the central Atlantic shore where *La Dauphine* touched in 1524: the Indians there looked "with great admiration" upon the young mariner whom they had rescued from the surf (the fire they built was not to roast him—as his watching shipmates feared— but to warm him). "They admired the whiteness of our skins," Captain Arthur Barlowe reported to Raleigh in 1584, "and wanted constantly to touch our chests."

But it was Amerigo Vespucci, in 1497, who first stated the case for the irresistibility of the white male for the red female, with the pronouncement: "They showed themselves very desirous of copulating with us Christians." "They" were the Indian maidens depicted in a copper-plate engraving by the Flemish publisher-engraver Theodore de Bry in illustration of the scene Vespucci had described: a half dozen of de Bry's fair, nude, Europeanized, Rubensian aboriginal females shown lining up on the seashore to offer themselves to the sheepish Italian. Hariot's caption for the engraving read: "A Renaissance Gentleman in America."[14]

It was a traditional Indian gesture of hospitality to offer an honored guest a pipe of tobacco to smoke and a comely young maiden to share his bed (whether a female captive or a slave rather than a maiden of the tribe or a wife or sister of the host is a point never clarified by early reporters). Smith made note (in his 1612 *Map of Virginia*) of that custom as he observed it among the Powhatans: ". . . and at night where his [the honored guest's] lodging is appointed, they set a woman fresh painted red with *Pocones*[15] and oile, to be his bedfellow."

These early observers of the Indian cultural patterns on the American continents were conspicuous for their lack of scientific training; the result was a gross misunderstanding of the aboriginal cultures. It came as a distinct shock to the European Christian invader to discover that polygamy was common to both North and South American aborigines (where Powhatan's count of wives was a modest one hundred, Mexico's Montezuma numbered his in the thousands). The vagaries of the American Indians' sexual mores bewildered the European Christian: whereas chastity before marriage, for example, was not generally speaking esteemed a cardinal virtue, still, infidelity after marriage was deemed a serious breach of the moral code, punishable, in many instances, by the loss of a nose, an ear, even a life. Henry Spelman stated that adultery was a capital offense ("to lye with another's wife is death if he be taken in the manner"), while Strachey implied that it was the adulterous woman who was punished ("the women very care-full not to be suspected of dishonestie without the leave of their husbandes"). (The Salish and Gros Ventre Indians, according to *David Thompson's Narrative*, decreed death for both parties taken in adultery.)

Further to confuse the newcomers, Indian sexual mores differed widely from tribe to tribe, from region to region. The only fault with which Verrazano and his crew could charge the Wampanoag Indians of Rhode Island (which Verrazano named in 1524) was the concern of the men of that tribe for the chastity of their women. The Ojibway and the Chipewyan tribes were said by early reporters to put the same premium on virginity. Iroquois maidens, also, had a reputation for chastity before their "corruption" by contact with southern tribes. And whereas the young women of the Cree, Assiniboin, and Sioux tribes— demoralized by contact with the invading whites—became notorious for their harlotry in the nineteenth century, pioneer travelers had earlier attested likewise to their integrity. Francis Parkman stated that "chas-tity in women was recognized as a virtue by many tribes," but most North American Indian tribes, certainly most of those west of the Rockies, took a highly permissive view of premarital contact on the part of the female. As Baron de Lahontan noted in his observations on the Canadian tribes, the Indian woman was "master of her own body" in a sense that the European woman was not. "The Maidens are entirely at their own disposal," Beverley observed at the close of the century, "and may manage their persons as they think fit."[16] "Libidinous beyond measure" was Vespucci's characterization of the Indian female—a total stranger to the Judaeo-Christian concept of sin in sex.

The lubricious white invader rarely analyzed the good fortune in female form awaiting him on the Western shore. Anthropologists sug-gest a complex, even mystical explanation for the ready sexual com-pliance of the Indian women, seeing it in a sacred or ceremonial context: the newcomer from across the water was taken as a god or superman to whom the women of the tribe were offered in the hope that offspring of the union would provide a new, superior, supremely valorous warrior caste for the tribe, that the power of the white man would be absorbed by the Indian woman, transmitted by her to her husband, to her people. Robert Beverley, describing this folkway as he observed it among the remnants of the Virginia tribes at the end of the seventeenth century and the beginning of the eighteenth, and referring to "A Brace of young Beautiful virgins" supplied as a gesture of hospitality to visiting "Men of great Distinction," saw and drew a parallel to the custom of classical times: "After this manner perhaps many of the Heroes were begotten in old time, who boasted themselves to be the Sons of some Way-faring God."

Was it as a "Way-faring God" that Captain Smith appeared to the Powhatans . . . and to Pocahontas? a white-skinned, blue-eyed, fair-haired, blond-bearded apparition, his carapace of armor glinting in the sun, his magical weapons firing thunder-bolts and lightning-flashes— a visitor to their shore from over the horizon, from some other world? steel-clad, dauntless in extremity—"all beard and certainty," as Hart Crane imagines Pocahontas's view of him—Smith must have appeared to Pocahontas as a superior being, a demigod if not a God, whose other-worldly power, valor, and wisdom might be transmitted to her people by their union, hers and his, in a mystic communion performed upon the altar-stones: her body (that, appropriately, of a princess of the blood), the means whereby the genius of his people would be bred into her people's bones. The rite performed by her before the pawcorance (or altar-stone) at Werowocómoco was entirely within the tradition of her tribe, her race. Later generations—if not Smith's own or those immediately succeeding his—would see in it a symbol of reconciliation between the races through sex and love (and marriage?). Later genera-tions could look back and perceive that there had existed, in the be-ginning, a possibility of assimilation, acculturation, integration—as sym-bolized by Pocahontas and the English captain—a possible alternative to dispossession and genocide.

CHAPTER V

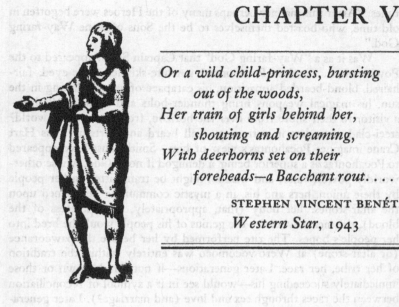

Or a wild child-princess, bursting
out of the woods,
Her train of girls behind her,
shouting and screaming,
With deerhorns set on their
foreheads—a Bacchant rout. . . .

STEPHEN VINCENT BENÉT,
Western Star, 1943

POCHOHUNTAS, a well featured but wanton young girle Powhatans daughter, sometymes resorting to our Fort, of the age then of 11. or 12. yeares, [would] gett the boyes forth with her into the markett place and make them wheele, falling on their hands turning their heeles upwardes, whome she would follow, and wheele so her self naked as she was all the fort over. . . ."[1]

It came as a shock to nineteenth-century romantics (among whom the cult of Pocahontas flourished) to read the above account by litterateur-pioneer William Strachey; it was written in 1612 but not published until 1849, this pen-picture of the Powhatan princess exposing herself shamelessly (or was it unashamedly?) in cartwheels, handsprings, somersaults through the air—dark hair streaming, dark eyes flashing, coppery body lithely arching, muscles rippling, "privities" undraped, in full view.

"Frolicksom" is the word Robert Beverley uses, a century later, to describe the women of Pocahontas's tribe: "The excess of Life and Fire, which they never fail to have, makes them frolicksom, but without any real imputation to their Innocence . . . ground enough for the English, who are not very nice in distinguishing betwixt guilt, and harmless freedom, to think them Incontinent," but not for Virginia-born Beverley. "The Indian Damsels are full of spirit," he wrote admiringly, "and from thence are always inspir'd with Mirth and good Humour. They are extreamly given to laugh, which they do with a Grace not to be resisted."

As for "the boyes" at James Fort with whom Pocahontas disported herself so freely, they were not to be outdone by any mere girl, and taking her dare, went forth with her into the wide, open trading area or "markett place" at the center of the enclosure, kicked up their heels, and set off tumbling, spinning like tops, like "wheeles," cartwheeling, "all the Fort over." Pocahontas had found several boys to romp with at Jamestown (four were listed on the first voyage of the *Susan Constant*). Nimble lads nine years old and up were much in demand in the seventeenth-century merchant marine for service, errands, and high work on the masts. (Columbus's *Niña*'s crew listed seven able seamen and seven grummets, the old name for ship's boys.) Tutored by the boatswain, the boys could hope to attain to the rating and pay of able seaman after one voyage.[2]

If "the boyes" at the fort tagged along after the spirited Indian princess, so, in all probability, did the men, lustful and leering.

If Pocahontas was "then of 11. or 12. yeares" only, nonetheless she was—as the result of her vigorously athletic Indian youth—a well-developed, well-formed, and probably shapely young female and, as Strachey pointed out, a "well featured" one—as such, sure to be a cynosure of eyes at the fort.

If the men, eyeing her, ogling her, restrained themselves, if they respectfully kept their distance, it was because they knew she was the Supreme Chieftain's favorite daughter, favorite child, pride and joy, as well as Councilor-Captain Smith's special friend—his savior, guardian angel, adopted sister or adopted wife or concubine; whatever she was to him, it was something very special.

But was she, indeed, only eleven or twelve years old? In corroboration of his estimate of her age at only eleven or twelve, Strachey contends that her naked state was proof of prepubescence: "Their younger women goe not shadowed* . . . untill they be nigh eleaven or twelve returnes of the leafe old"—the years being computed, poetically, in terms of the annual greening of the leaf. "But being past once 12 yeres they put on a kynd of semicinctum leathren apron (as doe our artificers or handicrafts men) before their bellies and are very shamefac'd to be seene bare."

---

* To "goe not shadowed" meant to be uncovered below the waist.

But Strachey's testimony on the subject of Pocahontas's age is not reliable, since his was strictly hearsay evidence: Strachey did not arrive in Virginia until 1610 with the second section of the Third Supply. He could only report what he had heard from the First Planters and the pioneers of the First and Second Supply.

Captain Smith, on the other hand, a witness who could speak with authority, spoke of her as "a childe of tenne yeares old" in his *True Relation* of 1608. But that was a year, a time, at which both author and editor may have found it politic to play down any romantic or sexual connection, to soft-pedal any idea of fraternization between European Christian and aboriginal pagan in the wilderness.

If Pocahontas was "a childe of tenne," then she was not yet pubescent, certainly not yet a woman, not yet an appropriate mate for a man of twenty-eight, such as Smith. But he flatly contradicts himself on that very point, in the letter he addressed to Queen Anne in 1616, referring to Pocahontas as having been "a childe of twelve or thirteene yeeres of age," thereby putting her over the borderline of pubescence; the age of twelve was considered the age of responsibility, of adulthood, by Indian tradition—the age, furthermore, of nubility.[3]

Further to compound the confusion, Richard Potts and William Phettiplace (two pioneers of the First Supply arriving at Jamestown with Captain Newport in early January, 1608) placed Pocahontas's age "at most not past 13 or 14 yeares." (Their account appeared in "The Proceedings of the English Colonie in Virginia," second part of *The Map of Virginia*, published in London in 1612.) At age thirteen or fourteen, Pocahontas would have been well into pubescence, nubility, maturity—a graduate of tribal puberty rites, ready for love and marriage, functioning as a responsible member of the tribe.[4]

With a variety of estimates ranging from ten to fourteen, the best guess as to Pocahontas's age in 1608 would be a minimum of twelve. An irresponsible child would not have been allowed to exercise the tribal right of adoption, to claim the life of a captive and make him a member of the tribe. Pocahontas's exercise of that right in the case of Captain Smith is the most convincing proof of her being at least twelve at the time. Nor would an irresponsible child have served—as Pocahontas did—as liaison between the Supreme Chieftain of the confederacy and the English commandant.

With both stores and shelter going up in flames in early January, with bitter midwinter cold to intensify the suffering and aggravate the want, the English colony on the James stood in jeopardy. It was the beneficence of Pocahontas that averted catastrophe in the crucial early months of 1608, as Captain Smith remembered:

Now ever once in foure or five dayes, Pocahontas with her attendants, brought him [Smith] so much provision, that saved many of their lives, that els for all this had starved with hunger. . . .

James towne with her wild traine she as freely frequented, as her father's habitation; and during the time of two or three yeeres, she next under God, was still the instrument to preserve this Colonie from death, famine and utter confusion; which if in those times, [it] had once beene dissolved, Virginia might have line [lain] as it was at our first arrivall to this day.

They emerged from the snowy woods into the clearing in front of the palisaded fort, Pocahontas walking ahead of the others to the gate, to be met and greeted by Captain Smith; her attendants waited at the forest edge for her summons, their shoulders bowed under the heavy carcasses of deer, the braces of wild turkey, the pottery jars of meal, the baskets of bread. (To protect themselves against the icy wind, "both men and women," as Strachey wrote, "putt on a kynd of leather breeches and stockings, all fastened togither, made of deere skynes, which they tye and wrappe about their loynes after the fashion of the Turkes or Irish Trouses.")

Pocahontas walked ahead, free, unencumbered by burdens; half-naked, but every inch a chieftain's daughter, unmistakably a person of rank enjoying the privileges thereof. A chieftain's wife, sister, or daughter, Strachey says, was attended by slaves and servants for menial tasks ("not ordynarily perfourmed to any other amongst them"), and she moved "with a kynd of pride," with "a shew of greatnes." Not for her, as for "the other both maydes and marryed women" to "come out of her Quintan or Boat, through the water"; instead, a weroansqua or a princess (like Pocahontas) was to be "carryed forth between twoo of her servants" to the riverbank (as was the weroansqua Strachey observed). Waited on hand and foot, in "Sommer tyme," she would be

lay'd without dores under the shadow of a broad leav'd tree, upon a Pallet of Osiers spredd over with 4. or 5. fyne grey matts, her self Covered with a faire white drest deare-skyn . . . and when she rose, she had a Mayde who fetch't her a frontall of white Corrall, and pendants of great . . . pearles, which she putt into her eares, and a Chayne with long lynckes of Copper, which came twice or thrice doubled about her neck . . . and thus attyred with some variety of feathers, and flowers stuck in their hayres, they seeme as debonayre, quaynt, and well pleased as . . . a daughter of the howse of Austria behoung with all her Iewells. Likewise, her Mayd fetch't her a Mantell . . . made of blew feathers, so arteficially and thick sowed togither, that yt showes like a deepe purple Satten, and is very smooth and sleek, and after she brought her water for her handes, and then a bunch or towe of fresh green ashen leaves, as for a towell to wype them. . . .

ASIDE FROM THE BENEFICENCE and bounty of a well-disposed Princess Pocahontas and her chieftain father, Captain Newport found few encouraging developments to cheer him in the weeks following his return to Jamestown. Any hope he (or the Virginia Company) cherished that a lode of gold or a passage to the "Other Sea" might have been discovered in his absence was doomed to disappointment by the reports of Captain Smith and the other members of the Council.

The Council, for that matter, was in sad disarray: ex-President Wingfield was still confined to quarters aboard the pinnace; incumbent President Ratcliffe was increasingly proving himself inept, improvident, lazy, vain, and so becoming steadily more unpopular; his henchman Captain Archer was now reduced in rank from Council member (to which he had never been entitled) to recorder; Captain Martin was forever incapacitated, afflicted by some ailment even more serious than his chronic gold fever. The advent of a new member could not but be highly welcome at that point. The newcomer was Captain Matthew Scrivener, a member of the First Supply on the *Susan Constant*, and Captain Smith could certainly use his support against the Ratcliffe faction.

Captain Smith, in his report to Newport, made much of Powhatan's favor, manifested to the colony in the person of Pocahontas. Powhatan was made out to Newport as another Montezuma: if the riches of Mexico were not at his disposal, his was the bounty of the Chesapeake:

> His [Smith's] relation of the plenty he had seene, especially at Werowocómoco, and of the state and bountie of Powhatan (which till that time was unknowne) so revived their dead spirits (especially the love of Pocahontas) as all mens feare was abandoned.

Especially the love of Pocahontas! At thought of her—her compassion and benevolence, her good offices as intermediary, her obvious determination to help them survive the winter, her manifestation of love for Captain Smith and, through him, for them all—at thought of her, their dead spirits revived.

A journey to Werowocómoco, to the court of the Supreme Chieftain, was proposed for late February, when Smith would present Captain Newport, his superior officer—"his Father," in Indian parlance—to Powhatan. It was not beyond the realm of possibility that Powhatan might open up to Smith and Newport the veins of the precious metals of his domain, or reveal the waterway leading to the Other Sea.

No such revelations were forthcoming, but "Powhatan strained himselfe to the utmost of his greatnesse to entertaine them": the same pomp and circumstance surrounded the emperor as upon the occasion of Smith's first visit to Werowocómoco in December: "Two in a ranke we marched to the Emperor's house," Smith recalled in his *True Relation* of 1608:

> Before his house stood fortie or fiftie great Platters of fine bread [Powhatan status symbols]. Being entrd the house, with loude tunes they all made signes of great joy. This proud salvage, having his finest women, and the principall of his chiefe men assembled, sate in rankes as before is expressed. . . . Four or five hundred people made a guard . . . for our passage: and Proclamation was made, none upon paine of death to presume to doe us any wrong or discourtesie. . . .

Powhatan's response to the Englishmen's gifts—a suit of red cloth, a white greyhound,[5] and a stovepipe hat—was the proclamation of "a perpetuall league and friendship." To seal the treaty, hostages were exchanged: a thirteen-year-old English boy "named Thomas Salvage was then given unto Powhatan, whom Newport called his sonne; for whom Powhatan gave him Namontack his trustie servant, and one of a shrewd, subtill capacitie." Each boy was to adapt to the other culture, to learn the language, to serve as interpreter.

"Three or foure dayes more we spent in feasting, dauncing, and trading, wherein Powhatan carried himselfe so proudly, yet discreetly (in his salvage manner) as made us all admire his naturall gifts, considering his education." His natural gifts appeared far more considerable than Captain Newport's when it came to trading: Powhatan, "scorning to trade as his subjects did," called Newport down for haggling over the value of copper and swords in relation to corn.

Smith saved the day by producing a sensational new trade item, a dazzle of Venetian glass, beads of blue "the colour of the skyes . . . a most rare substance," by Smith's ballyhoo, "not to be worne but by the greatest kings in the world." As a result, "Such strange Iewells" brought a prodigious "2. or 300. Bushells of corne." (The animus that Newport subsequently displayed against Smith sprang in all probability, from his embarrassment at being thus conspicuously outtraded by his second-in-command.)

As traders, Newport's crew proved as prodigal as their captain, so that when the *Susan Constant* sailed for England on April 10, the rate of exchange of Indian corn for English trade-goods had skyrocketed.

Captain Smith breathed a sigh of relief to see the ship pull out of Jamestown, for more reasons than one. For one, two arch-enemies of his were aboard: ex-President Wingfield and Captain Gabriel Archer. (Another passenger was Namontack, the shrewd and subtle young Indian hostage, sent to England by Powhatan, in Smith's opinion, as an intelligence agent, "to know our strength and Country's condition.") Yet another reason was that the vessel was laden with Captain Martin's "phantasticall gold" instead of the cargo of red cedar logs Smith had advocated. Martin's gold fever had infected the colony throughout February, March, and early April: "there was no talke, no hope, no worke, but dig gold, wash gold, refine gold, loade gold"—"such a bruit of gold," in fact, that the reconstruction of the fort, urgent as this was in the wake of the fire, was totally neglected. When the *Susan Constant* set sail, it was, in Smith's words, "a drunken ship with so much gilded durt" that, as he suspected, would prove worthless by assay.

But now,

> The spring approaching, and the Ship departing, Master Scrivener and Captaine Smith divided betwixt them the rebuilding James towne; the repairing our Pallizadoes; the cutting downe trees; preparing our fields; planting our corne, and to rebuild our Church, and re-cover our Store house.

Work was interrupted on April 20 by the appearance of sails on the river: fear of a Spanish raider sent the colonists rushing to man the cannon. But when the red cross of St. George was identified on the pennant flying at the masthead, the rush was to the waterfront instead, to cheer and greet the *Phoenix*, her captain, Francis Nelson, and the passengers aboard, new recruits from England come to swell the ranks of the hundred-odd Jamestown settlers.

In May, while the *Phoenix* waited at Jamestown for its cargo for the return passage to England, the colony was suddenly plagued by Indian raids, sneak attacks, and ambushes—with the purpose, apparently, of seizing English tools and weapons. Captain Newport, just before he sailed in early April, had committed the error of reciprocating Powhatan's gift of twenty turkeys with a gift of twenty swords. When Captain Smith refused to follow Newport's dangerous precedent, the consequence was that swords, axes, muskets, spades, and shovels were purloined, picked off stealthily, or wrested forcibly from unwary colonists as they cultivated their fields or hunted in the forest.

The Virginia Company injunction "not to offend the Naturals" still prevailed with most of the English high command, but Powhatan soon learned that Captain Smith was not a man to meddle with.

> This charitable humor prevailed, till well it chanced they meddled with Captaine Smith, who without further deliberation gave them such an incounter, as some he so hunted up and downe the Isle, some he so terrified with shipping, beating, and imprisonment: as for revenge they surprised two of our forraging disorderly souldiers, and having assembled their forces, boldly threatened at our Ports to force Smith to redeliver seven Salvages, which for their villanies he detained prisoners, or we were all but dead men.

Smith was no man to be threatened: "He sallied out amongst them, and in lesse than an houre"—rampaging, raiding, putting neighboring villages to the torch—had brought the "Salvages" to terms: the two captive Englishmen were returned and a peace parley initiated.

As to the seven Indians imprisoned in the fort, their interrogation was conducted under the threat of torture and death: they were treated to a demonstration of the English horror-machine known as the rack, they hearkened to the firing of "certaine vollies of shot" designed to cause "each other to think that their fellowes had been slaine." Mass confessions ensued: the Indian prisoners "all agreed in one point, they were directed onely by Powhatan to obtaine him our weapons, to cut our owne throats."

Whether these seven had acted on Powhatan's orders, at a confederacy directive, or on their own initiative independently of the confederacy, the reason for the intensification of Indian hostility should not have been difficult to comprehend: the steady reinforcement of the colony—the arrival of the *Susan Constant* and the *Phoenix* with their complement of new settlers—gave proof of the invaders' intention to stay, to settle, to dispossess. The native inhabitants were more than ever convinced that the invaders were "a people come from under the world, to take their world away."

At which point, it was, once again, Pocahontas who stepped into the breach, who served as intermediary between the Indians and the English, who carried messages back and forth between the fort on the James and the great-house on the Pamunkey, furthering negotiations between Powhatan and her friend and ward (and lover?), Captain Smith. Pocahontas, having committed herself in some way to Captain Smith—and to his compatriots—would exert her every effort to bring about a peaceful coexistence between her people and the strangers, the supermen from across the seas.

Sometime during the month of May, Powhatan "sent his messengers, and his dearest daughter Pocahontas with presents to excuse him of the injuries done by some rash untoward Captaines his subjects, desiring their liberties for this time, with the assurance of his love for ever." This is Smith's account, in his *Generall Historie*, of diplomatic negotiations between him and Powhatan. The account in his *True Relation* is much the same: "Powhatan understanding we detained certaine Salvages, sent his Daughter."

To accompany his paragon of a daughter, Powhatan sent "his most trustie messenger, called Rawhunt," who, for all his deformity of body ("much exceeding in deformitie of person"), was endowed with "a subtill wit and crafty understanding."

Rawhunt "told mee," Smith wrote, "how well Powhatan loved and respected mee; and in that I should not doubt any way of his kindnesse, he had sent his child, which he most esteemed, to see me. . . . His little Daughter hee had taught" a lesson in hauteur and imperiousness, that she should appear publicly to take no notice of the Indian prisoners, leaving their cause to be pleaded by friends and relatives ("not taking notice at all of the Indians that had beene prisoners three daies, till that morning that she saw their fathers and friends come quietly, and in good termes to entreate their libertie").

Pocahontas may not have stooped to plead the cause of the Indian prisoners, but it was into the custody of "Pocahuntas, the Kings Daughter," that they were given over by their English captors, to show their appreciation "of her fathers kindnesse in sending her."

"Pocahuntas also we requited with such trifles as contented her"—blue Venetian beads; mirrors (the first to reflect the aboriginal princess's face); hawks' bells (tiny, tinkling bells such as were fastened by falconers to the collars of their birds of prey)—all these trade-items were taken from the ships' stores and heaped into sweet-grass baskets for presentation to the Indian princess. "Bid Pokahontas bring hither two little Baskets," Smith wrote as a conversational exercise phrase in his "Vocabulary of Indian Words &c" appended to Book Two of his

Generall Historie. The English sentence was followed by the Algonkian: "*Kekaten Pokahontas patiaquagh niugh tanks manotyehs*"; "and I will give her white Beads to make her a Chaine": "*mawokick rawrenock audawgh*." With the aid of hostages exchanged between the red camp and the white, Pocahontas and Captain Smith made progress in each other's language.

Smith made it clear that it was for Pocahontas's sake alone that concessions had been made, that it was to her alone the prisoners owed their life and liberty: "he delivered them [to] Pocahontas; for whose sake onely he fayned to have saved their lives, and gave them libertie."

When on June 2, the *Phoenix* slipped her moorings, unfurled her sails, and headed downriver into the Bay toward the open sea, the perennially ailing Captain Martin was aboard,[6] en route back to England, as was the manuscript of Captain Smith's *True Relation*—his rough notes in letter form—entrusted to Captain Nelson for delivery "to a worshipful friend" of Smith's in London (who would see to its publication in a record ten weeks' time).[7]

The letter reflected the writer's optimism at that date: "Wee now remaining being in good health, all our men wel contented, free from mutinies" (for the first time, with trouble-makers Wingfield, Archer, and Martin gone, with President Ratcliffe's influence on the wane, and Smith's waxing strong), "and as we hope in a continuall peace with the Indians"—thanks, mainly, to Pocahontas and her good offices.

With the situation at Jamestown stable enough in early June to warrant his absenting himself, Captain Smith set out on the second from Cape Henry with a company of fourteen (seven "Gents" including a "Doctour of Physicke," four "Soulders," and two fishermen or sailors) on an exploratory mission around the Chesapeake, to the hitherto unexplored eastern and northern shores, to see "whether the bay were endlesse, or how farre it extended," as the Virginia Company Instructions had suggested. Now sailing, now rowing in "that open barge of two tunnes," Captain Smith "discovered," surveyed, mapped, and named (the very first isles that came into view, directly across the strait, he named in his own honor, "Smiths Iles," and they keep the name to this day).

The first people accosted, the Accomac tribe of "the Easterne Shore,"[8] members of the Powhatan Confederacy although separated by a wide stretch of water from their confederates, were handsome and hospitable (their king was "the comliest, proper, civill Salvage we incountred"): "They spoke the language of Powhatan" (by now familiar to Smith and some of his party) "wherein they made such descriptions of the Bay, Isles and rivers, that often did us exceeding pleasure"—one more reference out of many to the articulateness, the eloquence of the native American.

Other tribes encountered around the Bay were hostile or were suspected of hostility; still others, speaking in a non-Algonkian tongue, could not make themselves understood, except by resort to the universal Indian sign-language. Everywhere, the English barge stirred up ripples of excitement: "The people ran as amazed in troups from place to place, and divers got into the tops of trees." An encounter, no matter how cordially initiated, might suddenly erupt into violence: where the English even suspected an ambush, they would fire "five or six shot among the reeds," scattering the crowds that lined the shore (the scattering crowds leaving behind "a many of baskets and much bloud").

Some coasts of the Chesapeake were fairly thickly populated; others, uninhabited, awesome and forbidding in their solitude and silence: "woods extreame thicke, full of Woolves, Beares, Deare, and other wild beasts"; vast unpopulated stretches for which the explorers' name of "Limbo" was appropriate.

Their foremast toppled by a gale, their "small Barge" almost submerged by the "mighty waves" of that "Ocean-like water," and bailing water to keep afloat, the men "oft tired at their oares," finally importuned Captain Smith to turn back.

"Returne I will not," came Smith's reply—not until at least one of the Virginia Company's twin objectives had been achieved: to locate the mouth of the Patawomack (the Potomac) and locate the headwaters of the Bay.

He allayed the "childish feares" of his crew with the assurance that he would lose neither himself nor them in "these unknowne large waters, or be swallowed up in some stormie gust." Having convinced them that there was "as much danger to returne, as to proceed forward," he proved good as his word—"lost not a man" on that first exploratory mission into the Chesapeake.

Back across the Bay ("so broad that one could scarce perceive the great high Cliffes on the other side") Smith proceeded up the Potomac, as far up as the barge could go (about the site of present-day Washington).

If the hoped-for silver mine in that region proved disappointing (the ore that glittered, sad to say, was not silver), still, there was a fortune in fish and furs to console the Virginia Company stockholders: "Otters, Beavers, Martins, Luswarts, and sables we found: and . . . that abundance of fish lying so thicke with their heads above the water, as for want of nets we attempted to catch them with a frying pan; but we found it a bad instrument to catch fish with. Neither better fish, more plenty or variety, had any of us ever seene in any place then in the bay of Chesapeack; but they are not to be caught with frying pans.""9

Captain Smith "sported himselfe" spearing fish with his sword in the shallows until he tangled with a stingray: removing his catch from his sword-tip, he was stung—his hand and arm swelled morbidly, like balloons. Given up for lost, arrangements were made for his interment in a site of his own selection, a nearby island (to be known thenceforward as "Stingray Ile," and today as Stingray Point). But a stingray was no match for the Captain: Smith was tough as a boot, and had, "ere night," recovered sufficiently to "eate the fish to his supper"![10]

Before the summer and the food supply ran out, Captain Smith and his company hastened to complete their discovery to the far reaches of the Bay ("these foure branches of the Bayes head," by Captain Smith's description, touching on the state lines of the present-day Maryland, Delaware, Pennsylvania), mapping the Patuxent, the Rappahannock, and the Piankatank rivers as they rowed. It was a prodigious feat of exploration, given "this small number" and "that small barge," to have covered "about three thousand myles . . . in those great waters and barbarous Countries . . . till then to any Christian unknowne." They marked the trail they had blazed with crosses carved in trees, "to signify to any, Englishmen had been there."[11] Englishmen had been there, trading and raiding, leaving trade-goods or devastation in their wake, according to the reception accorded them.

Close to the borders of present-day Pennsylvania, they had come upon Iroquoian-speaking peoples: the "mightie," the culturally advanced Massowomekes and the "gyant-like" Susquehannocks, with their booming voices, their luted birchbark canoes, their "Tobacco-pipes three foot in length"; their tightly woven, arrow-proof shields, their brass and copper hatchets imported all the way from French trading-posts in Canada.

When the company of English explorers, Captain Smith at their head, finally rowed back up the James to Jamestown, on September 7, they came as conquering heroes, painted streamers flying at the masthead of their barge.

It could have come as a surprise to no one, on September 10, that Smith should have been elected to succeed to the presidency from which Ratcliffe had been deposed.

A man of action, Smith had seen to it, before the month was out, that

the Church was repaired; the Store-house recovered; buildings prepared for the Supplyes we expected; the Fort reduced to a

five-square forme; the order of the Watch renewed; the squad-
rons . . . trained; the whole Company every Saturday exercised in
the plaine by the west Bulwarke . . . where sometimes more than
an hundred Salvages would stand in an amazement to behold. . . .

No sooner was the month out than Captain Newport sailed in with
the Second Supply, some eighty hardy (or unwitting) souls—including
the first two women, a Mistress Forrest and her "Maide," Anne
Burras—who had come to join the one-hundred-and-thirty-odd survivors at Jamestown.[12]

Captain's Smith's hackles rose as Captain Newport read out the
new Virginia Company directives: "not to returne without a lumpe of
gold, a certaintie of the South Sea, or one of the lost company sent out
by Sir Walter Raleigh."

What struck Smith as stranger still: an even "more strange Coronation" had been decreed by the London power-structure: Powhatan was
to be crowned "Emperour" as a vassal of the English monarch. A
coronation robe and a copper crown were among other imperial regalia
being unloaded from the hold of Newport's vessel, the *Mary and
Margaret*. The whole idea struck Smith as not merely nonsensical but
perilous, in that it might well result in making an already difficult
chieftain more difficult still to deal with.

Smith was "directly against it," as he would write to the company,
but he could not disregard explicit instructions from London, so he set
off overland for Werowocómoco, with a hand-picked party of five, to
invite Powhatan to come to Jamestown for the investiture.

Smith's small party included Captain Waldo, a recent arrival on
the *Mary and Margaret*, a recent addition to the Council (hailed by
Smith as "ancient Souldier" and "valiant Gentleman"); another gentleman, Master Andrew Buckler; a "Souldier," Edward Brinton (expert
marksman and veteran of the first landing party); and as fourth member,
Samuel Collier, Smith's page, one of the four ship's boys of the first
expeditionary force. In addition to the four Englishmen, there was
Namontack, the young Indian hostage who had just returned with
Newport from a visit in England.

Smith and his party were not to find Powhatan at Werowocómoco.
With his warriors, he was at some thirty miles' remove from his principal seat (off on a hunting expedition or on confederacy business).
Messengers were dispatched from Werowocómoco to inform him that
a party of Englishmen awaited his return.

It was Pocahontas who received them in her father's stead, who
gave them a reception no Englishman could have anticipated. "In the

meane time Pocahontas and her women entertained Captaine Smith in this manner:

"In a fayre plaine field they made a fire"—a ritual fire built within a ring of tall posts, each with a grotesquely carved and painted mask as terminal, about which dancers and singers circled in a ritual song and dance, to the accompaniment of drums, flutes, and rattles.[13] It was a scene strikingly similar to one observed and described by Thomas Hariot—observed and illustrated by John White*—in the Carolinas, a quarter of a century earlier. But Hariot understood better than Smith what he saw; Hariot realized that it was "a great and solemn feast," a calendric occasion, scheduled for "a certain time of year"; timed, in all probability, to coincide with a seasonal crop festival, a harvest festival to which "all their neighbors from adjoining towns" were invited, all gathering "on a broad open plain enclosed by tall posts carved into faces resembling those of veiled nuns."[14]

Just beyond the fire and its ring of painted posts, Smith and his four companions were directed to reed mats. But no sooner had they settled themselves upon the ground on their mats than "suddainly amongst the woods, was heard such a hydeous noise and shreeking, that the English [the five of them] betooke themselves to their armes, and seized on two or three old men by them, supposing Powhatan with all his power come to surprise them."

Their alarm was unfounded. This was no surprise attack, no ambush, as they should have known by the presence of old men, women, and children in the audience.

Pocahontas herself came to reassure Captain Smith, to offer her life as pledge for their safety: "But presently Pocahontas came, willing him to kill her if any hurt were intended; and the beholders, which were men, women and children, satisfied the Captaine there was no such matter."

Whereupon, presumably, the party's French pistols were put aside, and the entertainment began: "Then presently" (according to the Generall Historie[15]) they were presented with this "anticke":

> Thirtie young women came naked out of the woods, onely covered behind and before with a few greene leaves, their bodies all painted, some of one colour, some of another, but all differing, their leader [presumably Pocahontas] had a fayre payre of Bucks hornes on her head, and an Otters skinne at her girdle, and

* See John White's sketch of Religious Dance, The New World, Stefan Lorant, pp. 196-7.

another at her arms, a quiver of arrows at her backe, a bow and arrows in her hand; the next had in her hand a sword, another a club, another a pot-sticke; all horned alike. . . .

These fiends with most hellish shouts and cryes, rushing from among the trees, cast themselves in a ring about the fire, singing and da014ncing with most excellent ill varietie, oft falling into their infernall passions, and solemnly againe to sing and daunce; having spent neare an houre in this Mascarado, as they entred, in like manner they departed.

As a matter of fact, there was some difference of opinion among Englishmen: the Indian women's voices raised in song were not "hellish" but highly pleasing to the ear of William Strachey: "When they sing they have a delightful and pleasant tang in their voyces," he commented during his sojourn among the Virginia Indians, a few years subsequent to Smith's.

This masquerade over, the dance coming to an end, the voices falling silent, the fire dying down (down, but not out, the embers cherished all the year round, as sacred as the sun whence they derived), Smith and his companions had not long to wait before Pocahontas and her chorus reappeared, having removed their ritual paint and paraphernalia, their greenery and headgear, and having resumed their customary attire.

Having reaccomodated themselves, they solemnly invited him [Smith] to their lodgings, where he was no sooner within the house, but all these Nymphes more tormented him than ever, with crowding, pressing and hanging about him, most tediously crying, Love you not me? love you not me?

(The last repetitive amorous inquiry, in all probability, is a euphemism for a more ribald, more direct solicitation; some coarse seventeenth-century English catch-phrase, very likely, taught the Indian Nymphes by English seamen and adventurers—a titillation to English ears to hear their own obscenities repeated back to them on a foreign tongue, in a female treble.[16])

Smith describes an ultimate male fantasy: to be accosted, solicited, importuned to sexual riot and abandon in the wildwood by voluptuous, copper-skinned, half-naked young nymphs, "crowding, pressing, and hanging about him," thrusting sex upon him; stroking, fondling, obscenely posturing, lewdly gesturing ("falling into their infernall passions").

Smith's use of the word "Nymphes" suggests that he was thinking in terms of pagan practice (he might equally well have used the word maenads or bacchantes), and the metaphor was apt: the Powhatans were probably celebrating the autumnal corn harvest with a fertility dance as ritually orgiastic as the Dionysian revels or the Bacchanalia that celebrated the autumnal harvest of the grape in ancient Rome or Greece. Study of surviving American tribal cultures shows that the seasonal crop festivals were the occasion for sexual license: according to the Papago and Mohave ritual, coupling came as the climax of the corn festival, the dancers seeking mates at the signal of the medicine-men, outside their own clan or division, in the view that new blood would produce stronger, more valiant fighter stock; the replenishment of warrior ranks was a constant preoccupation of Indian tribes across the continent.

With the advent of corn culture—the gift from Middle America—the East Coast tribes of North America, sometime in the first century A.D., changed from small, nomadic hunting-and-gathering societies into sizable, more or less settled farming-hunting-fishing societies, their residence fixed in villages adjoining their cultivated fields, still within easy reach of their hunting and fishing grounds. A people without writ-ten records, dependent on oral tradition, it must have seemed to them that there had never been a time when corn had not been their main-stay. And had they been asked to date the origin of their corn culture and its traditions, they probably would have replied (as Pueblo peoples reply to that question today), "from the beginning," their own ancient mythology and ritual having been expanded to incorporate the myth and rite which had come north to them along with the seed corn from the south.

The Powhatans—by the time the English arrived among them in 1607—could not remember a time when they had not made a feast of the season's first tender roasting ears,[17] sucking up the sweet juices of both cob and stalk; could not remember a time when they had not pounded the dried kernels for meal and baked the meal in bread and cakes, could not remember a time when they had not stewed corn for soup or combined it with beans for succotash (another Algonkian word, another Algonkian recipe).

From what must have seemed time immemorial, it had been the custom of the women of the Virginia Algonkian tribes to plant and reap the fields of their werowance; to shuck, shell, and dry, to prepare the crop for storage in his granaries—performing, as it were, annual feudal services or corvées for their overlord, scrambling for the beads he tossed out to them, in royal largesse.

The last crop of the tidewater season, planted on an appointed day in the month of June, ready for harvesting in October, would have been the occasion for celebration among the Powhatans as for all corn-grow-ing peoples of the continent, one of the most sacred in the calendric round attending the growth of corn, usually taking the form of an agro-sexual ritual, performed, appropriately, by the women who were the cultivators. And it was very probably just such an autumn-harvest fer-tility festival which Captain Smith witnessed at Werowocómoco in October of 1608.

Reading Smith's description of the multihued dancers in the fire-light at Werowocómoco—"their bodies all painted, some of one colour, some of another, but all differing"—what comes to mind is the dance of the varicolored Corn Maidens, representing the six varieties of corn, as it was performed in the Zuñi kivas as late as the twentieth century. If the ancient harvest tradition was the same among the Northeast Wood-land tribes and the western Pueblo people, then the "leader" described by Smith (and generally accepted as Pocahontas) would have been por-traying the Yellow Corn Maiden (leading lady of the pageant), her body streaked with bright yellow to symbolize the first, the earliest species of corn developed.

What Smith never understood—no more than did any of the other early New World explorers, save perhaps Hariot—was that the orgiastic pageants they witnessed among the Indians were ritualistic, sacred, and ceremonial in context. What the Christian European—especially the English Puritan—could never comprehend, could never condone, was an ethic where sex was free of religious stricture, an ethic where sex was not associated with sin. His insistence on interpreting the alien culture solely in terms of his own could only result in gross cultural misunder-standing. It would require centuries for the European newcomer to the continent to attain to a scientific, an objective—much less an empathic —point of view; centuries would have to pass before anthropology would make clear that the communal orgies, the acts of sexual license accompanying the Indians' fertility, hunting, mourning, and martial rituals were characteristic of primitive peoples in many parts of the world.[18]

Whether or not Captain Smith and his four compatriots understood the esoteric significance, the traditional symbolism, of the autumn har-vest fertility festival celebrated in the fire-ring at Werowocómoco, cer-tainly it spoke directly to the passions, and it is unlikely that they could have resisted the amorous overtures of the "thirtie" voluptuous, nude, paint-daubed "Nymphes" who sought to involve the white strangers in the communal sexual commerce. Human nature being what it is, male concupiscence being what it is, the answer to "Love you not me?" had to be in the affirmative.

If those five Englishmen "loved not" those thirty young wood-nymphs, if they turned away from such embracements, then they were unnatural men, exceptions to the rule, for they were men without women—men who had been at sea or in the wilderness, deprived of heterosexual relations for months (months in the case of the more recent arrivals, a year or more in the case of Smith and his page-boy, Samuel Collier, and the marksman Brinton). Even Collier, by then fourteen or fifteen years old, was not too young to have responded to the invitation of those bare-breasted bronze maidens—an invitation so explicit as to be clear even to a gawky ship's boy.[19]

Young Collier would have taken the lead from his elders, would have followed his superior officers away from the banquet area; would have disappeared, like them, into the shadows, each with the maiden of his choice—or perhaps a brace of dusky nymphs—on his arm.

Collier's initiation into "savage" sex would have revealed no sensational practices, those of the American aborigine differing insignificantly from those of the European (insofar, at least, as sexual manners can be determined through the reportage of seventeenth- and eighteenth-century mountain men and fur traders, whose journals and memoirs constitute the main source of information available on the subject). The techniques of intercourse among American Indians included neither bizarreries nor acrobatics as in the case of various primitive societies in Africa and Oceania. The practice of sex among American Indians was, by preference, in seclusion and darkness; love play offered no startling variations to the European.

As for Pocahontas, given her role in this pageant, there can no longer be any question of her nubility. As of the autumn of 1608, she was, clearly, no longer a child, but a mature woman, playing a woman's role in an orgiastic tribal fertility rite—"the infernall passions" into which the dancers fell, by Smith's description, quite possibly enactments of the procreative act, as in the Hopi kivas.

As for Captain Smith, gallant as he may be elsewhere on the subject, protesting his profound respect for the princess as well as for the woman, here, in these passages from *The Map of Virginia* and the *Generall Historie*, he steps out of character—the character of the parfit, gentil knight he has assumed vis-à-vis Pocahontas. Here, he is cynical. He smirks as he relates his encounter with the thirty naked dancing girls and their leader:

> This salutation ended, the feast was set, consisting of fruit in baskets, fish and flesh in wooden platters; beans and pease there wanted not (for 20 hogges), nor any Salvage daintie their inven-

tion could devise: some attending [serving] others singing and dancing about them.

This mirth and banquet being ended, with firebrands (instead of torches), they conducted him to his lodging.

The paragraph ends abruptly; the ending is inconclusive, tantalizing to even the most sluggish imagination. The last glimpse to be had of Pocahontas, by Smith's account, is as she lights his way to the longhouse, to the raised platform bed strewn with mats, pine-boughs, and raccoon-skins where he was to pass the night. There is no hint as to whether she leaves him there or stays to share his couch, whether it is a consummation of the intimate communion they shared at the altarstone the previous winter, or the continuation of an established, yearlong liaison.

Smith, as if his revelations were already far more extensive than he had intended, breaks off abruptly, in mid-sentence; retires into his customary reticence on the subject of interracial sex.[20]

The firebrands are extinguished, darkness and silence overtake the longhouses of Werowocómoco.

The following paragraph begins: "The next day came Powhatan."

CHAPTER VI

Noah an' Jonah an' Cap'n John
Smith,
Mariners, travelers, magazines
of myth,
Settin' up in Heaven,
chewin' an' a-jawin',
Strummin' golden
harps, narreratin' myth! . . .

DON MARQUIS,
"Noah an' Jonah an'
Cap'n John Smith," 1921

THE CORONATION PROVED A FIASCO.
First in a series of misadventures came Powhatan's rejection of the invitation to journey to Jamestown for the investiture. He would not budge from Werowocómoco. Just as the King of France refused to "visit" beyond his own demesne, so too did the ruler of the Powhatan Confederacy: "If your King have sent me presents," came the lordly reply to Captain Smith's proposal, "I also am a King, and this is my land. . . . Your Father [Captain Newport] is to come to me, not I to him, nor yet to your Fort, neither will I bite at such a bait. . . ."

There was nothing for it but to mount two sizable expeditions: "the Presents were sent by water (which is neare an hundred myles) and the Captains [Newport and Smith] went by land with fiftie good shot."[1]

Powhatan condescended to try out the "Bed and Furniture," the

"Bason and Ewer" sent to him as gifts from the King of England, but he balked at being garbed in the "scarlet Cloke and apparell" until "perswaded by Namontack they would not hurt him." It was the copper crown,[2] however, that created the major problem.

Powhatan was importuned to kneel—in the feudal tradition—so that Captain Newport, representing the suzerain James I, could settle the coronet on Powhatan's brow. But that chieftain knew neither "the majesty nor meaning of a Crowne, nor bending of the knee." And not all their "perswasions, examples, and instructions" could force him to his knees.[3] "At last, by leaning hard on his shoulders, he a little stooped, all three" (Newport, Smith, and Namontack, all three together!) "having the crowne in their hands put it on his head. . . ." At last, the deed was done.

The first act was over but the comedy of errors was not yet played out. At the signal of a pistol shot, the boats were notified that the King was crowned, and a "volley of shot" rang out in salute from the harbor, causing the King "to start up in a horrible feare"!

Reassured by Namontack and the others, Powhatan recovered his composure: "Then remembring himselfe, to congratulate their kindnesse, he gave his old shooes and his mantell to Captaine Newport."[4] Otherwise, Powhatan's generosity and gratitude were not conspicuous: a niggardly few bushels of corn, less than a dozen, were his sole contribution to the nearly empty Jamestown larder.

The coronation, as an attempt to syncretize the monarchical concepts of the two cultures, had proved not only ludicrous, it was, as Smith had feared, deleterious to the English interest—the deference shown the chieftain further inflated his autocratic ego and encouraged him in his intransigence. But if Smith's misgivings on this score had been well founded, he could scarcely expect congratulations from Captain Newport, who had insisted—over Smith's protests—on carrying out the Virginia Company's instructions to the letter.

Relations between the two English commanders further deteriorated. Smith's name was conspicuously absent from the roster of adventurers designated by Newport to accompany him upriver, in November, on an exploratory and trading mission to the fall-line of the James.

Another fiasco for Newport: not a glitter of gold along those banks, nor even of silver; and as final disappointment to his hopes, no corn. The Indians encountered en route pleaded a dearth in their own granaries at the onset of winter; apologetic or defiant, they could not be induced to trade.

Foraging parties dispatched by President Smith from Jamestown, in other directions, encountered similar rebuffs: the Weanocs, the

Chickahominies, the Appomatocs, and the Nansemonds all acknowledged that Powhatan had laid an interdict on trade. Difficult as it was for the English to distinguish friend from foe among the redskins, they resorted—in desperation—to promiscuous violence, coercion, and extortion. But the destruction of native houses, canoes, and fishing weirs served to produce only a few paltry bushels of corn.

It would appear that a joint resolve had been taken by the tribes, that a concerted effort was finally under way to rid the land of the invader by denying him the native rations without which he apparently could not survive. It would appear that the militant faction in the confederacy had finally prevailed in the councils. Smith perceived that this unusual instance of concerted action had come as the result of a high-level policy decision.

"The President perceiving that it was Powhatan's policy to starve us," resolved to beard the lion in his den, to "go toward Powhatan," to confront him at Werowocómoco, to appeal the case to the highest authority.

Smith's stubborn will and instinct for survival again asserted themselves. Let the fainthearted wring their hands and sit on them! Not Smith! ("No perswasions," he blustered in his *Generall Historie*, "could perswade [him] to starve.")

He would bide his time until the *Mary and Margaret* sailed in December, 1608, relieving him of his major opposition: both Captain Newport and Councilman Ratcliffe/Sicklemore (that "poore counterfeited Imposture," Smith scathingly labeled him, whose ceaseless machinations against him Smith had successfully frustrated) left for England.

A letter addressed by Smith to the Virginia Company—sent with Newport—was, as Smith himself characterized it, "a rude Answer": in reference to Ratcliffe, Smith wrote: "I have sent you him home least the company should cut his throat." Nor did Smith mince words concerning the folly of the coronation, tactlessly reminding them that he had been "directly against it." Impolitic to the last line, Smith harshly criticized as well the caliber of the colonists being recruited by the company for the Virginia adventure: "When you send againe I intreat you rather send but thirty Carpenters, husbandmen, gardiners, fisher men, blacksmiths, masons, and diggers up of trees, roots, well provided; then a thousand of such as we have. . . ."

Smith's sketches for his "Map of Chesapeake Bay and The Rivers," along with the manuscript copy of his *Relation of the Countries and Nations*, had likewise been confided to Captain Newport—a bulky packet for delivery to Smith's London publisher.[5]

With the departure of Newport and Ratcliffe, the Jamestown

Council was reduced to a membership of four: Captains Waldo, Winne, and Scrivener along with the president, Captain Smith. In the fourth month of his presidency, Smith faced a second bitter winter in the wilderness outpost, with some two hundred souls in his charge and provisions insufficient to sustain a fraction of that number.

Making ready, just before Christmas, for the journey to Werowocómoco, assembling the company of forty-six experienced soldiers and sailors he would lead there, Smith delayed only long enough to attend the wedding—perhaps to officiate, the president of the Council substituting for the missing vicar[6] at the first Christian marriage to be celebrated in Virginia—that of Anne Burras (maid to Mistress Forrest) and John Layden (a "Labourer" and veteran of the first landing).

Struggling against wind, snow, and sleet, the pinnace—under Sir George Percy's command—and the barge, under Smith's, made their way slowly to Werowocómoco, arriving on January 12, only to find the river frozen solid for half a mile out from shore, making the landing very difficult.

Once ashore, once the formalities of welcome had been observed —the two traditional shouts of greeting ringing out on the icy air, the welcome mats unrolled and spread, the giant baskets of bread, turkey, and venison arranged at the entrance of the visitors' longhouse—then, and only then, could the interview begin, Powhatan and Smith, face to face.

Powhatan's first question brusqued the formalities of welcome. It was abrupt, disconcerting: what he wanted to know was "when we would be gone." It was the question uppermost in the Indians' minds.

The colloquy dragged on and on endlessly, strange, rambling, desultory. If Smith's account of it is confusing to the reader, this is probably a reflection of Smith's own perplexity over the import of Powhatan's discourse.

Despite the fact that Smith had met all Powhatan's preconditions for a conference—had dispatched workmen and tools for the construction of the English house required by the chieftain, had provided the rooster and the hen, the beads and copper further stipulated by Powhatan—the chieftain now demanded "fortie swords" for "fortie Baskets" of corn, spurning to trade for copper, "saying he could rate [eat] his Corne, but not the Copper."

Smith rejected Powhatan's new terms, his "strange demands," replying: "As for swords and gunnes, I told you long ago I had none to spare." The intent of "the subtill Salvage" was clear: to disarm the English. If the invaders' superiority in armament could be equalized, then the Indians' superiority in numbers would prevail.

If, in the beginning, their superiority in numbers over the invaders had given the Indians a false sense of security, if Indian apprehensions had been further lulled by the invaders' ineptitude in coping with an environment in which the aborigines prospered, there now came second thoughts, strong misgivings: what if this feeble colony on the James should prove the exception, what if it should not falter and fail and be abandoned as had all the earlier European settlements on that stretch of the Atlantic coast? Namontack, on his return from England with Captain Newport, may have brought news disconcerting to Powhatan and the tribal council, reports of a population infinitely outnumbering that of the tidewater and capable of endless reinforcement, reports of more people in London alone than stars in the sky over Chesapeake Bay, more people than leaves on the tallest oak in the Virginia forests. If it had been Powhatan's policy, initially, to exploit the whites—to allow them to survive as long as they could be held in subservience, to fit them into the pattern of native warfare as allies or as purveyors of superior armament for use against the traditional enemies of the Powhatans—now that policy was subject to reappraisal.

Powhatan (by Smith's account) voiced such fears:

> Yet Captaine Smith, sayth the King, some doubt I have of your comming hither, that makes me not so kindly seeke to relieve you as I would: for many doe informe, your comming hither is not for trade, but to invade my people, and possesse my Country.

That was it, then: the native inhabitants had begun to take alarm at the signs of permanence now evident at Jamestown: the quickening maritime traffic up the James, the steady flow of reinforcements and supplies to the colony, the ever-widening range of English activity in the region (exploration as well as trade), the coercion and extortion exercised in trade relations. . . .

Even so, as the colloquy at Werowocómoco proceeded on that January day in 1609, Captain Smith "wrangled out of the King ten quarters* of Corne for a copper Kettell." If that was only a pittance, Smith agreed to accept it only because of the Powhatans' grain shortage, and only on condition that Powhatan would promise "as much more the next yeare."

Smith's threat was veiled: he would not "dissolve that friendship we have mutually promised," was how he phrased it, "except you constrain me by our bad usage."

* A quarter, as a British measure of grain, was the equivalent of eight bushels.

Whereupon "Powhatan began to expostulate the difference of Peace and Warre after this manner":

I know the difference of Peace and Warre better than any in my Country. . . . But now I am old and ere long must die; my brethren, namely Opitchapam, Opechancanough, and Kekataugh, my two sisters, and their two daughters, are distinctly each others successors. I wish their experience no less than mine, and your love to them no lesse than mine to you. . . . What will it availe you to take that by force you may quickly have by love, or to destroy them that provide you food. What can you get by warre, when we can hide our provisions and fly to the woods? whereby you must famish by wronging your friends. . . .

Powhatan's threat, like Smith's, was veiled: the implication, a variation of the "scorched earth" policy—although Powhatan claimed, like Smith, to prefer a peaceful solution: "Thinke you I am so simple," Smith quotes him as arguing,

not to know it is better to eate good meate, lye well, and sleepe quietly with my women and children, laugh and be merry with you, have copper, hatchets, or what I want being your friend: then be forced to flie from all, to lie cold in the woods, feede upon Acornes, rootes and such trash; and be so hunted by you, that I can neither rest, eate, nor sleepe; but my tyred men must watch, and if a twig but breake, every one cryeth there commeth Captaine Smith: then must I fly I know not whether: and thus with miserable feare, end my miserable life. . . .

And yet "to flie from all" was the very action Powhatan would take within a matter of hours. It was a decision the old chieftain reached suddenly and effected secretly, shortly after his colloquy with the Englishman: "to take his luggage, women and children" (all his children, including Pocahontas), and all his wives save for "two or three," cleverly deployed ("left . . . behind with the Captaine") lest his "suspition" be aroused. Powhatan withdrew from Werowocómoco, and the vicinity of the Englishmen, deep into the forest fastnesses, to the remote village of Orapaks upstream on the Chickahominy, a relatively secure location at a distance of some thirty miles from his stronghold on the Pamunkey.

With this action early in 1609, the pattern of Indian-white relations was set for centuries to come: incursion and withdrawal.

But if Powhatan had moved to put more distance—fifty miles—

between himself and Jamestown, between the native red men and the invading whites, he had not moved far enough. The fifty miles were too few. If Powhatan withdrew from Werowocómoco to Orapaks to leave the white man a broader purlieu on the peninsula—acres enough to house, fields enough to feed Jamestown's growing population—then it was not sufficiently broad to accommodate the ever-increasing numbers. Powhatan had not allowed for the steady stream of immigration just begun, the boatloads already launched, those yet to come.

"My countrie is large enough to goe from you," Powhatan would declare confidently, although there was no room for confidence; his "countrie" was not large enough; not all the vast continent would prove large enough for him and his people "to goe from"—to escape being overtaken and overrun by—the multitude on its way. What Powhatan could not foresee was that the greatest migration of people in recorded history was under way, and that he and his people stood athwart its course. As it moved across his tidelands country, across the Appalachians, across the Mississippi, across the Plains, across the Rockies . . . not even Pacific palisades would be distant enough to put space enough between Powhatan's people and the oncoming whites.

If, by early 1609, Werowocómoco had proven to be in too close proximity to the white man's outpost on the James, then Orapaks would prove, by 1622, too close as well. By midcentury, the frontier would have been pushed to the fall-line, the retreating Algonkians of the tidelands driving the Iroquoian and Siouan tribes out of the piedmont to make room for their retreat under the steady encroachment of the insatiably land-hungry tobacco planters.

Powhatan had made his break for Orapaks while Captain Smith stood by, beside the river at Werowocómoco, waiting for the Indians to clear a passage in the ice to permit the barge to approach the bank to take on the "ten quarters of Corne" Smith had "wrangled out of the King."

"Whilst he [Powhatan] secretly fled, and men as secretlie beset the house," the intrepid Captain fought his way out, single-handed. "With his Pistol, Sword and Target, he made such a passage amongst those naked divels that they fled before him . . . so that without hurt, he obtained [reached] the Corps du guard."

With the barge stranded on the ebb-tide, the Captain and the eight men who had accompanied him ashore from the pinnace had no choice but to pass another uneasy night in the strangely silent, half-empty longhouses of Werowocómoco.[7]

Powhatan, "all this time [at Orapaks] was making ready his forces to surprise the house and him [Smith] at supper."

"Notwithstanding the eternall all-seeing God did prevent him, and by a strange meanes." God's means was, once again, Pocahontas; Pocahontas, once again acting in her role of savior, of guardian angel to the Captain.

> For Pocahontas his dearest jewell and daughter, in that darke night came through the irksome woods, and told our Captaine great cheere [the customary banquet] should be sent us by and by: but Powhatan and all the power he could make, would after come kill us all. . . . Therefore if we would live, shee wished us presently to bee gone. Such things as shee delighted in, he would have given her: but with the teares running downe her cheekes, shee said shee durst not be seene to have any: for if Powhatan should know it, she were but dead, and so she ranne away by her selfe as she came.

A story that bears repetition, it is twice told by Smith: as above, and again, as below, in the letter to Queen Anne (dated 1616, although it appears for the first time in print in 1624 in the *Generall Historie*):

> . . . When her father with the utmost of his policie and power, sought to surprize mee . . . the darke night could not affright her from comming through the irkesome woods, and with watered eies gave me intelligence, with her best advice to escape his furie; which had hee knowne, hee had surely slaine her.

If Pocahontas had come—as presumably she had—from Orapaks, whither she had removed in her father's entourage, she had come some thirty miles over narrow trails difficult to discern in the gloom of night and under the pall of snow, had come alone through deepest forest "irkesome" with "Beasts of Prey,"[8] irksome with cold, with sleet—bramble and branch abristle with stalactites of ice.

Since the plot to surprise and slay the Englishmen had reached Pocahontas's ears, it follows that either she must have eavesdropped at her father's council or he must have spoken out in her presence, in the certainty that her first loyalty was to him and to her people, regardless of any emotional involvement with the man she had in some wise committed herself to in the adoption ritual of the previous year.

It must be assumed that she was risking her life in betraying Powhatan by this warning to his intended victim—and that she knew it. No wonder, then, that she was offended, and wept, at Smith's offer to reward her heroic service with gewgaws, with bells and beads. Was this

his sole response to her noble intervention in his behalf? Was he so unresponsive, so indifferent to her sacrifice and devotion, as to try to pay her off with trinkets? (Captain Smith was no more remarkable for his sensitivity or sensibility than for his tact.)

"For if Powhatan should know it, she were but dead"; her father and people would kill her, she had to explain, doubtless vexed at Smith's failure to recognize what should have been obvious—that for her to wear his baubles, his distinctive English trade-goods, would be to proclaim her perfidy. She dared not "be seene to have any"!

The risk she ran in defying her father's orders was so great, the offense against him and her people so heinous, that the question arises as to whether it could have been her intention—whether she would have dared—to return to Orapaks from her perfidious errand at Werowocómoco. Or had it been her intention to defect, to transfer not only her allegiance but her person from the red camp to the white?

What could have possessed her to take action so drastic, a step so final, so irreversible, to make a commitment so total, to renounce all the familiar ways, places, faces, gods—for the unknown, the unfamiliar? A strong physical attraction, very possibly, or the lure of the exotic. (Examples abound in myth and literature: Ariadne forsaking her own to follow Theseus; Medea, to follow Jason; Madame Butterfly flying to her Pinkerton. There are more such heroines unsung than sung: Celtic maidens shipping out after Viking lovers, Gallic and Iberian maids off with Greek and Roman sailors in their triremes, vahines of the South Pacific island-hopping to keep up with their English, French, German, or American suitors.)

But the biographer finds more validity in the suggestion that Pocahontas was moved by an extraordinary curiosity, that she experienced —was vouchsafed—a rare flash of insight into the riches and splendors of that other world, that other society, that other culture; that she was imbued with a profound yearning, an irresistible impulse to make the great leap forward, to plunge ahead alone—centuries, perhaps millennia —ahead of her own people in their measured ascent to that rung of the cultural ladder. (Intrepidity was requisite to the decision, intrepidity no less pronounced than Smith's. There was, furthermore, a cultural shock implicit in such a radical transition. If jet lag is defined as the body's inability to adjust in rapid transit from one time zone of the earth to another, then cultural shock might be defined as the inability of the mind and imagination to transfer suddenly from one cultural level to another—from a woodlands culture, as in Pocahontas's case, to the Renaissance.)

Pocahontas must have believed that such an option was open to her when she flew—in defiance of her father—to Smith's rescue, that cold winter's night, in January, 1609. She must have gone in expectation of finding a welcome there with him.

Whereupon the first question to arise is whether, at that point, she discovered the option not to be open, after all; whether, at that point, she encountered rebuff, discouragement.

There is significance in Smith's reference (remembering always that the only account is his) to "the teares running downe her cheekes" ("her watered eies"): Pocahontas will be seen to be highly emotional—emotionally overwrought—at her every encounter with this man. Not that this fact should excite great wonder: the emotional stress and strain to which she must have been subject in coming to so traumatic a decision is not difficult to imagine. Nor is it difficult to guess what anguish it must have cost her to betray not only her people but her fond—perhaps overfond?—her doting and indulgent father.

When Pocahontas—her face stained with tears—left Smith that night, when she slipped out of his wigwam into the wintry night, she left alone ("by her selfe as she came"), unescorted, unprotected, without the retinue customarily attending the chieftain's daughter—but she left Smith forewarned, alerted to the perils of the night.

So that when "eight or ten lusty fellowes" arrived bearing "great platters of venison and other victuall" to Smith from Powhatan, he accepted that "great cheare" but, thanks to Pocahontas's warning, "hee knew they came to betray him at his supper." Thanks to Pocahontas, he was on his guard against "all their other intended villanies," he "cocked matches" throughout the hours of the night to set off his matchlock at a moment's notice,[9] and did not relax his vigilance until the midnight tide came in ("not till it was high-water") and the barge could take off to join the pinnace where she waited in the open water of the river.

It is possible only to conjecture on the cause of the sudden deterioration of red-white relations, the sudden eruption of hostilities between Powhatan and Captain Smith at this juncture. David Beers Quinn suggests the possibility that it came in the wake of a confrontation between the two men on the subject of the Lost Colony, the possibility that at some phase of this conference between Powhatan and Smith, Powhatan either boasted or admitted and stoutly defended his active role in wiping out the Roanoke Island settlement or the few settlers who had made their way north (if, indeed, they did) from the Carolina Outer Banks to the Chesapeake Bay area. If it was not from Powhatan's own lips that Smith heard this shocking news, it may have been from those of one of the Jamestown colonists who had heard the rumor in some native village where he had spent time as a captive, hostage, or runagate. Altogether, an "iffy" supposition. If news of the fate of the Raleigh colony did come to Smith's ears, he gave no hint of it in any of his several published accounts of that period. His silence on the matter must be considered strange, indeed, since the news value was sensational: the solution to a mystery that had haunted the English nation for a quarter of a century.

Whatever the explanation of Powhatan's sudden withdrawal from Werowocómoco, and for his attempt on Smith's life, the latter, once safely aboard the pinnace, headed upstream. Foolhardy as it might seem after so narrow an escape, Captain Smith now moved still deeper into enemy territory, into the clutches of Opechancanough. It was desperation—the dire need for provisions to bring the colony through the dead of winter—that compelled Smith to try his hand at trade with Powhatan's brother, the most notoriously hostile chieftain in all the confederacy and a proponent of destruction of the invading force from the day of landfall.

This was truly leaping from the frying pan into the fire. Pamunkey country bristled with peril. Dangers multiplied, crises proliferated. Smith's every chapter boasts a brush with death; his every moment must be thought to be his last (although he lives to tell it, even write and publish it). Exclamation points fly as thick as arrows in his *Historie*; hyperbole jostles hyperbole off the pages of his *Map of Virginia* (although it may be The Reader, held too long breathless in suspense, who chokes and purples—falls, perhaps, the only casualty of this installment).

Indian warfare, like Smith's rhetoric, was largely based on blow and bluster, flourish and fanfare; threat and counter-threat constituted half the battle. Tactics consisted primarily of surprise: the ambush, the raid, the hit-and-run attack, engagement followed by swift disengagement—no set battle-piece, no sustained attritional combat: the feat of touching the enemy (making "coup") in the thick of battle was accounted as glorious as the taking of his scalp.[10]

When Smith (with his handful of stalwarts) looked up to find himself surrounded by hordes of painted, howling Pamunkey braves, he accepted the odds unflinchingly: "And wee are sixteene, and they but seaven hundred at the most," he declared, rallying his fifteen compatriots with the cry, "Let us fight like men, and not die like sheepe!"

Smith cleverly created a diversion by challenging Opechancanough to a trial of strength—they two alone to face one another, naked and unarmed, on an island in the river: "Our game shall be, the Conqueror take all"—all at stake, the copper and the corn and their lives.

But Opechancanough declined to engage in single combat as prescribed by the chivalric code.

Outraged, Smith seized the Pamunkey chief by his scalplock, shoved a pistol into his ribs, and marched him out in ignominy to help load the barge with corn, shouting: "You promised to fraught my Ship ere I departed, and so you shall; or I meane to load her with your dead carcasses. . . ."

As if the situation on the Pamunkey were not desperate enough, there came news of a disaster on the James: eleven men including Master Scrivener and Captain Waldo (two of the four remaining Council members) had been drowned when their skiff capsized among the ice floes on the river.

The bearer of the sad news was the intrepid Richard Wiffin, the only man at the fort to volunteer to undertake so hazardous a mission through the (to him) trackless, impenetrable, enemy-infested forest ("Dangers and difficulties" lurked "in all parts as he passed"). And never would he have made it through to Smith had not Pocahontas intervened to hide and guide him on the night when he finally made his way—only a few paces ahead of his pursuers—into Werowocómoco, to which Powhatan had returned immediately after Smith's departure. Wiffin found the chief village of the Powhatans in a ferment of "preparation for warre," and must have been a dead man in that armed camp, save for the princess (who had by then also returned from Orapaks).

It was from Pocahontas that Wiffin must have learned of Smith's departure and present whereabouts, from her he had directions for the trail he was to follow: "Pocahontas hid him for a time, and sent them who pursued him the cleane contrary way."[11]

Conjecture as to her motivation flourishes: certainly Wiffin was nothing to her—whatever Smith was!—although there is the possibility that her aid to Wiffin was to the purpose of aiding Smith. Was she, as has been suggested, a traitor to her race, the red race's Uncle Tom? (If so, not the first: that had been Cortez's Malinche—both Indian women infatuated, enamored perhaps of whites, both dazzled by white skin, both subject to an overpowering physical attraction, to the lure of the exotic, both in a total surrender to "Way-faring gods.")

Upon receipt of Wiffin's message, Smith hastened back to Jamestown to bolster the authority of Captain Winne (the sole surviving Council member at the fort), stopping only briefly, en route, to trade with the Youghtanund and Mattaponi tribes, in the hope of adding to the hoard of corn already aboard the barges.

That hope was dashed: Smith was met with "such complaints and teares from the eyes of women and children, as he had beene too cruell to have beene a Christian, that would not have been satisfied and moved with compassion"—"satisfied," that is, that a scarcity existed, "compassionate" enough to exact a tribute of only one-half the Indians' remaining stores, charitable enough not to chastise them for the paucity of their contributions.[12]

In spite of an occasional show of clemency, the six weeks' foraging foray under Smith's command had produced provisions enough to tide the colony over the waning winter: "479 Bushels of Corne" had been stowed aboard the barges, along with "neare 200 lb. waight of deere suet" (approximately a pound per capita of the Jamestown population in that first week of February, 1609). ("Men may think it strange," Smith reminds the reader in his *Generall Historie*, "that there should be such a stirre for a little corne, but had it been gold with more ease wee might have got it, and had it wanted, the whole Colony had starved.")

But this was not the time for Smith to rest upon his laurels: with just such gusto as he tackled the enemy, he now tackled the tasks that awaited doing at Jamestown: a sweet-water well was dug within the confines of the palisade; the church was reroofed, twenty houses were built, a block-house was constructed ("in the neck of our Isle," at the point where the narrow ribbon of land running from the peninsula joined the mainland) and as promptly garrisoned, as a check-point for Indian traffic in and out of the citadel. Fishing-weirs (commandeered from the Indians) were installed in the river. Last but not least, the planting area on the island was enlarged (another indication of permanence to alarm the vigilant Indian sentinels). "Thirtie or forty Acres of ground we digged and planted," in accordance with advice from Indian prisoners and visitors "on how to order and plant our fields"—instruction in successful native gardening techniques (such as the hilling of corn, the planting of beans in the same hole to climb and run on the corn stalks).

Clapboard and wainscoting—the colony's sole exportable commodities, to date—were cut and stacked to serve as cargo at some future date. It was a chore to which Captain Smith expected even the "proper Gentlemen" of the colony to turn their hands, no matter how delicate. He pooh-poohed the gentleman's blistered palms and chastised his profanity ("a Cann of water powred downe his sleeve" for every oath!).[13]

But Smith could neither jolly nor coerce those indolent, insolent, improvident English gentlemen into honest labor—into labor of any kind. They were untrained, undisciplined; many were ne'er-do-wells—or worse. "Many in Virginia," Smith complained, were "merely projecting, verball, and idle contemplators." "Many unruly Gallants were packed thither by their friends," as Smith's *Generall Historie* observes, "to escape ill destinies"; others were shipped off by their families, as a last resort, to the farthest shore . . . which happened to be Virginia—under an alias, like Ratcliffe/Sicklemore, to live down an Old World scandal in the New; like Lady Finch's reprobate son, sent out to

Virginia for a lesson in discipline (one he did not learn, killed in a drunken brawl within a week of his return to England). "Many of the men sent hither have bin Murtherers, Theeves, Adulterers, idle persons, and what not besides."[14]

Virginia was, from the beginning, a dumping ground for undesirables from England's overcrowded (or what were then considered overcrowded) shores: the Virginia Company attracted the landless, the jobless, the disinherited; younger sons and wastrels were enlisted, even "vagabonds and condemned men" (although "some did chuse to be hanged ere they would goe thither"). It was "the scumme of the world," in Smith's own words, which had been recruited.

The Puritan colonies of New Plymouth and Massachusetts Bay looked askance at their neighbor to the south: it was "the Refuse of the English Nation," in Cotton Mather's words, by which Virginia was "first Peopled"—a fact which might well have accounted for some of that colony's early troubles. New England was a totally other kettle of fish: the odds were on the godly, their chances of success far brighter.

Captain Smith was to find that it would take more than "a Cann of water" to discipline those "proper Gentlemen" at Jamestown—or any of the rest, for that matter. There was insubordination, there were malingerers among the laborers and soldiers at the fort in the spring of 1609. In an emergency, Smith would have to resort to sterner measures.

An emergency arose in April with the discovery that the casked corn had spoiled: not only weevils but rats had gotten into the stores, so contaminating the grain that "the Hogges would scarcely eate it."[15]

To grapple with this emergency, Captain Smith now stood alone: Captain Winne, the only other Council member, having gone, somehow, sometime, that spring, to his grave (if a hero's, unsung; with only a fleeting reference in the Generall Historie to his passing).

The law Smith laid down was martial law: "he that will not worke shall not eate." There was none to dispute him: "power," he declared, "resteth in my selfe." He would use that power to change the scheme of things whereby the many lived on the labors of the few, whereby the many drones were maintained by the few workers of the hive, who caught and preserved the sturgeon when they ran, who dug "tockwhagh roots" to make into a not very palatable, bitter bread used only as a last resort against starvation by red men and white. Henceforward, Smith declared, "the labours of thirtie or fortie honest and industrious men shall not be consumed to maintaine an hundred and fiftie idle loyterers."[16] A work-sheet was to be posted: "a Table, as a publicke memoriall of every mans deserts," and he that would not bestir himself was to "be banished from the Fort as a drone."

"This order many murmured was very cruell, but it caused the most part so well to bestirre themselves, that of 200" (out of the two hundred souls, that is, confided to Smith's care upon the departure of Captain Newport in November, 1608), "there died not past seven, except they were drowned" (not counting, that is, the eleven lost in the boating accident in January).

If Smith's measures were harsh, the emergency was of the direst. And if the colony at Jamestown survived that winter of 1608–9, it was thanks, in large measure, to Smith's iron discipline. It was Smith's will and instinct for survival, extended to include the colony, that preserved it through what has come to be referred to by historians as the Epic Period of Jamestown, the years 1607 through 1609.

With the first corn harvest as far off as August, President Smith took a tip from the Indians, divided the colony into small self-sustaining units—twenty or thirty to a group—and dispersed them to live on the natural bounty of the land and of the sea, as was the Indian way in lean seasons. "One group was sent down the river to live upon Oysters, and 20. with liutenant Percy to try for fishing at Poynt Comfort" (although "in sixe weekes they would not agree once to cast out the net. . . ." Those "loyterers," rather than exert themselves, "would all have starved or have eaten one another"!).

Some colonists were billeted with friendly Indian tribes to await the first corn crop. Some colonists defected, seduced by the prospect of a warm wigwam, a warm bedfellow, the relatively easy life of the Indian village in comparison to the grim existence of the Fort.

With some settlers living among the Indians and some Indians living among the settlers (as guides, informants, prisoners), interaction of an individual nature could be said to have been in process: the Indians thereby increased their technological skills, accommodating themselves readily enough to the use of European implements and armament such as firearms and tools (the technological gap, in that preindustrial era, was less wide than might be imagined), while the English, at the same time, learned the secrets of exploiting their new environment (the Indian techniques of hunting, fishing, and farming). In this process, the two groups may be said to have learned something of each other's cultures, although, in the final analysis, efforts to bridge that cultural gap were unavailing—both sides were unwilling to surrender their own values and traditions as social entities.

Relations between reds and whites were, from the first, touchy, subject to constant stress and strain, uncertain, complex, variable; now friendly, now hostile, as is characteristic of contact between races at widely divergent cultural levels. Such interaction as did occur between reds and whites failed to dispel mutual suspicion. An uneasy peace prevailed under the muzzle of the English cannon in the early spring of

1609: "They did knowe wee had such a commanding power at James towne they durst not wrong us of a pin."

But hostility flared into sporadic skirmishes, raids, and rampages; injury or trespass by the Indians provoked retaliation by the English; flimsy truces were trumped up to maintain trade relations. The ever-harsher measures to which the English resorted in coercing the Indians to trade elicited fresh threats of withdrawal: "If you proceed in revenge," a young Paspahegh orator warned Smith in the wake of a punitive English raid on his village, "we will abandon the Country." His implication was clear: that without the Indians' relief, the English could not survive.

In early July, the hard-pressed colony looked up to see friendly sails approaching up the river (England's colors flying at the masthead rather than the dreaded Spaniard's). Hails and halloos rang out from the bank where every man Jack of the one hundred and eighty still alive at Jamestown gathered to greet Captain Samuel Argall and his crew after a record-breaking nine-and-a-half-week crossing from Portsmouth over a new trial route north of the Spanish West Indies.[17]

Argall's was a "ship well furnished with wine and much other good provision. Though it was not sent us, our necessities was such as inforced us to take it."

Even headier than the wine in Argall's hold was the news he brought of a mammoth Third Supply—seven ships, five to six hundred new colonists—en route to Virginia.[18] This mighty new colonial undertaking had come in response to mighty propaganda campaigns launched by the Virginia Company, and coordinated by Thomas Hariot and Richard Hakluyt, the latter firing the opening salvo, in April, with the publication of his *Virginia Richly Valued*. Fiery sermons on Virginia were to be heard from every major pulpit—exhortations to colonize and proselytize—John Donne's among the most celebrated. Broadsides were scattered about London to announce the golden opportunities awaiting the colonist on the New World's golden strand; tracts were printed by the dozen, notably Alderman Robert Johnson's *Nova Brittania: Offering Most Excellent Fruites by Planting in Virginia*.[19] Plays about Virginia abounded on the London stage. Poems were indited, notably Michael Drayton's "Ode to the Virginian Voyage," an appeal as direct as a recruiting sergeant's:

> *Britons, you stay too long,*
> *Quickly aboard bestow you,*
> *And with a merry gale*
> *Swell your stretched sail,*

With vows as strong
As the winds that blow you. . . .

To finance such a major expedition, a new stock issue had been floated with a subscription list of over fifty city companies (the companies of Grocers, Drapers, Haberdashers, Fishmongers, Goldsmiths, Vintners, Brewers, Pewterers, to name only a few of the more familiar trades and guilds) and over six hundred and fifty individual subscribers whose names read like a Who's Who of Jacobean England: courtiers, noblemen, prelates, mercantile and financial magnates—a register of English society toward the end of the age of Shakespeare. If Shakespeare's name is missing from the list, those of his patrons, the Earls of Southampton, Pembroke, and Montgomery appear among the stockholders, as do the names of Sir Francis Bacon and Sir Oliver Cromwell (whose nephew-namesake would become Lord Protector). The names of the Archbishop of Canterbury and the Lord Mayor of London graced the list of subscribers which included, all in all, twenty-one peers of the realm, ninety-six knights, twenty-eight esquires, fifty-eight gentlemen, one hundred and ten merchants, and two hundred and eighty-two "Others" (ordinary citizens, presumably), forming an impressive array of support representative of the entire nation—a mercantile venture transformed into a national enterprise.

Captain Argall brought the colony news of the reorganization of the Virginia Company, news of a Second Charter granted by the King ("the effective instrument in the creation of Virginia"), the transfer of control from the Royal Council to the Virginia Company Council, with a membership of fifty-four.

As concerned the colony itself, the most significant feature of the new Charter was the appointment of a Lord Governor for Virginia— Lord De La Warre—to take over the responsibility of government from the Jamestown Council, the latter ordained to play, in future, a minor and merely supportive role.

By mid-August, six of the original seven ships[20] of the Third Supply came straggling into the Bay and up the James—storm-battered, "much weather-beaten": mainmasts toppled, sails ripped, hulls leaking; of the three-hundred-odd passengers aboard, few were on deck to see the landing: most were too ill to stand, weak, shaken, injured, yet counting themselves lucky to have survived a crossing fatal to so many. (The "Calenture"—sunstroke—had taken a heavy toll in the seas just north of the Tropic of Cancer; thirty-two persons had been "throwne overboard," had fallen or been blown into the water. One small craft, the *Unity* was so "sore distressed" that "of seventy landsmen, she had not ten sound; and all her Sea men were downe but onely the Master and his Boy with one poore sailer."[21])

As the *Blessing*, the *Lion*, the *Falcon*, the *Unity*, the *Swallow*, and the *Diamond*, in that order, came gratefully to rest at their moorings off Jamestown, two old and mortal enemies of Smith's reappeared on that shore: Captain Gabriel Archer aboard the *Blessing*, and aboard the *Diamond*, Ratcliffe/Sicklemore (that "poore Counterfeited Imposture" whom Smith had shipped home to the Virginia Company the previous December). The *Diamond* "was said to have the plague in her": the plague could have taken Ratcliffe, for all Smith cared! When Captain Martin (the Goldbug-bitten) disembarked with Archer and Ratcliffe, his face could have struck Smith as only slightly more congenial than the other two.

The hurricane which had struck the full fleet off the Bahamas had separated these six ships from the flagship, the *Sea Venture*. Never sighted again by any one of the six, she had clearly been blown off her course; might have perished, might well have to be accounted lost.

If so, the loss was staggering: venturing all their eggs in one basket, the entire high command of the expedition had sailed aboard the flagship *Sea Venture*—no one of the three high-ranking officers had been willing to yield precedence to the other. If the *Sea Venture* was lost, Sir Thomas Gates, the Governor's Deputy, the first in command, was lost. And with him, his deputy, Sir George Somers, Admiral of the Fleet. And with them, Vice Admiral Newport, master-mariner of the flagship. And with the leadership of the expedition were lost the Instructions and Commissions—all the official documents—drawn up, signed and sealed by the Virginia Company in London for the administration and direction of the colony across the sea.

With no duly constituted authority on the ground, the power struggle could not but wax ferocious. "Now did we all lament the absence of our Governour" (as Captain Archer made lament by letter, dated August 30, to the Virginia Company), "for contentions began to grow, and factions. . . ."

Factions rent the colony. Archer and Ratcliffe had lost no opportunity, en route, to stir up anti-Smith sentiment among the newcomers. All "joyned together," now, to effect Smith's overthrow.

Smith had his faction, too; his support was strongest among the veterans who realized that they owed their lives to his leadership and acknowledged the debt. Of course, stern disciplinarian that he was, Smith had his enemies; hackles rose at the brash self-confidence and self-assertiveness that were his hallmark.

Archer and Ratcliffe relished the opportunity to inform President

Smith that a new form of government had been decreed for the colony, the presidency superseded by the governorship.

Smith refused to be superseded until the official papers were produced, contending that—in the absence of the appointed governor and the governor's deputy, in the absence of the proper documents relieving him of his authority—authority resided with him as the last duly elected chief officer. In any event, he would not yield that authority until the expiration of his one-year term (due to expire shortly, in September), and certainly not to such trouble-makers as Ratcliffe and Archer. ("Happy had we bin had they never arrived . . . for on earth was never more confusion or miserie than their factions occasioned.")

Digging in his heels, ignoring calls for his resignation in favor of the Honorable Francis West (brother of the governor, Lord De La Warre), President Smith addressed himself to the emergency: some three hundred newcomers (women and children among them) streaming ashore without so much as a roof over their heads, and winter coming on.

With the population more than doubled (only one hundred and eighty–odd survivors at the Fort prior to the arrival of the Third Supply), the narrow Jamestown island would no longer suffice.

President Smith sallied forth in search of wider territory; he sent one group of one hundred and twenty men, under Sir George Percy and Captain Martin, to establish a satellite colony in Nansemond territory. Upstream, near the falls—to accommodate another one hundred or so Englishmen, under the command of Francis West—Smith wangled a "readie built" village (sturdy wigwams, cleared fields and all!) out of young Tanx-Powhatan, promising the great Powhatan's son not only English copper but English military support against the dread Monacan raiders from the piedmont.

"But both this excellent place and those good Conditions did those furies refuse, contemning both him, his kinde care and authoritie"— "those furies" none other than Smith's thankless compatriots, relentless enemies, obstructionists all, blocking him at every turn.

His subordinates—out of ineptitude or malice—frustrated every design his ingenuity could devise: the moment the Honorable Francis West, Sir George Percy, and Captain Martin took over at the Nansemond colony and the Powhatan village, trouble erupted between red and white. West, Percy, and Martin promptly proved that they lacked Smith's talent for getting along with the Indian—lacked, for that matter, any genuine desire to get along with what they considered an inferior race, evidencing a pronounced racial contempt and a strong sadistic streak, perpetrating senseless cruelties, wanton atrocities.

The Indians reciprocated in kind, and the tempo of bloodshed quickened.

When Smith journeyed back upstream in late August to patch up relations and resume trade with the Powhatans, the latter complained that their traditional enemies, the Monacan raiders from the piedmont, were less formidable than the Englishmen Smith had brought them "for Protectors."

As a pledge of goodwill, Smith left Tanx-Powhatan a hostage, in the person of young Henry Spelman, a recent arrival in the Third Supply, scapegrace scion of a distinguished family, who had left England under a cloud: "Beinge in displeasure of my frendes," as he says straight off, straight out, in the opening line of his *Relation of Virginea*, "and desirous to see other cuntryes"—a concise statement of the motivation of a substantial number of Virginia colonists. (Spelman, nephew of Sir Henry Spelman, the historian-antiquarian, is the semi-literate litterateur whose travel journal has been frequently quoted in earlier chapters.)

As soon as Smith could arbitrate the differences at the Powhatan village near the falls, he turned his barge around to rush back downstream to Jamestown where an unremitting vigilance had to be maintained to frustrate the mutinies being hatched against him.

But misfortune befell him en route: "But this hapned him in that Iourney. Sleeping in his Boate . . . accidentalie, one fired his powderbag" (Smith's powder-bag ignited by a flying spark from a careless sailor's pipe or by a clumsy soldier's matchlock matches). The freak accident caused a dreadful wound,

> tore the flesh from his body and thighes, nine or ten inches square in a most pitifull manner; but to quench the tormenting fire, frying him in his cloathes he leaped over-board in the deepe river, where ere they could recover him he was neere drowned.

Smith made it back to the fort, but not back to his feet. The mortal combat in which he was engaged with his implacable foes would have to be waged from his couch.

Flat on his back, he looked less formidable. Ratcliffe, Archer, "and the rest of their Confederates" waxed ever bolder. "It would be too tedious, too strange, and almost incredible; should I particularly relate the infinite dangers, plots, and practices, he daily escaped amongst this factious crew."

The several accounts—Smith's *Generall Historie* and his *Map of Virginia*, Captain Archer's letter to the Virginia Company, and the one addressed by Ratcliffe/Sicklemore to the Earl of Salisbury, the Secretary of the Virginia Company—offer wildly conflicting testimony, agreeing on one point only: that chaos and confusion were rampant. Amid the charges and countercharges, the plots and counterplots, the truth is not easily determinable. Ratcliffe and Archer were suddenly seized and placed under constraint, arrested for some unspecified, some more than usually audacious act of sedition. While they waited

> to come to their trials, their guiltie consciences fearing a just reward for their deserts, seeing the President unable to stand, and neere bereft of his senses by reason of his torment, they had plotted to have murdered him in his bed.

A fate he escaped thanks only to the assassin's last-minute change of heart: "But his heart did faile him that should have given fire to that mercilesse Pistoll."

Archer and Ratcliffe "joyned together to usurpe the government," to suppress Smith's presidential commission and press it on a not totally reluctant Francis West.

"The President had notice of their projects." Forewarned, Smith might have made a last-ditch stand, as his faithful old guard urged him to let them make in his behalf ("though his old souldiers importuned him but permit them to take their heads that would resist his command, yet he would not suffer them"), yet he would not allow them to risk their lives while he stood hors de combat, immobilized, helpless and disabled on the sidelines.

It was unlike Smith to retire from the field, thus to leave it to his enemies. But he was at the limit of his strength, at the end of his resources ("so grievous were his wounds, and so cruell his torments" and "neither Chirurgian [surgeon], nor Chirurgery in the Fort to cure his hurt"). He was no coward, but neither was he fool enough to go up against insuperable odds. He would return to England, recover from his wound, regain his strength—political as well as physical—come back to fight another day, and win! Or such may have been the conclusions of his sickbed cogitations.

His decision made, he summoned the six sea-captains on the very eve of their departure: "sent for the Masters of the ships, and took order with them for his returne to England"; arranged to sail with one of them—very possibly his friend Captain Nelson of the *Falcon*—very possibly on the morning tide.

But no sooner had Captain Smith been carried aboard ship, no sooner had the mooring cables been loosened than an order was issued from the fort to the captains to stay the departure of the vessels.

Ratcliffe and Archer needed time "to perfit some colourable complaints against Captaine Smith"—to justify themselves for having deposed him from the presidency, to "excuse themselves by accusing him." "Three weekes longer, they stayed the 6 ships" while they drew up a formal complaint to be transmitted to the Virginia Company in London via the eastbound fleet. ("This man is sent home," Ratcliffe wrote of Smith, "to answere some misdemeanors, whereof I perswade me he can scarcely clear him selfe from great imputation of blame.")

Malcontents and malfeasants, perjurers and pilferers—"all those Smith had either whipped, punished, or any way disgraced"—were invited to lodge complaints, to make "foule slanders" against the former president. "Some that knewe not anything to say, the Councel instructed and advised what to sweare." Some swore that Smith had "caused the Salvages to assault them"; others, that "hee would not let them rest in the fort . . . but forced them to the oyster banks." Hearsay evidence was accepted against him; even hearsay on hearsay.

The self-constituted Council (consisting, at that point, of Ratcliffe, Archer, Martin, West, and Percy) dared lodge the complaint that Smith "would not submit himselfe to their stolne authority." He stood accused by some of being too hard on Indians; by others, of being too soft.

But the gravest charge brought against the captain was the one that linked his name with that of Pocahontas:

"Some propheticall spirit calculated [that] hee had the Salvages in such subjection, hee would have made himselfe a king, by marrying Pocahontas, Powhatan's daughter." The implication, not only of miscegenation but of treason! Crimes well calculated to horrify Puritan and Royalist alike!

Smith partisans indignantly refuted the charge:

It is true that she was the very Nomparell of his [Powhatan's] kingdome, and at most not past 13 or 14 yeares of age. Very oft shee came to our fort, with what shee could get for Captaine Smith; that ever loved and used all the Countrie well, but her especially he ever much respected: and she so well requited it, that when her father intended to have surprized him, shee by stealth in the darke night came through the wild woods and told him of it. But her marriage could no way have intitled him by any right to the kingdome, nor was it ever suspected hee had ever such a thought; or more regarded her, or any of them, than in honest reason and discreation he might. If he would, he might have married her, or have done what him listed, for there was none that could have hindred his determination.

This chapter of Smith's *Map of Virginia* bears the signatures of Richard Potts and W. Phettiplace. Their bias as stalwart Smith supporters is apparent, but there is validity to their contention that Smith's marriage to Pocahontas would have brought him no closer to the Powhatan chieftaincy since she did not stand in the traditional line of succession—unless, of course, Smith's firepower in support of the princess might have altered tradition.

No matter what conjecture flourished at Jamestown, at that hour, on the subject of Smith's ulterior motives, no matter what "foule slanders" assailed his name in connection with Pocahontas, the fact remains that when the six ships of the Third Supply finally pulled away from the fort (sometime during the first fortnight in September, 1609), and headed downriver, into the Bay, into the open sea, toward England, Smith had not even bidden farewell to the Powhatan princess to whom he owed his very life.

The departure of the fleet would have been duly reported, by lookouts posted all around the Bay, to the Supreme Chieftain at Orapaks, but Smith had not so much as sent a message to Pocahontas to apprise her of his departure from her shore.

She felt the slight, as is made clear by the reproach she would later make him for his negligence: "They did tell us alwaies you were dead"! ("They" can be taken to mean none other than Ratcliffe, Archer, and Martin, the new Council members, and Sir George Percy, the new president, the compromise candidate who had won when Francis West proved too controversial a figure to gain majority support among the power-mongers. It would have been to the councilors' advantage to convince the Indians that they could no longer look to Smith as arbiter.)

Pocahontas, believing Smith to be dead, and being under injunction of her father to sever relations with the English colony, would never again—of her own free will and accord—set foot in Jamestown.

CHAPTER VII

*Besids, what could they see but a
hidious and desolate wildernes, full
of wild beastes and willd men? and
what multituds ther might be of them
they knew not. . . .*

GOVERNOR WILLIAM BRADFORD
reporting the landing of the
Mayflower *at Plymouth, November, 1620*

WITH SMITH'S DEPARTURE FOR ENGLAND in the autumn of
1609, and with Pocahontas's severance of relations
with the colonists, Jamestown's long winter of agony was to begin.
Seventeenth-century chroniclers would refer to the winter months of
1609–10 as the Starving Time.

In contrast to her long record of friendship and benevolence toward the newcomers, Pocahontas now held aloof from them. In the
colony's grimmest hour, she was conspicuous by her absence: "all
which time shee was not heard of" (as Smith would later note in his
Generall Historie).[1] The rumor of Smith's death, current among the
Indians in the weeks after his accident, may have robbed Pocahontas
of her incentive to safeguard the colony. The alternate explanation of
his disappearance—that he had sailed without so much as a word of
farewell to his benefactress—may have aggrieved her and turned her
against his people. Whether Pocahontas was indifferent to the fate of
the colony once Smith was no longer in command, whether she
sought to avenge herself on Smith for his desertion (if such it was)
through his hapless fellow countrymen, whether fearful of incurring

her father's and her people's wrath, she made no move, in this crisis, to relieve the plight of the strangers on her shore; she must have listened impassively to the casualty reports coming in from the fort on the James to her father's new headquarters at Orapaks.

Try as they might—digging graves and performing burials in the dark of night—the English could not conceal the colony's mounting death toll from the ring of red men closing in around the fort. Famine and disease took their toll within the palisades; the Indians, theirs, without. To venture out into the woods in search of fish or game was to risk sudden death: as slippery and silent as shadows, and as inescapable, the natives on patrol in the woods and waterways overtook, ambushed, and assaulted hunting and fishing parties and stragglers.

"For the Salvages no sooner understood Smith was gone," according to Smith's *Generall Historie*, "but they all revolted and did spoile and murther all they incountered." A satellite colony of Englishmen at Nansemond, downstream from Jamestown, was surprised, surrounded, overwhelmed; Captain Sicklemore (alias Ratcliffe), on a trading mission up the Pamunkey River, decoyed from his barge by Powhatan, "with about thirtie others as carelesse as himselfe, were all slaine." Ratcliffe's mission deep into enemy territory had been undertaken in desperation, an alternative to starvation.

"Now wee all found the want of Captaine Smith, yea his greatest maligners could then curse his losse" (again according to Captain Smith's *Generall Historie*, in an account purportedly written by an eyewitness, anonymous but clearly loyal to the departed Captain). Instead of the "corne provision and contribution" President Smith had managed to obtain in trade "from the Salvages" during his term of office, his successor, President Percy, could provide the unlucky colonists with "nothing but mortall wounds, with clubs and arrowes."

Powhatan had, by then, become implacable: "Powhatan still, as he found meanes, cut off their Boats, denied them trade." All the Jamestown livestock ("Hogs, Hens, Goats, Sheepe, Horse or what lived") was slaughtered, "till all was devoured; then swords, armes, pieces, or any thing, wee traded with the Salvages" (whenever, that is, they could be induced to trade). What with the "crueltie" of the natives ("whose cruell fingers were so oft imbrewed in our blouds"), what with the "indiscretion" of "our Governours," the casualty rate soared during the winter of 1609–10—nine out of every ten succumbed. Out of the "five hundred" colonists left by Captain Smith at Jamestown in October, 1609, "within six moneths after Captaine Smiths departure, there remained not past sixtie men, women and children, most miserable and poore creatures."*

---

* Excavations undertaken at Jamestown in 1965 yielded a grisly reminder of the

"Nay, so great was our famine" (according again to the *Generall Historie*), "that a Salvage we slew and buried, the poorer sort tooke him up againe and eat him; and so did divers one another boyled and stewed with roots and herbs: And one amongst the rest did kill his wife, powdered [salted] her, and had eaten part of her before it was knowne[2]; for which hee was executed, as hee well deserved. . . . This was that time, which still to this day ["this day" of publication in 1624] we called the starving time."

Spain, controlling the Atlantic coast with missions and presidios strung out from Florida to the Carolinas, gloated over reports of calamity at the only English base of operations in the Western Hemisphere: "The Indians hold the English surrounded in the strong place which they had erected there, having killed the larger part of them," Alonso de Velasco, the Spanish Ambassador, gleefully reported to his monarch, Philip III, from London in 1610. "Unless they succour them with some provisions in an English ship . . . they must have perished before this." He concluded, "Thus it looks as if the zeal for this enterprise was cooling off and it would . . . on this account be very easy to make an end of it altogether by sending out a few ships to finish what might be left in that place."

By mid-May of 1610, it was clear that without prompt succor from English ships, without reinforcements, without provisions and ammunition, the Spaniards could write finis to the English colonial venture in Virginia.[3] The beleaguered outpost on the James could not have survived another ten days in such "extremities of miseries" as then afflicted it. Sir George Percy, the president—ill as he was, almost too weak to draw his sword from its scabbard—had to flourish that naked blade to enforce his orders on the sullen, stricken men under his command. Another ten days, and the "sixtie men, women and children, most miserable and poore creatures" huddled in the compound of the five-cornered fort would have succumbed to the ultimate pangs of hunger or to the final ferocious Indian assault on the crumbling bulwarks of the palisade. There were now scarcely men enough to man the guns, scarcely ammunition enough to load them. "This," in the words of the anonymous chronicler of the *Generall Historie* (who must have participated in that final agony) ". . . would [shortly] have supplanted us all with death."

"But God that would not this Countrie should be unplanted, sent Sir Thomas Gates, and Sir George Sommers with one hundred and

---

Starving Time: seventy skeletons were dug up just behind the presumed location of the original fort. The shallow graves and the absence of caskets indicate hasty burial; the few survivors were too weak to dig deep, and had to work in haste at night.

fiftie people . . . to preserve us. . . ." The anonymous chronicler of the *Generall Historie*, characteristically of his century, saw the hand of God in their deliverance. To him and the handful of anguished survivors on the Jamestown waterfront, the sight of sails on the river on May 23—two friendly English pinnaces, rather than Spanish raiders—appeared a manifestation of Divine Providence clearly favoring and fostering the Anglo-Saxon, Protestant settlement of North America.

Here, at last—some nine months behind the other ships of the Third Supply with which they had sailed from England—here, at last, came the duly appointed high command of the Virginia Colony: Sir Thomas Gates (to serve as deputy governor until the arrival of the Governor-General, Lord De La Warre) and Sir George Sommers as deputy to Gates.* They were survivors of the shipwreck of the *Sea Venture*, flagship of the Third Supply, which had been separated from the rest of the fleet in the previous summer's tempest, blown off course to founder on the Bermuda reefs. Beached on that balmy and bountiful isle—to which all passengers and crew had safely (providentially?) made their way—the castaways set to work to construct two pinnaces.

Sailing from Bermuda on May 10, 1610, aboard the *Deliverance* and the *Patience*, the two pinnaces constructed there, the survivors of the *Sea Venture* dropped anchor at Jamestown on May 23, and came upon a scene of utter desolation: the fort in disarray, disrepair; the few still alive there in a state of shock.

"Viewing the Fort, we found the Pallisadoes torne downe," Gates would sorrowfully report to London,

> the Ports open, the Gates from off the hinges, and emptie houses (which Owners' death had taken from them) rent up and burnt rather than the dwellers would step into the woods a stones cast-off from them, to fetch other fire-wood; and it is true, the Indians killed without, if our men stirred beyond the bounds of their Block-house, as [many as] Famine and Pestilence did within. . . . In this desolation misery our Governour found the condition and state of our colonie.

The high Council—Gates, Sommers, Secretary William Strachey, and Admiral Newport—concluded that the situation was hopeless. The "sixtie men, women and children" they found alive at Jamestown had

---

* Governor-General Lord De La Warre, Deputy-Governor Gates, and Gates's deputy, Sommers, had been appointed in London in 1609 by the Council for the Virginia Company under the Second Charter. Lord De La Warre was scheduled to follow to take over his duties in person within a few months after the sailing of the Third Supply.

reached the limit of their endurance. And it was unrealistic to expect that one hundred and fifty newcomers—having endured their own ordeal by storm and shipwreck—could now cope with conditions as grim as those confronting them at Jamestown.

A decision was reached by the high council to abandon the colony. A deciding factor was Powhatan's uncompromising hostility, the confederacy's new policy of war to the death: "The Indians . . . were forbidden likewise (by their subtile King at all to trade with us); and not only so, but to endanger and assault any Boate upon the River, or stragler out of the Fort by Land. . . ."

Four or five days later, on the morning of June 7, 1610, to a doleful roll of drums, the order was given to abandon camp, to board ship. As soon as the last colonist came aboard, the two small pinnaces moved slowly back down the James to anchor for the night at Mulberry Island, just above the river's mouth.

Within hours of that sailing, Indian runners would have raced to Powhatan at Orapaks with the news. Within minutes, bands of neighboring Paspahegh tribesmen rushed howling past the stockades, past the unmanned bulwarks, through the unhinged gates, into the deserted compound to ransack and rummage the ruins, to comb through the rubble for lost or forgotten valuables, to brandish firebrands and celebrate the retreat of the invaders back over the horizon whence they had come.

If the Powhatans found cause for rejoicing at the news of the English exodus, so would the Spaniards. With England's colonial expansion in America thwarted or fatally retarded, the whole Atlantic seaboard would lie open to Spain. Spain could move up from her bases in the South; the entire continent was within the grasp of Spain—and only the steadily expanding native confederacies to dispute it with her.[4]

But rejoicing by Spain or the Powhatans was premature. Fate decreed that England was not to lose her tenuous hold on the continent.

Even the most confirmed skeptic could not but see it as an act of Divine Providence that the fleet of Governor-General De La Warre himself should have loomed up in the Bay just hours before the deputy governor and his two pinnaces sailed out! At the crack of dawn of June 8, the flagship *De La Warre*—heading upriver under the command of Captain Argall, the De La Warre coat of arms proudly emblazoned on her waistcloth—confronted the *Deliverance* and the *Patience*, heading downstream.

Lord De La Warre came in the very nick of time. A day later, even a few hours later, and the two pinnaces would have left the river, left the Bay, disappeared over the horizon of the open sea; he would have found only a ghost town on the James, the five-cornered fort deserted, sacked, put to the torch, reclaimed by the forest and by the natives of the forest.

But "God would not have it so abandoned" (according to William Box, chronicler of this Fourth Booke of the *Generall Historie*, a man ready to "acknowledge God's infinite providence").[5]

If it was the hand of God that turned the pinnaces round at Mulberry Isle, their crews took over from there, steering upstream in the wake of the *De La Warre* and the other ships of the governor's fleet.

His Lordship, stepping ashore at Jamestown on the tenth of June, came in all his splendor, in a costume of slashed velvet, ruffed, bejeweled, accompanied by Captain Argall, commander of the fleet, and followed by fifty red-liveried attendants. His standard-bearer read aloud the Governor's Commission to an audience of several hundred gathered in the ruins of the church.*

After a thanksgiving service conducted by the Reverend Bucke, Lord De La Warre announced his appointments to the Council.[6]

If the governor's "Oration" met with "a generall applause," there was a less enthusiastic audience response to his stern command to diligence in the rehabilitation of the colony: two new forts, he announced, were to be erected at Point Comfort (Fort Henry and Fort Charles, in honor of the two sons of James I); at Jamestown, the palisade and bulwarks were to be restored, reinforced; sturdy new housing was to go up, "covered above with strong boards, and some matted round with Indian mats"; the church was to be enlarged and rebuilt; more land was to be cleared, more fields to be planted. This ambitious program was to be accomplished by means of a six-hour workday—from which not even the gentlemen were to be exempt! ("Nor should it bee conceived that this business excludeth Gentlemen, whose breeding never knew what a daies labour means . . . cannot digge, use the Spade, nor practice the Axe. . . .")

But if the gentlemen could not swing an axe or wield a spade, neither could (or neither would) the "Others"—a bad lot, for the most part, "the very excrements of a full, swelling State," "the scumme of England," shiftless, insubordinate, unskilled. Although they were listed on the manifest as "Labourers," they "never did know what a dayes work was," "were for most part footmen" hired by the gentlemen-adventurers "to attend them." So what you had "were poore Gentlemen, Tradesmen, Serving-men, libertines, and such like, ten times more fit

* The one hundred and fifty new colonists arriving with De La Warre, the one hundred and fifty survivors from Bermuda, the sixty-odd pitiful survivors of the garrison found alive by Gates and Sommers.

to spoyle a Commonwealth, then either begin one, or but helpe to main-taine one." The caliber of men recruited for Virginia was such as to imperil the entire colonial enterprise.[7]

If anyone could have curbed what De La Warre called "the haugh-tie vanities" of the gentlemen, or spurred the rabble out of its "sluggish idlenesse," it would have been just such an illustrious nobleman as De La Warre, selected for the highest command post by reason of his lofty rank and station—in the Jacobean society, like the Elizabethan, social authority was equated with political authority; leadership de-volved upon commanders whose "Eminence or Nobillitye" was such that "everye man subordinate is ready to yield a willing submission."

In the event, however, not even a peer of the realm proved capable of enforcing discipline on that raffish crew. Even under De La Warre's administration, the colony never became self-sufficient: in even those famous fishing waters, inept and ill-equipped fishermen returned with a meager catch; in even that balmy clime and fertile soil, indifferent farmers could not produce crops to supply the community (the Anglo-Saxon concept of private property was ill-accommodated to a com-munal endeavor and a common store, "as though the sap of their bodies should bee spent for other mens profit," as one chronicler of the *Gen-erall Historie* complained).

No longer was there relief to be had from the Indians. Powhatan's ban on trade with the foreigners was observed by most of the tribes; confederacy policy had coalesced. Ever more brutal coercion to trade on the part of the English proved ever more ineffectual. The Indian policy of steadily deeper withdrawal into the interior served only to enrage the invader, but his wanton destruction of Indian villages and fields proved a self-defeating tactic.

From the day of Captain Smith's departure, red-white relations had deteriorated. Smith's efforts toward peaceful coexistence had ap-parently been abandoned by his successors. The Indians vainly sought a definition of the invaders' territorial ambitions. To an ultimatum from Lord De La Warre, Powhatan replied with one of his own: "that either we should depart this country, or confine ourselves to James-town only." Otherwise, "he would give a command to his people to kill us, and do unto us all that mischief which they at their pleasure could. . . ."

Ultimatum answered ultimatum. Atrocity provoked atrocity. The execution of the children of a captured Paspahegh weroansqua was "ef-fected by throwing them overboard and shooting out their brains in the water." Only Captain Percy's demur saved their mother from the stake, his recommendation "either by shot or sword to give her a

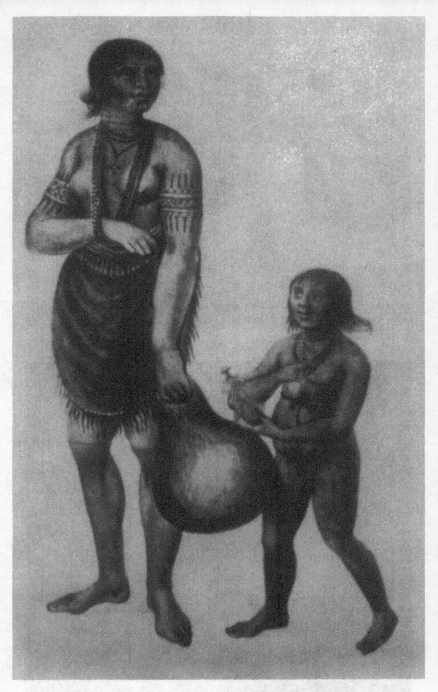

The wife and daughter of a chief from the village of Pomeiock.
The daughter is holding a doll which was probably a gift from a
colonist. This watercolor was painted by John White ca. 1585.
(SMITHSONIAN OFFICE OF ANTHROPOLOGY)

An idealized portrait of Pocahontas, first published by McKenney and Hall in The Indian Tribes of North America, *1836.*
(SMITHSONIAN OFFICE OF ANTHROPOLOGY)

OPPOSITE ABOVE:
John White's watercolor of Pomeiock. A group of Indians are crowded around the fire in the center, while others are splitting logs or carrying wood; one man is walking his dog.
(THE BRITISH MUSEUM)

OPPOSITE BELOW:
A Shoshoni maiden swinging from a tree. This romantic vision was painted by Alfred Jacob Miller ca. 1830.
(WALTERS ART GALLERY, BALTIMORE, MARYLAND)

An early engraving of Captain Smith being rescued by Pocahontas.

The capture of Pocahontas. Argall bribes the Indians with a copper kettle to get her aboard the ship and off to Jamestown. Engraving by Theodore de Bry, 1619.

The marriage of Pocahontas.
(THE BETTMANN ARCHIVE)

Pocahontas in England longs for home. A 1906 watercolor.
(PICTURE COLLECTION, NEW YORK PUBLIC LIBRARY)

*Pocahontas: the frontispiece
of John Smith's* Generall
Historie of Virginia,
*London, 1627. Engraving by
Simon Van de Passe.*

*Matoaka als Rebecka daughter to the mighty Prince
Pouhatan Emperour of Attanougskomouk als virginia
converted and baptized in the Christian faith, and
wife to the worᵗ Mᵗ Joh Rolff.*

*Van de Passe's engraving of
John Smith.*

A fanciful portrait of
Pocahontas, possibly a model
for a tavern sign; it was
probably painted in Holland
or England around 1650.
The artist's name was not
recorded.

(SMITHSONIAN OFFICE OF
ANTHROPOLOGY)

A statue of Pocahontas commissioned by
Cassell and Co., London, 1956.
By David McFall, R.A.

The Marriage. From the 1913 film Jamestown.
(MUSEUM OF MODERN ART/FILM STILLS ARCHIVE)

Indians in dance costume on the Pamunkey Reservation,
King William County, Virginia. Photograph by D. L. Gill, 1899.
(SMITHSONIAN OFFICE OF ANTHROPOLOGY)

quicker dispatch." In retaliation, the twang of the bowstring made the wildwood a deadly danger for the white man to traverse: the victim, never seeing the hand on the bow, hearing only the howl of triumph at the lucky shot—the shout of "Paspahegh, Paspahegh" making clear in whose name vengeance had been wrought. When Lord De La Warre, in defiance of Powhatan's warning to confine himself to the Jamestown area, pushed up to the falls of the James, Indian bowmen picked off three or four members of the governor's party.

Within a few weeks, De La Warre was gone, suffering from a whole catalogue of ailments contracted in the line of duty.

Although that nobleman's administration could not be said to have accomplished any significant improvement in the colony, even so, his illness and departure (in March of 1611, aboard the flagship *De La Warre*) constituted a severe blow not only to the colony in Virginia but to the parent company in London. News of the governor's return to England in ill health climaxed a long run of adverse publicity—the shipwreck of the *Sea Venture*, the Starving Time, the Indian troubles, the accelerating mortality rate—inevitably damaging to the reputation and financial status of the Virginia Company. Enthusiasm for the whole colonial enterprise perceptibly cooled, volunteers reneged on their enlistment to settle there, subscribers to the joint stock company reneged on their subscriptions.[8]

Sir Thomas Dale, a distinguished soldier and veteran of the Flanders campaigns, was rushed across the Atlantic—with the title of Marshal of Virginia—to take over from Sir George Percy, into whose faltering hands the reins of government had again been entrusted by his kinsman De La Warre.

Arriving in Virginia on May 12, 1611, with a fleet of three ships carrying three hundred new colonists, Marshal Dale found the colonists in want and turmoil, "found them growing againe to their former estate of penurie . . . being so improvident as not to put Corne in the ground for their bread" and "their houses ready to fall on their heads." And no wonder, since "most of the companie were at their daily and usuall works, bowling in the streets," to quote Captain Ralph Hamor, contemptuous after a year's experience with those incorrigibles at Jamestown.

According to "Hamors Booke,"* an account incorporated into John Smith's *Generall Historie*, it was the same old story of idleness,

---

* Hamor originally wrote a pamphlet entitled *A True Discourse of the Present Estate of Virginia*, published in London in 1615. Large portions of this work were subsequently incorporated into *The Generall Historie* (1624) under the title "Hamors Booke."

ineptitude, irresponsibility, and insubordination that had plagued the colony from the beginning.

Marshal Dale's "first care therefore was to imploy all hands about setting of Corne"—under the lash, if need be. Likewise under duress, he set them other "necessarie workes, as felling of Timber, repayring their houses. . . ."

A military man and stern disciplinarian, Dale did not hesitate to impose martial law on the colony.[9] "Lawes of Blood," the colonists called them: Death was the penalty for lèse majesté (disrespect to the sovereign or the sovereign's representatives). A thief could expect his ears cut off or his hand branded—or worse: "And some which robbed the store, he [Dale] caused them to be bound fast unto trees and so starved them to death." The crime of desertion entailed penalties still more "bloody and severe" (in the view of colonial historian William Stith)—no pity was to be shown the runagate: "Some he [Dale] appointed to be hanged. Some burned. Some to be broken upon wheels. Others to be staked, and some to be shot to death." (The defector was left with little choice: death at the hands of the English executioner was scarcely preferable to death at the hands of the savages' executioner.)

Dale's reign of terror was instituted as a reaction to his confrontation with that "headie, daring and unruly multitude." Captain Hamor, for one, heartily approved: "so as if his Lawes had not beene so strictly executed, I see not how the utter subversion of the Colonie should have beene prevented. . . ." Only an "absolute and powerfull government" could deal with anarchy.[10]

Dale came, furthermore, as a scourge upon the Indians, raiding without apparent provocation all the way up the James to the fall-line. By means of the four new forts he proposed to build, he hoped to control the entire peninsula: "I should so overmaster the subtle, mischievous Great Powhatan," as he wrote to assure Lord Salisbury in London, "that I should leave him either no room in his country to harbor in, or draw him to a firm association with ourselves."

But there was scant hope of accommodation, of association of any kind with the Great Powhatan. He was inaccessible, unapproachable, implacable. From the January day in 1609 when he had slipped away from Werowocómoco and the English-occupied coastal area, the white men at Jamestown had not laid eyes on him again.

NOR ON POCAHONTAS, presumably with her father at Orapaks or Rasawrack, somewhere in the green depths of the trackless Virginia forests. Had there come about, since Smith's leaveless leave-taking, a hardening of what he called her "compassionate pitifull heart"? With his going, had there fallen a chill upon what he called "her extraordinarie affection to our Nation"? How else explain her abandonment of that nation in its hour of greatest peril? With the loss of Pocahontas, the English colony had lost its most effective intermediary with the opposing forces.

Newcomers knew her only from the tales told by the "Ancients," tales of the friendly and frolicsome Indian princess sporting with the cabin-boys about the fort or consorting more gravely with Captain Smith, heaping gifts of game and grain upon him and his half-famished comrades, bedecking herself gaily with the glass and copper beads he gave her in return.

The Pocahontas legend was already in the making by the time the new secretary, William Strachey, reached the colony in 1610. Strachey set it all down in his *Historie of Travell into Virginia Britania*, written upon his return to England in 1611.

One report that reached him shortly after his arrival in Virginia concerned her marriage. With communication practically severed between the two camps, it is no wonder that details were scarce: "young Pocahunta," Strachey wrote, is "now marryed to a private Captayne called *Kocoum* some 2. yeares synce."* With Pocahontas presumably nubile in 1608 (the date of the autumn harvest festival at Werowocómoco), the only wonder can be that a marriage had not taken place earlier; in her society, marriage was not long delayed after the puberty rites.

It is the identity of the groom that arouses wonder: Strachey's reference to "a pryvate Captayne" seems to imply that Kocoum was not a chieftain, but merely a war-party leader. Whereas the hand of the favorite daughter of the Supreme Chieftain would surely have been sought in marriage by every ambitious subchief in the Powhatan Confederacy.

Powhatan's youngest daughter—succeeding to his favor after the marriage and departure of Pocahontas—was later to be married to "a great Werowance" who paid "two bushels of Rawrenoke"[11] for the privilege of allying himself through marriage with the Supreme Chieftain. Pocahontas—so long recognized as her father's "delight and darling"—must have appeared no less a catch than her little sister, no less a matrimonial prize to the politically ambitious. In all likelihood, Poca-

---

* Strachey's account was completed, apparently, in 1612; his reference to "some 2. yeares synce"—that is, two years prior to his writing—would seem to establish the date of the alleged marriage as 1610. Strachey is the only contemporary to report this development; neither Smith, Hamor, Rolfe, Dale, Whitaker, Argall, nor Spelman refers to an early marriage between Pocahontas and a man of her own people.

hontas would have attracted an even greater werowance, commanded an even higher bridal price.

Willful and headstrong as Pocahontas had already shown herself to be, overindulged from earliest childhood by an aging and doting father, it is possible that her marriage was of her own making, to a man of her own choosing, without regard to his rank or station—a choice from which she could not be dissuaded. It may be that she refused to be a party to her father's matchmaking, refused to be traded off for several bushels of shell beads.

That she dared act in defiance of her father had already been made clear in 1609 when she raced through the snowy woods to Werowocómoco to forestall her father's design for the death of Captain Smith. For her to have defied her father in her choice of a mate would have been entirely in character. She was independent in her thinking, she was fearless, defiant of convention and authority, and she was moved by emotion and by passion, as is evident in almost every line of the few that have come down to us about her. The conclusion is inescapable that if she married Kocoum, it was in response to a strong sexual attraction.

Their coming together would have been unchallenged. An Indian girl had absolute liberty of action in this regard. The Baron de Lahontan, observing Huron maidens in Canada in the early eighteenth century, commented that "a young woman is allowed to do what she pleases. . . . Neither father, nor mother, brother nor sister, can pretend to control her. A young woman, they say, is master of her own body." Robert Beverley's analysis of the mores of the Virginia Indians, as he observed them at the turn of the seventeenth-eighteenth centuries, indicates a similar permissiveness among the tidewater tribes: "the Maidens are entirely at their own disposal," he wrote, "and may manage their persons as they think fit." The young man was likewise free to pay court to any maiden who attracted him, according to Henry Spelman's observations on the mating customs, "for if he taketh likinge of any woman he makes love to hir, and seeketh to hir father or kindsfolke to sett what price he must pay for hir. . . ."

Indian youth responded freely to love and sex. There was nothing in their religious tradition or behavioral code to restrict them. Responding early to physical and emotional stimuli, they early assumed marital bonds.

In the best Powhatan tribal tradition, it would have been her suitor's valor as a warrior, his skill as a hunter, that first attracted Pocahontas: "In the tyme of hunting," as Strachey wrote, "every man will stryve to doe his best to shew his fortune and dexterity, for by excelling therein, they obteyne the favour of the women"—the best hunters, clearly, made the best providers for wife and family. It was by their prowess on the warpath and in the hunt that they attracted brides of their choice.[12]

If he was a conventional Powhatan suitor, "the pryvate Captaine called *Kocoum*" would have paid court to Pocahontas by emptying his game bag and spreading his catch at the entrance to her father's longhouse: "They expresse their loves to the maidens of their choice" (to quote Strachey again on the courtship customs of the tidewater Indians) "by presenting them with the fruictes of their Labours, as by Fowle, Fish or Wild Beasts." Nor could the parents deny an earnest suitor the right to pay their daughter court: "the Parents must allowe of the Sutor," while in return "for their good wills, the Woer promiseth that the daughter shall not want of such provisions nor of deares skynns fitly drest to weare." And not merely the necessities, but the luxuries as well, were promised by the ardent suitor: "he promiseth to doe his endeavour, to procure her beades, perle and Copper. . . ." Then, to seal the bargain, it was customary for the Powhatan swain to produce some negotiable "token of Betroathing," some article valid as a medium of exchange to ratify the espousal, the "Arra sponsalitia," in Strachey's classical turn of phrase.

Whereupon "the acquaintaunce" would be given time to develop, "to be contynued betweene them"; "so after as the liking growes and as soon as he hath provided her a howse (yf he have none before) and some platters, morters, and Matts," why, then, "he takes her home."

Henry Spelman described a somewhat more elaborate "cerimony" or "manner of mariing": The bridal price

> beinge once agreed on, the kindred meett and make good cheere, and when the sume agreed on be payd she shall be delivered to him for his wife, The cerimony is thus The parents bringes their daughter betwene them . . . (for ye men goes not unto any place to be maried But ye woman is brought to him wher he dwelleth). At hir cumminge to him, hir father or cheef frend of ye man Bringeth a longe stringe of Beades and measuringe his armes leangth thereof doth breake it over ye hands of those that are to be married while ther handes be ioyned together, and gives it unto y*e* womans father or him that brings hir. And so with much mirth and feastinge they goe togither.

Planter-historian Robert Beverley, applying himself earnestly in the late 1600s to a study of the customs and folkways of the surviving

Virginia Indians, described the Indian marital compact, emphasizing that marriage was considered secular and economic, while birth, death, and puberty came under the domain of the supernatural. In the very next breath, however, he tells us that the Indians

> esteem the Vows made at that time as most sacred and inviolable. Notwithstanding they allow both the Man and the Wife to part upon disagreement; yet so great is the disreputation of a Divorce, that Marry'd People, to avoid the Character of Inconstant and Ungenerous, very rarely let their Quarrels proceed to a Separation. However, when it does happen, they reckon all the ties of Matrimony dissolv'd, and each hath the liberty of marrying another.

A childless marriage, to be sure, as Beverley observed among the Virginia tribes, was more easily dissolved than a marriage with children—parents' love for their children was the strongest bond between man and woman, and children provided a cogent reason for the preservation of the family unit:

> In these Separations, the Children go, according to the affection of the Parent, with the one or the other; for Children are not reckon'd a Charge among them, but rather Riches, according to the blessing of the Old Testament; and if they happen to differ about dividing their Children, their method is then, to part them equally, allowing the Man the first choice.

The marriage covenant between Pocahontas and the "pryvate Captayne called *Kocoum*," if Strachey was right in saying one had been made, had apparently been dissolved—there is no further mention of his name, no suggestion of any offspring—when next, in 1613, the English came upon Pocahontas, far from her home, on the banks of the Patawamake River (the Potomac), the guest of the "great King Patawomeck."

It might be supposed that Kocoum was a Patawamake, and that Pocahontas had gone to his land, as Spelman says was customary for the bride to do. Or, as Captain Ralph Hamor heard the story (from an officer with the English expedition up the Potomac in the spring of 1613), she had traveled there to represent her father on a trading mission: "It chaunced," according to Hamor's *True Discourse*, that

> Powhatans delight and darling, his daughter *Pocahuntas*, (whose fame hath even bin spred in England by the title of *Nonparella*

of Virginia) in her princely progresse, if I may so terme it, tooke some pleasure (in the absence of Captaine Argall) to be among her friends at *Patawomecke* (as it seemeth by the relation I had) imploied thither, as shopkeepers to a *Fare*, to exchange some of her fathers commodities for theirs.

Whether she went as her father's ambassadress to an intertribal trade fair (as Hamor's informant, Ensign Swift, understood the situation), or had been sent as an emissary to collect tribute owed by the distant Patawamakes to the Supreme Chieftain, or had followed her husband to his native village—however it was, she had, by 1613, left her old haunts, the peninsula between the James and the York-Pamunkey.

There is evidence that her going was the result of an estrangement between herself and her once-doting father, presumably because he had found out about her warning to Captain Smith. Her championship of Smith, her undisguised pro-English sympathies, could only have been construed as treason to her father and her people in their open hostility toward the English invader. If, in her defection from her father's camp to Smith's, she had exceeded for once her own uniquely privileged position, then she might have been obliged to go temporarily into hiding, to seek shelter with trusted friends, to wait quietly, out of sight, on some distant shore, until such time as the Supreme Chieftain's wrath against her had subsided.

"Absconding" is the word used by William Stith[18] to describe her departure, a word implying furtiveness. "Hard by Patowomack," he wrote,

> Pocahontas lay concealed, thinking herself safe, and unknown to all but trusty Friends. What was the reason of her absconding from Werowocomoco, cannot easily be judged; except it was to withdraw herself from being a Witness to the frequent Butcheries of the English, whose Folly and Rashness, after Smith's Departure, put it out her power to save them. . . .

As if to say that if she could not mediate between the two camps, could neither moderate the strangers' folly nor mitigate her own people's fury, then she would not stay to watch the slaughter.

Stith's conclusions on this matter are significant because of his special insight into Pocahontas's life and times—natives of the same peninsula, their centuries overlapping, the branches of their family trees intertwined: the historian's aunt, Anne Stith, was the second wife of Colonel Robert Bolling, whose first wife had been Pocahontas's granddaughter. Stith was heir to family legend and tradition; he had heard stories told at first or second hand, from the lips of the Powhatan princess's direct descendants. And not only that, Stith had access to historical materials since fallen prey to the ravages of time and thus no longer available to researchers, to "authentick Manuscripts" such as "the London Company's Records," "Sir John Randolph's Collection of publick Papers, and the Capitol Records," such as manuscripts and records found by Stith in the Byrd library, documents lost or destroyed since Stith's time.[14]

In judging what Stith called "the Reason of her absconding from Werowocomoco," it may be, as he suggests, that an alienation had come about between the once-inseparable father and daughter, and that fear of Powhatan's displeasure had prompted Pocahontas to leave. If fear is too strong a word, then it was, perhaps, a vague dissatisfaction with her own people and a sense of insecurity in her relation with the alien society that possessed Pocahontas in the months following Captain Smith's sudden disappearance from the scene—a malaise that would account for her restlessness, her possible excursion into wedlock and out again, and, eventually, her flight from her home grounds to the remotest perimeter of the world open to her. (Voluntarily to desert one's homeland is a very un-Indian thing to do: given the intimate association in the Indian's mind between tribal tradition and topography, between the creation myth and the familiar landmarks, it is out of character for him to abandon his natal horizon; he loses his gods in losing the places sacred to them.)

If it was not a breach between Powhatan and Pocahontas that precipitated her flight from home, it may have been the trauma she had experienced when Captain Smith—to whom she had so wholeheartedly committed herself—suddenly disappeared from her life, without even a message to explain his going, without so much as a good-bye. Whether it was a sailing vessel or death which had removed him from her shore, their extraordinary relation, which had had its origin at the altar-stone in 1608, came to an abrupt and sudden end. Her pride wounded—if not her heart—disappointed and disillusioned at the denouement of her liaison with the foreigner, Pocahontas may have married Kocoum on the rebound and followed him to his wigwam on the Potomac.

(Pocahontas could not have known what events would later prove: that Captain Smith was not a marrying man, having loved and left ladies on several continents.[15] If a romantic attachment existed at the time of his death, in 1631, it was no more than that; the lady in question was not Mrs. Smith, but a "Mistris Tredway," so named but not otherwise identified as the recipient of a small bequest in the Last Will and Testament drawn up on his solitary deathbed.[16])

Even though Pocahontas, after Captain Smith's leaveless leave-taking, no longer cared to consort with his fellow countrymen at Jamestown, even though she no longer dared defy her father's orders by going there to relieve the white men's wants, neither would she refuse her aid to those who sought her out in the forest, performing one last signal service for the stranger before departing her home in the vicinity of the fort.

It was once again Pocahontas's intervention—in defiance of her own father and people—that preserved the life of an Englishman in flight from her father's vengeance.

The man—or, rather, the youth—was scapegrace Henry Spelman, assigned by Governor Percy, in 1609, to serve as hostage to the chief. When Spelman, along with Thomas Savage and another boy named Samuel, made a dash for freedom out of Powhatan's stronghold at Orapaks, they were overtaken in their flight by redskin braves. Thomas Savage reconsidered, and returned voluntarily to the lodge of the chieftain, who had consistently shown him signal favor. Samuel fell to the tomahawks of the pursuers. Spelman managed to escape into the forest, where Pocahontas found him and, throwing off the pursuit, guided him through the maze of trails and waterways that led to the Potomac River: "and Pokahontas the Kings daughter saved a boy called Henry Spilman that lived many yeeres after, by her meanes, amongst the *Patawomekes*."[17]

Her trusted friend, the "Great Kinge" of Patawamake, would shelter them both from the wrath of Powhatan.

Although they were members of the Powhatan Confederacy, the Patawamake tribe was large and strong enough—and distant enough from the center of power—to maintain a certain autonomy in domestic affairs. Their werowance had been independent enough to act in contravention of confederacy policy by trading with the white invader when Captain Argall sailed up the Potomac in the winter of 1610–11. He would offer an even more striking demonstration of his independence in giving refuge to Powhatan's absconding daughter and Powhatan's runaway English prisoner.

Pocahontas, writes Stith, thus thought "herself safe" with the werowance of the Patawamakes, lying "concealed" in his dominion, "unknown to all but trusty Friends."

She could never be sure who betrayed her.

CHAPTER VIII

*Be not you discouraged, if the
promises which you have made to
yourselves, or to others, be not so
soon discharged; though you see not
your money, though you see not your
men, though a flood, a flood of blood
have broken in upon them, be not
discouraged. . . . Only let your principal end be the propagation of the
glorious Gospel. . . .*

JOHN DONNE, *"A Sermon upon
the Eighth Verse of the Acts of
the Apostles," 1622*

SHUT OFF FROM TRADE with all the Indians of the immediate
vicinity—the James, the York, the Pamunkey, and Chickahominy valleys—and desperate for provisions for the coming winter,
Lord De La Warre dispatched Captain Samuel Argall up the Potomac
in late 1609 to try his luck with the tribes along that river.

As luck would have it, the Patawamakes, situated at the edge of the
confederacy territory and serving as a buffer between the Algonkian-
speaking Powhatans and the Iroquoian-speaking Massawamekes and
Susquehannocks (who inhabited the Delaware and Pennsylvania areas),
dared defy the trade boycott leveled against the English by the confederacy, and loaded Argall's ship with four hundred bushels of corn
in exchange for such coveted English trade-goods as copper, beads,
and bells.

The success of the trading mission up the Potomac ("a goodly River" boasting "the goodliest Trees for Masts," "Hempe better then English," "an excellent fishing Banke") was one of the few achievements poor, sickly Lord De La Warre could report "to the Lords and others of the Counsell of Virginia"* upon his return to England in the early summer of 1611:

> The last discovery, during my continuall sicknesse, was by Captaine Argoll, who hath found a trade with Patomack (a King as great as Powhatan, who still remaines our enemie, though not able to doe us hurt).

Captain Argall, having ferried the ailing governor back to England, sailed west again in the summer of 1612—his third westbound crossing to Virginia, made in a record seven weeks' time—to serve under the new governor, Sir Thomas Gates. Gates returned from London in late summer of 1612 to take over command from the interim governor, Sir Thomas Dale—who could, in turn, resume his title of marshal and his military duties, such as the fortification of the peninsula and the construction of the new town, Henrico, upstream on the James from Jamestown.

Although Gates had sailed into the Chesapeake with "six tall Ships, with three hundred Men, an hundred Cattle, two hundred Hogs, and with all Manner of other Munition and Provision," it was clear that the provisions would never last the winter without replenishment of grain through trade with the Indians. It could not be with the Powhatans, "for the Indians about James-town," according to Stith, "were in a ticklish state, and little to be depended upon."

If not with the Powhatans, then perhaps with the Patawamakes. Captain Argall, in late December, 1612, nosed the prow of his good new ship, the hundred-thirty-ton *Treasurer*, past Point Comfort, into the Bay, and back up the Potomac River to Pastancie at the mouth of Potomac Creek.

The tribes of that region had shown a disposition to be friendly from the first, and as Stith's *History of Virginia* has it,

> Captain Argall soon entered into a great Acquaintance and Friendship with Japazaws, King of Patowmack, an old Friend to

---

* "A Short Relation made by the lord De-La-Warre, to the Lords and others of the Counsell of Virginia, touching his unexpected returne home, and afterwards delivered to the generall Assembly of the said Company at a Court holden the twenty five of June, 1611."

Captain Smith, and so to the whole English Nation, ever since the first Discovery of the Country.[1]

To seal the pact of friendship, hostages were exchanged and the *Treasurer* was loaded with eleven hundred bushels of much-needed corn.

By March of 1613, the granaries at Jamestown and Henrico were empty again, and Captain Argall headed back up the Potomac, all the way up to the river's head of navigation on that trip ("about 65. leagues into the Land, and navigable for any ship"), to the site of present-day Washington.[2]

En route downriver again, it struck Captain Argall as noteworthy that he had "found a Myne" and that he had come upon a herd of buffalo, "a great store of Cattle as big as Kine" (a rare sight in that area).

But the word that riveted Captain Argall's attention was the word that came to his ear at Pastancie when he stopped to pick up Ensign Swift, whom he had left there, in December, as a hostage with his friend Japazaws: the word that Pocahontas was hiding somewhere in the region ("lay concealed" somewhere "hard by Patowomack," "thinking herself safe, and unknown to all but trusty Friends").

The "trusty Friends" who betrayed her, according to Ensign Swift, were the venal Japazaws and his equally venal wife, although it may well have been Swift himself who, having heard the rumor during the months he spent in the Potomac region, passed it on to his commanding officer when the *Treasurer* appeared in the river in the early spring of 1613.

It was from Ensign Swift that Captain Ralph Hamor, the new Recorder of the Colony, heard the story and recorded it:

> Captaine Argall, having entred into a great acquaintance with Iapazaws . . . heard by him there was Pocahontas, whom Captaine Smiths Relations intituleth the Numparell of Virginia, and though she had beene many times a preserver of him and the whole Colonie, yet till this accident shee was never seene at James towne since his departure.
>
> Being at Patawomeke, as it seemes, thinking her selfe un-knowne, was easily by her friend Iapazaws perswaded to goe abroad with him and his wife to see the ship: for Captaine Argall had promised him a Copper Kettle to bring her but to him, promising no way to hurt her, but keepe her till they could con-

clude a peace with her father; the Salvage for this Copper Kettle would have done any thing, it seemed by the Relation.

For though she had seene and beene in many ships, yet hee caused his wife to faine how desirous she was to see one, that hee offered to beat her for her importunitie, till she wept. But at last he told her, if Pocahontas would goe with her, hee was content: and thus they betraied the poore innocent Pocahontas aboord, where they were all kindly feasted in the Cabbin. Iapazaws treading oft on the Captaines foot, to remember he had done his part; the Captaine when he saw his time, perswaded Pocahontas to the Gun-roome, faining to have some conference with Iapazaws, which was onely that she should not perceive hee was any way guiltie of her captivitie: so sending for her againe, hee told her before her friends, she must goe with him, and compound peace betwixt her Countrie and us, before she ever should see Powhatan; whereat the old Iew[3] and his wife began to howle and crie as fast as Pocahontas, that upon the Captaines faire perswasions, by degrees pacifying her selfe, and Iapazaws and his wife, with the Kettle and other toies, went merrily on shore; and shee to James towne.

A messenger forthwith was sent to her father, that his daughter Pocahontas he loved so dearely, he must ransome with our men, swords, peeces, tooles, &c. hee trecherously had stolne.

The abduction having been plotted and carried out, the ransom note was drawn up and sent off.

The idea of an abduction did not spring full-fledged from Argall's head: Lord De La Warre's commission from the Virginia Company contained just such a suggestion in connection with the conversion of the infidel:

Yt is very expedient that your Lordship with all diligence endeavor the conversion of the natives and savages to the knowledge and worship of the true God and their redeemer Christ Jesus as the most pius and noble end of this plantation, [which] the better to effect, you are to procure from them some of their Children to be brought up in our language and manners and if you think it necessary you first remove from them Quiacooks or priests by a surprise of them and detayning them prisoners and in case they shall be wilful obstinate, then to send us some 3 or 4 of them into England [so that] we may endeavor their conversion there.

The suggestion of kidnapping in connection with the conversion of the heathen was heard even from the pulpit: in May of 1609, the Reverend William Symonds reminded his Virginia-bound congregation that "a captive girl brought Naman to the Prophet. A captive woman was the means of converting Iberia. . . . God makes the weake things of the worlde confounde the mighty."

Captain Argall may well have attended that service in London, and the Reverend Symonds's words may still have been ringing in his ears, four years later, in the Virginia wilderness. Thus, no sooner did Argall hear the news of Pocahontas's presence on the Potomac shores—far from home, unprotected, easy prey—than he was struck by the possibilities inherent in her capture. She would make an illustrious convert, to be sure, but there was more to it than that. The Powhatan princess was a prize: "Powhatan's delight and darling, his daughter Pocahontas" would be a trump card in the hands of the English. With Pocahontas in their power, the English might bring her father to terms, to the peace table he had thus far so obdurately shunned.

What a coup for Argall if he could deliver the Supreme Chieftain's daughter, unharmed, to the authorities at Jamestown, to Governor Gates and Marshal Dale! To bring it off, he needed the connivance of Japazaws and his wife. Alternating threat with promise, Argall won them over to his kidnap scheme. Not only did he guarantee Pocahontas's safety, he gave assurance of the respect to be shown her by a class-conscious English society fully mindful of her rank. She would be received in Jamestown not as a prisoner, but as an honored guest.

There was no stratagem, as Argall himself wrote in his letter to London, to which he would not stoop to achieve his ends:

> Whilst I was in this businesse, I was told by certaine Indians, my friends, that the Great Powhatans Daughter Pokahuntis was with the great King Patowomeck, whether I presently repaired, resolving to possesse my selfe of her by any stratagem that I could use, for the ransoming of so many Englishmen as were prisoners with Powhatan: as also to get such armes and tooles, as hee, and other Indians had got by murther and stealing from others of our Nation, with some quantitie of Corne, for the Colonies reliefe.
>
> So soone as I came to an anchor before the Towne I manned my Boate, and sent on shoare, for the King of Pastancy and Ensigne Swift (whom I had left as a pledge of our love and truce, the Voyage before) who presently came and brought my pledge with him: whom after I had received, I brake the matter to this

King, and told him, that if he did not betray Pokohuntis into my
hands; wee would be no longer brothers nor friends.

To do him justice, Pocahontas's "trusted Friend," Japazaws, at
first resisted Argall's overtures.

Hee alleaged, that if hee should undertake this businesse, then
Powhatan would make warres upon him and his people; but upon
my promise, that I would joyne with him against him, hee repaired presently to his brother, the great King of Patowomeck,
who being made acquainted with the matter, called his Counsell*
together: and after some few houres deliberation, concluded
rather to deliver her into my hands, then lose my friendship: so
presently, he betrayed her into my Boat,† wherein I carried her
aboord my ship. . . .

With the connivance, perhaps, of Pocahontas herself? Several
curious lines crop up in the Hamor texts to suggest that Pocahontas
was not entirely an unwilling victim.

The first suggests that she was not unaware of the danger she ran
in boarding the *Treasurer*: "fearefull perhaps to be surprised" is how
Hamor puts it—fearful, that is, of being taken by surprise, being seized
and carried off, once she stepped aboard the English ship. If anyone had
warned her of the danger of an abduction, the warning was disregarded;
she flew in the face of danger.

It is possible that whereas she would not openly desert her father
and her people, would not of her own free will walk into the enemy
English camp, still she might have exposed herself, consciously or unconsciously, to the risk of an abduction that would have had the same
end result. Forcibly removed and transplanted, she would not be subject to the charge of treason, could not be called a defector, a renegade.
But she had long since made the transfer of her allegiance.

Pocahontas offered little or no resistance, "was easily by her friend
Iapazaws perswaded to goe abroad with him and his wife to see the
ship," went voluntarily toward her encounter with the English captain.
She was, after a four years' absence from Jamestown, "desirous to renue
hir familiaritie with the English, and delighting to see them." If she had
lent herself willingly, unresistant, to the scheme for her own kidnapping, then the "howles" and cries described by Hamor in the *Generall*

* The Patawamake tribe evidently referred matters of state to a Council of Elders.
† A light rowboat was used between the shore and the sailing vessel at anchor in the
river.

Historie were window-trimming, merely part of a charade intended to show that she had been seized, taken against her will. If she showed herself "exceeding pensive and discontented," it was not for long; and "upon the Captaines faire perswasions, by degrees pacifying her selfe," she was soon restored to her normal composure, her ineffable dignity.

Once her treacherous host and hostess were back ashore at Pastancie, Pocahontas found herself alone with the white men, the *Treasurer*'s crew of sixty and their captain, who made "much adoe" over their illustrious captive, according her "extraordinarie curteus usage," lodging her "in the Gunners roome," the best accommodation aboard, save for the captain's own cabin.

Captain Argall, before raising anchor at Pastancie on April 13, had "dispatched" a messenger to Powhatan,

> to let him know, that I had taken his Daughter: and if he would send home the Englishmen (whom he deteined in slaverie, with such armes and tooles, as the Indians had gotten, and stolne) and also a great quantitie of Corne, that then, he should have his daughter restored, otherwise not. This newes much grieved this great King, yet, without delay, he returned the messenger with this answer. That he desired me to use his Daughter well, and bring my ship into his River, and there he would give mee my demands; which being performed, I should deliver him his Daughter, and we should be friends.

At Jamestown, Captain Argall quite properly turned over the ransom negotiations to Governor Gates, inquiring of him, "upon what condition he would conclude this peace and what he would demand."

Hamor's account of the ransom negotiations is more expansive than Argall's:

> A messenger forthwith was sent to her father, that his daughter Pocahontas he loved so dearely, he must ransome with our men, swords, peeces, tooles, &c. hee trecherously had stolne.
>
> This unwelcome newes much troubled Powhatan, because hee loved both his daughter and our commodities well, yet it was three moneths after [not, that is, until July] ere hee returned us any answer: then by the perswasion of the Councell,[4] he returned seven of our men, with each of them an unserviceable Musket, and sent us word, that when wee would deliver his daughter, hee would make us satisfaction for all injuries done us and give us five hundred bushels of Corne, and for ever be friends with us.
>
> That he sent, we received in part of payment, and returned

him this answer: That his daughter should be well used; but we could beleeve the rest of our armes were either lost or stolne from him, and therefore till hee sent them, we would keepe his daughter.

Powhatan's daughter was assuredly being "well used" by her captors, as Hamor wrote in his Booke in the *Generall Historie*; those caste-conscious English officers would not have been remiss in according the proper deference to a person of her rank and station. A daughter of the Supreme Chieftain of the tidewater could expect to be—and was—"very well, and kindely intreated." Both Governor Gates and Marshal Dale showed their distinguished hostage attention and courtesy. Dale undertook to act as her guardian, zealously performed his duties in that capacity, and later, after her marriage, served as friend of the family, patron, and sponsor.

If he was a scourge upon the Indians, a bloody despot to the English colonists under his command, he must have shown Pocahontas only his better nature, must have shown himself consistently considerate and gentle in his dealings with his celebrated captive. A highly controversial figure, a harsh and stern disciplinarian—reports of his brutality published in England redounded to the disrepute of the Virginia Company, with the result that he was bypassed in all the company's future colonial assignments—the Marshal was apparently always on the best of terms with the Powhatan princess, and cordial relations continued between them throughout her life.[5]

Pocahontas found Jamestown much changed since her last visit there in 1608. Few of the "Ancients" remained, few of the veterans of the First and Second Supplies—Smith had returned to England in 1609, Percy in 1612, and Spelman in 1611; Captain Gabriel Archer had died in the Starving Time; the gentle Reverend Hunt had succumbed, one of the many casualties of 1608. Among the "Boyes" with whom Pocahontas had so indecorously disported herself, at least one, Samuel Collier, would have been on hand to greet her when she was brought to Jamestown in 1613.[6]

If Pocahontas found few familiar faces in Jamestown in 1613, the settlement itself was scarcely more recognizable. Between the three of them, De La Warre, Gates, and Dale had not only made improvements, but had extended the perimeters of the colony on the peninsula onto the mainland. "The Towne it selfe," according to Hamor, who saw the progress,

> by the care and providence of Sir Thomas Gates, who for the most part had his chiefest residence there, is reduced into a hand-

some forme, and hath in it two faire rowes of houses, all of framed timber, two stories and an upper Garret, or Corne loft high, besides three large, and substantiall Store-howses, joyned togeather in length some hundred and twenty foot, and in breadth forty, and this town hath been lately newly and strongly impaled, and a faire platforme for Ordenance in the west Bulwarke raised: there are also without this towne in the island, some very pleasant, and beautifull howses, two Blockhouses, to observe and watch least the Indians at any time should swim over the back river, and come into the Island, and certain other farme howses. . . . This Ile, and much ground about it, is much inhabited. . . .

New arrivals had moved out from behind the cramped five-cornered palisaded area constituting the original fort, and development would continue along the shore to the south of these first dwellings outside the fort proper. A larger church had been built outside the fort, and a market-square had developed around it. The New Town (James City, as distinguished from James Fort) was to consist chiefly of houses built along the main road (much as English villages had sprung up at crossroads or along main thoroughfares). Some of the refinements of English life began to appear on the frontier: the governor's house at Jamestown boasted a garden where "many forward apple and peare trees come up, of the kernels set the yeare before." "The Great Road," begun by the early settlers, ran from James Fort across the isthmus to the mainland; later extended, it passed the "Glasshouse"* to the mainland; eventually, in its final extension, it followed an Indian trail to a point midway in the Peninsula between the York and the James.

The report of the capture of the Indian princess and her arrival at Jamestown constituted the gladdest tidings to reach London from the colony in that year of 1613—a boon to the morale of the tottering Virginia Company.

In London, John Chamberlain (man-about-town, born gossip, born reporter) made haste to relay the good news to a young friend on diplomatic assignment across the Channel: "There is a ship come from Virginia," he wrote to Sir Dudley Carleton at the Hague on August 1, 1613,[7]

with newes of their well-doing, which puts some life into that action, that before was almost at the last cast. They have taken a

---

* A glass factory. As early as 1608, according to John Smith, "a tryall of glass" was made in Jamestown at the Glasshouse. European craftsmen ("Eight Dutchmen and Poles") were sent to the colony in an effort to produce exportable commodities—glass, potash, pitch, and tar.

daughter of a king that was theyre greatest ennemie, as she was going ᵃ feasting upon a river to visit certain frends: for whose ransome the father offers whatsoever is in his power, and to become theyre frend, and to bring them where they shall meet with gold mines. They propound unto him three conditions: to deliver all the English fugitives, to render all manner of armes or weapons of theyrs that are come to his handes and to give them 300 quarters of corne. The first two he performed redilie, and promiseth the other at theyre harvest, yf his daughter may be well used in the mean time.

"But this ship," as Chamberlain wryly concluded (he was a stockholder in the Virginia Company, and nervous about the returns on his investment), "brought us no commodities from thence but only these fayre tales and hopes." The Virginia Company was in serious financial straits, could not pay off its debts with "fayre tales and hopes." Great expenses had been incurred in dispatching the several large expeditions to Virginia; subscribers to the joint stock issue were delinquent in the face of the bad news from the colony; it was impossible to float another issue. After 1612, the company's financial plight was such that the public lottery would prove its sole fund-raising capability. By the new Charter of 1612, the company was granted not only the lottery privilege but also the title to colonization of the Bermudas (then known as the Summer or Sommers Isles, in honor of Sir George Sommers*).

In the meantime—possibly by the time the news-bearing ship had reached England in late July—Pocahontas had been transferred from Jamestown to a new community, a model city being constructed under the direction of Marshal Dale, some fifty or more miles upriver by foot, eighty or more by canoe or skiff (a site some ten miles below the present city of Richmond).

Between 1611 and 1616, the center of gravity in the colony seemed to move upriver, out of reach of Spanish raiders, onto higher ground more defensible against Indian attack, with air more wholesome than that from the pestilential marshes around Jamestown.[8]

Upon a site of his own choosing, Dale had carved "his new towne" out of the wilderness in record time, thanks to the assistance of "three hundred and fiftie men" likewise of his own choosing, furnished him by Governor Gates in the autumn of 1611. "Within ten or twelve daies," Captain Hamor recalled,

* The Bermuda venture instantly prospered. With the climate ideal and nature bounteous on the uninhabited Bermudas, the colony there encountered no such hardships as had the one in Virginia.

he had invironed with a pale, and in honour of our noble Prince Henry, called it *Henrico*. The next worke he did, was building at each corner of the Towne a high commanding Watch-house, a Church, and Store-houses: which finished, hee began to thinke upon convenient houses for himselfe and men, which, with all possible speed he could, he effected, to the great content of his companie and all the Colonie.

This towne is situated upon a necke of a plaine rising land, three parts invironed with the maine River, the necke of land well impaled, makes it like an Ile; it hath three streets of well-framed houses, a handsome Church, and the foundation of a better laid (to bee built of Bricke). . . . Upon the verge of the River there are five houses, wherein live the honester sort of people, as Farmers in England, and they keepe continuall centinell for the townes securitie.

About two miles from the towne, into the Maine, in another pale, neere two miles in length, from River to River, guarded with severall Commanders, with a good quantitie of Corne-ground impailed, sufficiently secure to maintaine more than I suppose will come this three yeeres.

On the other side of the River, for the securitie of the towne, in intended to be impaled for the securitie of our Hogs, about two miles and a halfe, by the name of Hope in Faith and Coxendale, secured by five of our manner of Forts, which are but Palisadoes, called Charitie Fort, Mount Malado (a guest house [hospital] for sicke people) a high seat and wholsome aire, Elisabeth Fort, and Fort Patience: And here hath Master Whitaker chosen his Parsonage, impaled a faire framed Parsonage, and one hundred acres called Rocke hall. . . .[9]

It was Master Whitaker—the Reverend Alexander Whitaker—into whose tender care the Princess Pocahontas was confided by Marshal Dale. It was Whitaker to whom Dale entrusted the conversion of this first Virginia Indian to enter the fold. What a prize—this daughter of the Supreme Chieftain of the tidewater—if she could be brought to the faith!

Whitaker's fair-framed parsonage and his hundred-acre Rock Hall farm promised the ideal retreat for the distinguished hostage and prospective convert: across the river from Henrico, the parsonage was to be protected by no less than "five of our manner of Forts"—one of the best fortified points in the colony. Powhatan would find it difficult to penetrate those defenses to snatch her away, should such an exploit be undertaken.

Pocahontas might conceivably have stayed on at Jamestown under the aegis of Sir Thomas Gates, with the worthy Reverend Bucke as her religious mentor, but the conversion seemed the special project of Sir Thomas Dale. The marshal was "a man of great knowledge in Divinity," as his friend Reverend Whitaker pointed out in his *Good Newes from Virginia*, "and of a good conscience in all his doing, both of which Bee rare in a martiall man."

And surely Whitaker was the ideal man, the man most appropriate to the lofty mission, picked by Dale to accompany him as chaplain on the marshal's westward journey in early 1611. A Puritan clergyman with superlative credentials and prestigious background—"a Schollar, a Graduate" of St. John's College, Cambridge, where his father was Master and Regius Professor of Divinity, "well borne and friended," as the eminent divine William Crashaw described him[10]—young Whitaker, twenty-six when he departed for the New World, could well have anticipated every success in his ecclesiastical career. Only a strong vocation could have called him to arduous service in a primitive wilderness outpost, in preference to the comfortable vicarage in the serene English countryside which might have been his lot, had it been his inclination. It was clearly upon a divine imperative that young Whitaker went to what he called "this barbarous Countrey of Virginia" to become "Apostle to the Indians." He took a brighter view of the Indians than did most men of his day and time. "One God created us," he would write in his *Good Newes from Virginia* sermon, in 1613; "they have reasonable soules and intellectuall faculties as well as wee; we all have Adam for our common parent." A handsome concession on the part of a seventeenth-century Puritan divine; one wonders whether it was the reasonable soul and intellectual faculties perceptible in his protégée that gave him his good opinion of the red race.[11]

Religion was a major preoccupation of the Virginia colony. Twice-daily church attendance was compulsory: the first time a man failed to attend services, he forfeited a week's food allowance; a second offense brought on a flogging; habitual offenders were shot, hanged, or burned at the stake. By Dale's blue laws, profanity was punishable by the lash; a blasphemer's tongue was run through with a bodkin; in the case of repeated offenses, the dealth penalty was applicable.

"Every Sabbath day wee preach in the forenoone," Whitaker wrote to a relative in England,

> and Chatecize in the afternoone. Every Saturday night I exercise in Sir Thomas Dales house. Our Church affaires bee consulted on by the Minister, and foure of the most religious men. Once

every moneth wee have a Communion, and once a yeer a solemn Fast.

The solemn congregation at Henrico would have been joined by Pocahontas as soon as the Reverend Whitaker's course of instruction had prepared her to follow the services of the Church of England and to observe the Christian ritual.

And as soon as her nakedness had been covered. When she came into their midst, the Reverend Whitaker undoubtedly assigned some good English housewife in his parish the task of fashioning proper European-style garments to the Indian girl's measurements—her wisp of a fringed doeskin apron would have been exchanged for a long, billowing skirt and a long-sleeved, clinging, cylindrically shaped bodice.

There may have been resort to gentle and subtle persuasion, but it is inconceivable that Pocahontas's conversion could have been anything but a voluntary act. She appeared disposed, from the beginning, from her very first contact with the stranger—with Smith, specifically—to adopt that stranger and his way of life, disposed to become European-ized, Anglicized, eventually Christianized; disposed to renounce her own people, own land, own religion, own heritage, in the transition. Where Captain Smith and Captain Newport and Namontack, all three in unison, had had difficulty forcing Powhatan to his knees in the per-formance of the coronation ceremony at Werowocómoco in 1608, Pocahontas seems to have taken without protest to the genuflections requisite to the Anglican service in the chapel at Henrico, as to the bowing of her head when grace was said before the meal in the Rock Hall parsonage. Nor is there any evidence of mental or spiritual reser-vations on Pocahontas's part, any sign of a divided loyalty in her profession of faith in the Church of England. Hers was apparently a whole-hearted, whole-souled conversion. Events in the future would show her to be a devoutly practicing Christian.

Pocahontas, at Henrico in 1613, had much to learn under the Reverend Whitaker's tutelage: first of all, perhaps, to read in order to be able to follow the services in the English Book of Common Prayer, and to study the Ten Commandments, the Apostles' Creed, and the Catechism. (A Horn Book, in all probability, was her primer: the seventeenth-century abecedarium consisted of a small wooden paddle across which was stretched a sheet of parchment just large enough to hold the alphabet printed in both upper and lower case, lists of the vowels and consonants and combinations thereof, and the ten lines of the Lord's Prayer. The entire printed surface was protected by a thin layer of the transparent horn whence the Book derived its name.)

Pocahontas doubtless attended the Reverend Whitaker's Sabbath-afternoon catechizing sessions, which became standard procedure in Virginia parishes for the instruction of young people in the Church Catechism in preparation for their admission to Holy Communion.[12]

Demurely covered from neck ruff to wrist-band, her lithe waist confined in bone corseting, her agile body weighted down by a farthingale (a framework of whalebone over which the crinolines and skirt were extended), Pocahontas went decorously—if uncomfortably—about her appointed rounds of prayer and study at Rock Hall.

On the theory that the ability to adjust to a change of environment is a gauge of intelligence, Pocahontas gave evidence of a high intelligence, adjusting smoothly and swiftly to an alien culture, religion, life style. Her intellectual curiosity apparently aroused about this other world, and highly susceptible to its influences, Pocahontas moved into it eagerly and with remarkable ease, quickly conforming to life in the Anglican parsonage.

She proved an ideal pupil. Her spiritual mentors rejoiced at "her desyre to be taught and instructed in the knowledge of God, her Capablenes of understanding, her aptnes and willingnes to receyve any good impression," as would be said of her by John Rolfe, a planter in the Henrico area, who had the privilege of assisting in the great work, the opportunity to observe at first hand the astonishingly rapid progress of the young neophyte.

"How carefull they were to instruct her in Christianity" ("they" being Dale, Whitaker, and Rolfe, the writer being John Smith, in his *Generall Historie*), "and how capable and desirous shee was thereof."

"She was the first Christian Indian in these Parts," Stith proclaimed, "and perhaps the sincerest and most worthy, that has ever been since"—in the hundred-odd years between her conversion, 1613–14, and the publication of Stith's *History* in 1747. "She on her Part," as he repeated the legend transmitted by her direct descendants, "expressed an eager Desire, and shewed great Capacity in learning. After she had been tutored for some time, she openly renounced the Idolatry of her Country."

If Pocahontas had much to learn at Henrico, she had much to unlearn: the sum and total of her entire young life, every impression of all the eighteen or so years she had lived, the totality of her mental, emotional, and spiritual experience from the cradleboard on—every normal, natural instinct and impulse henceforward had to be repressed, denied.

Such a denial of identity is necessarily traumatic. Not only was courage required for the sudden transition from a familiar world to one totally strange, totally unknown, but there was sacrifice entailed, as well. No longer to run free in the wildwood was a sacrifice, as it was no longer to swing on the grapevine, no longer to cartwheel with the boys, no longer to leap and spin in maenadic dance, no longer to dive and swim in river and bay—but, instead, to sit sedately, ladylike, in church or classroom, hands folded demurely in her lap, skirts smoothed over ankles primly crossed. To give up the games and sports, the athletic life customary to a wildwood youth, could not but have constituted a grievous deprivation to Pocahontas, whose every muscle had been attuned to strenuous exercise. To bind her unbound breasts, to cinch her supple waist in whalebone must have been an acute discomfort for her, as it must have also to fetter her arms with sleeves, her feet with shoes. The transformation from unconstrained pagan maiden to sedate Christian neophyte could not have been accomplished without a measure of distress.

It must be remembered, too, that her adoption of a new faith was not for any lack of spiritual sustenance or ardor in the old; her previous religious experience had been neither mean nor sterile: the Powhatan tribal cosmology was elaborate, intricate, the mythology often lyrical, the ritual rich in pageantry, appealing to the spirit as well as to the senses. The Indian's conviction of man's oneness and harmony with nature was vivid and compelling; the Indian's appreciation of beauty in the natural world was intense; his reverence of nature in all its aspects— earth, sky, water—his respect for all creation, inanimate as well as animate, were inherent in his basic concept of the world and of life. ("There is as yet in Virginia," Strachey acknowledged, "no place to be discovered so savage and simple, in which the Inhabitants have not a Religion." The well-formulated religious concepts of the Powhatans included a supreme being, a creator "who governes all the world," so benign as to require no propitiation.[18])

Pocahontas's ready conversion to Christianity and her eager adaptation to an alien way of life manifest, according to recent and persuasive psychoanalytical theory, all the aspects of a grief process. If Pocahontas believed Smith dead—as she herself would, one day, say she had—if she was grieving for a foreigner, then the pain of her grief could have driven her to seek a foreign land, a religion and customs hitherto strange to her; her behavioral pattern subsequent to her abduction—like her flight from home at the first news of Smith's disappearance—may be construed, psychologically, as an attempt to reunite with the foreigner whose loss she mourned.

Indifferent to the intricacies of motivation behind Pocahontas's amenability to civilizing influences, Marshal Dale and the Reverend

Whitaker rejoiced to be able shortly to announce the date for their illustrious neophyte's public profession of faith and baptism—the ceremony to take place, in all probability, in the "faire and handsome Church" at Henrico.[14]

It was a triumph for Dale—the colony's first convert to Christianity, herald of assimilation—and he proudly proclaimed it by letter to the Bishop of London:

Powhatans daughter I caused to be carefully instructed in Christian Religion, who after shee had made some good progresse therein, renounced publickly her countrey Idolatry, openly confessed her Christian faith, was, as she desired, baptised.

Already a turncoat, Pocahontas now published her apostasy: having forsaken her people, she now publicly renounced her gods.

The Reverend Alexander Whitaker gave Dale full credit, writing to his cousin, the Minister of Black Friars' Bridge, London: Pocahontas "confessed the faith of Jesus Christ, and was baptized; which thing Sir Thomas Dale had laboured a long time to ground in her."

Captain John Smith, it is to be remembered, gave credit not merely to one man, nor even to two, but to three men, including John Rolfe along with Dale and Whitaker as responsible for the evangelical mission: "How carefull they were," Smith insisted, "to instruct her in Christianity."

Only a scriptural scholar such as Whitaker could have been responsible for choosing the Christian name to be taken at the baptismal font: Rebecca. There was intuition as well as erudition in Whitaker's choice of the new name for the Powhatan princess: the verses in the Book of Genesis that tell the story of Rebecca can be read as an augury.

Whitaker seems to have had a forewarning—if not foreknowledge —of the interracial marriage she was to make, the vast and proud progeny of mixed blood—red and white—that were to be her heirs in Virginia and throughout the South. Verse 60, Chapter 24, of Genesis is prophetic:

Be thou the mother of thousands of millions, and let thy seed possess the gate of those which hate them.

And in Chapter 25, Verse 23:

And the Lord said unto her, Two nations are in thy womb, and two manner of people shall be separated from thy bowels;

and one people shall be stronger than the other people; and the older shall serve the younger.

The man she was to marry—the Englishman whose blood was to be mingled with hers in a proud and numerous heritage—was already in Virginia, the first to experiment with a tobacco crop in the impaled fields around Henrico, the pioneer in tobacco culture, the savior of the colonial economy.

CHAPTER IX

There was a bed of leaves, and
   broken play;
There was a veil upon you,
   Pocahontas, bride—
O Princess whose brown lap was
   virgin May;
And bridal flanks and eyes hid
   tawny pride.

HART CRANE,
The Bridge, 1930

THE MAN Pocahontas would marry was John Rolfe.
   Master Rolfe, accompanied by his wife, had sailed from England for Virginia in June of 1609 aboard the *Sea Venture*, the ill-fated flagship of the Third Supply, whose passenger list included Deputy Governor Sir Thomas Gates, Admiral Sir George Sommers, and Vice-Admiral Christopher Newport, along with such lesser lights as Secretary William Strachey and Captain Ralph Hamor.
   During the eight months spent by the castaways on the islands of Bermuda—on whose reefs the *Sea Venture* had foundered in July—Mistress Rolfe gave birth to a daughter, who was christened by the Reverend Richard Bucke on February 21, 1610, as duly noted by Sir Thomas Gates in his report on the shipwreck:

> We had the childe of one John Rolfe christened . . . to which Captain Newport and myselfe were Witnesses, and aforesaid Mistress Hortan, and we named it Bermuda.[1]

The infant's name would appear on Gates's list of the casualties occurring during the castaways' sojourn on that isle. If Mrs. Rolfe had died in childbirth, her name should have appeared on that list. Since it does not, it may have been an oversight on the deputy governor's part, or it may be that she died en route from Bermuda to Virginia in the spring of 1610, or conceivably fell victim to one of the perils—famine, pestilence, Indian arrows—awaiting the newcomers in Jamestown.

Whatever her cause of death, whatever its date, Mistress Rolfe was no longer among the living in 1613, when John Rolfe appeared upon the scene, a widower, free to pay his court to the dusky young Indian princess who was to be his neighbor in the parish of Henrico.

John Rolfe was, by that date, in his middle to late twenties. His birthdate cannot be positively established, any more than can his origins. His ancestry has been the subject of endless research, speculation, and conjecture: generations of historians and genealogists have sought and failed to make positive identification of this particular John Rolfe with any of the several branches of the Rolfe family in England. In this instance, legend and tradition have carried the day despite lack of solid documentation: such standard works of reference as the *Dictionary of National Biography* and *Dictionary of American Biography* capitulate to tradition and show the Virginia adventurer John Rolfe as stemming from the Rolfe family of Heacham in Norfolk County on the North Sea coast, one of three sons born to John and Dorothy Rolfe, his birthdate shown on the Parish Register as 1585.

The Heacham Rolfes could be designated landed gentry, thanks to John Senior, a self-made man, whose mercantile successes had made possible the acquisition of land (and with it, the designation of "gentleman"). The identification of John Rolfe of Virginia fame with the Rolfes of Heacham has been accepted primarily, perhaps, because it rings true: the Heacham Rolfes typified the middling people, the sturdy, industrious, pious Puritan stock that made up the backbone of early colonial America. John Rolfe of Virginia was, clearly, a gentleman of just such stock. Although Rolfe family descendants have sought to prove that John Rolfe had attended—like so many other Norfolk and Suffolk County Rolfes—one of the English universities, none of the possible matriculates has been positively identified with the renowned colonist. Nevertheless, Rolfe's *True Relation* and a number of holograph letters of his which have survived bear witness to the fact that he was an educated man.

If he was only a second-generation gentleman, he was—unlike the many other indolent gentlemen in Virginia—industrious, ambitious, and ingenious. If he was a scion of the Heacham Rolfes, he may have found his inspiration in the lines of Latin on his father's tomb in Heacham Church, an epitaph extolling the virtues of the deceased and claiming that he "increased his family estate with the export and import of things which England either abounded with or wanted."

The cultivation of tobacco in Virginia as a profitable commodity for export became the consuming interest of John Rolfe's life. The development of a superior leaf of tobacco could spell the difference between survival and collapse, success and failure, for the struggling colony and for the financially embarrassed Virginia Company (no fortunes, clearly, were to be expected from such commodities as sassafras, silkworms, clapboard). Himself a heavy smoker, a confirmed addict, John Rolfe was just the man to recognize the sales potential of a good grade of the "esteemed weed" (as he called it) in the English and European market.

Once in Jamestown, his first move would surely have been to procure a pipeful of the regional smoke, which was the hardy, shrubby *Nicotiana rustica*, the sole species indigenous to Virginia, a coarse and acrid leaf little improved by the rude curing methods traditional to the tidewater Indians.[2] "There is here a great store of Tobacco which the Salvages call *Apooke*, howbeyt yt is not of the best kynd," as William Strachey described the native growth in his *Historie*; "yt is but poore and weake, and of a byting tast."

The very first puff—burning the tongue, rasping the nose and throat—convinced Rolfe that the hot, rank species native to Virginia could not compete with that being cultivated by the Spaniards in their West Indies plantations—the mild and fragrant *Nicotiana tabacum*, originally from Brazil, the prized leaf in demand all over Europe.

By 1611 or 1612, within a year or two after his arrival in Virginia, John Rolfe had managed somehow, somewhere, to obtain a handful of that coveted *Nicotiana tabacum* seed. How he ever laid hands on those precious, fine, tiny, prolific seeds from the West Indies, remains as much of a mystery as his origins. Certainly the Spanish tobacco growers would have jealously guarded their monopoly of the lucrative market, and never knowingly have relinquished so much as an ounce of such a treasure to a possible competitor. The seeds were more precious than gold, their tobacco plantations yielding the Spaniards, in the long run, a greater fortune than even their mines of gold and silver.[3]

Whether acquired by hook or crook, that pinch of gold-brown dust had been planted by Rolfe in the sandy soil of the Peninsula between the James and the York by the summer of 1611 (or 1612); the first broad hairy leaf of the new variety unfurled and flourished in the balmy, steamy tidewater growing season—a successful first trial. Rolfe had proven that a top-grade tobacco could be grown on the east coast of North America as well as in the West Indies; Virginia and England could compete with Spain for the European tobacco market. John Rolfe had successfully launched the first American enterprise; the crop he pioneered would develop a new agricultural economy capable of maintaining England's overseas colonies. The introduction of tobacco culture on the banks of the James represents, says P. A. Bruce in his *Economic History of Virginia*, "by far the most momentous fact in the history of Virginia in the seventeenth century."

LEGEND AND TRADITION insist that Rolfe came upriver from Jamestown to make his tobacco experiments in the fertile fields being cleared and fenced by Sir Thomas Dale around Henrico, and that it was there, in 1613, that Rolfe encountered the famous hostage, the pagan princess being coached by the Reverend Whitaker at Rock Hall.

A gentleman as pious as Rolfe consistently shows himself to be in his deeds and words would have attended twice-daily services at the Henrico Church where Pocahontas was to worship. Rolfe would have put in an appearance "every Saturday night" at the house of Sir Thomas Dale—as would Dale's Indian protégée—where the Reverend Whitaker was wont (as he wrote) to "exercise" (an exercise of worship, as the seventeenth-century use of the word implied). Rolfe may have qualified as one of the "four of the most religious men" of Henrico parish who joined with the minister in consultation on "Church affaires," meeting—in all likelihood—at Rock Hall, where the notable Indian proselyte was lodged. Rolfe would have gone without fail to the Henrico Church for the monthly communion service, which would likewise have been attended by Pocahontas—or, rather, by the Lady Rebecca, as she would be known to the English after her baptism.

Thrown into daily contact with Pocahontas at either the church or the parsonage or at the home of Sir Thomas Dale, Rolfe was promptly struck, as he himself remarked in a letter he later addressed to the governor, by the princess's eagerness to learn, her thirst for knowledge, and her aptitude at absorbing it. In Rolfe's breast was kindled the same desire that burned in those of Dale and Whitaker—to claim this notable pagan soul for Christ. Rolfe would join his friends Dale and Whitaker in their holy mission to pronounce her the first Indian convert in Virginia.

Rolfe began to take a hand, to play an important role in Pocahontas's Christianization and Anglicization: it was thanks to John Rolfe "and to his friends" (as even John Smith would concede) that

Pocahontas "was taught to speake such English as might well bee understood, well instructed in Christianitie. . . ."

The governor and the minister undoubtedly welcomed Rolfe's cooperation in their holy mission: "For, after all that can be said" (and would be said, at the turn of the century, by Virginia's Colonel William Byrd II—with, very probably, this very case in mind), "a sprightly lover is the most prevailing missionary that can be sent amongst these or any other infidels."

"What shoulde I doe?" Rolfe would cry out in his soul-searching trial and tribulation, inquiring of himself and of Sir Thomas Dale, his commanding officer,

> shall I be of soe an untoward a disposicon to refuse to leade the blynde into the right waye? shall I be soe unnaturall not to gyve breade to the hungry, or soe uncharitable not to Cover the naked?*

Not that "the naked," in this instance, was not covered. Yet not all the yards of cambric, not all the whalebone, could conceal the natural grace with which Pocahontas moved: her physical attractions were remarked by Rolfe, moved him to concupiscence ("these passions of my troubled Soule," he called them), to consuming carnal desire— "the unbridled desire of Carnall affection," to use his own words to describe his own sad state of emotional and moral turmoil. (He "underwent great torment and Pain," as William Stith would later empathetically recount Rolfe's temptation in the wilderness, "out of his violent Passion, and tender Sollicitude for her." Captain Smith, less empathetically than Stith, one suspects, refers to "the strange apparitions and violent passions he [Rolfe] endured for her love. . . .")

If the widower Rolfe found himself irresistibly attracted to the exotic creature with whom fate had thrown him into a dangerous propinquity, he was convinced that she was not indifferent to him, but responded warmly to his discreet advances; he speaks, in his famous letter to Dale, of her "greate apparance of love to me." Whiteness had exerted a fatal fascination upon her, apparently, from the first day she laid eyes upon the first white man of her acquaintance—the day she had been moved to save Captain Smith's life at the altar-stone. From that first encounter, she had manifested a decided inclination, positive penchant for fair-skinned men.

---

* For the full text of Rolfe's letter, see Appendix C.

In 1609, it was John Smith to whom she had been so strongly attracted, so irresistibly drawn.

In 1613, it was John Rolfe who won her affections. In explanation of this transfer of affections from Smith to Rolfe, not even the layman in psychological theory has difficulty in recognizing that Pocahontas saw Rolfe as a reincarnation of Smith, that her marriage to Rolfe would be to recapture a lost love.

From the instant John Rolfe recognized his emotional involvement—"from the very instant that this beganne to roote it selfe within the secrett bosome of my hart," love rather than lust, as he insisted—his conscience, a Puritan conscience if one is to judge by his scriptural exegesis, caused him a veritable torment, day and night, waking and sleeping ("the many passions and sufferings wch I have daylie, howerly, yea in my sleepe endured"). In what he called "this my godly Conflict," he sought divine guidance in "dailye and earnest prayers," as he confessed by letter to Marshal Dale, a formal letter inscribed, "To you . . . (most noble Sr) the Patron and father of us in this Countrye," wherein he set forth his honorable intentions toward the marshal's Indian ward, and requested official authorization to take her as his bride.

Rolfe was, to quote him verbatim, "in love." Which is how his friend Captain Ralph Hamor saw him: "Long before this time, a gentleman of approved behaviour and honest carriage, maister John Rolfe had bin in love with Pocahuntas and she with him."

The romance had flourished during months of close association and companionship—heads bent together over the Book of Common Prayer, the Bible, the Horn Book with its English alphabet—in the Henrico Church and the Rock Hall parsonage, at Dale's mansion; Rolfe refers to "the effects of my longe Contynued affection."

As a Biblical scholar, and a Calvinist (if one is to judge by his citation of that authority), Rolfe was well aware of the Old Testament injunction against the taking of strange wives: "Woe am I ignorant," as he would write to Sir Thomas Dale when finally he unburdened his soul, "of the heavy displeasure wch Almighty God Conceyved against the Sonnes of Levie and Israell for marrienge of straunge wyves. . . ." Rolfe could have quoted, chapter and verse, Ezra 10:2: "We have trespassed against our God, and have taken strange wives of the people of the land."[4]

Pocahontas—princess though she might be, Lady Rebecca though she might become after her christening, object of deferential treatment throughout the colony—could only be categorized as one of the biblically proscribed "strange wives of the people of the land," dark and sultry, voluptuous, forbidden, but perennially tempting to the fair Anglo-Saxon newcomer. Pocahontas was, as Philip Young suggests, the

> progenitress of all the "Dark Ladies" of our culture—all the erotic and joyous temptresses, the sensual, brunette heroines, whom our civilization (particularly our literature: Hawthorne, Cooper, Melville, and many others) has summoned up only to repress. John Smith is the first man on this continent known to have made this rejection; his refusal to embrace "the wild spirit" embodied in the girl was epic, and a precedent for centuries of denial.[5]

Rolfe would vigorously deny that it was any base carnal desire that motivated his decision to marry the dark lady at Henrico, would deny, too, that it was any "dark happiness in the flesh" he hankered after when he made his proposal of marriage to Pocahontas via Governor Dale. No, Rolfe protested in that interminable missive to the governor, "tis not my hungrye appetite to gorge my selfe with incontinencye," not to sate his lust upon a strange wife but to proselytize among the people of the land, that he proposed to take the Powhatan princess to wife. His protestations ring with the sense of mission that imbued the seventeenth-century English colonization movement, the mission to convert the heathen, to civilize the wilderness.

In disclaiming lust as his motivation, Rolfe even found it necessary, sad to say, to disparage the object of his affection's physical attractions: had it been merely a question of "suche desire," he might have satisfied it, he insists, "with Christians more pleasinge to the eye."

Rolfe likewise found it necessary—likewise, sad to say—to apologize to family and friends for the lady of his choice (or for his choice of a lady); he did not plan permanently to expatriate himself, and was not indifferent to censure of interracial marriage. Miscegenation was one of the ugliest words in the lexicon. Rolfe was very conscious of his status as a gentleman and loath to be criticized for having demeaned himself by marriage to a redskin savage. (He could not guess that the criticism to be leveled at him in England by his monarch would represent the directly opposite point of view.) "Nor am I in soe desperate estate," he points out,

> that I regarde not what becometh of me, nor am I out of hope but one daye to see my Countrye nor soe voyde of ffriends, nor meane in Birth but there to obtayne a matche to my greate content nor have I ignorantly passed over my hoapes there, or re-

gardlessly seeke to loose the love of my ffriends by taking this Course. . . .

This course of action implied no mad, headlong, reckless impetuosity on his part; smug, insular, caste-conscious, it was out of character for Rolfe to commit a grand folly. Rolfe respected the conventions, shared the racial and social prejudices of his day and time and class; now he implored the understanding of his friends and fellows, although he could not allow "the base feare of displeasinge the worlde" to keep him from his appointed task ("I will hartely accept it as a godly taxe appointed me").

After long months, perhaps even years, of widowerhood and celibacy, John Rolfe was perhaps reluctant to admit that the dusky maidens of the wildwood appeared less dusky than at first encounter. (To Italian Verrazano's eye, the redskins' skin-tone was "russet" or "brasse"; to Englishman William Strachey, it was "mulberry"; poet Vachel Lindsay's word is "rosy copper red"; poet Muriel Rukeyser's, "persimmon.") John Rolfe might well have said (along with the Pilgrim Hampden in Joseph Croswell's play, *A New World Planted*),

> I know she's browner far than European dames,
> But whiter far, than other natives are.

The problem of mixed marriage troubled the hero in Croswell's drama as it had John Rolfe in real life; playwright Croswell justified the marriage of the protagonist to an Indian princess (named Pocahonta) by making her a distinguished person, daughter of a chieftain, noble, beautiful, intelligent.

If Rolfe's real-life princess's endowments were equally notable, Rolfe would further justify his marriage by Christianizing, civilizing, Anglicizing her—eliminating all the wild, the gamy elements of her personality; bleaching her out, so to speak, to approximate a Caucasian, thus exorcising the stigma of an interracial union.

There can be no question but that Rolfe met with encouragement from Reverend Whitaker, without whose sanction he would not have been free to frequent the parsonage, to visit Pocahontas, and assist her in her study of the English language and the Bible. And Governor Dale must have made clear from the beginning his approbation of a courtship involving an important political prisoner, else the rector would never have given Rolfe access to her, would never have facilitated the frequent meetings whereby friendship ripened into love.

The matter, evidently, was discussed by the three of them, as

Rolfe makes clear when he writes: "And thus with my readinge and conference with honest and religious psones have I receaved noe small incouragement."

In the last analysis, however, it was within his own soul that Rolfe's dilemma had to be resolved, in solitude that the interior debate most hotly raged: "a mighty warre in my medytacons," by his own characterization; agonizing, he had "throughly tryed & pared" his "thoughts even to the Quicke."

That of which he most wanted to convince Dale—and himself— was that his heart was pure, his motives lofty; that his proposed union with a "straunge" wife was indeed

> for the good of the Plantacon, the honor of or Countrye, for the glorye of God, for myne owne salvacon, and for the Convertinge to the true knowledge of God and Iesus Christ an unbelievinge Creature, namely Pohahuntas. To whom⁰ my hart and best thoughts are and have byn a longe tyme soe intangled & inthralled in soe intricate a Laborinth that I was even awearied to unwynde my selfe thereout.

If there are passages in Rolfe's letter that alienate the twentieth-century audience by their cant and arrogance, this particular passage reminds the reader that the Puritan ethic condemned both sex and beauty.

But the sharpest pang Rolfe suffered was the nagging fear that the inspiration to this union might have been demonic rather than divine: was it God or Satan? he asked himself, who did

> provoke me to be in love with one, whose education hath byn rude, her manners barbarous, her generacon Cursed, and soe discrepant in all nutriture from my selfe, that often tymes with feare and tremblinge I have ended my pryvate Controversie with this, Surely theise are wicked instigations hatched by him whoe seeketh and delighteth in mans distruction. And soe with fervent prayers to be ever preserved from such diabolicall assaults I have taken some rest. . . .

Diabolical assaults were a reality: the Devil was no abstraction to men of the Reformation; had he not goaded Luther into hurling that famous ink-pot? The Devil was as much alive to the seventeenth-century Protestant mind as to the medieval Catholic. The first Americans explained every occurrence in terms of the familiar dichotomy of good and evil, of God and Satan, the one or the other responsible for every happening, every event—the hoof of Satan discernible in every disaster, every temptation; the hand of God visible in every blessing, every miracle of deliverance. The precariousness of life in the wilderness served to intensify the fears and superstitions of the adventurers; the skies and waters were scanned for signs, omens, portents, for a flaming comet or a hurricane or a monstrous beast.

To determine whether the forces of good or evil were impelling him to take this strange wife, Rolfe had recourse to a trial separation in order to determine whether—out of range of the strong physical attraction she exerted upon him—he would waver in his high resolve. He did not waver: not "even when shee hath byn farthest sepa[ra]ted from me, wch in Comon reason (were it not an undoubted woorke of god) might breede a forgettfullness of a farre more woorthy Creature. . . ."

The conviction that it was "an undoubted woorke of god" came, at last, to a sorely tried Rolfe, along with the conviction that the union would redound to the glory of both God and country: to bring Pocahontas into submission to Christ and to bring Powhatan into submission to James I must fulfill the fondest hopes of English patriots, zealous Christians: to claim the first heathen soul in Virginia—so noble a soul as Pocahontas's!—for Christianity, to effect a reconciliation between the races through love and marriage, to bring about a peace between red men and white in Virginia as a consequence of the union between Englishman and Powhatan princess constituted "soe good effects that yor selfe" (Dale, that is, to whom Rolfe wrote) "and all the worlde maye truely saye, this is ye woorke of God and merveilous in our eyes."

The time had come for an official pronouncement on a matter so weighty, so politically significant. Rolfe quite properly addressed himself to the colony's deputy governor, none other than Sir Thomas Dale, upon whom the high command had devolved after the departure of Sir Thomas Gates in the early spring of 1614.

> Howebeit I freely subject myselfe to yor grave & mature Judgement, deliberacon, approbacon, and determynacon . . . either pswadinge me to desist, or encouraginge me to psist herein. . . .

To persist rather than to desist was evidently Dale's counsel to Rolfe. Else the governor would never have included Pocahontas's suitor in the party he assembled in April of 1614, to accompany the Powhatan princess on a visit to her chieftain-father.

"Sir Thomas Gates having imbarqued himselfe for England" (as Dale described events in a letter to London dated June 16, 1614),

> I put my selfe into Captaine Argalls ship, with a hundred and fifty men in my frigot, and other boats went into Pamaunkie river, where Powhatan hath his residence, and can in two or three daies, draw a thousand men togeather, with me I carried his daughter, who had been long prisoner with us.

Despite the fact that his beloved daughter was being held hostage by the English, no word, no sign had come from Powhatan in many months, no further reply to the English ransom demands.

The flotilla rode at anchor in the Pamunkey, uneasy at the unnatural silence on the river: nothing stirred in the green depths of the forest, no footfall disturbed the sandy beaches; no pole, no paddle rippled the waters.

Powhatan let them wait a short while longer.

"It was a day or two before we heard of them," Dale reported: "At length they demaunded why we came."

> I gave for answere that I came to bring him his daughter, conditionally he would (as had been agreed upon for her ransome) render all the armes, tooles, swords, and men that had runne away, and give me a ship full of corne for the wrong he had done unto us: if they would doe this, we would be friends, if not burne all. . . .

Take it or leave it.

In reply to Dale's ultimatum, Powhatan's emissaries "demaunded time to send to their King," who was apparently cautiously keeping his distance.

To this request for "time," Dale assented—two hostages having been exchanged as pledge of good intentions on both sides, Dale's "two men" detailed "to carrie" his "message to Powhatan."

It developed that "the great King was three daies journey off," but that his brother "Opochankano was hard by, to whom they would have had them deliver their message, saying, that what he agreed upon and did, the great King would confirme."

There is plausibility to the theory that Powhatan had disqualified himself from negotiations in which he could not trust himself to put the best interests of his people above the best interests of his favorite daughter. No less plausible is the theory that he had been disqualified by the tribal council which was mistrustful of his judgment where his so dearly beloved daughter was concerned.

Chief Opechancanough—important not only as Powhatan's brother and successor to the chieftaincy of the confederacy but also in his own right, as chieftain of the powerful Pamunkey tribe and leader of the confederacy's militants—may well have forced Powhatan's hand in that particular situation.

"This Opocankano," Dale acknowledged,

> is brother to Powhatan, and is his and their chiefe Captaine: and one that can as soone (if not sooner) as Powhatan commaund the men. But my men refused to doe my message unto any save Powhatan, so they were brought back, and I sent theirs [their hostages] to them.

The tension exploded into overt acts of war:

> so as we went ashore they shot at us, we were not behinde hand with them, killed some, hurt others, marched into the Land, burnt their houses, tooke their corne, and quartered all night ashoare.

"The next day we went further up the River." The Indians never let the flotilla out of sight: "they dogged us, and called to know whither we went; wee answered, To burne all, if they would not doe as we demaunded, and had beene agreed upon. . . ."

There was a semblance of compliance:

> They would they said, bring all the next day so wee forbare all hostilitie, went ashoare, their men in good numbers comming amongst us, but we were very cautious, and stood to our Armes.

At this point, Governor Dale and Captain Argall decided to allow their hostage to show herself on the deck, even on the shore, although her demeanor was to prove strange in the extreme.

> The Kings daughter went ashoare, but would not talke to any of them, scarce to them of the best sort, and to them onely, that if her father had loved her, he would not value her lesse then old Swords, Peeces, or Axes: wherefore shee should still dwell with the English men, who loved her.*

---

* "And now she had no Manner of Desire," as William Stith's *History* tells the story, "to return to her Father; neither could she well endure the brutish Manners, or Society, of her own Nation."

Powhatan was finally roused to reply, taking negotiations out of Opechancanough's hands:

> At last came one from Powhatan, who told us our Swords, and Tooles within fifteene dayes, should be sent to James Towne, with some Corne, and that his daughter should be my child, and ever dwell with mee, desiring to be ever friends, and named such of his people, and neighbour Kings, as hee desired to be included and have the benefit of the peace, promising if any of our men came to him, without leave from mee, he would send them backe; and that if any of his men stale from us, or killed our cattell, hee would send them to us to bee punished as wee thought fit. With these conditions wee returned, and within the time limitted, part of our Armes were sent, and twentie men with Corne, and promised more, which he hath also sent. . . .

Wily Opechancanough appeared to assent to the *volte face* in policy: Dale took his assent at face value:

> *Opachankano* desired I would call him friend, and that he might call me so, saying, Hee was a great Captaine, and did alwayes fight: that I was also a great Captaine, and therefore he loved mee; and that my friends should bee his friends. So the bargaine was made, and every eight or ten dayes, I have messages and presents from him, with many appearances that he much desireth to continue friendship.
>
> Now you may judge, Sir, [Dale was addressing the Bishop of London] if the God of Battailes had not a helping hand in this, that having our Swords drawne, killing their men, burning their houses, and taking their corne: yet they tendred us peace . . . by which many benefits arise unto us. First, part of our Armes . . . redelivered, some repaire to our Honor. Our cattell to increase, without danger of destroying, our men at libertie to hunt freely for Venison, to fish, to doe anything else, or goe any whither without danger; to follow the husbanding of our corne securely, whereof we have about five hundred Acres set. . . . And which is not the least materially, wee may by this peace come to discover the Country better. . . .

It was to be known as the Peace of Pocahontas. If it did not last forever, it lasted her lifetime.

In this Peace, John Rolfe played a part. Governor Dale's choice of John Rolfe as one of the emissaries to Powhatan struck Rolfe's friend

Captain Hamor as eminently appropriate—Rolfe, by then, was openly acknowledged as the fiancé of Powhatan's daughter, Pocahontas.

It was at this juncture, according to Hamor, that John Rolfe made formal application to the deputy governor of the colony for the hand of Pocahontas, for official permission to wed the celebrated hostage.

It may have been that Rolfe, confronted with the possibility of losing Pocahontas if she was returned to her people in the course of the ransom negotiations, was startled into making the final formal demand for her hand in marriage, although it seems far more likely that he had been planning that move with Hamor, Dale, and Whitaker over the past several months.

According to Hamor, it was he himself who—at the very hour of the parley on the Pamunkey—presented Rolfe's petition to Marshal Dale:

> which thing at the instant that we were in parlee with them, my selfe made known to Sir Thomas Dale by a letter from him, whereby he intreated his advise and furtherance in his love, if so it seemed fit to him for the good of the Plantation.

At the self-same hour, Pocahontas was left to impart the news to her family: "and Pocahontas her selfe acquainted her brethren therewith."*

Governor Dale's approval was a foregone conclusion:

> which resolution Sir Thomas Dale wel approving, was the onely cause hee was so milde amongst them, who otherwise would not have departed their river without other conditions.

Powhatan's approval of the match might have been less confidently expected. His reaction to the news was anxiously awaited in the English camp. It came speedily, and it was favorable:

> The bruite of this pretended marriage came soone to Powhatans knowledge, a thing acceptable to him, as appeared by his sudden consent thereunto. . . .

---

* Hamor's *True Discourse* tells us that "two of Powhatans sonnes being very desirous to see their sister who was there present ashore with us, came unto us, at the sight of whom, and her well fare, whom they suspected to be worse intreated, though they had often heard the contrary, they much rejoyced, and promised that they would undoubtedly perswade their father to redeem her, and to conclude a firme peace forever with us. . . ."

CHAPTER X

To Pocahontas

Why, sweet Nymph, that heart-fetch'd sigh,
Which thy heaving bosom rends?
Whence that pensive, down-cast eye,
Whose magic glance soft transport sends!

Sure thy roving thoughts recal,
A faithless Lover to thy mind;
Whose heart thy charms did once enthrall,
But now inconstant as the wind.

Ah! disclaim his fickle love,
Take some more deserving swain;
The tale he whisper'd in the grove,
Heed not when he tells again.

JOHN DAVIS, *Travels of Four*
Years and a Half in the United
States of America During 1798,
1799, 1800, 1801, 1802

THE UNITED STATES OF AMERICA had been united only briefly when a young Englishman named John Davis set out to cross them on foot. Peripatetic, romantic, literarily prolific, Davis found material for four novels in the Pocahontas-Smith-Rolfe triangle. Davis's novel (entitled *Travels of Four Years and a Half in the United States of America*) would have us believe that Master John Rolfe wooed his Indian bride upon what she believed to be the grave of Captain John Smith! In Davis's version of the Pocahontas-Smith interlude, Captain Smith had craftily "devised an expedient" to "cure her of her passion." He embarked

> privately for England, and enjoined the Colonists . . . to represent that he was dead; for Smith knew the mischief every woman feels an impulse to perpetrate whose passion has been scorned; but he also remembered the position, that where there was no hope there could be no longer love; and the breast, which knowing him to be living, would glow with an impatience of revenge, would, on the belief of his death, be accessible only to the softness of sorrow. The project of our adventurer was founded on an acquaintance with the human heart; for when Pocahontas again, under pretence of carrying provisions to the fort, gratified her secret longing to meet her beloved Englishman, she yielded to every bitterness of anguish on hearing of his death.

She "prostrated herself on the pretended grave, beat her bosom, and uttered the most piercing cries."

"Though the breast of Rolfe possessed not the ambition of Smith," as Davis compares the two Englishmen who played on Pocahontas's affections, "it was infinitely more accessible to the softer emotions." (Davis's obsession with breasts and bosoms is already discernible: those of his redskin females are usually described as "throbbing," "heaving," or "in convulsive throes.") According to Davis, John Rolfe

> beheld with interest the tender sentiments which Pocahontas cherished for Captain Smith . . . and his own heart became infected with a violent passion. . . . He wandered dejected by moon-light along the banks of the river; and he who once was remarked for dressing himself with studied elegance, now walked about with his stockings ungartered. . . .
>
> The mind of Rolfe warmed with the ideal caresses of Pocahontas, produced often in his walks a poem to his Indian beauty. Of these effusions, I have three in my possession; they rise, I think, above mediocrity. . . .

Davis published Rolfe's verses in his novels: if they rose, in his estimation, above mediocrity, it was because they were the product of his own pen! The first of the three, indited "To Pocahontas," begins with the inquiry,

> Why, sweet Nymph, that heart-fetch'd sigh,
> Which thy heaving bosom rends?

The second of the three "effusions" Davis credits to Rolfe is likewise titled "To Pocahontas" ("But more than mortal is the bliss / Of him who ravishes a kiss /In playful dalliance; from those lips"). "The third and last poem of Mr. Rolfe," John Davis tells us unblushingly, "was produced on the banks of the river Powhatan" ("Here as I pensive wander through the glade / I sight and call upon my Indian Maid," / "Thy form, O! Pocahontas, fills my mind," etcetera).

It was during one of those nights when Mr. Rolfe was sitting woe-begone under an oak, sighing and groaning, and coupling love with dove, that a foot wandering among the trees disturbed his profound thoughts. . . . It was SHE! It was Pocahontas strewing flowers over the imaginary grave of Captain Smith. Overcome with terror and surprize, to be thus discovered by a stranger, the powers of life were suspended, and she sunk into the arms of Rolfe. . . . The impassioned youth clasped the Indian Maid to his beating heart, and drank from her lips the poison of delight. The breast of a woman is, perhaps, never more susceptible of a new passion than when it is agitated by the remains of a former one. When Pocahontas recovered from her confusion, a blush burnt on her cheek to find herself in the arms of a man; but when Rolfe threw himself before her on his knees, and clasping his hands to the moon, discovered the emotions that had so long filled his breast, the afflicted girl suffered him to wipe the tear from her eye that overflowed with sorrow, and no longer repulsed the ardour of his caresses. The day was now breaking on the summits of the mountains in the East; the song of the mocking-bird was become faint. . . . Pocahontas urged to go; but Rolfe still breathed in her ear the music of his vows, as he held her in his arms, or still rioted in the draught of intoxication from her lips. . . .

If Davis's fictional John Rolfe "rioted in the draught of intoxication from her lips," the real John Rolfe sedulously avoided any mention thereof in drafting his letter to Governor Dale: no good Puritan, no decent seventeenth-century Protestant would admit of delight in sex or beauty. (When John Winthrop of Massachusetts lost his young wife, he saw a connection between her attractions and her early death: "It made me delight too much in her to enjoy her long" was how he stated it, and his contemporary, John Rolfe, would have thoroughly understood his meaning.) The consciousness of original sin, of sin in sex—even marital sex—would have been one a Puritan husband would have needed promptly to inculcate in a pagan wife totally devoid of such consciousness.

Captain Hamor resented the widespread criticism that greeted Rolfe's marriage to a once-naked redskin heathen, and defended his friend for having crossed the color line. To clarify Rolfe's motives in making such a marriage, Hamor decided—on his own, without consulting Rolfe on the matter—to publish Rolfe's controversial letter to Dale in his (Hamor's) *True Discourse*, introducing it thus:

> And least any man should conceive that some sinister respects allured him hereunto, I have made bold contrary to his knowledge in the end of my treatise to insert the true coppie of his letter, written to Sir Thomas Dale to acquaint him with his proceedings, and purpose therein, the rather to give testimony to the misconstruing and ill censuring multitude of his integritie, in the undertaking a matter of so great a consequent, who in my hearing have not spared to speak their pleasures. . . .

Rolfe's letter constituted his best defense against racist censure of English society: "his owne letter hits them home, and the better sort, who know to censure judiciously cannot but highly commend and approve so worthy and undertaking." (One can only hope that Rolfe's letter, as published in Hamor's treatise in 1614, never came into Pocahontas's hands. Even the most primitive feminine vanity must have been offended.)

Rolfe may have envisioned himself and his high-born Indian bride as setting a precedent of love to transcend the barriers of race, a precedent of marriage to reconcile the races, to accommodate the Old World to the New, to bring the pagan to Christianity—assimilation and conversion through wedlock.

It was not, at that historical juncture, an impossible dream. Sex has always provided the most effective means of interracial communication. A century after Rolfe's noble experiment, two distinguished Virginians, Robert Beverley and Colonel William Byrd II, were still propounding assimilation of the native red man by the invading white through intermarriage. As late as the early eighteenth century, marriage between Indians and whites represented the great hope for saving the savage of the New World for the Old World's God and civilization.

"Intermarriage had been indeed the Method proposed very often by the Indians in the Beginning, urging it frequently as a certain Rule that the English were not their Friends, if they refused it," according to Robert Beverley. It is significant that the attitude of tolerance toward intermarriage in the colony was changing at that very hour: Beverley's pro-integration passage was deleted from the 1722 edition of his 1705 *History and Present State of Virginia.* "And I can't but think," he wrote in 1705,

> it would have been happy for that Country, had they embraced this Proposal. For, the Jealousie of the Indians, which I take to be the Cause of most of the Rapines and Murders they committed, wou'd by this Means have been altogether prevented, and consequently the Abundance of Blood that was shed on both sides wou'd have been saved; the great Extremities they were so often reduced to, by which so many died, wou'd not have happen'd; the Colony, instead of all these Losses of Men on both Sides, wou'd have been encreasing in Children to its Advantage . . . and, in all Likelihood, many, if not most of the Indians would have been converted to Christianity by this kind Method. . . .

"For my part," wrote Colonel William Byrd II of Westover, second of that distinguished line in the colony, as proud of his library as of his plantation, "I must be of opinion . . . that there is but one way of converting these poor infidels and reclaiming them from barbarity, and that is charitably to intermarry with them. . . ."

As unorthodox as the notion may have seemed to the Puritans of New England (where miscegenation was consistently discouraged), Colonel Byrd believed that intermarriage would have brought political and social as well as religious advantages to the hard-pressed colonies: "the poor Indians would have had less reason to complain that the English took away their land if they had received it by way of a portion with their daughters." Elsewhere the enlightened Virginian planter had remarked that, "morals and all considered, I cannot think the Indians were much greater heathens than the first adventurers, who, had they been good Christians, would have had the charity to take this only method of converting the natives to Christianity." Doubtless Rolfe's thinking was along the lines that Byrd and Beverley articulated a very few generations later.

Rolfe's decision to wed once taken, Dale's approval once besought and bestowed, notification was given to Powhatan, who was prompt to signify his approval: ". . . some ten daies after [, he] sent an olde uncle of hirs, named *Opachisco*, to give her as his deputy in the Church, and two of his sonnes to see the marriage solemnized, which was accordingly done about the first of Aprill," according to Hamor's *True Discourse*.

Pocahontas's venerable uncle was sent to Jamestown as Powhatan's deputy because the Supreme Chieftain "would not trust himself at her wedding" (if Beverley's account to that effect is trustworthy). The overlord of the confederacy had been consistent in his refusal to set foot in English territory: he had refused to go to Jamestown for his "coronation" in 1608, he refused to go there for his daughter's wedding in 1614. (This, at face value, would seem to be the purport of Beverley's 1705 account, although it is open to another interpretation: that Powhatan would have been too emotionally disturbed to witness his favorite child's public renunciation of her people and her gods. Her defection to the enemy might seal a peace between them and her people, but her father could not bear to stand witness to it.)

The new church at Jamestown was to be the scene for the wedding ceremony. It was a timber-and-frame edifice (as compared to the original "cruck" church of 1607, described by Captain Smith as covered with rushes, boards, and earth); it was some sixty feet by twenty-four in size, boasting casements on hinges and, at the west end, two bells, and had been erected in 1610, at Lord De La Warre's instruction, outside the original palisaded fort area.

Although no hard facts are available, it is generally assumed that it was the Reverend Richard Bucke, the rector of Jamestown and senior prelate of the colony, who officiated at the altar, uniting the celebrated pair according to the Church of England ritual. It would have been only natural for the bridegroom to turn to an old and trusted friend on so momentous an occasion: Bucke and Rolfe had been shipmates on that tempest-tossed *Sea Venture* crossing of 1609; Bucke had christened the Rolfes' daughter, Bermuda, shortly after her birth, shortly before her death, on that island; Bucke would be called to witness Rolfe's last will and testament. Bucke was, in Rolfe's words, "a verie good preacher."

On the other hand, it was true that it was the Reverend Alexander Whitaker who had taken the illustrious captive under his care and tutelage at the Rock Hall Parsonage, Whitaker who had undertaken her education and conversion, Whitaker who had—presumably in the church at Henrico—baptized her.

But it may be that the two ministers presided jointly at both ceremonies. Whitaker, writing his cousin, describes both sacraments in one sentence: "But that which is best, one *Pocahontas* or *Matoa*, the daughter of *Powhatan*, is married to an honest and descreet English gentleman, Maister Rolfe, confessed the faith of Jesus Christ, and was baptized."

If Whitaker gave his patron, Sir Thomas Dale, full credit for the work in the vineyard of the Lord as in the colony of the King, Dale did not, himself, disclaim it, pointing out to the London bigwigs that it was on his authority that "Powhatans daughter" had been

> caused to be carefully instructed in Christian Religion . . . baptized . . . and since married to an English Gentleman of good understanding (as by his Letter unto me, containing the reasons for his marriage of her you may perceive). . . . Her Father and friends gave approbation to it, and her Uncle gave her to him in the Church. . . .

The bridegroom slipped the wedding ring upon the finger of the bride, saying "With this ring, I thee wed"; pronounced the words, "With my body, I thee worship. . . ."

The marriage constituted, in Governor Dale's opinion, "another knot to binde this peace the stronger."

The marriage ushered in the Peace of Pocahontas, as it came to be known in the colony—literally and figuratively, a honeymoon between the races.

"Pocahontas being thus married in the Year 1613" (Robert Beverley, writing in 1704 or 1705, confused the date of the wedding, making it a year earlier than it was, a date incontrovertibly established as 1614), "a firm Peace was concluded with her Father, tho' he would not trust himself at her Wedding. Both the English and the Indians thought themselves intirely secure and quiet."[1]

Given Powhatan's astuteness as a leader, and his great dedication to the welfare of his own tribe and the other tribes of the Powhatan Confederacy over which he ruled, it is unlikely that—however great his attachment to the daughter married to a white man—he would have entered into a peace with the whites for reasons of sentiment. Harmony during the years of this peace was possible because enough land still remained in the area to satisfy the needs and way of life of both the native and the invader. Territory lost by the Powhatans to the English along the James River could be offset by expansion to the west, into a virtually unoccupied strip of land—one to ten or twelve miles wide—a no-man's-land that ran east of the fall-line, the full length of the confederacy's holdings, a barrier between the tidewater Powhatans and their traditional enemies of the Virginia piedmont, the Monacans and Manahoacs. One of the unsentimental reasons for Powhatan's receptiveness to a period of peace with the English was that it allowed him time to take action against his ancient piedmont enemies; although no historical data is available on that score, there is conjecture to the effect that the Powhatan Confederacy played its part in the downfall of those Siouan-speaking tribes to the west.[2] It was the best interests of his people that inclined Powhatan toward a peaceful solution—if only a temporary one—with the English: the sprawling confederacy which he had been building at the hour of the English landings needed further solidification.

The period of détente that followed Pocahontas's marriage to John Rolfe in April, 1614, was one for which not only Governor Dale but Captain Ralph Hamor, too, wanted credit. If Rolfe chose a best man for the wedding, it must have been Hamor, the friend who had encouraged Rolfe's romantic leanings, who had acted as intermediary between the suitor and the governor.

The marriage ceremony was performed "about the first of Aprill," as Hamor noted in his *Discourse*, "and ever since we have had friendly commerce and trade, not onely with Powhatan himselfe, but also with his subjects round about us; so as now I see no reason why the Collonie should not thrive a pace."

Even independent tribes, such as the Englishmen's immediate neighbors, the Chickahominies, now showed a disposition to be friendly:

Besides this, by the meanes of Powhatan, we became in league with our next neighbours, the Chicahaminias, a lustie and a daring people, free of themselves [not subject, that is, to the confederacy]. "These people, so soone as they heard of or peace with Powhatan, sent two messengers with presents to Sir Thomas Dale, and offered [their] service, excusing all former injuries, hereafter they would ever be King James his subjects. . . .

As for the bridegroom whose nuptials had ushered in an era of peace for the colony—he himself voiced the general rejoicing at the termination of hostilities: "Whereupon"—upon his nuptials—

a peace was concluded, which still continueth so firme, that our people yearely plant and reape quietly, and travell in the woods a fowling and a hunting as freely and securely from feare of danger or treacherie as in England.

What satisfaction Rolfe must have experienced, what justification for his daring action, as he addressed his *True Relation of the State of Virginia** to his sovereign in 1616:

> The great blessings of God have followed this peace, and it, next under him, hath bredd our plentie—everie man sitting under his fig tree in safety, gathering and reaping the fruits of their labors with much joy and comfort. . . .

The fig tree under which John Rolfe sat in safety with his Indian bride flourished in the rich soil of Varina Plantation on the banks of the James River near Dale's new "city" of Henrico—or so Virginia tradition vigorously asserts. No records substantiate the tradition: early records show other holdings of John Rolfe's (a property patented downriver on the south bank, another large parcel of land on Mulberry Island close to Chesapeake Bay), but Varina House in Henrico County is, to this day, identified as the Rolfes' honeymoon cottage, and Varina Farm—the surrounding acreage—as the site of Rolfe's earliest tobacco-culture experiments, the name "Varina" being the English designation for the top-grade leaf of the Spanish tobacco trade. (The house standing there today is a large, square two-story brick building with four chimneys; the old section of the house—the part associated with the Rolfes—consists of a wing attached by a long passage to the present mansion.) Varina was the gift—again according to tradition current in Virginia—of the Supreme Chieftain Powhatan to his favorite daughter on the occasion of her marriage; a gift of land, among the Indians, was traditionally signified by delivering a basket filled with soil from the gift property.

Wherever their land and house, whether at Varina or on Mulberry Island or Hog Island, the Rolfes lived happily, according to Sir Thomas Dale: "She lives civilly and lovingly with him, and I trust will increase in goodnesse, as the knowledge of God increaseth in her." To live "civilly," by Dale's definition, was to observe the amenities, the mores and manners of the English society of that day and time: to dress, to keep house, to attend divine services, to deport herself in decorous seventeenth-century English fashion.

To live "lovingly" with a man in the seventeenth-century term of reference could have differed little from that term of reference in the

---

* Rolfe's *True Relation of the State of Virginia in 1616* was published in 1617 by his new-found friend, the Reverend Samuel Purchas, paraphrased and incorporated into the third edition of Purchas's *Pilgrimage*, a highly successful anthology of early travel narratives.

twentieth: when Governor Dale declares that Pocahontas lived "loving-ly" with John Rolfe, he could only have meant that their marital relation was characterized by tenderness and affection, that it was clear to an observer on a footing of intimacy in the household that the pair dwelt harmoniously and fondly—even passionately—together. Captain John Smith (though far removed from the honeymoon scene: in England in 1613, in New England on a journey of exploration and mapping in 1614) comments in his *Generall Historie* of 1624 on "the true affection she constantly bare her husband"; it "was much." And as for John Rolfe, "the strange and violent passions he endured for her love, as he deeply protested, was wonderful. . . ."* Smith's conclusions are based upon "a Letter written by Sir Thomas Dale, another by Master Whitaker, and a third by Master John Rolfe." Smith cannot be expected to be an entirely objective witness on the matter of the transfer of Pocahontas's affections to another. His choice of words is interesting: he characterizes Pocahontas's emotion toward Rolfe as a mild—if "true" —"affection," in striking contrast to the "violent passions" possessing Rolfe.

Better surely to marry than to burn, Smith seems to be saying, but to marry and still to burn may still be sinful. A Puritan husband was expected to betake himself to the marriage bed for the purpose of pro-creation, not for rapture and delight—whether or not an Indian mate could be persuaded to that point of view.

A child was conceived in the Rolfes' marriage-bed in the months following their April wedding, born within a year of that date, some-time in the late winter or early spring of 1615: a boy, christened Thomas, presumably in honor of Sir Thomas Dale.

The connubial bliss of his protégés may have been what stimulated Sir Thomas to seek a Powhatan princess for his own couch. Dale em-ployed none other than Captain Hamor—to act as emissary to Powhatan in the spring of 1614 to procure him such a mate: "It pleased Sir Thomas Dale," Hamor wrote in his *True Discourse*, and it pleased Hamor ("my selfe being much desirous before my returne for England, to visit Pow-hatan & his Court, because I would be able to speak somewhat thereof by mine own knowledge")

to imploy myselfe, and an english boy for my Interpreter on[e] Thomas Salvage (who had lived three yeers with Powhatan,

---

* Smith would have been familiar with Rolfe's "deep" protests from a reading of Rolfe's letter to Dale, included in Hamor's *True Discourse*, published in London in pamphlet form in 1615.

speakes the language naturally, one whom Powhatan much affecteth) upon a message unto him, which was to deale with him, if by any meanes I might procure a daughter of his, who (Pocahuntas being already in our possession) is generally reported to be his delight and darling, and surely he esteemeth her as his owne soule) for surer pledge of peace. . . .

I departed the fifteenth of May early in the morning with the English boy, and two Indian guides . . . and came to his court or residence (as I judge some three score miles distant from us, being seated at the head almost of Pamaunkie River, at a towne called Matchot) the next night after, about twelve of the clocke, the former night lodging in the open woods, feareles and without daunger; when we were come opposite to his Towne, the maine river betweene him and us, least at any time we should martch by land unto him undiscovered: my Indian guides called for a Canoa (a boate made onely of one tree, after the fashion of a hollow trough) to transport us, giving them to know that there was two English sent upon businesse to Powhatan from the English Weroance, which once knowne, a Canoa was presently sent, and we ferried over, Powhatan himselfe attending at the landing place to welcome us.

Powhatan's greathouse was close by, "not full a stones cast from the waterside," the outside "guarded with an hundred bowmen, with their quivers of arrowes at their backes, which at all times, & places attend his person." Once within, Hamor reports, the Supreme Chieftain ensconced himself in state to receive the delegation from Jamestown:

himselfe sat downe on his bedsteade side. . . . On each hand of him was placed a comely and personable young woman, not twenty yeeres old the eldest, which they call his Queenes. . . . The first thing hee offered us was a pipe of Tobacco . . . whereof himselfe first dranke, and then gave it to me, and when I had drank what I pleased, I returned his pipe, which with his owne hands he vouchsafed to take from me.

The ritual of welcome complete, the parley could begin:

then began he to inquire how his Brother Sir Thomas Dale fared, after that of his daughters welfare, her mariage, his unknowne sonne, and how they liked lived and loved together: I resolved him that his brother was very well, and his daughter so well

content that she would not change her life to returne and live
with him, whereat he laughed heartily, and said he was very glad
of it.

—a reaction perhaps typical of the permissiveness that had always
characterized his relation with his daughter and encouraged her defiance
of parental authority.

In the face of the ungracious message from his daughter, Powhatan
sent gifts to her and to his son-in-law via the two Englishmen: "he gave
each of us a Bucks skin as well dressed as could be" ("white as snow,"
Hamor describes them elsewhere) "and sent two more to his sonne and
daughter. . . ."

Once the exchange of gifts—Powhatan's to Hamor and to Savage,
to Pocahontas and John Rolfe; Dale's via Hamor to Powhatan—had
been accomplished, Captain Hamor could proceed, through his interpreter, to the official business: first, the delivery of Dale's message to
the chief: "Sir Thomas Dale, your Brother, the principal commander of
the English men, sends you greetings of love and peace," Hamor intoned
ceremoniously, and then got down to particulars:

> The bruite of the exquisite perfection of your yongest daughter,
> being famous through all your territories, hath come to the hear-
> ing of your Brother Sir Thomas Dale, who for this purpose hath
> addressed me hither, to intreate you by that brotherly friendship,
> you make profession of, to permit her (with me) to returne unto
> him, partly for the desire which himselfe hath, and partly for the
> desire her sister hath to see her of whom, if fame hath not been
> prodigall . . . your brother (by your favour) would gladly make
> his neerest companion, wife and bedfellow. . . .

Powhatan graciously acknowledged the compliments of Sir
Thomas, replying,

> I gladly accept your Kings salute of love & peace. But to the
> purpose, my daughter whom my brother desireth, I sould within
> these few daies to be wife to a great Weroance for two bushels of
> Roanoake (a small kind of beades made of oystershels, which
> they use and passe one to another, as we doe money) . . . and it is
> true she is already gone with him three daies jorney from me. . . .

Powhatan, in declining Dale's offer, was no less artfully deceptive
than Dale in making it: the governor could not have "intended to

marry" the Indian princess whose hand he ostensibly sought. There was already a Lady Dale, in England, very much alive (if not well enough to have come to the wilds of America with her lawful husband).

Hamor made a valiant effort to persuade Powhatan to renege on the marriage contract on the excuse that the little princess was not yet "full twelve yeeres old, and therefore not marriageable." As for the bride price, the two bushels of Roanoke already paid to Powhatan, that could be returned to the "great Weroance," on the assurance that Governor Dale would "treble the price of his daughter, in beades, Copper, Hatchets and many other things more usefull for him. . . ."

Powhatan was proof against all persuasion:

> His answere hereunto was, that he loved his daughter as deere as his owne life, and though he had many Children, he delighted in none so much as in her, whom if he should not often beholde, he could not possibly live, which the living with us he knew he could not, having with himselfe resolved upon no termes whatsoever to put himselfe into our hands, or come amongst us, and therefore intreated me to urge that suite no further, but returne his brother this answer. . . .

This answer was that the English governor must content himself with one Powhatan princess; in Pocahontas, he already had his pledge of peace: "I desire no firmer assurance of his friendship, then his promise which he hath already made unto mee," said Powhatan;

> from mee, he hath a pledge, one of my daughters which so long as she lives shall be sufficient, when she dieth he shall have another childe of mine, but she yet liveth: I holde it not a brotherly part of your King, to desire to bereave me of two of my children at once. . . .

And from that position neither threat nor entreaty could budge him, although he made clear that his intentions were peaceful: Powhatan instructed Hamor to advise Dale

> that if he had no pledge at all, he should not neede to distrust any injurie from me, or any under my subjection, there have bin too many of his men and my killed, and by me occasion there shall never bee more . . . for I am now olde, and would gladly end my daies in peace, so as if the English offer me injury, my country is large enough, I will remove my selfe farther from you. . . .

What Powhatan could not foresee, in 1614, was that his country would not be large enough to accommodate the tobacco economy that was to result from the experiments being undertaken at that very hour by his son-in-law John Rolfe in the cultivation of that "golden weed." Virginia, thanks to Rolfe, would become a tobacco colony. Tobacco in Virginia would dominate and regulate colonial life to a greater degree than any other agricultural product of a modern community; tobacco would become an alternative currency in Virginia—bridal prices, the salaries of ministers and militia, even taxes paid in choice Virginia leaf.[3] Because tobacco is a spendthrift crop—a crop to "use up" the soil, to deplete and exhaust it rapidly—ever-new, ever-broader acreage would be required by the tobacco planters. In seventeenth-century Virginia, tobacco plantations averaged five thousand acres, the largest spread over thirty-seven thousand acres. (Colonel William Byrd II's land inheritance, in 1704, exceeded twenty-six thousand acres.) Insatiably land-hungry tobacco planters exercised a constant pressure on the coastal Indians' territories, pushing the native tribes ever farther into the interior.

To say merely that John Rolfe was industrious is not to do him justice: he was enterprising, imaginative, innovative. Shortly after his arrival on the James, he was struck by the idea that if the superior South American variety of tobacco—the "west-Indie *Trinidado*," as Hamor called it—could be successfully grown in the tidewater, it might prove to be the colony's first exportable commodity and the salvation of the colonial economy.

Once the idea entered his head, Rolfe promptly put it into operation, literally and figuratively dug into the sandy peninsula soil to plant his minuscule Trinidado seeds. Rolfe was not only a visionary; he was that rare combination, a man of vision and a man of action. If he is one of the most underrated, least appreciated of American folk-heroes, it may be because he was slighted, put down by the romantic nineteenth-century novelists, playwrights, and poets who concluded somewhat arbitrarily that Pocahontas had married the wrong man.

Captain Ralph Hamor wanted to make sure that his friend John Rolfe won recognition for introducing the highly profitable *Nicotiana tabacum* to the North American mainland, for experimenting with its culture and promoting its sale. "I may not forget the gentleman," Hamor wrote in his *True Discourse*,

> worthie of much commendations, which first tooke the pains to make triall thereof, his name Mr. John Rolfe, *Anno Domini* 1612, partly for the love he hath a long time borne unto it, and partly

to raise commodity to the adventurers, in whose behalfe I witnesse and vouchsafe to holde my testimony in beleefe, that during the time of his aboade there, which draweth neere upon sixe yeeres, no man hath laboured to his power, by good example there and worthy incouragement into England by his letters, then he hath done. . . .

If tobacco was to be King in Virginia, John Rolfe must be recognized as the Father of the King!

The precious seeds once in hand, Rolfe made "triall" of the planting, trying various depths, various distances from the river, various exposures, combinations of sun and shade; and he experimented with planting at various months of the spring.

The month of March or April would have been Pocahontas's suggestion to her husband as the best time to plant tobacco, the time traditional with the tribesmen of the tidewater. Although the cultivation of tobacco fell to the men of the tribe—it was the sole crop not raised by the women—Pocahontas must have possessed, and imparted to Rolfe, a great store of valuable information relative to its origin and culture, as developed from time immemorial by the red men. According to Virginia Indian tradition, tobacco came fourth in the order of creation: "The people of the South-parts of Virginia . . . say that God in the creation did first make a woman, then a man, thirdly great maize or Indian wheat [meaning corn], and fourthly, Tobacco. . . ."[4]

In view of her people's centuries-old experience with that crop, Pocahontas must have shared her husband's interest in that experimental tobacco patch laid out in their riverside garden. If he took advantage of his wife's knowledge of the ancient Indian practices, Rolfe would have chosen virgin ground, a recently cleared woodland tract with a sunny southern or southwestern exposure on a slope above a stream or river; he would have hilled the tobacco seed as the Indians did with both tobacco and corn.[5] Chances are that Rolfe would have adopted the Indian practice of "topping" the plant—removing the seed-head to concentrate nourishment in the leaves. ("Weed" is a misnomer: the tobacco plant is neither tough nor rank like a weed, but fragile, demanding what one tobacco expert calls "a kind of brooding care.")

Soil and climate favored Rolfe's experiment; the summer air of Virginia proved as balmy and propitious as that of the Caribbean: *Nicotiana tabacum* flourished in its new habitat, the James Valley; in the sandy loam of the Peninsula, the fragile seedlings shot up four or five inches in six to ten weeks.

To the North American Indian familiar only with the scrubby

native species (*Nicotiana rustica*), the import offered cause for astonishment, its stalk attaining a height of four to six feet (sometimes as much as nine feet, "taller than a tall man"), its leaves spreading broad and generous, a magnificent botanical specimen in comparison to the lowly —if hardy—native species.[6]

"Yt growes not fully a yard above grownd bearing a little yellow flower like to henn-bane," William Strachey wrote disdainfully of the local specimen in his *Historie of Travell*,

> whereas the best Tobacco of *Trinidado* and the *Oronoque*, is large sharpe and growing 2. or 3. yardes from the grownd, bearing a flower of the breadth of our Bel-flowers in England.

Not that the significant difference lay in the size or color of the flower (pink in *N. tabacum*) or the height of the stalk but, rather, in the quality of the leaf; *N. tabacum* was wonderfully aromatic, sweet though strong, subtly pleasant in comparison to the sharp, rank, acrid *N. rustica*.[7]

The flavor and fragrance of tobacco were, to be sure, not as important to Indians as to Europeans: it was ceremoniously and shallowly puffed by the Indians rather than deeply inhaled, as it was by the Europeans, for the pleasure of taking smoke into the lungs. Tobacco, in the Indian tradition, was a sacred plant—smoking it was perhaps originally a priestly rite and function—reverently cultivated by the men and priests, used ritually, magically, and even medicinally. The Indians of southern Virginia "use it for the curing of wounds and in smoke as we do," according to Alexander Brown's seventeenth-century source.

A patient and persevering John Rolfe continued to cross-breed and to improve his crop already thriving along the banks of the James. Readily adaptable though tobacco may be "to highly varying climates," yet "it shows a remarkable sensitivity to soil characteristics, climate, and the cultural routine," as Jerome E. Brooks, a contemporary tobacco authority, states. Tobacco is a chancy crop, and the success of the experiment was in great part due to Rolfe's determination, despite April hail or August drought or September frost, despite tobacco worm or tobacco wilt.

August was, traditionally, the month tidewater Indians harvested their tobacco crop. As for their curing methods, there had to be room for improvement—or so it struck Strachey: "The Salvages here dry the leaves of this *Apooke* over the fier and sometymes in the Sun, and Crumble yt into Powlder, Stalkes, leaves, and all."

One curing method Rolfe (and any pioneer planters who joined him in the experiments) found was to pile the leaves in heaps and cover them with hay to be cured by sweating in the sun. But within the next few years, as early as 1617, it was established that a far better way was to string the leaves on lines or racks to dry and cure. It enhanced the subtly pleasant taste, brought out the flavor; it intensified the aroma and accentuated the pervasively sweet scent for which the Virginia leaf was to become world-famous.

Once Rolfe and the other pioneer Virginia planters had gotten the hang of the curing process, "no country under the sun" would be able to produce "a more pleasant sweet or strong tobacco," as Captain Hamor predicted in 1615.

Rolfe himself would make so bold as to address his tobaccophobe of a sovereign on the prospects of a successful tobacco economy for the Virginia Colony, inscribing his letter to "The King's Most Sacred Ma'tie" in 1616. Rolfe assured James I that the "esteemed weed . . . which thriveth there so well that no doubt but after a little more triall and expense in the curing thereof, it will compare with the best in the West Indies."

And so it would. The tobacco culture John Rolfe launched and promoted in the colony would eventually produce a grade to compare favorably with the best from the plantations of the West Indies.

To compare meant to compete. By 1617, the Virginians exported twenty thousand pounds of their best leaf to compete with the Spanish for the opulent English market; in 1618, forty thousand pounds were shipped. Over the next ten years, the contest for preeminence in the world tobacco trade raged between the two major producers, Spain and the American colonies. The Spaniards' monopoly had been dramatically broken.

Even the Indians of the tidewater conceded the superiority of the tobacco being grown by the newcomers. They raised only enough of the native variety to supply ceremonial needs. For a better "smoke," the Powhatan tribesmen bought from the English colonists.

If it was a "colony founded on smoke," that fact was deplored, above all, by King James. The sovereign of this first English colony in America wished ardently and openly that its economic salvation had been founded on any other commodity, rather than "the vile weed" (as colonial Governor Berkeley called it). James I abhorred tobacco, perhaps because it was not one of his indulgences—not even his handsome young male favorites dared smoke in the royal presence. ("Surely Smoke becomes a kitchin far better than a Dining Chamber," to quote from His Majesty's diatribe on the subject.) Only a witch was more odious to James than a smoker; both were objects of his most violent antipathy; against both he had tiraded in print: *A Counter-Blaste to Tobacco* was his first publication (1604) upon ascent to the throne of England. But, as impotent as was King Canute to halt the tide, King James was powerless to control the wave of tobacco-smoking engulfing England. Neither James's tract nor the stiff duty he imposed (a tax of 6s 8d upon every pound of the Devil's concoction imported into the British Isles) could turn the tide of addiction. Rail though he might against the "barbarous Indians" and "the vile barbarous custome" of theirs, his subjects were not to be discouraged from their ruinously expensive habit, some spending as much as "four hundred pounds a yeere upon this precious stinke." It was clear to the King that smoking was a pernicious as well as an expensive habit: autopsies had already revealed, the *Counter-Blaste* pointed out, "an unctuous and oily kinde of Soote as hath bene found in some great Tobacco takers." Smoke, His Majesty predicted, would "infect the aire"; smoking was a habit "dangerous to the Lungs," "hurtfull to the health of the whole body. . . . A man [may] smoke himselfe to death with it (and many have done). . . ." (Among the first heavy smokers to fall ill of a disease associated with tobacco use would be Raleigh's friend and pensioner, Thomas Hariot, who had picked up the habit in the Carolina islands and would die in 1621 of symptoms suggesting cancer of the throat.) If the King of England, Scotland, Ireland, and Virginia could not put a stop to this "stinking smoke," this "vile custome," no one could. No one could.

CHAPTER XI

*Were there two sides to Pocahontas?
Did she have a fourth dimension?*

ERNEST HEMINGWAY,
*quoted by Philip Young in
"The Mother of Us All:
Pocahontas Reconsidered," 1962*

UPON THE AWESOME OCCASION OF BIRTH, as at death, the human instinct is to seek one's own kind, to cling to the rock of tradition.

Pocahontas—amenable though she showed herself generally to the white man's culture and religion—could have been expected to turn to her own people at the birth of her son in early 1615, to want the birth to take place in the isolation traditional to her people—the mother segregated from the men of the tribe, the same taboos operative at parturition as at puberty, the same inimical female magic in operation to estrange the male in both crises ("nor will the men at such a tyme presse into the nursery where they are," as William Strachey ascertained to be the case in Pocahontas's tribe*).

Even if there had been a trained midwife in any of the small English settlements along the James in 1615, she would have commanded no more technical skills, no more obstetrical instruments than her counterpart among the Indians; neither could cope with serious obstetrical emergencies.

It may be true, as both Captain Smith and Captain Hamor testify,

---

* Although Strachey does not elaborate on the subject, "the nursery" to which he refers was usually an isolation hut or primitive bower deep in the forest. Among the Sioux, there was a secluded bed of sand on which the mother knelt or lay, pressing her feet against two pegs driven into the ground, grasping two other pegs with her hands in the throes of labor.

that Pocahontas appeared to shun her fellow tribesmen in the months following her conversion and marriage, and yet she surrounded herself with a number of her own people—attendants, servants, relatives—to the final day of her life (entrusting her child to the care of a sister). Whatever bold pronouncements she may have made in public in repudiation of her own people (she could not "well endure the society of her owne nation," to hear Captain Smith tell it), in private, she clung fast to them.

She would have looked for a familiar face—an aunt's, sister's, cousin's—as the ordeal of childbirth began for her. So speedily and easily did Indian women usually deliver that she may have slipped away with her chosen Indian companion to a secluded spot in the environing forest and have returned home with the infant before her husband was even aware her labor had begun.*

"Their women (they say)," as Captain Smith writes in his *Map of Virginia*, "are easilie delivered of childe," presumably as the result of prenatal diet and exercise, techniques of muscle contraction and relaxation, in all probability similar to those practiced today in the regimens of natural childbirth. (Women of the Seneca tribe believed, apparently with good reason, that such a regimen made the child stronger, and the birth easier for the mother, although whatever her pangs, they were borne in stoic silence, fortitude constituting a cardinal virtue to the woman in travail as to the warrior under torture. It would appear that the extensive Indian pharmacopeia† included herbal preparations for relief of pain in childbirth; if none were administered by Christian Europeans, it may be because it was deemed by them that labor was a woman's proper expiation for original sin.)

Pocahontas's labor over, she and the aunt or sister serving her as midwife, following Powhatan tribal tradition, would have dipped the newborn babe in the waters of the James, would have wrapped it in soft, warm skins and fastened it to the cradleboard before returning home from the forest to lay it before its father.

To the white man's eye, some of these Powhatan tribal practices at childbirth seemed strange: "The manner of the Indians treating their young Children is very strange," Robert Beverley exclaimed.

---

* White men often expressed amazement at the ease with which Indian babies were born, as did Ezra Stiles (eighteenth-century president of Yale University): "I have often been told that a pregnant Squaw will turn aside & deliver herself, & take up the Infant and wash it in a brook and walk off." Among nomadic Indian tribes, the mother—her child strapped to the cradleboard—rejoined the others on the trail within hours after parturition.

† About one hundred and seventy drugs still listed in the Pharmacopeia of the United States of America and the National Formulary were in use by North American Indians at the time of the arrival of the white man.

The first thing they do, is to dip the Child over Head and Ears in cold Water, and then to bind it naked to a convenient Board, having a hole fitly plac'd for evacuation. . . . They always put Cotton, Wool, Furr, or other soft thing, for the Body to rest easy on, between the Child and the Board. . . .

Beverley described (and illustrated) the wooden board used by the Indian mother to transport and cradle her baby while she worked in the field or wigwam, or trudged the trail. The infant, within its cocoon of warm, soft things, was lashed to the small, lightweight plank which could be secured with thongs against the mother's back or suspended from the limb of a tree or deposited upon a rack of poles. The Indian mother unfastened the child several times daily to nurse it, to change its diapering of moss, to allow it to stretch and squirm.

There are specific references to Pocahontas as a mother. William Stith, familiar as he was with Rolfe family tradition, attests to Pocahontas's strong maternal instincts: "She was likewise delivered of a Son, of which she was extremely fond." And, in the words of Captain Smith, who saw her with young Thomas, this was "a childe which she loved most dearely," with an intense maternal love expressed, almost inevitably, Indian-fashion.

When it came to motherhood, Pocahontas's reactions would have been understandably primitive; here it was a question not of manners but of instincts and early experience, unlikely to be curbed or suppressed or redirected in a matter of months. Pocahontas's every instinct would have led her to relate to her child as an Indian mother, passionately fond, doting and indulgent, yielding him her breast generously and frequently, and for a matter not of months but of years.* The Indian mother was permissive in many other ways, as chary of discipline as she was of caresses (caresses perhaps unnecessary between nursing mother and child, suckling perhaps the supreme caress), and she was everywhere observed to be tender, devoted, attentive, reveling in the company of her child and keeping it constantly close.

And once the child had outgrown the cradleboard, it was carried everywhere its mother went, if not in the mother's arms, then in a very "unusual fashion" described by Thomas Hariot in his caption for a John

---

* In seventeenth-century Europe, the noble or bourgeois mother usually weaned her child within a few months or turned it over to a foster-mother. Weaning was not normally attempted by the aboriginal mother until the child had reached the age of two or even three years. As for the Indian mother's permissiveness, it is to be noted that even in the matter of controlling its excretory functions, the Indian child was left to achieve that control of its own accord, in its own good time, in company with its peer group.

White watercolor showing a Pomeioc mother with her child on her back: the intricate entanglement of limbs, the mother's with the child's, symbolic of the intimacy and warmth of that relation. As such, evidently, it impressed Robert Beverley in the late seventeenth century:

> They carry them at their backs in Summer, taking one Leg of the Child under their Arm, and the Counter-Arm of the Child in their Hand over their Shoulder, the other leg hanging down, and the Child all the while holding fast with its other Hand.

With the possible exception of such irrepressible maternal instincts, Pocahontas had made an apparently excellent adjustment to the white man's world: "During this time," as Captain John Smith would testify,

> the Lady Rebecca, alias Pocahontas, daughter of Powhatan, by the diligent care of Master John Rolfe her husband and his friends, was taught to speake such English as might well bee understood, well instructed in Christianitie, and was become very formall and civill after our English manner.

It is to be supposed from Smith's comment that Pocahontas had, by 1616–17, when Smith saw her again, become fairly fluent in English: if it was an English spoken with an accent, still it was intelligible. Although Smith gave credit to "Master John Rolfe her husband and his friends" for their "diligent care" in the instruction, still he would not fail to remind The Reader of the *Generall Historie* that he himself was the man who had initiated that language-study course.

Linguists say that a new language is relatively easy for a child twelve years of age or less to learn; beyond that age, facility in a second language is less readily achieved, and the speech characteristics of the mother tongue, less easily overcome. Pocahontas was twelve or more when she learned her first words of English from Captain Smith and the English hostages at her father's encampment. Once she became totally immersed in the English community in 1613, however, she probably became fairly fluent in English, with only a trace of Algonkian accent lingering in her speech. Her English would have been smooth and flowing, pleasing to the Anglo-Saxon ear. Many western Indian tongues, such as the Navajo, strike us as harsh, nasal, guttural; not so the Algonkian,* which is free of glottalized consonants, and of glottal catches, a

---

* Although the Virginia Algonkian languages became extinct in the eighteenth century, along with the tribes who spoke them, it is possible for linguists to reconstruct much of their phonology and structure by reference to other Algonkian tongues such as Cree, Fox, Menomini, Ojibwa, and Cheyenne, which are still in use, and under study, today.

language in which the vowels are more prominent than the consonants, and consonant clusters are relatively few. Unlike Navajo and Chinese, Algonkian is not a tonal language; the absence of great variations in pitch contributes further to its smoothness. Pocahontas, therefore, in learning English, would have encountered no great problems with intonation. In all likelihood, Pocahontas's voice level was agreeably low, as is true of almost all American Indian groups.

Smith remarked that Pocahontas was "well instructed in Christianitie"—well grounded in Christian doctrine and familiar with Anglican ritual. Sir Thomas Dale and the Reverend Whitaker found cause to beam with pride at the sight of the once savage princess taking her seat beside her Christian husband, following the services in the chapel at Henrico, kneeling, bowing her head, nibbling the consecrated bread, sipping the communion wine, as the rubrics of the Book of Common Prayer directed.

For Smith to say that the Lady Rebecca, alias Pocahontas, "was become very formall and civill" was for him to say that she had, by then, forsworn savage paint and nakedness for prim and proper European garb, that she no longer sprawled, Indian-style, on a mat upon the ground with her food, but sat decorously at table, instead, to eat and drink (happily, she was spared the necessity of learning to wield a knife and fork, implements not yet in general use even in Europe at that date).

Smith's phrase, "after our English manner," implied that Rolfe's bride had adapted herself to English household routines, to milking the cows, to churning the butter, to making the cheeses fancied by her husband.

Not that the popular Indian specialties were discarded by the Rolfes or their fellow colonists subsequent to the importation of the cow, the chicken, and the hog. The succotash, the maple sugar, the corn pone and corn bread, the turkey and cranberry which were favorites of Pocahontas's people became favorites of her husband's. Such native arts as the clambake and the barbecue, as planked shad and baked beans (beans cooked twenty-four hours in a warm place without fire) were not lost on the newcomers: certain specialties of Indian cuisine became part and parcel of our national cuisine. Indian women were not only skillful at cooking such tasty dishes, but cleanly in their food preparation, according to most early reporters.

Whether or not Pocahontas ever actually turned her hand to domestic chores is not known, although reports would indicate that her Indian handmaidens stayed with her after her marriage, followed her wherever she went, on all her travels. A princess by birth, enjoying the privileges of her high rank and station, relieved by servitors from the household and agricultural drudgery that devolved upon the ordinary tribeswoman, Pocahontas would seem to have retained this privileged status throughout her life, in the English community as in the Indian, depending upon a retinue of servants to fetch and carry for her in her husband's brick-and-timber cottage[1] on the James as at her chieftain-father's longhouse on the Pamunkey.

Even though Pocahontas may never have deigned to stoop to labor in the fields, she would nevertheless have been informed enough on the subject to give valuable pointers to her husband and his fellow colonists on the agricultural techniques best suited to the region, on the vagaries of tidewater weather and its effects on the crops of the area, on the use of fishheads as fertilizer, on the custom of hilling the corn, of planting beans along with the corn to climb and run on the cornstalks, and sometimes pumpkin and squash in the same field—a mixed seeding that was to become a unique feature of American agriculture.

Although Indian women engaged in neither hunting nor fishing, Pocahontas was heir to the secrets of her natal woods and waters and could share them with her husband and his compatriots: she knew and could point out the migratory habits of the game animals and birds of the tidewater, the timetable of the spawning runs of the fish in the estuaries. What a boon to the tenderfoot to be told when to tap the maple tree, in what thicket to flush the largest turkey, in which clearing to find the first ripe blueberry bush, which roots and leaves and bark to gather to compound the manifold, effective Indian herbal medicines.

Without fear and without molestation, then, in the year 1614, the colonists could range all the lands and waters within the boundaries of the Powhatan Confederacy, to farm and to hunt and to fish, to gather and to store the vast bounty of the Chesapeake ("comparable to the best in Christendom," according to John Rolfe's propaganda pamphlet, *The True Relation*). Beginning on the April day in 1614 when Pocahontas became the first Indian bride of an Englishman in the Virginia Colony, through all the years of their marriage, peace prevailed between the newcomers and the natives, the Peace of Pocahontas, the blessings of which were to be enjoyed by "everie man" in the colony, not by the bridegroom Rolfe alone, "sitting under his fig tree in safety."

THE COLONY'S FIRST FIVE YEARS had ended in horror and terror, in agony and misery; if its sixth year was beginning on a note of promise, that promise was on the lips of Pocahontas. The Virginia Company of London acknowledged its indebtedness to the Powhatan princess by allocating an annual stipend to be paid her for her lifetime.

It was decided in London to put her on the payroll and on parade. What better way for the Virginia Company to bring home to Englishmen the successes achieved in the New World in the realm of evangelization and race relations than by bringing home to England the first Virginian convert, the first native bride of an English subject? No more effective propaganda campaign could have been devised than the one to transport this paragon Indian princess to the British Isles and to present her, in the ruddy flesh, to London, to King and Court, to the stockholders of the Virginia Company.

To bring the Lady Rebecca along with her husband and child, of course—a trio comprising the first legitimate mixed-blood family (red and white) in English history. Not that Pocahontas's husband came along merely as an escort to his lady; John Rolfe was no nonentity, but now Secretary of the Virginia Colony, having succeeded his friend Ralph Hamor in that post when the Captain left the colony in 1614. Rolfe carried significance in his own right: he typified the industry and enterprise that would make England's overseas colonies economically independent of the mother country, even a rewarding investment for the mother country, thus setting England upon the course of empire.

It was in his capacity as secretary of the Colony that Rolfe was urged by Sir Thomas Dale to draw up a report on the state of the colony in 1616.[2] The state of the colony was good; prospects were encouraging; if the past had been grim, the future loomed bright: not only peace but law and order now prevailed under Governor Dale, who had put an end to the anarchy (the "envie, dissensions and jarres," to quote Rolfe) that had been rampant under the benighted regimes of Council and President.

Sir Thomas Dale—at the end of a strenuous five-year tour of duty in the wilderness, and with numerous successes chalked up to "his singular industry and policy as deputy," was making preparations in early 1616 to return to England, and to take his famous protégée Pocahontas —his main claim to fame—with him: "She will goe into England with mee," he announced by letter to the Bishop of London, "and were it but the gaining of this one soule, I will think my time, toile, and present stay well spent." From London, the Virginia Company signified approval of Dale's project.

As the company must have seen it, the publicity attendant on the appearance of the celebrated Indian princess in London could be counted on to benefit the forthcoming Virginia Lottery, which (since 1615, when the default of company subscribers assumed serious proportions) had become the company's most effective fund-raising method. The first Virginia Lottery had taken place in St. Paul's Churchyard in

1615; holders of the winning tickets were paid off in shares of the Virginia Company's stock.

Despite the glowing terms of Rolfe's prospectus, the colony's and the company's sole great resource, at that date, consisted of land—land bought by the sacrifices of the first ten years. The Virginia Company had become a land-company: all its plans, after 1616, were dependent upon the hope that it might use its power to give title to that land as an inducement for investments in the colony.

In the spring of 1616, Governor Dale made one or two last punitive raids upon the Kiskiacks and Warrasqueocs, named George Yeardley, a career soldier like himself, to succeed him as chief officer of the colony, and then boarded Captain Argall's ship, the *Treasurer*, which lay awaiting passengers, her crew at their posts, her ensigns flying, her hold well stocked. Small barrels and heavy canvas rolls of Rolfe's choicest Virginia leaf tobacco had already been stowed below.

Whether the *Treasurer* lay moored to the trees at Jamestown or rode at anchor off Point Comfort, a large audience of colonists and natives would have been attracted to the waterfront at the hour of her sailing. A strange procession formed to embark with the Governor: the Princess Pocahontas, her baby, and her husband; her sister Matachanna ("one of Powhatan's Daughters," by Stith's book) and Matachanna's husband, Uttamatamakin, a tribal councilor and priest whose name appears variously, in sundry chronicles and histories, as Uttamaccomack, Tomakin, Tomocomo, or Tomo; and about a dozen native attendants ("several young Indians of both Sexes," according to Stith; "divers men and women of thatt countrye to be educated here," according to Lord Carew, the Queen's Vice Chamberlain; "some ten or twelve old and younge of that countrie," according to the indefatigable letter-writer John Chamberlain), all in native dress, barbaric regalia, paint-daubed and befeathered, an entourage without which Pocahontas evidently would not travel (although the usual number may have been increased by the authorities to dramatize Pocahontas's London appearance, to underline her imperial status).

As if the composition of the *Treasurer*'s passenger list were not already bizarre enough, there came aboard a distinguished Spanish prisoner, Don Diego de Molina and, with the Don, a prisoner less distinguished—one probably in irons—a renegade Irishman named Francis Lymbry, who had served as pilot of the Spanish caravel on which Molina had sailed from Cuba into the Chesapeake on a spying mission in 1611, both men having fallen into the hands of the English in the course of a shore excursion near Point Comfort.

Pocahontas was only too familiar with the *Treasurer*, aboard which

Captain Argall had transported her to Jamestown after her abduction
on the Potomac, three years earlier. But that had been a short journey
—a mere matter of days—for the most part along calm riverine waterways, and had not prepared her for the hardships and discomforts of
a seven-weeks' North Atlantic crossing. It requires a mighty effort
of the imagination to conceive, today, of conditions aboard those tiny
(one hundred tons, more or less—more often less), frail, crowded,
reeking and vermin-infested ships of the early seventeenth-century
merchant marine.

To the eyes of Pocahontas and the Powhatan Indians in her retinue,
at embarkation, the hundred-thirty-ton *Treasurer* with its three (or
four) lofty, flag-strung masts, its huge square-rigged linen-flax or
canvas sails, its towering and gilded sterncastle, doubtless loomed large,
at first view—far larger than the largest (forty-foot) dugout war-
canoe—but they would soon, before they were many hours out of the
Bay, have discovered it to be dismayingly small, oppressively crowded,
with its complement of a hundred-odd, including passengers and crew.

Even an old sea-dog like Captain Smith conceded that the sailor's
life in the Great Age of Colonization (as in the Great Age of Exploration) was grim: "the labour, hazard, wet and cold is so incredible that
I cannot expresse it," he warned the prospective mariner in his *Accidence for Young Sea-Men.*

The best the young sailor could expect in the way of accommodations was to lash his sea chest and swing his hammock against a bulwark
on the main deck (a lower deck laid a few feet over the ballast) or to
stretch out to sleep on a pallet or a mound of canvas. He could be
grateful to have a roof over his head (the spar deck was open, exposed
to the elements) even if the headroom was scant (not more than four
or five feet between one deck and another).

Only an officer could lay claim to a bunk, and only the captain
could lay claim to a proper cabin ("the Captaines Cabben or great
Cabben," by Smith's denomination), high and dry in the "Captaines
Castle."

From his perch on the quarter deck high above the stern, the captain could keep an eye on the nearby "stearage roome" (where the
navigational instruments and charts were kept), could dominate the
ship and the crew. ("Swabber make cleane the shippe. . . . Boteson and
the rest, repaire the sayles and shrouds. . . . Carpenters about your
leakes. . . . Boy, Holla, Is the kettle boyled? . . . Boy fetch my celler of
Bottles," Smith has the captain shout down to the lad serving as cabin-
boy, who answers with a "Holla Maister . . . Yea, yea.")

Only a distinguished passenger such as Governor Dale could have expected Captain Argall to share those choice accommodations of his in the lofty sterncastle. The rest could have hoped for a makeshift cabin or a bunk, at best.

The Lady Rebecca was an exception, and would have expected special consideration to be shown her and her family in the matter of accommodations. On board this same ship, in 1613, en route from the Potomac to the James, Captain Argall had "lodged" his illustrious captive "in the Gunners roome" (according to Captain Hamor's account), and she would have been content with no less on this voyage.

The other members of Pocahontas's party would have bunked with the petty officers in the forecastle or found space to spread their fur bed-rolls alongside the seamen's—'tween decks, in the hold, on the main deck, wherever they could. In the case of Uttamatamakin, it took some time to convince that dignitary that he was expected to sleep on a heaving deck, that the *Treasurer* would sail on, night as well as day, when what "hee expected"—according to the Reverend Samuel Purchas, to whom he would express his astonishment later in London—was that "they should have anchored by the shoare" at nightfall, as was the Indian custom in the course of protracted over-water journeys, returning to *terra firma* not only to sleep at night but to perform the necessary excretory functions.

Aboard ship in the seventeenth century, there were no facilities for the performance of such functions, none save "the Beake-head which," as Captain Smith explains, "is without the ship before the fore-Castle, and of great use, as well for the grace and countenance of the ship, as a place for men to ease themselves in."[3]

Cooking facilities aboard ship in the seventeenth century were primitive, too. "The Cooke roome" to which Smith refers was located forward, the cooking fire laid directly on the sand and stone of the ballast, and a smoke-pipe leading to the spar deck immediately above serving as an exhaust, to clear the air below. "The Cooke is to dresse and deliver out the Victuall"—which was limited in the extreme, little more to the taste of the white men aboard the *Treasurer* than the red. Some ships boasted an oven, but the staff of life aboard ship was the jaw-breaking hardtack (or "ship's biskit"), and that sure to be moldy and maggoty before the long weeks of the Atlantic crossing were over. What the maggots spared, the rats and roaches spoiled. The Indian contingent aboard the *Treasurer* may have considered itself lucky to have packed along some of its own dried, stripped venison or smoked fish, as an alternative to the ship's fare of gruel and corned meat (the meat on an eastbound crossing consisted, probably, of some form of game packed in brine). If the few butts of water loaded on the *Treas-*

urer ran dry, the only hope lay in a rainstorm to refill them. The Indians would not have consoled themselves, as did the Englishmen, with the plenteous barrels of beer and wine stowed in the hold. (The Powhatan tribes did not survive the original white onslaught long enough to acquire the taste for alcohol that would prove fatal to so many other tribes, the length and breadth of the continent.)

Shipboard life in the early seventeenth century was one to try the stomach and test the stamina of all but the hardiest seamen: "Some masters," warned Captain Smith, "care not much whether the passengers live or die." A babe in arms, a child such as Thomas Rolfe, about a year old, in the spring of 1616, when he was brought aboard the *Treasurer*, could scarcely have been expected to survive the hardships of that voyage, had he not still been at nurse. Aboard the *Treasurer*, as in the wilderness, it was a case of the survival of the fittest.

Stomachs strong enough to stand the dysentery and scurvy that were the inevitable consequence of spoiled food and dietary deficiencies might not have been proof against motion sickness in the shuddering roll and pitch of the tiny vessel overtaken by heavy seas or storm.

In a storm, superstitious Indians aboard the *Treasurer* might have had recourse to a Powhatan tribal conjuration described by Captain Smith in his *Map of Virginia*:

> They have also another superstition that they use in stormes, when the waters are rough in the rivers and sea coasts. Their Conjurers runne to the water sides, or passing in their boats, after many hellish outcries and invocations, they cast Tobacco, Copper, *Pocones*, and such trash into the water, to pacifie that God whome they thinke to be very angry in those stormes.

Aboard the *Treasurer*, the exercise of such a sacerdotal function would have devolved upon Uttamatamakin.

Should a storm break—in spite of pagan incantations and Christian prayer—the passengers could hurry below, to take cover from rain and wind, to shudder and retch in the clammy, fetid darkness of the lower decks.

The crew was not so privileged. At the first thunderclap, first lightning flash, came the crew's call to stations. Pity the poor mariner! is the theme of Captain Smith's *Accidence*:

> Men of all other professions, in lightning, thunder, stormes and tempests, with raine and snow, may shelter themselves in dry houses, by good fires, and good cheere; but those are the chief

times, that Sea-men must stand to their tackelings, and attend with all diligence their greatest labour upon the Deckes.

Barefoot on the slippery decks, rain-soaked, shivering with cold, the crew fought out the storm. In high wind or dead calm—the latter as dread as the former—the mariner's was a hard life.

Once "Faire weather" had returned, it was, Smith said, "Out with all your sailes"! "Steare study before the wind"! At the master's commands, one thinks to see the experienced "Saylers"—the "antient men" —"hoysing the sailes, geting the tackes aboord, hawling the Bow-lines, and steering the ship"; one thinks to see "the yong men called Fore-mast men, to take in the Topsayles . . . Furle, and Sling the maine Saile . . . and take their turne at Helme"; one thinks to see the nimble lads—the ship's boys or grummets—scrambling like little monkeys into the highest rigging.

Scoff though they might, those weatherbeaten English mariners and sailors, at savage superstitions such as scattering tobacco on the waves, yet they clung resolutely to superstitions of their own. To avoid antagonizing touchy supernatural forces in their own universal scheme, sailing on a Friday—the day of Our Lord's crucifixion—was taboo. No blasphemy, no obscenity, no gambling ("neither dicing, carding, tabling nor other divelish games," by Sebastian Cabot's shipboard rules and regulations) was countenanced on the high seas, lest the wrath of heaven fall upon them and the vulnerable craft they sailed.

The dangers of the deeps were ever-present to the mind of sixteenth- and seventeenth-century seamen: they remembered John Cabot, lost with his four ships and all hands; they remembered the Portuguese brothers Corte-Real, lost with their two ships and all hands; Sir Humfry Gilbert, lost, his pinnace, *Squirrel*, pooped and swamped ("devoured and swallowed up by the Sea"), somewhere north of the Azores, as recently as 1583.

As for John Rolfe, a survivor of the *Sea Venture* shipwreck, the memory of that disaster of 1609 was still horrifyingly fresh in his mind as he sailed east on the *Treasurer* in 1616.

According to the Laws of Oleron (the traditional laws of the sea), profanity, ribaldry, and gaming—offenses against the Almighty—were punishable, as were offenses against the captain, by the hand of the ship's officer called the marshal.

Whatever minor infractions of the law may have occurred aboard Captain Argall's ship in the course of that eastbound voyage in 1616, whatever minor penalties may have been imposed in accordance with the code of the sea, the record does not show. What the record does show is that the marshal of the *Treasurer* was called upon to inflict the supreme penalty (that of death) for the ultimate infraction of the code (that of treason) upon the prisoner Francis Lymbry, the renegade Irishman—more Spanish by then, perhaps, than the Spaniards with whom he had been captured near Point Comfort in 1611, and with whom he had languished over the last five years behind a Jamestown palisado.

Why Lymbry was not returned to England for due process of law (as must have been originally intended), what emergency arose in mid-Atlantic to prompt Governor Dale and Captain Argall to take justice into their own hands, remains a mystery. If evidence of high treason came into Dale's hands at sea—proof that Lymbry had served as a pilot with the Spanish Armada in its attack upon England in 1588 —then, surely, Dale (in whom justice was seldom tempered with mercy) was not the man to hesitate at ordering Lymbry to be strung up on the yardarm—a hanging, to break the monotony of shipboard life, a grisly spectacle to lead Uttamatamakin to question whether the savages' methods of execution were more savage than those of the civilized Englishman.

More and more critical of the English in general—and of Dale, in particular—as Tomakin was to show himself in the course of his sojourn in England, Pocahontas was apparently to see only the gentler aspects of the governor's nature. It was only natural that she should have responded with gratitude and affection to the consideration and attention he consistently showed her throughout the years of their association. And it was only natural that Dale should have been solicitous of his imperial protégée, the star of the band of native Americans he planned to present as a major attraction for the Virginia Company in London.

In the absence of an ordained minister to conduct the twice-daily religious services on the *Treasurer*, Sir Thomas Dale fully qualified as "a man of great knowledge in Divinity," as the Reverend Alexander Whitaker said of him. Equally well qualified as a religious scholar was Pocahontas's husband, John Rolfe, eternally quoting Calvin and spouting Scripture, as is evident from even a cursory perusal of his "honorable intentions" letter to Sir Thomas Dale and in his *True Relation* (a document he must have been in process of drafting, even then, during that crossing, to have it ready for presentation to the sovereign, as he would, in London, a few months later. Either Rolfe or Dale would have conducted religious services aboard the *Treasurer*.

"Boteswaine call up the men to Prayer and Breakfast," Smith has the command ring out. If Governor Dale's notorious blue laws had made church attendance compulsory in the colony on the James, he would have countenanced no less assiduity in the devotions of the congregation aboard ship, floating perilously upon the North Atlantic. Every Christian, including Pocahontas, of course, would have been expected to attend daily or twice-daily services.

Since no opportunity to proselytize among the heathen was to be neglected, the party of Powhatans accompanying Pocahontas was sure to have been drawn into the circle of worshipers. Facts support the theory that Tomakin provided a center of resistance to proselytization efforts, that he held himself aloof—and those of his fellow-tribesmen subject to his influence. A man of faith as steadfast as any Christian martyr, a man of inquiring and probing mind, Tomakin could hold his own against Dale and Rolfe, as he would later hold his own in religious disputation with the premier prelates of London (as the latter would admit).

Sir Thomas Dale—an Indian-fighter, "Indian-hater par excellence," one of the first of the breed so categorized by Herman Melville—would have been quick to interpret Tomakin's stubborn resistance to Christian doctrine as savage insolence. If Dale was slow to castigate him—as he had castigated so many, up and down and across the Peninsula—it was because of Tomakin's rank and eminence, his standing as the Emperor Powhatan's official envoy on this mission to King James I.

To read between the lines is to read a lurking antagonism between Tomakin and Pocahontas, as well: his own unshakable loyalty to tribe and to tribal tradition constituted a reproach to her for her apostasy. It is not too far-fetched to assume that Tomakin and the Englishmen were still disputing Pocahontas's soul between them, that Powhatan may have delegated the faithful and devout Tomakin to accompany his renegade daughter to England for that very purpose; that Dale began, even before the ocean voyage was half over, to regret having accepted Tomakin as a member of his party, and to resent that fiercely independent spirit of Tomakin's which not all Dale's power could curb.

As the long days of the North Atlantic crossing (forty or fifty[4] even by Argall's short new route that led due east from the Virginia coast to the Canaries before turning north) dawned and darkened, as the *Treasurer* left the soundless deeps and came onto soundings that marked the continental shelf of Europe, a sense of excitement seized homecoming passengers and crew, communicated itself even to the party of American natives to whom Europe was an unknown, unfamiliar, unimaginable shore.

"One to the top to looke out for Land"! The order would ring out from the lips of master or mate to one of the agile ship's boys, the shouted command from the sterncastle to nip up quickly to the crow's nest, topmast.

Coming north from the Canaries, Lands End or Lizard Point in Cornwall was the first headland of the home island to gladden an English lookout's eye, as the vessel entered the chops of the English Channel.

No man alive knew better that narrow, treacherous waterway than the commander of the *Treasurer*. Captain Argall knew the Channel's every swift, high tide, its every buoy, every landmark.

A veteran navigator such as Argall tried to time his entrance into the Channel to coincide with the full of the moon; from the towns along the coast, he could expect no more in the way of lighting than an occasional warning fire burning in an iron cresset on a pole; to warn off passing ships, he kept a lighted "lanthorn" in a bucket at his prow.

According to the Reverend Samuel Purchas,

> Sir Thomas Dale . . . arrived at Plimmouth in May or June 4.1616. to advance the good of the Plantation, Master Rolfe also with Rebecca his new convert and consort, and *Uttamatamakin* (commonly called *Tomocomo*) one of Pohatans Counsellours came over at the same time.

Dale, under a dateline of June 3, sent notice of the *Treasurer*'s arrival in Plymouth to Sir Ralph Winwood, First Secretary of State, in London.

News of the arrival of the ship from Virginia had reached the capital by June 20, on which date Sir George Carew, Vice Chamberlain to Queen Anne, notified the English Ambassador in India that

> Sir Thomas Dale retourned frome Virginia, he hathe brought divers men and women of thatt countrye to be educated here, and one Rolffe who married a daughter of Pohetan (the barbarous prince) called Pocahuntas hath brought his wife with him into England.

At Plymouth, chief port of Devonshire, the official greeting would have been tendered Governor Dale, Captain Argall, and company by Sir Lewis Stukely, Vice-Admiral of Devon, then at the high point of his career, basking in the royal favor; he had been one of the first Englishmen to be knighted by King James as the latter crossed the border into England from his Scottish homeland in 1603.

The theory that Governor Dale and his party continued on from Plymouth toward London by water, aboard the *Treasurer*, is substantiated by Dale's letter to Winwood, in which he wrote: "I shall with the greatest speed the wind will suffer me present myself unto you." If so, Captain Argall headed his ship around Start Point and continued east past the Isle of Wight, past Beach Head and Dungeness into the Strait of Dover, rounded North Foreland Cape, past the Isle of Sheppey, and, at last, into the mouth of the Thames, past Gravesend, and so up to London.

Or perhaps only as far as Gravesend, the watergate of London, where large sailing vessels often moored to unload cargo while their passengers transferred to barges for the remaining twenty-five miles upriver to the capital. Sir Thomas Dale, as the governor of England's only New World colony, had a right to expect an official welcome at Gravesend, as was customarily tendered there to distinguished arrivals from overseas, a right to expect a royal barge to fetch him and his party for the short journey up the narrowing Thames to London.

By June 22, London must have witnessed the arrival of the exotic boatload from the western world, must have buzzed with news of it.

John Chamberlain rushed off a report to his friend Sir Dudley Carleton, England's Ambassador to The Hague, dating his letter "From London this 22th of June 1616" and announcing:

> Sir Thomas Dale is arrived from Virginia and brought with him some ten or twelve old and younge of that countrie, among whom the most remarquable person is *Poca-huntas* (daughter of Powatan a kinge or cacique of that countrie) married to one Rolfe an English man. . . .
>
> I heare not of any other riches or matter of worth, only some quantitie of sassafras, tobacco, pitch, and clap-board, things of no great value unless there were more plentie and neerer hand. All I can learne of yt is that the countrie is goode to live in, yf yt were stored with people, and might in time become commodious, but there is no present profit to be expected. . . .

And there was the rub, as far as John Chamberlain and his fellow stockholders in the Virginia Company were concerned: it was the profit, not the glory, they were looking for; they had begun to despair of ever seeing a return on their investment, were unwilling to risk more, reluctant to follow up bad money with good. The Virginia Company, teetering on the verge of bankruptcy, could only hope that the Princess Pocahontas and her troupe of redskins would stimulate the interest—and the investment—needed to keep the colony alive.

CHAPTER XII

*Savages we call them, because their
Manners differ from ours, which we
think the Perfection of Civility; they
think the same of theirs.*

BENJAMIN FRANKLIN

NOT ALL JOHN ROLFE'S WORD PICTURES could have prepared
Pocahontas for the sight of London.

She and her party of Powhatan tribesmen must have gazed in
wonder, gaped in astonishment at first view of London.

London stared back.

If Lady Rebecca Rolfe disembarked at the City primly gowned,
robed from head to toe, sleeved from neck to wrist, the red flesh of
her companions was bare save for splashes of paint, sprigs of feathers,
swatches of rawhide, exposed for all of London to goggle at.

From the first, the savages of the New World had created a sensation in the Old; from the first, from the day in 1493 when the first
six savages in Columbus's train had been paraded before the Court of
Ferdinand and Isabela in Barcelona, the Spaniards had marveled—and
after the Spaniards, the Portuguese, the French, the English would
marvel—at these exotic creatures from overseas, their skin red as sal-
mon, gaudy as parrots in their body-paint and feathers, their status—
whether human or subhuman—still under debate in the Church at
Rome. Europe found itself in a quandary to explain the species and the
origin of the aborigines, their place in Christian cosmogony.

The Reverend Alexander Whitaker, fresh from his months as
preceptor to Pocahontas, was one to declare, Yes, the Indians have an
immortal soul. Yes, they belong to the race of Man, all men the product
of a single Creation: "One God created us," Whitaker proclaimed in

his *Good Newes from Virginia*, "we all have Adam for our common parent; yea, by nature the condition of us both is all one."

If the red men of America belonged to the human race, then Christian Europe was confronted with the necessity of Christianizing and civilizing them in order to complete and perfect their humanity. To do so, America had to be colonized: the evangelical mission motivated, to great extent, the colonization of the newly discovered continent. To recognize that the evolution and development of man might take an alternate path from that of Judaeo-Christian man, to concede the Indians' pagan state "as an equal though totally other human possibility" was beyond the capacity of Renaissance Europe.

In Europe, in France above all, speculation about the aborigines of the newly discovered continent raged. Montaigne postulated a natural man living in a state of nature—in a Golden Age—uncorrupted by the vices of society, and thus a nobler creature than civilized man. Jean Jacques Rousseau would later further idealize and romanticize the Noble Savage, theorizing that somewhere in the development of civilized man, a wrong turn had been taken, and that this accounted for the vices of society. It was the proposition of Rousseau's *Social Contract* that the direction might be reversed by a return to nature. Rousseau's oversentimentalized concept of primitive man influenced Europe for generations to come, was responsible for the persistent convention of primitivism in the art and literature of the nineteenth and twentieth centuries. François René de Chateaubriand continued in the tradition of Rousseau, romanticizing the American Indian in highly popular novels such as *Atala* (1801), *René* (1802), and *Les Natchez* (1826).

The early colonist, the frontiersman, on the ground in America, in mortal combat with the redskin, could not afford to indulge in the European's abstract, philosophical speculations. There, on the spot, in the wilderness, the idea of Savagism was invented—the idea of the bloodthirsty, brutal, brutish Savage obstructing the progress of civilization in the New World. The rationale of progress justified extermination of the Savage and seizure of his land.

The first of that strange breed from that far shore to be seen in England was a chieftain from Brazil exhibited as a curiosity at the court of Henry VIII. The first North American Indians to touch England's shores arrived with Cabot in 1497, and made no favorable impression, to judge by the report of Richard Hakluyt, who likened their "demeanour" to that of "bruite beastes." The Court of Queen Elizabeth, on the other hand, lavishly admired the young chieftain Manteo, who had sailed—one of the few to board ship voluntarily—from his home island of Roanoke with Raleigh's Captain Barlowe in 1584; when he returned to the Carolina Outer Banks in 1585 with John White and Thomas Hariot, it was as Lord of Roanoke, a title bestowed upon him by the Virgin Queen. In 1603, Londoners were treated to a demonstration of the Indians' skill in handling a canoe: three native "Virginians" paddled along the Thames in a bark brought from their homeland. In 1605, Plymouth harbor was agog at the arrival of Captain George Weymouth's ship *Archangel* with a fascinating human cargo: five New Worldlings, Abnakis, specimens collected on the coast of Maine. Sir Ferdinando Gorges, commander of the Plymouth Fort, was quick to perceive their propaganda value in the promotion of the North Virginia (or New England) colonization project of which he was a principal agent, and managed somehow to talk Weymouth out of three of the five red men for publicity purposes of his own in the capital: they "had been shown in London for a wonder," to quote Gorges himself.

Indians from the New World became the rage in Elizabethan England: Shakespeare must have seen them himself, or read a broadsheet heralding such an exhibition. He makes a rather scornful reference in *The Tempest* to those sensation-seeking Londoners who would "not give a doit [the smallest of current coins] to relieve a lame beggar, but will lay out ten to see a dead Indian." Again, in a mob-scene in *Henry VIII*, Shakespeare refers to the novelty of the Indian in London; in this instance, a live Indian with a phallus larger than life to titillate the noble ladies: "Or have we some Indian with the great tool come to court, the women so besiege us?"

The Indian craze had not abated at the Court of James I: on the occasion of the marriage of his daughter Princess Elizabeth to the Prince Palatine in 1613, both theatrical *divertissements* arranged for the pleasure of the wedding guests—a masque by Sir Francis Bacon, another by George Chapman—boasted Indian themes: "the chief masquers in Indian-habits" designed by master-architect–stage-designer Inigo Jones: "attired like Virginian priests," "their hair black and large, waving down to their shoulders," "On their heads high sprigged feathers . . . like the Virginian princes they represented," "strange hoods of feathers and scallops about their necks," "altogether estrangeful and Indian-like," according to the record kept by His Majesty's Master of the Rolls, the Court official in charge of such festivities.

And even long after James's day, as late as 1635, during the reign of his son, Charles I, a London correspondent of John Winthrop Jr.'s was writing to the governor of the Saybrook Colony (in Connecticut) to urge him "to send over some of your Indian Creatures alive"!

When it came to live red Indians, Jacobean London was no more blasé than Elizabethan London: crowds gathered, flocked to see, paid to see, dogged the step of every redskin that set foot within the City's walls.

And Pocahontas caused a furor in 1616, the female the rarest of the rare species*—if not the first then surely the second Indian woman to be seen in the land and, of a certainty, the first princess of the race. "As wonders last," the wonder of Pocahontas would not have dimmed in the usual "nine daies," not even in nine months, had she sojourned that long in England. As long as she stayed, wherever she went, she attracted attention, stirred up interest, stimulated gossip and speculation, dominated the news, monopolized conversation, challenged the imagination.

As for Pocahontas and the Indians accompanying her, those first days in London—that sudden transition from the banks of the James to the banks of the Thames—could not but have been a bewilderment. Until the day of disembarkation, their idea of a large settlement had been Werowocómoco, a huddle of garden-arbors on the Pamunkey, with a total population of perhaps two hundred, at the most.

London, as early as the first decade of the 1600s, could claim a population of a quarter of a million, and that figure was on the increase, a population bursting the bounds of the medieval city walls, overflowing in all directions from the original, ancient, central City, a rising tide of population that neither plague nor royal decree could turn back, expanding to the east, to the west, spreading across to the opposite bank of the Thames—with London Bridge and a lively traffic of tilt-boats and wherries to connect the north bank to the south. The ancient city provided a spectacle to astound even the jaded eye of the world-traveler, second to none as a world capital, of "utmost renown" even in Tacitus's day. A Dutch map-maker, in the mid-seventeenth century, paid tribute in verse (in Latin, Dutch, and French) to *Londinum celeberrimum Angliae emporium*:

> *If London appears to you as huge, splendid, beautiful,*
> *If her palaces, her bridge, her spreading walls,*
> *If her temples and her towers announce her fame,*
> *It is not surprising. Twenty centuries have polished*
> *The city to such perfection. . . .*

If even such sophisticated travelers as map-makers, diplomats, traders, and explorers were impressed with London, what must have

---

* The first female Indian to have visited England is said to have been an Abnaki, one of the five brought back by Captain Waymouth from Maine in 1605, known by the name of Mistress Penobscot, probably from near the bay of that name.

been the reaction of Pocahontas and her party as they came within sight of the vast, sprawling, swarming metropolis? Plunged suddenly into the maelstrom of a giant city, transplanted from the simplest pastoral existence into the most tumultuous urban life, what would have been the first impression of those denizens of deep forest as their barge rode up the Thames, past Greenwich and its palaces, past the Isle of Dogs, into the Pool of London?

The first sight of many was the great, grim, gray Tower, anchoring down the eastern end of the medieval city wall—William the Conqueror's crenelated, moated fortress-prison glooming down upon the river from its strategic eminence on Great Tower Hill.

Just beyond the Tower loomed the Bridge—London Bridge, the only one spanning the Thames in 1616, a marvel of engineering for its time, twenty great masonry arches supported by twenty-one stone piers. From end to end, tall and narrow merchant's houses jostled one another for foundation space—London Bridge was as densely populated as London tenements. To the left, the tower of the southern gatehouse of the Bridge caught every eye; it bristled with heads—human heads, heads of felons and traitors, severed by the executioner, impaled on spikes as a warning to the vagrant to keep out of London-town—a display to remind Pocahontas and her fellow-tribesmen of the enemy scalps flaunted on poles at Powhatan victory celebrations.

And to the right, the great bulk of St. Paul's Cathedral, high on Ludgate Hill, dominated the scene. Ludgate Hill was a veritable forest of church-spires, but St. Paul's—of lead-coated timber—scraped the sky. That twelfth-century Gothic mammoth (even without benefit of Wren's famous dome) was already London's most distinctive landmark.

Impossible to encompass it all, take it all in, the first trip up the Thames above London Bridge; constant distractions were offered to the eye of the sightseer, endless points of interest attracted his attention. See the bear-garden, the brew-house, the octagonal Globe Theater, the Archbishop's Palace! Look to the north, at the Temple Gardens in full panoply of summer! Here, a glitter of gold domes and gilt weather-vanes, catching the sun; there, bright banners and pennants fluttering in the breeze. The river, a spectacle in itself: with its ripples of swans, its brisk traffic of small craft above the Bridge: a criss-cross of wherries, tilt-boats, shallops, ferrying their fares to and fro; a procession of barges, upstream and down; the riverside in perpetual motion, too: longshoremen loading and unloading cargo at the numerous quays, hithes, wharves, slips; fishermen flinging their iridescent scaly catch on the public docks.

Then, suddenly, at the river bend, along the Strand—a riverside road connecting the City of London with the City of Westminster—

the eye discovered a splendorous row of palaces—the mansions of the mighty few—set deep in lavish gardens running down to the riverbank, to ornate watergates and water-stairs.

Most ornate of all, as befitted the majesty of the crown of England, there rose the marble flight of Whitehall Stairs, riverside entrance to Whitehall Palace, largest—if most hodgepodge—in Christendom.

Just beyond, ancient Westminster Hall managed to hold its own in grandeur; just behind the Hall's two square towers and steep roof, Westminster Abbey (without its two eighteenth-century towers) and St. Margaret's were discernible from the river.

If neither Sir Thomas Dale's rank nor mission warranted an official reception at Tower Wharf (to the accompaniment of a salute from the Tower artillery), then he and his party from Virginia would have come ashore, less ceremoniously, at one of the public wharves, such as Dowgate, Ebbgate, Queen Hithe, in the heart of London, close to the foot of Ludgate Hill. If government officials did not meet the travel-weary passengers off the *Treasurer*, surely Virginia Company officials were on hand to conduct Lady Rebecca Rolfe, her husband, John Rolfe, and little son, Thomas, to their lodgings at the Belle Sauvage Inn, halfway up Ludgate Hill, in the shadow of St. Paul's.

If the name Belle Sauvage translates loosely, from the French, as Savage Belle or Beautiful Indian Maid, it was by one of those strange coincidences to which a whimsical fate seems addicted, for the inn where Pocahontas was to stay in 1616 had been named long before, in 1529. The Belle Sauvage was one of the oldest inns in London, already a well-known, well-established, well-patronized hostelry.

The seventeenth-eighteenth-century London inn was at the vortex of the capital city's life and traffic: Londoners and provincials, strangers from abroad—the travel-weary, the hungry, the thirsty, the lonely, the lusty—all headed for the inn, to take shelter for the night, to eat and drink, to make merry, to greet an arrival or to speed a departing visitor. A bawdy, brawling, motley crew thronged the inn's galleried wings, its dining and sleeping quarters; comings and goings kept the inn-yard astir—coaches, carriages, horsemen clattering in and out—a crew more motley still with the arrival, in late June of 1616, of a party of red-skinned Americans!

The yard of the Belle Sauvage accommodated not only the usual stables, carriage-houses, ovens, and kitchens, but a stage, as well, serving not only as a hostelry, a neighborhood club, a coach depot, but even as a theater! In the sixteenth century, in the early days of the London theater, before there were buildings specifically dedicated to the presentation of spectacle and drama, strolling players gave performances in the yard of the Belle Sauvage upon some sort of scaffolding erected to serve as a stage. (Christopher Marlowe's *Dr. Faustus*, for one, was produced there, with the Devil himself in the role of the Devil, if we are to believe the horrified report of a Puritan in the audience, one William Prynne, who would have denounced the play no matter who had played the role.) And, in default of dramatic works, entertainment-mad Londoners flocked to the Belle Sauvage to see animal acts or professional sword-play.

All in all, the inn was a rackety, rowdy, uproarious, inappropriate shelter to offer the Lady Rebecca Rolfe, who had known only greenwood solitudes. Burly Ben Jonson—who may or may not have encountered her there, the legend of their encounter notwithstanding—was struck with the incongruity of the place as her abode—a princess from the American wilderness, "in womb of tavern," a tavern "unfit too for a princess," as he put it, in a line from his comedy *The Staple of News* (the first literary allusion to Pocahontas):

> *No, I have known a princess, and a great one,*
> *Come forth of a tavern. . . .*
> *. . . . . the blessed*
> *Pokahontas, as the historian calls her,*
> *And great king's daughter of Virginia,*
> *Hath been in womb of tavern. . . .*

It is reasonable to assume that the "tavern" had been the choice of some functionary of the Virginia Company charged with meeting the distinguished party from Virginia and arranging for their lodgings. Clearly, the company (on the instructions of Sir Thomas Smythe, treasurer and chief executive) had assumed financial responsibility for Pocahontas's sojourn in England: it was "the Company which allowed provision for herself and her son," according to the Reverend Samuel Purchas, who, as the colony's chief propaganda officer, was in a position to know; a fact confirmed by Captain John Smith, in the Fourth Book of the *Generall Historie*: "the Treasurer and Company tooke order both for the maintenance of her and it"—the "childe."

The allowance made by the company for Pocahontas's expenses in England was proof of the fact that she had been brought there by the board of governors on company business, for propaganda purposes. At long last, with the arrival of the Princess Pocahontas and her party of mild-mannered savages, came the perfect occasion for the governing board to dispel the rumors and scandal, to improve the image of the company, the image of the colony, the image of the blood-thirsty savage.

The Lady Rebecca Rolfe, ladylike in her high-necked, full-skirted, long-sleeved English gown, speaking softly not some barbarian gibberish, but an acceptable, comprehensible English, civil and mannerly in her demeanor, submissive, adaptable, tender, arm in arm with her Anglo-Saxon husband; in her person, living proof that the savage could be gentled, the infidel brought to Christ, the red assimilated with the white, the perfect spokesman for Virginia Company policy, the symbol of peaceful coexistence, the dove of Powhatan! A madonna figure, at her breast a child in whose veins the blood of England mingled with that of the native American; in his bloodstream, the two races addressed the future with hope and mutual regard.

It would have been only proper for the Virginia Company to have sent representatives to greet so distinguished a visitor as Lady Rebecca Rolfe. A returning colonial governor—a Sir Thomas Dale—deserved no less of an official welcome, and certain honors were due the captain of the company's good ship *Treasurer*. If not Sir Thomas Smythe in person at quayside, then perhaps his deputy, Alderman Robert Johnson, or some other high-ranking member of the Council.

As for Lady Dale, it would have been unnatural had she not gone to the waterside to meet her husband after a five years' separation, and later to the Belle Sauvage to extend offers of courtesy to her husband's protégés, the Rolfes, to admire and fondle her husband's namesake, the small boy, Thomas Rolfe. (Pocahontas and Matachanna, remembering Governor Dale's request for the hand of their youngest half-sister, transmitted to Powhatan by Captain Hamor early in 1614, might have been astonished to discover that the Governor was already much married, his Lady very much alive.*)

John Rolfe's brother Henry, a London merchant and member of the Virginia Company, could have been expected to be on hand to greet his brother, his celebrated new sister-in-law, and his nephew Thomas.

Diplomatic protocol required of Baron De La Warre—for life, Lord Governor of Virginia, and still hoping to return there to resume active duty—that he seek out and show honor to the daughter of the

---

* The Dales had been separated for the entire duration of their marriage, which had taken place just before Sir Thomas's departure for Virginia in 1611, accounting perhaps for his forgetting about his marital status. William Stith, in his mid-eighteenth-century *History of Virginia* exonerates Dale of deception in this matter, implying that the governor sought the hand of the young Powhatan princess not for himself, but "for some worthy English Gentleman."

Supreme Chieftain of that Virginia territory, required that he bring Lady De La Warre along with him, as well as one or more of their five daughters, to salute the Virginian princess.

Lord and Lady De La Warre, with their lofty Tudor Court connections—he, a member of his cousin Elizabeth's Privy Council, a holdover on that of his cousin James's as well—were ideally suited to sponsor the Powhatan princess at Whitehall Palace, and did so (according to Captain John Smith's report), extending Pocahontas their protection, serving as her liaison with the Stuart Court of James I.

The great world of London society took its cue from the De La Warres: "divers persons of great ranke and qualitie had been very kinde to her," again according to Captain Smith, "divers other persons of good qualities" sought to make the acquaintance of the redskin celebrity.

Those who did were impressed.

One of the first to seek her out and to sing her praises was the Reverend Samuel Purchas. Rolfe's wife, Purchas wrote in his *Pilgrimes*,

> did not only accustome her selfe to civilitie, but still carried her selfe as the Daughter of a King, and was accordingly respected, not onely by the Company, which allowed provision for her selfe and her sonne, but of divers particular persons of Honor, in their hopefull zeale by her to advance Christianitie.

Armchair traveler that he was, Samuel Purchas welcomed the opportunity to talk, face to face, with these natives of the western world of which he had hitherto only read, to interview Pocahontas—a question-and-answer session conducted entirely in English—and to interrogate Uttamatamakin through an interpreter made available, as Purchas gratefully notes, by Marshal Dale.

With arrangements under way for the Powhatan princess to be received in audience by the monarch and his Danish consort, Queen Anne, it was necessary for her to be coached in the elaborate etiquette of the Stuart Court.

The responsibility of selecting a proper costume for Pocahontas for her reception at Whitehall Palace devolved, in all likelihood, upon her sponsor and social arbiter, Lady De La Warre, although it was, in all likelihood, the Virginia Company that footed the bills.

It is logical to assume that this was the costume Pocahontas wore when she sat for the portrait which has come down to us both as an engraving and an oil—her white lace cuffs and whisk, or shoulder collar, stiffly starched, her white ostrich plume fan tightly clutched in her right hand, her high hat (in high fashion at the Stuart Court), a rigid beaver form trimmed in red to match the red brocaded velvet of the gold-stitched short mantle that sparks the somber gold-buttoned under-dress.[1]

Although the artist who painted the oil did not sign his canvas, the name of the artist who made the drawing for the engraving is writ clear in the lower left-hand corner of the print: SI. PASS: SCULP (SI. PASS, short for Simon Van de Passe, a young Dutch artist; SCULP., short for *sculpsit*, "designed or executed"). Compton, the name of the Dutch engraver who issued the small quarto-size print, appears in the lower right-hand corner. Whether or not Simon Van de Passe was the artist responsible for the unsigned oil painting of Pocahontas as well as for the signed engraving remains a subject for debate among the authorities of the National Portrait Gallery in Washington, where the Pocahontas canvas presently hangs (a gift of Andrew Mellon, who acquired it from Francis Burton Harrison, a descendant of Poca-hontas's, who had acquired it from the Elwin family of Booton Hall in Norfolk, England, collateral descendants of the Rolfes of Heacham).

In the view of the art experts of the National Portrait Gallery, "there can be no doubt that the two works of art, one on canvas, the other on paper, are closely related." The weight of evidence supports the theory that the same artist did them both, and since the engraving is known to have been made in 1616, then it would follow that the oil was painted in the same year—one or the other, very possibly from life.

Proof that the Pocahontas oil likeness was painted no later than the eighteenth century would seem to be confirmed by Elwin family tradition, which insists that the portrait was hanging in Booton Hall, the family's ancestral home in Norfolk, as early as the 1760s or 1770s.

As for the differences to be observed between the engraving and the oil, they are more consistent with a derivation of the painting from the engraving "than with the reverse filiation." There is less detail in the ornamentation of the clothing in the painting than in the engrav-ing: the hat shown in the painting lacks the plume that decorates it in the engraving, and the hat-band lacks the beaded edge; the bracelet on the right wrist in the engraving does not appear in the painting. A distinct pattern discernible in the damask of the jacket in the engraving is lost in the painting, where the fabric becomes a crimson velvet.[2]

But these are minor differences. The difference that is significant is the difference in the features of the subject's face, the difference in expression. The head is carried proudly, if stiffly, in the painting, as in the engraving; the air of dignity is common to both. But the cast of the features is less typically Indian in the painting than in the engraving.

Whereas the face of the subject in the engraving is definitely not that of an Englishwoman, that of the painting has only a slightly foreign aspect. The painter's hand has softened the features of the face, rendered the cheekbones less typically high, the slant of the eye less pronounced; the brows are less darkly, starkly defined. (While the complexion of the woman in the painting is not Anglo-Saxon fair, neither is it distinctly tawny, ruddy; it would be stretching a point to call it "redskin.") There is a diminution of individuality in the painting when it is compared to the engraving. In the engraving, the eyes are piercing; the set of the jaw, defiant, stern. The woman of the engraving—however much of a curiosity she may be—faces down the alien world, returns stare for stare.

"Here is a fine picture of no fair Lady"! John Chamberlain wrote scathingly, on February 22, 1617, to his friend Carleton, enclosing a copy of the Van de Passe engraving (which obviously enjoyed a wide circulation in the English capital).

There is a racist ring to Chamberlain's comment, his disparaging reference to the color of her skin. "No fair Lady," she suffers in comparison, in his view, with the fair-complexioned, blonde, blue-eyed Anglo-Saxon beauties. Chamberlain was a snob as well as a racist; his letter sneers at what he considers the Indian woman's airs, pretensions: her title of Lady Rebecca, "Daughter to the mighty Prince," her court costume—with its implication of Whitehall Palace entrée—an impudence in itself. "And yet," he continued sarcastically,

> with her tricking up and high style and titles, you might think her and her worshipful husband to be somebody, if you do not know that the poor company of Virginia, out of their poverty, are fain to allow her four pounds a week for her maintenance.

Chamberlain's investment in Virginia Company shares entitled him to be critical of the company's largesse to the Indian woman (the four pounds a week seemed "handsome" to William Stith, relating the events, something more than a century later: "the Treasurer and Company gave Order, for the handsome Maintenance of both her and her Child").

John Chamberlain might look down his nose at her, but the "Virginian woman" was attended by peers of the realm: "accompanied with that honourable Lady the Lady De la Ware and that honourable Lord her husband, and divers other persons of good qualities," by Captain Smith's reportage.

And not only lords and ladies, but the most venerable prelates

of the Anglican Church lionized the "Daughter of the mighty Prince."
Among the "particular persons of Honor" to do her honor was the
Reverend Purchas's superior in the ecclesiastical hierarchy: "I was
present," Purchas writes,

> when my Honorable and Reverend Patron, the L. Bishop of
> London, Doctor King entertained her with festivall state and
> pompe, beyond what I have seene in his great hospitalitie af-
> forded to other Ladies. . . .

The scene of the "festivall" given in Pocahontas's honor was grand,
indeed; the Bishop of London's palace was described by a contemporary
as "a large thing for receipt [receptions], wherein divers Kings have
been lodged, and great house-hold hath been kept."
It remained only for King James I and Queen Anne to receive and
distinguish the redskin visitor from the farthest shore.

CAPTAIN JOHN SMITH would claim credit for Pocahontas's reception
at Whitehall Palace by Queen Anne. As soon as news of Pocahontas's
coming had reached his ears, even "before she arrived in London,
Captaine Smith," to quote the Captaine,

> to deserve her former courtesies, made her qualities knowne to
> the Queenes most excellent Maiestie and her Court, and writ a
> little booke to this effect to the Queene: An abstract whereof
> followeth:

> TO THE MOST HIGH AND VERTUOUS PRINCESSE,
> QUEENE ANNE OF GREAT BRITTANIE

> Most admired Queene,
> The loue I beare my God, my King and Countrie, hath so
> oft emboldened mee in the worst of extreme dangers, that now
> honestie doth constraine mee [to] presume thus farre beyond
> my selfe, to present your Maiestie this short discourse: if in-
> gratitude be a deadly poyson to all honest vertues, I must bee
> guiltie of that crime if I should omit any means to bee thankfull.

> So it is,
> That some ten yeeres agoe being in *Virginia*, and taken
> prisoner by the power of *Powhatan* their chiefe King, I receiued
> from this great Saluage exceeding great courtesie, especially

from his sonne *Nantaquaus*, the most manliest, comeliest, boldest spirit, I euer saw in a Saluage, and his sister *Pocahontas*, the Kings most deare and wel-beloued daughter, being but a childe of twelue or thirteene yeeres of age, whose compassionate pitifull heart, of my desperate estate, gaue me much cause to respect her: I being the first Christian this proud King and his grim attendants euer saw: and thus inthralled in their barbarous power, I cannot say I felt the least occasion of want that was in the power of those my mortall foes to preuent, notwithstanding al their threats. After some six weeks fatting amongst those Saluage Courtiers, at the minute of my execution, she hazarded the beating out of her owne braines to saue mine; and not onely that, but so preuailed with her father, that I was safely conducted to *Iames* towne: where I found about eight and thirtie miserable poore and sick creatures, to keepe possession of all those large territories of *Virginia*; such was the weaknesse of this poore Commonwealth, as had the Saluages not fed vs, we directly had starued. And this reliefe, most gracious Queene, was commonly brought vs by this Lady *Pocahontas*.

Notwithstanding all these passages, when inconstant Fortune turned our peace to warre, this tender Virgin would still not spare to dare to visit vs, and by her our iarres haue beene oft appeased, and our wants still supplyed; were it the policie of her father thus to employ her, or the ordinance of God thus to make her his instrument, or her extraordinarie affection to our Nation, I know not: but of this I am sure; when her father with the vtmost of his policie and power, sought to surprize mee, hauing but eighteene with mee, the darke night could not affright her from comming through the irkesome woods, and with watered eies gaue me intelligence, with her best aduice to escape his furie; which had hee knowne, hee had surely slaine her.

Iames towne with her wild traine she as freely frequented, as her fathers habitation; and during the time of two or three yeeres she next vnder God, was still the instrument to preserue this Colonie from death, famine and vtter confusion; which if in those times, [it] had once beene dissolued, Virginia might haue line as it was at our first arriuall to this day.

Since then, this businesse hauing beene turned and varied by many accidents from that I left it at: it is most certaine, after a long and troublesome warre after my departure, betwixt her father and our Colonie; all which time shee was not heard of.

About two yeeres after shee her selfe was taken prisoner, being so detained neere two yeeres longer, the Colonie by that meanes was relieued, peace concluded; and at last reiecting her barbarous condition, was maried to an *English* Gentleman, with whom at this present she is in *England*; the first Christian euer of that Nation, the first *Virginian* euer spake *English*, or had a childe in mariage by an *Englishman*: a matter surely, if my meaning bee truly considered and well vnderstood, worthy a Princes vnderstanding.

Thus, most gracious Lady, I haue related to your Maiestie, what at your best leasure our approued Histories will account you at large, and done in the time of your Maiesties life; and howeuer this might bee presented you from a more worthy pen, it cannot from a more honest heart, as yet I neuer begged any thing of the state, or any: and it is my want of abilitie and her exceeding desert; your birth, meanes and authoritie; her birth, vertue, want and simplicitie, doth make mee thus bold, humbly to beeseech your Maiestie to take this knowledge of her, though it be from one so vnworthy to be the reporter, as my selfe, her husbands estate not being able to make her fit to attend your Maiestie. The most and least I can doe, is to tell you this, because none so oft hath tried it as my selfe, and the rather being of so great a spirit, how euer her stature: if she should not be well receiued, seeing this Kingdome may rightly haue a Kingdome by her meanes; her present loue to vs and Christianitie might turne to such scorne and furie, as to diuert all this good to the worst of euill: where finding so great a Queene should doe her some honour more than she can imagine, for being so kinde to your seruants an subiects, would so rauish her with content, as endeare her dearest bloud to effect that, your Maiestie and all the Kings honest subiects most earnestly desire.

And so I humbly kisse your gracious hands.

For all Captain Smith's fine words, however, he failed to go to greet the Indian princess in whose behalf he had addressed the sovereign. Months went by, strange to say, without his attending in person upon the woman to whom he owed his life. All London flocked to see Pocahontas; only Smith was missing, and conspicuous by his absence.

One senses an implicit rivalry between the two men in her life, between John Smith and John Rolfe. Mutual friends may have fanned the flames of a mutual distrust, a hostility, a rivalry between the Englishman who had first captured Pocahontas's affections and the second to do so. To recognize one's self as second choice cannot predispose one in favor of the first choice. Rumors had circulated, even in Virginia, and must eventually have reached Rolfe's ears, to the effect that Captain Smith could have taken the Indian princess as his bride, had he cared to make their relationship permanent: "If he would, he might have married her, or have done what him listed"—an innuendo to taunt the man who had married her.

Resentments rankled in the breasts of both men. From Smith's point of view, in 1616, John Rolfe appeared to have carried off all the prizes: Smith may have envied Rolfe his bride—a celebrity, a nine-day wonder in England, richly dowered with New World properties; Smith may have envied Rolfe his recognition and position in the colony and in the company, his post and title of Secretary-Recorder of Virginia; may have envied Rolfe his rich cargo of the golden leaf in the hold of the *Treasurer*.

Even on the issue of tobacco (a divisive one, from the beginning), the two men squared off in opposition, Rolfe championing tobacco and its advantages to the colonial economy, Smith—as rabidly antitobacco as the monarch—flourishing his pen to propagandize against "the filthy weed."

Captain Smith, let it be noted, lost no opportunity, in the letter he addressed to Queen Anne, to point up John Rolfe's humble social status: Pocahontas's "husband's estate," in Smith's words, "not being able to make her fit to attend your Maiestie. . . ."

Fortune had vouchsafed Captain Smith few favors; the Virginia Company, none. If he had been the hero of the original expeditionary force of 1607—his valor and leadership, in great part, responsible for Jamestown's survival—no hero's welcome awaited him upon his return to England in 1609. He returned very much under a cloud, "sent home," as his inveterate enemy Captain Ratcliffe spitefully advised the Earl of Salisbury, "to answer some misdemeanors, whereof I persuade myself he can scarcely clear himself from great imputation of blame." If Smith managed to stave off formal charges, managed to escape a court of inquiry, he never quite succeeded in clearing his name of the charges of insubordination, of mutiny. While none could dispute Smith's leadership capabilities, neither could anyone dispute his tactlessness, his knack for making enemies. Risking his life to save another's, Smith promptly fell out with him. The heroic gesture came more easily to Captain Smith than the conciliatory, the diplomatic. He was infinitely tactless, brash; he had accumulated enemies in the Virginia Company as in the colony.

Despite Smith's numerous petitions, no reassignment to active duty in the colony was forthcoming, nor the offer of any administrative or executive position on the company's London staff. If Sir Thomas Smythe was Smith's "honorable good friend" (as Smith described him), he gave no evidence of friendship for Smith in the course of the years 1609–16, when the reins of power still resided in Smythe's hands.

Chafing at inactivity—Smith's sporadic excursions into writing and publishing could not yet provide a livelihood—and despairing of his future with the Virginia Company, John Smith managed to find investors to finance a small expedition to the northeast coast of America, in 1614. For lack of the hoped-for gold and whales, the backers of the venture had to console themselves with dried cod and beaver pelts.

Captain Smith found his consolation in surveying and mapping that northeastern seaboard from Penobscot Bay (Maine) down to Cape Cod. He returned to England in the summer of 1614 totally committed to the idea of establishing an English colony on the coast of New England (Smith's name for the region, confirmed by Prince Charles), and succeeded in communicating his enthusiasm to Sir Ferdinando Gorges, a leader in the Plymouth Company (a company representative of the commercial interests of the ports of Plymouth, Bristol, and Exeter), which held the "colonial rights" of exploration, trade, and settlement to that part of the North American eastern seaboard designated as "northern Virginia"; London's Virginia Company held the colonial rights to "southern Virginia."

The Plymouth Company bestowed on Captain Smith the resounding title of Admiral of New England, in token of their confiding to him "their authority in those parts"; he, on his part, engaged himself "to undertake it for them."

Smith's first expedition under Plymouth Company auspices—setting out in midsummer, 1615—was inauspicious in the extreme, dogged by disaster. Only Smith could have survived such a series of misadventures: first storms, then corsairs conspired to keep him from the Western Hemisphere.

No wonder that fresh funds for a second expedition to New England did not materialize as rapidly as Smith had hoped. He champed at the bit, fretted at the delays. The Plymouth Company was proving no more reliable than the Virginia Company, Sir Ferdinando Gorges no more trustworthy than Sir Thomas Smythe: "all their great promises nothing but air," by Smith's bitter complaint. He was frustrated, impatient, bitter, in the summer of 1616, when Pocahontas landed in England. He was on tenterhooks of anxiety, waiting for the long-promised ships in which he hoped to make the voyage back to New England.

His sixty-odd page *Description of New England*—written during his months of captivity aboard a French corsair in 1615, and off the press as a small quarto volume in the summer of 1616—could distract him only briefly from his main purposes in life: exploration and colonization.*

His mind was on his next sailing.

And he had little opportunity to make contact with Pocahontas when she arrived in London in midsummer. London was no longer the center of activities for Smith; by then, he was commuting between London and the West Country ("Much labour I had to bring the Londoners and them to joyne together, because the Londoners have the most Money, and the Westerne men are most proper for fishing. . . ."); Plymouth, rather than London, was his headquarters: it was only a "small time I staid in London," as he put it.

The press of preparations for this projected New England voyage —fund-raising among "divers Merchants of the West," enlistment of colonists and crew—was the excuse Smith offered for his failure to go in person to offer his services, to pay his respects, to greet the stranger on his shore who had been savior and guardian-angel to him:

> Being about this time preparing to set saile for New England, I could not stay to doe her that service I desired, and she well deserved. . . .

* Four years later, the Pilgrims would take Smith's tip that Massachusetts was "the Paradise of all those parts," that Plymouth (which Smith had named as he had New England) offered "an excellent good harbor, good land; and no want of anything but industrious people. . . ." The Pilgrims would take Smith's map, if not Smith; it was a remarkably accurate map, the distances generally corresponding with those known to be true today. Both the map and the portrait for this book were engraved by Simon Van de Passe.

CHAPTER XIII

. . . an huntinge kinge, a dauncinge queen . . .

THE CLIMATE OF ENGLAND—exceptionally fine as it was that year of 1616—did not agree with the Virginia Indians.

It would be the death of them. Out of the original party of a dozen or so, not more than half would survive.

There was, despite the fine weather of 1616, a great deal of illness prevalent in the British Isles in the summer the Virginia party landed there: "We have a new ague or sickness," John Chamberlain reported in a letter dated August 24, 1616,

> that begins to spread itself in many places, and . . . hath taken away diverse of good note, and upon short warning. . . . And it is the more strange for that we have had the finest and most seasonable weather now this whole twelvemonth that ever I knew. . . .

Abruptly transplanted from their tranquil forest habitat, the Virginia Indians could not accommodate themselves to the uproar of life in a metropolis. According to Brown's *First Republic*,

> In the course of a few months, in 1616, at least three of the Indians brought from Virginia by Dale, had died at the house of Sir Thomas Smythe, in Philpot Lane, Langborne Ward, London, and were buried at St. Dionis church, in the same ward. They did not stand the climate of England much better then the English did that of Virginia, although they were amply provided for in every way.

Funeral expenses for three was only the beginning: one after another, the party of Virginia natives fell ill, requiring medical attention for which the Virginia Company grudgingly had to pay, as company records show. Four years later, as late as 1620, the Company was still paying out money "for the adminstring of Physick and cordialls" for "the health" of "one of the maydes which Sir Thomas Dale brought from Virginia . . . now verie weake of a consumption."[1] It was probably "a consumption" from which the Powhatan tribesmen and tribeswomen suffered; there was a high incidence of consumption in the seventeenth century in England, especially among young women. (The American Indians lacked immunity and thus were highly vulnerable to a number of diseases, including tuberculosis, smallpox, measles, malaria, and typhoid, common in the Old World, thus far unknown to the New.) It was not bubonic plague that struck down Pocahontas's attendants in 1616; the red plague cross had not flown in London since 1603, the year of James I's accession (a year in which London recorded a death toll of thirty thousand), and would not fly again until 1625.

If the Virginia Company had only gotten its money's worth in publicity out of the redskin troupe, it would not have begrudged the poor Indians their "Physick and cordialls." The troupe had been imported as the main attraction for the forthcoming Virginia Lottery (to be held in St. Paul's Churchyard, like the last), but those few that managed to survive, languished—and who would pay to see a show with sickly, drooping savages?

Pocahontas, Matachanna, Uttamatamakin, and the rest must have breathed uneasily under the blanket of London fog with its noxious vapors ("this misty and unsavoury town," in the words of John Chamberlain; this "filthie toune," in the words of James I, who spent no more time than necessary in his capital city). When the elements conspired, the smoke from thousands of chimneys hung like a pall over London, as did the fumes from the open sewers. (Sanitation measures were rudimentary: a squad of scavengers assigned to every ward of London barely managed to dispose of the household refuse and the ordure littering the streets.)

The squalor, the stench, the din, the crowd, the crush of London were enough to take aback the rustic, the forest-dweller: he quaked at the thunder of hooves on cobble, the clatter of cart- and carriage-wheels*; he cringed at the press of people, the swirling throngs, the multitudes swarming, pushing through the dark, narrow, winding streets. On the even narrower lanes and alleys, the upper story of a house on one side jostled the upper story of the house across; the tene-

---

* The horse and the wheel must have ranked as the two chief wonders of the Old World to the native of the New, window glass probably as the third.

ments rose tall and narrow, bleak half-timbered houses with pointed roofs, several stories high, one story overhanging the other, peopled from cellar to attic, a family to a room.[2]

If moccasined feet winced on the cobblestones, ears attuned to wildwood silence were shattered in the cacophony of city racket. To the clatter of traffic and the clamor of bells was joined the babel of street vendors, the patter of costermongers, peddlers, and tradesmen who took to the streets to cry their wares. And the calls of the watch rent the night; the last word was the city crier's "and so goodnight, and so goodnight."

The ill health—whether a manifestation of psychic or physical malaise—which afflicted Pocahontas and the other Indians of her party throughout their London sojourn was probably in great part attributable to their confinement in what must have seemed to them insufferably close quarters, denied the exercise to which life in the vast spaces of their homeland had accustomed them. Children of the tidewater— water as much their element as earth—they missed, perhaps above all, their sunrise river plunge, the salute to their sun god with which their day traditionally began. The Thames near London unfortunately did not permit swimming, already polluted by the flow of open sewers and garbage from the city, human, animal, and household waste emptying into the river.

Tradition rather than personal hygiene prompted the Powhatans' morning swims, but even so, their skin may have been subject to discomfort, deprived of the habitual daily immersion. They were nicer in the matter of bodily cleanliness than were their English hosts: homilies notwithstanding, cleanliness had not yet taken rank as a virtue next to godliness. If the colonists in Virginia turned up their noses at the rancid bear-oil with which the Powhatan tribesmen anointed themselves as a discouragement to vermin, the Powhatans, in their turn, must have sniffed disdainfully at the host of Englishmen whose only ablutions consisted of dabbing at the hand or wrist with a cloth dipped in water— fennel- or rose-water, preferably; Queen Anne's rose-water imported from Antwerp. As for King James, if his skin was "as soft as taffeta sarsanet," it was "because he never washed his hands, only rubbed his fingers' ends slightly with the wet end of a napkin." Baths were taken, at the most, once a year, unless on doctor's prescription, as a cure for gout or rheumatism. (A bath rashly taken by Queen Anne at Hampton Court was popularly considered responsible for her death in 1619; a shivering fit overtook her as she emerged, and ended in smallpox.) The pomander-ball strung about an English lady's neck, the nosegay fastened in her corsage were not designed to enhance her costume but to mitigate the unpleasant odors which assailed her nostrils in any seventeenth-century crowd or gathering; to that purpose, articles of clothing, especially gloves, were scented. In English households which could afford such amenities, the floors were strewn with herb-scented rushes.

Pocahontas was apparently still in good health when the summons came to Whitehall Palace, possibly from the Queen. Robert Beverley, toward the close of that same century, wrote:

> Pocahontas had many Honours done her by the Queen upon account of Capt. Smith's Story; and being introduced by the Lady Delawarr, she was frequently admitted to wait on her Majesty, and was publickly treated as a Prince's Daughter. . . .

Certainly Captain Smith liked to think that it was his "little booke," his character reference which had won Pocahontas the Queen's favor: ". . . and as since I have heard, it pleased both the King and Queenes Majestie honourably to esteeme her. . . ."

Although it may have been John Smith's petition that originally attracted the Queen's attention, stirred her imagination, undoubtedly others besides the humble captain put in a good word for Pocahontas at the Stuart Court. Sir Thomas Dale had a good friend high in the hierarchy of power—Sir Ralph Winwood, Secretary of State—to whom he would naturally have appealed in behalf of his protégée. And it was certainly in the interest of Sir Thomas Smythe as treasurer of the Virginia Company to promote the reception of the Indian princess at Whitehall: to attract royal favor for the Virginian princess was to attract royal favor for the Virginia Colony.

Nor would the project have been overly difficult of achievement: a real live redskin princess from the far side of the earth promised more of a novelty at Court than even a dwarf or blackamoor (both of which had been fixtures at Queen Elizabeth's Court) and, as such, would have tickled the fancy of the frivolous, flighty, pleasure-loving consort of King James. To be amused was all to Anne, to relieve her tedium was her chief preoccupation. Her ladies in waiting were expected to romp with her in children's games like "Rise, pig, and go!" or "One penny, follow me!" (to the scorn of an intellectual like the Lady Arabella Stuart when she was importuned by the Queen "to play the child again").

But if the pedantic James's wife was a flibbertigibbet, she was also good-natured, well-intentioned, agreeable, kind, although her good nature, sad to say, was eroding under the stress and strain of a steadily deteriorating marital relation. Platinum-haired, fair-skinned, blue-eyed, a typical Scandinavian in coloring, the Danish princess had been pretty enough in her teens to attract James's eye, although he was not, even in his youth, highly susceptible to feminine charms. His homosexual tendencies became more pronounced after he had fulfilled his duty to the kingdom—the production of two male heirs—and retired from the marriage bed. Anne was, apparently, despite the gossip, giddy and flirtatious rather than adulterous.

Pocahontas—ushered into the presence of the Queen in 1616—beheld a woman of forty-two, a statuesque if raddled blonde, magnificently appareled, dazzlingly bejeweled, her extravagance and indebtedness on this count yet another source of marital discord. Despite her six children and numerous miscarriages, Anne of Denmark's fine figure was intact: Paul Van Somer's portrait makes much of her wasp waist, the swell of fine white bosom.

As apt a pupil of her noble sponsors as of her religious sponsors, quick to accommodate herself to the intricacies of Court etiquette, Pocahontas evidently performed her deep obeisance before Queen Anne with grace and dignity. Reflecting honor on the De La Warres and on Captain Smith, Pocahontas is said to have carried herself nobly at her Whitehall début, as in all subsequent encounters with the sovereigns and the courtiers: "Upon all which Occasions," Robert Beverley reported,

> she behaved her self with so much Decency, and show'd so much Grandure in her Deportment, that she made good the brightest Part of the Character Capt. Smith had given of her. . . .

The fact that Pocahontas was "frequently admitted to wait on her Majesty" is proof that, in her very person, she offered a piquancy, a novelty well calculated to divert a queen to whom diversion was the aim of all existence. (Not that Pocahontas appeared at Whitehall in her savage finery of paint and feathers; she made her bow to royalty in conventional Court costume—her bosom perhaps less bare, her face less gaudily rouged than those of the ladies of Anne's suite—but, even so, her exotic look, her skin glinting bright as burnished copper, her dark eyes flashing, her barbaric origins, her reputation as heroine to Smith and savior to the colony lent her a fascination and assured her a welcome at Whitehall.)

It also suggests that Her Majesty's reception was cordial: Anne was naturally inclined to a cordiality, a geniality, rare in a royal personage. Rarer still was her approachability, frequently remarked and acknowledged by those admitted to her presence. Stranger though Pocahontas was in a strange land, she could not but have been sensible to the favor shown her by Anne. It was human nature to respond in kind to such a welcome. Pocahontas, furthermore, was young, young enough to be Anne's daughter (Anne's daughter Elizabeth was approximately the same age), and inclined, by nature, to be playful, sportive (as the Powhatan meaning of her name suggests). Chances are that she enjoyed frolicking with Anne and her ladies in the boisterous juvenile games spurned by Lady Arabella Stuart. Blithesome both, Queen Anne and her young visitor from the Western Hemisphere were likely to have been congenial.

There is not only Captain Smith's word for it that Pocahontas enjoyed her success at the Stuart Court, that she found in it "great satisfaction and content." William Stith concurs: "she was wonderfully well pleased and delighted" with her reception at Whitehall. She had reason to be equally pleased and delighted with the reception tendered her by the Bishop of London. As Purchas observed her on that occasion, she moved with ease, with poise and confidence in those lofty ecclesiastical circles, as she had in the royal ones—a suggestion that she felt at ease in those strange new surroundings.

The splendor of neither the episcopal palace nor the royal palace seemed to abash Pocahontas—or, for that matter, Uttamatamakin. He no more than she lost his composure; neither was apparently ever at a loss for words in those exalted precincts.[8]

Whitehall may have suffered in comparison with the Escorial or the Louvre, but these visitors from the New World had no such basis for comparison. What they saw on the north bank of the Thames was a vast rookery of a palace, a maze of two thousand and more rooms connected by irregular passageways and courtyards sprawling across twenty-three acres, an example of ramshackle Tudor architectural procedure.

Lords and ladies, entering or leaving their carriages at the Court Gate, must have stopped in their tracks at the sight of the two outlandish figures emerging from the De La Warre coach—Uttamatamakin the more bizarre of the two, with his scanty leather breech-clout, his brick-red chest festooned with beads and copper, his paint and feathers, his priestly coronet of stuffed snake and weasel skins ("their tayles tied together" to meet "on the crowne of his head in a tassell").

As grotesque a figure as he seemed, he could have been no more of a curiosity to the Jacobean courtiers than they to him and to Pocahontas. The splendor of the seventeenth-century English nobleman was dazzling, as seen, for example, in the portrait painted of him by the Dutch artist Daniel Mytens: there he stands (the third Earl of Dorset, one of the premier noblemen of James's realm), in his voluminous, richly embroidered breeches, a glittering doublet cinching his narrow waist, a brocaded cape heavy with gold burdening his left shoulder, gold clocks running up his white silk hose, spectacular lace pompon "roses"—big as cabbages—adorning his slippers, his locks elaborately curled and frizzled, his moustachios and goatee neatly, foppishly waxed, the tassels of his earrings dangling down upon the starched and wired lace ruff, his monstrosity of a white-plumed Court hat within reach on the table behind him. (Looks were deceiving: When the Jacobean courtier mounted his gorgeously caparisoned charger to enter the lists in the palace tiltyard, there was nothing effete about him; he showed himself an intrepid horseman, a master with a lance; only an expert rider could keep up with the monarch in the saddle from dawn to dusk, on the hunt, only a trained athlete could compete with his peers in the White-hall tennis court and bowling alleys.)

At Whitehall Palace, visiting dignitaries such as Pocahontas and Uttamatamakin, having passed through the Court Gate, crossed the Great Court and mounted the broad flight of stone stairs that led to the Great Guard Chamber, where two hundred of "His Majesties great Beefe-eaters," in their flamboyant red uniforms, stood guard over the inner sanctum, the private purlieus of the palace.

Only in the convoy of the captain of the guard could visitors proceed beyond that point.

At the door of the Presence Chamber, the Lord Chamberlain—principal officer of the Court—awaited them.

William Herbert, Earl of Pembroke—Privy Councillor, Knight of the Garter, one of the wealthiest, most powerful peers in England—was the Lord Chamberlain whose duty it was to usher Pocahontas and Uttamatamakin into the presence of James I, and there to perform the elaborate ritual of presentation. He it was who had appointed the day and hour for Pocahontas's audience at Whitehall Palace. A longtime proponent of western exploration and colonization, a member of the Royal Council for Virginia, as well as a stockholder in the Virginia Company, he would doubtless have been curious about this dark lady from the Americas, and would have readily obliged Lord and Lady De La Warre and high officials of the Virginia Company by arranging to bring Virginia to the King's attention.

Pocahontas—well coached by the De La Warres in the intricacies of Whitehall protocol—followed the Lord Chamberlain into the large and impressive hall known as the Presence Chamber, there to perform the prescribed obeisance and to kiss the remarkably soft, white hand His Majesty extended to her.

If Pocahontas, rising from her knee at James's sign, saw the sovereign as Mytens saw and painted him, at some time close to that date, she saw him seated in his armchair, resplendent in pale, gleaming velvet, his great cape thrown back over his shoulders to reveal the Garter ribbon draped about his neck just below his white lace ruff, his satin slippers fastened with enormous bows, his fantastic plumed Court hat reposing on the sumptuously draped table at his elbow.

Neither the magnificence of his raiment, however, nor all the trappings of majesty with which he was invested, could make of James I a truly imposing figure. Impossible for Pocahontas and Uttamatamakin not to have made the comparison with her father, who, naked as he was in his savage state, yet revealed himself every bare inch a king, awe-inspiring personification of power and authority: "such Majestie as I cannot expresse," to quote an awe-struck John Smith, "nor yet have often seene, either in Pagan or Christian."

This Christian James was of medium height, thickset and stocky, neither as tall nor as stalwart as the Indian chieftain. James had the intellectual's high forehead, a full face, fair and flushed and pox-pitted, set off by a sparse, square-cut brown beard and mustache. As magnificent as he seemed on horseback—a royal centaur—on foot, he appeared a poor thing. A victim of rickets and rickety, his gait was shambling, jerky: "that weaknesse made him ever leaning on other mens shoulders," in the words of Sir Anthony Weldon in his description of *The Court and Character of King James*, with both of which he was familiar, "his walke was ever circular, his fingers ever in that walke fidling about his codpiece."

A man of wide erudition, a scholar, pedant—"The Wisest Fool in Christendom," as Henri IV of France is said to have said of him— King James's lively intellectual curiosity had been attracted to the flora and fauna of the newly discovered western continent: Captain John Smith had been requested, upon his return to England from the west in 1609, to purvey a pair of flying squirrels from the Virginia forests to the monarch as an item of rare curiosity.

How much more of a curiosity, this pair of human creatures, New World aborigines, a male and a female specimen, the latter capable of conversing with James, in his own tongue, without the need of an interpreter! Although, to be sure, English was no more James's native tongue than it was Pocahontas's, a possible cause for difficulty in their colloquy: James's Scots brogue was pronounced, while Pocahontas, fluent though she may have become in English, would have yet spoken it with some trace of a foreign accent.

Questions on a variety of subjects would have come to James's inquisitive, wide-ranging mind in the course of his interview with

Pocahontas and Uttamatamakin. James's burning interest in religion and the chase would have prompted questions on those two topics: what the natives of America believed and how they worshipped, what wild game the North American continent provided and how the natives hunted it.

Uttamatamakin and Pocahontas, conversely, would have been interested in the methods of hunting pursued by their hosts, the way the deer were chased past screened ambushes whence the King and courtiers—ladies as well as lords—shot at the game with their crossbows; the chase on horseback and with a pack of hounds, a sport exclusively for the gentlemen, the quarry finally overtaken by the hounds and dispatched; the English practice of using trained hawks and falcons for hunting was entirely unknown to the Indians.

King James, presumably, was briefed by Lord De La Warre and by Sir Ralph Winwood, the Secretary of State, prior to his audience with the Virginians, on the matter of red-white relations in that land, on the matter of the economy of the new colony on the James.

If, thanks to John Rolfe, tobacco was proving the colony's first profitable export commodity and the economic salvation of the Virginia Company, Rolfe would receive small thanks for it from his sovereign.

He would receive none, in fact; would not even be received in audience with his wife, was pointedly excluded from the audience granted her and Uttamatamakin. It was not only Rolfe's modest social status (a mere gentleman-farmer) which precluded Rolfe's being given entrée to the Court, he had forfeited his King's good graces by his marriage. James was jealous of the prerogatives of royalty; he deemed it presumptuous of John Rolfe to have aspired to the hand of an absolute ruler's daughter, and threatened to visit his displeasure on this subject for his impudence.

At least, so went the report in Virginia, and so it came to the ear (and pen) of Robert Beverley:

> In the mean while, she [Pocahontas] gain'd the good Opinion of every Body, so much that the poor Gentleman her Husband had like to have been call'd to an Account for presuming to marry a Princess Royal without the King's Consent; because it had been suggested that he had taken Advantage of her being a Prisoner, and forc'd her to marry him. But upon a more perfect Representation of the Matter, his Majesty was pleased at last to declare himself satisfied."*

* The above paragraph, relating to the fuss and pother of the King's displeasure over Rolfe's presumptuousness in marrying into the imperial Powhatan family, ap-

Whoever it was—whether a resentful Captain Smith or some other—who had "suggested" that Rolfe "had taken Advantage of her being a Prisoner," Beverley does not reveal. Nor does Beverley tell the reader who it was who made "a more perfect Representation of the Matter"; Pocahontas herself might have spoken in her husband's defense on this point, but, above all, one would expect that Sir Thomas Dale would have risen promptly to the defense of Rolfe, who had quite properly applied directly to the governor for official consent to the union. Whereas Dale had no access to the King, he might have turned to Lord De La Warre to request that nobleman to make his representation in this matter for him.

Denied an audience with his sovereign, Rolfe respectfully submitted to His Majesty, during the course of 1617, a copy of his *True Relation*, a report on the state of His Majesty's Colony of Virginia, with special emphasis on the success of the tobacco experiments made by Rolfe. If the King made any acknowledgment, there is no sign of it. A formal petition submitted to the monarch in 1621, over the signatures of John Rolfe and Sir George Yeardley, then governor of the colony, and urging measures of relief for the Virginia tobacco growers and shippers from crippling taxes and restrictions, would prove likewise unavailing. King James's antipathy to the "vile weed" was so violent that he failed to recognize the fact that in tobacco England had actually found the ideal colonial commodity; an article, moreover, which could develop a tremendous export market on the Continent, eventually a worldwide market. But John Rolfe would not live to see that day: in his time, every effort was made to discourage the tobacco traffic; the diversification of commodities was urged on the colony and restrictions placed on tobacco acreage by colonial governors; in his day, the collection of duties and other taxes was granted by the crown to monopolists, a corrupt system not to be eliminated until 1643. It must be considered an irony of colonial and economic history that the Virginia tobacco monoculture triumphed over a hostile and restrictive official policy.

The monarch might fulminate against what he called the "vile custome," but his subjects went right on "quaffing the fume"; despite him, "the art of whiffing" became the rage in upper-class London, in James's own Court. Every dandy boasted a collection of silver pipes (or clay pipes trimmed with silver), carried his smoking paraphernalia in a fine ivory or gold or silver box, patronized a favorite tobacconist;

peared in Beverley's 1705 London edition of *The History and Present State of Virginia*. In the revised edition of 1722, the Virginia planter-historian added a final sardonic sentence to this paragraph: "But had their [the Indians'] true condition here been known, that pother had been saved."

James's own Lord Chamberlain, the Earl of Pembroke, was an addict, enjoying the dubious distinction of being known as England's first chain-smoker. Not only lords but ladies as well had taken up the smoking fad, though not always openly, according to a Venetian envoy in his report from London in 1618: "Gentlewomen moreover and virtuous females accustom themselves to take it as medicine but in secret, the others do it at pleasure."

It is unlikely that Pocahontas joined the Court ladies of her acquaintance in a pipe. Early chroniclers make clear that Indian women were nowhere in the Americas observed to indulge. Smoking was a ceremony limited exclusively to the men of the tribe; even the cultivation of the sacred herb was forbidden the women. There is no reason to think that Pocahontas would have been tempted to take up the smoking habit in England. (One wonders what she made of these noble Christian English ladies puffing away at their pipes, baring their breasts in an exposure she had been taught to abhor, tinting their hair red or yellow, blueing their veins, daubing their cheeks and lips with rouge no less garish than the pocones root she had been persuaded to forswear when she had adopted civilized ways.)

King James was a man of many prejudices; in addition to his prejudice against tobacco, he admitted a strong color bias, an antipathy for red men, by reason of their association with tobacco. His Majesty's *Counter-Blaste to Tobacco* attacked not only the Englishman who had popularized tobacco in England—Sir Walter Raleigh, "the first Author" and "father"—but the cultivators of the weed, as well, the Indians who had developed its use, or so James contended, as an antidote for the ravages of "the pox"; James's tract made the charge that the aborigines of America had infected the invading Europeans with venereal disease (instead of vice versa, for which a better case can be made). *Counter-Blaste* inveighed against "the wilde, godlesse, and slavish Indians" with their "barbarous and beastly manners."

Pocahontas, therefore, must have appeared to him as a rare exception, a paragon. Had her manners been "barbarous and beastly," he would never have invited her as his guest at the most notable occasion of the year, at the most brilliant event, the most prestigious festivity of the Court calendar, the grand and gala Twelfth Night masque to be presented before the most exclusive of audiences in the Banqueting House—the climax, the high point of the whole glittering Yuletide season. Extending from Christmas to Twelfth Night, the holiday season included three festivals, Christmas Day, Twelfth Day, and New Year's Day (that festival being kept on January 1st, according to the old Roman practice, even though the calendar new year did not actually begin until Lady Day—the day after March 24, 1616, for example, becoming March 25, 1617).

Throughout the twelve days of Christmas, the Jacobean Court was to be seen at its most splendid, most frivolous, most bibulous, most profligate: for the great lords, the stakes were always high, but the holiday season was the time for "Golden Play," with a minimum wager of £300 required of every player who approached the Whitehall gaming tables. It was traditional for the King's favorite to place the bets for the monarch (in the happy prospect that, should he be lucky, the winnings would be his to keep).

The Yuletide of 1616–17 was to be celebrated with especial éclat: James was entering upon his fiftieth year as King of Scotland (having acceded to that throne at the age of one year, one month). Not only that, sixteen-year-old Charles, King James's only surviving son, was making his Court début that season, as Prince of Wales (the official investiture having taken place in the Banqueting House in November). Furthermore, January was scheduled as the month for the apotheosis of that golden boy, Sir George Villiers—latest of the King's favorites, most nobly endowed of the lot, as the most powerful—his elevation to the rank of Earl of Buckingham to be announced on January 5.

Whitehall Palace and the City of London alike were caught up in a round of gaiety and festivity. The petty nobility and the country gentry, yearning for sophisticated pleasures, thronged London to participate in the holiday excitement—in the varied diversions of the city if not the Court—and had to be coerced, by royal proclamation, into returning to the shires ("to repayre to their Mansion houses in the Country, to attend their services, and keepe hospitality, according to the ancient and laudable custome of England").

To spend the holiday season in the capital was to be privileged, indeed. The humblest citizen of London shared with the noble courtier the dazzling display of fireworks set off as finale to some palace fête. The night skies flared for all to see (within sight of the river where the combustibles and explosives were set off on barges anchored across from Whitehall): wheels and rockets, showers of brilliant light; a set piece of the British lion, a favorite motif with the English Court, a burst of sound and color, a crackle and flame and sputter to intimidate a native of the New World never before exposed to pyrotechnical displays.

Even pagans like the Indians must have sensed the stir of excitement, the good will and good cheer of the Christmas season in Merry Old England. They would have taken a naïve, childish delight in the jollities and the decorations of the Christmastide: the holly and mistletoe adorning every door were familiar to the tribesmen from their home forests (though never for use in such a context), but not the Yule candle flickering through every mullioned window of every London home, not the Yule log burning on even the modest hearth, not the "Kissing Bough," a luminous candlelit globe of evergreens trimmed with bright red apples, a holiday motif predating the Christmas tree in England. The season was marked by joyous sounds as well as sights, as strangers from another continent discovered: carolers' voices rang out in every ward of London town, and the churchbells began to "ring in Christmas" as early as December 21, St. Thomas's Day, continuing on throughout the holidays, despite the Puritans' objections to the din. The natives of the New World would have been amused at the antics of Father Christmas (a newcomer to the scene in Queen Elizabeth's time) as at those of that old-time Christmas figure, that medieval buffoon, that high priest of revelry, the Lord of Misrule or Christmas Prince.*

New Year's, rather than Christmas, was the day for gift-giving: the King made gifts of gold (£10 to barons, £20 to earls) along with pieces of gilt plate. The great lords sought to impress the sovereign with gifts that had novelty as well as intrinsic value; the country gentry and commoners presented to the monarch tokens of marzipan, green ginger, hippocras. The De La Warres might have prompted Pocahontas to present the monarch and his wife with some gift typical of Virginia and the Powhatans—a porcupine-quill-embroidered pouch, a fringed white doeskin, a pearl necklace, a reed quiver, a woven sweetgrass basket.

The Pocahontas Vase—as it is referred to by its owners, the Elwin family, collateral descendants of the Rolfes of Heacham—may have been a New Year's gift, in 1617, from King James to his Indian visitor and guest but, if so, his was no royal gesture. The object is a small earthenware vase, pale mushroom in color, with a silver rim, a salt-glazed porcelain of a type produced in the Rhine Valley as early as the end of the sixteenth century; of no intrinsic value, then; of no value now, save for its provenance, if ownership could be definitely traced back to the Indian princess at James's Court.

Word went out at Whitehall in November of 1616 that the festivities were to be on a lavish scale: no expense was to be spared on the masque which would come as the high point of the glittering season, a showcase for the Earl of Buckingham's talents as a dancer.

Ben Jonson was commissioned to set the theme, to write the libretto for the opus; Inigo Jones, to design the costumes and scenery, to devise the ingenious mechanisms by which his stunning stage effects

---

* The Lord of Misrule was a master of the revels appointed at the Inns of Court and in great houses at Christmas time.

were accomplished; Nicholas Lanier, to compose the score to accompany Jonson's book and lyrics.

The King's Master of the Revels gave notice to the King's Men and other professional London companies of actors to stand by to join the noble amateurs in the Court performances. Twelve French musicians were engaged at a cost of £100. Finishing touches of gold and silver leaf were to be applied to the Banqueting House, center of Whitehall revelry and ceremonial: orders "for painting and gilding with part gold and silver . . . with pyramids and balls at the top, likewise gilded" were issued by the Paymaster of the Works early in November.

With the glamorous and graceful Buckingham to dance the leading role, the King was sure to be in attendance: "His Highness means to be [at the masque] in person," the word went out early in November: "This will increase His Majesty's debt by two thousand pounds"— thus a report to Sir Dudley Carleton at The Hague from his financial agent, Edward Sherburne.

Two thousand pounds . . . and more! Total expenses for the one-night extravaganza probably ran as high as £4,000 (£32,000 in modern values). So be it! *The Vision of Delight* was to be a starring vehicle for the King's radiantly handsome young favorite. Traditionally, the Royal Exchequer bore the burden of the Christmas theatrical productions but, in this case, the King may have loosened the strings of his own privy purse to supplement the budget.

These sumptuous and extravagant theatricals at Whitehall's Banqueting House served a purpose beyond mere diversion for the courtiers; they epitomized the pomp and grandeur of the English Court, enhanced the prestige of the British crown. International politics influenced the guest list for the King's masques and the seating arrangements for those guests.

If the Princess Pocahontas, on Twelfth Night (January 6, 1617), had the seat of honor beside the King of England at the premiere of Ben Jonson's *Vision of Delight*, she had French-Spanish squabbling to thank for it: Don Diego de Sarmiento had won King James's promise that if he, the Spanish Ambassador, could not attend, neither could the French. If neither the Spanish nor the French, then neither the Savoyard nor the Venetian. Solely the Powhatan was represented in the Banqueting House on that gala occasion.

This development was newsworthy in the extreme. John Chamberlain flashed the news to his friend Carleton at The Hague by letter dated January 18: "The Virginian woman Pocahontas, with her father-counsellor, hath been with the King and graciously used, and both she and her assistant well placed at the masque. . . ."

"Well placed," in terms of the Court protocol of 1617, meant that the Lady Rebecca and Uttamatamakin were seated on the royal dais, in the "great Neech"—at the monarch's right—the Queen and Prince of Wales were seated at the monarch's left. Pocahontas's place was one of prominence, such as the King was accustomed to give to the representative of a foreign potentate. And it was Uttamatamakin, Pocahontas's "father-counsellor," rather than her husband, who accompanied the chieftain's daughter to her seat on the royal platform. Her husband, John Rolfe, was relegated to the balcony of the Banqueting Hall, along with the twelve French musicians and other lesser mortals.

It would have been Pocahontas's assumption that she would have a place of prominence; she was accustomed to being treated as a privileged person, above the rank and file. In her father's longhouse on the Pamunkey, she had always taken her place close to his mighty person, along with his favorite wives and other daughters, on the raised platform described by Captain Smith. There, her finery had consisted of white feathers on her head, "and a great chayne of white beads" about her neck. At King James's Whitehall Palace on the Thames, it is reasonable to assume that Pocahontas wore the Court costume in which she sat to have her portrait painted.

One thing is certain: the skirt she wore was not a farthingale. That wide-spreading hoopskirt—"that impertinent garment," as James scathingly called it—had been banned at Court by special proclamation: to reduce the number of farthingales was substantially to increase the number of spectators James's Banqueting House would accommodate.

Space was at a premium not because the Banqueting House was small but, rather, because the audience was so numerous and the revels area so large: in addition to the stage proper—the platform behind the proscenium arch and curtain—a tremendously large area had to be allowed for the dancing in which the masquers invited the spectators to join, this green-carpeted dance-floor stretched from the proscenium arch at one end to the royal dais at the other.

The Banqueting House was a stone-and-brick building erected by James I in 1606 to replace the dilapidated structure raised there by Queen Elizabeth in 1581; this replacement of James's had the look of a Roman basilica or Egyptian hall, stretching—undivided, unfurnished—approximately one hundred ten feet long and fifty-five feet wide, a double cube. Tiers of seats (or benches) for the noble audience must have risen nearly halfway up the wall, along the long sides of the hall. When not in use as a theater—when the staging platform was dismantled and cleared away—the Banqueting House came into its own, lived up to its name as scene for royal feasting, toasting, dancing.[4]

Most authorities now agree that the Twelfth Night masque in 1617 was Ben Jonson's *Vision of Delight*, a divertissement, a dramatic confection as blithe and graceful as the season it celebrated—although contemporary critics were not unanimous in their praise.

Friends of John Chamberlain fortunate enough to have seats for that performance were less than ecstatic, according to a Chamberlain news bulletin of January 18: "I have heard no great speach nor commendations of the maske neither before nor since. . . ."

The classical allusions, the poetry of Ben Jonson's script, may have been lost on Pocahontas, but no eye, no ear, no matter how primitive, could resist the enchantment of Inigo Jones's repertoire of theatrical illusions, his kaleidoscope of changing scenes (behind the frame of the proscenium arch, Jones managed to create an illusion of depth by means of scenery painted in perspective, various scenes painted on "shutters," or wings, arranged in a projecting series on each side of the stage, one moved aside to reveal another), his sensational scenic effects and devices —feats of levitation in *The Vision of Delight*, the chariots of the Moon and Night, with their charioteers, rising high above the heads of the audience. The sound and spectacle of the masque, with its lavishness of costume, its song, dance, and music entranced most of the audience, the sophisticated along with the naïve.

On opening night of *The Vision of Delight*, the painted curtain fell (lowered from above, rather than raised, as today) to reveal what Jonson's libretto describes as "The Scene: A street in perspective of fair building discovered," for which Inigo Jones's pen-and-brown-ink sketch titled "A Street in Perspective" is doubtless the plan: a street scene of "fair" classical buildings, a tower, a house with scaffolding on top of it, a church, colonnades, a triumphal arch at the far end.

From "as afar off" (according to Jonson's stage directions), appeared the first character, "Delight, accompanied with Grace, Love, Harmony, Revel, Sport, Laughter." These characters "Spake in song, *stilo recitativo*." The audience ooh-ed and ah-ed at the first of Jones's stunning stage effects: "Night" in her chariot lifted straight up in the air; "Here the Night rises, and took her chariot bespangled with stars." ("See, see, Delight sings, her sceptre and her crown are all of flame.")

"By this time," Jonson directs, "the Night and Moon both being risen, Night, hovering over the place sung. . . ."

Working on a deep stage, Inigo Jones had perfected Italian stage techniques: in *The Vision of Delight*, the Street Scene yielded to billowing cloud effects: "The scene here changed to cloud," from which a new character, Fantasy, emerged bearing a mixed bag of dreams—

> *dreams that have wings,*
> *And dreams that have honey, and dreams that have stings.*

The anti-masque of *Phantasms* that followed Fantasy on stage was more fantastic still. No classical education was required of Pocahontas and Uttamatamakin to join that highly cultivated noble audience in laughter at the grotesquely clumsy and bulbous Chinese figures pirouetting about the stage with exotic hawklike birds.

A burst of "loud music" from the twelve French musicians in the balcony announced the climax of *The Vision of Delight*: at center stage, "a bower" of flowers ("honeysuckle," "bryony and jessamine") wondrously swung open (another ingenious contrivance of Jones's), and "the masquers" were "discovered," costumed "as the glories of the spring."

Every eye (including His Majesty's, including Pocahontas's) was on the premier dancer, the leader of the troupe, for he was none other than the King's radiant new favorite, the newly created Earl of Buckingham, "the handsomest bodied man in England," for whose dancing talents this spectacle had been designed as setting.

As the glamorous young Earl of Buckingham and his fellow-masquers descended from the platform stage at the north end of the Banqueting House and advanced across the dance floor to approach the royal dais at the south end, the poetry of the masque reached apogee, swept up the sovereign—to incorporate the regal symbol in the masque's dramatic theme.

This was accomplished by a line of "Fantasy's":

Fant'sy:

Behold a king
Whose presence maketh this perpetual spring. . . .

King of the less and greater isles,
And all those happy when he smiles.
Advance, his favour calls you to advance,
And do your this night's homage in a dance.

"Here they danced their entry," according to the script. Anon, "They danced their main dance." And finally, "They danced with ladies."

The lady with whom the glorious Buckingham danced was none other than Her Majesty, Queen Anne, as John Chamberlain duly noted in his letter of January 18: "the newmade earle and the earle of mongomerie [Montgomery] dawnced with the quene."

"They danced with the ladies" (again according to Jonson), "and the whole revels followed"—the finale to which the masque inevitably led, the noble masquers inviting partners from the noble audience to join in the dance upon the green-carpet area that stretched from the royal dais to the stage.

Was Princess Pocahontas one of those led out by a masquer to join the revels? It was customary for the masquers to invite the distinguished persons on the royal dais to be their partners, and agile dancer that Pocahontas was, she may have been coached for the occasion, may have learned the steps of the lively *galliard* and the running *corranto* from Lady De La Warre or from one of the five West girls[5] known to have been among the revelers in the Banqueting House on Twelfth Night, 1617.

CHAPTER XIV

Pocahontas, daughter of King
Powhatan of the Virgin Virginia forest,
Dazzles London with eyes like dark fish
Glittering in the unpolluted James.
The King of Scotland, Britain and the western
Prize extols a proud neck
Rising from the latest fashion in ruffs.
The ladies are jealous of her dancing feet,
The lords confused. She is all the
Rage, but the rage in her heart is
Homesickness, Jamessickness, malaise for the
High masterful trees
Trailing wild grape charged with a secret juice,
For a free run in a buckskin skirt
Under a burn of unimprisoning blue
Where fierce-eyed eagles soar to salute the sun. . . .

VIRGINIA MOORE,
"Pocahontas in London," 1968

As ROBERT BEVERLEY heard the story toward the end of the century, Pocahontas "was carried to many Plays, Balls, and other publick Entertainments, and very respectfully receiv'd by all the Ladies about the Court." And William Stith may have based his account on family tradition:

Pocahontas was eagerly sought, and kindly entertained every where. Many Courtiers, and others of his Acquaintance, daily flocked to Captain Smith, to be introduced to her. They generally confessed, that the Hand of God did visibly appear, in her Conversion; and that they had seen many English Ladies, worse Favoured, of less exact Proportion, and genteel Carriage, than she was. She was likewise carried to Court, by the Lady Delawarr, attended by the Lord, her Husband, and divers other Persons of Fashion and Distinction. The whole Court were charmed and surprised, at the Decency and Grace of her Deportment; and the King himself, and Queen, were pleased, honourably to receive and esteem her. The Lady Delawarr, and those other Persons of Quality, also waited on her, to the Masks, Balls, Plays, and other public Entertainments.

No mean accomplishment, so swiftly and smoothly to have made the startling transition from primitive tribal life on the Pamunkey to the upper levels of a highly cultivated, class- and tradition-conscious English society. The tenor of the reports—those made by Smith, Purchas, and Chamberlain in her own day, by Beverley within her century, by Stith within the next century—suggest that Pocahontas was the sensation of the London social season, the toast of the town, the darling of the Court; that she, furthermore, thoroughly enjoyed the fuss made over her, basking in the attention and the admiration.

But sometime after that gala season ended, sometime during that late winter or early spring, Pocahontas's health and high spirits visibly deteriorated. By a decision of her husband's—or a decision made by her husband in concert with the Virginia Company officials who had assumed responsibility for the Virginia contingent—a remove was made by the Rolfe family and their attendants from the damp, chill, noxious air of the crowded city to the countryside, to a village in Middlesex. Pocahontas's husband, according to Robert Beverley's account, "took Lodgings for her at Branford, to be a little out of the Smoak of the City"; or, as William Stith phrased it: "Being offended by the Smoke of the Town, she was immediately removed to Brentford. . . ."

Stith's reference to the smoke's being offensive suggests that Pocahontas's ailment was a respiratory one. Strangers unused to the rigors of an English winter were highly susceptible to rheums and coughs, bronchial and pulmonary infections. Pocahontas, like the other Powhatans who sickened there, would seem to have had what was then termed "a delicate chest"; her throat, her lungs irritated by the noxious coal-fire fumes overhanging the capital in winter.

Although Brentford was only some nine miles up the Thames from the heart of the City (today a part of greater London), in that day and time, a change of air—by so little as even a very few miles—was frequently prescribed for a patient, as beneficial to the health.

But it had been not only the oppressive city air from which Pocahontas and the other Indians had suffered; it had been the confinement, the close quarters, the lack of exercise—the walking, running, paddling, swimming, especially the swimming—to which they had been accustomed since childhood. In the environs of the village of Brentford, there was not only fresh air, there were open spaces, broad fields and orchards, even woodlands to rejoice the Indians' hearts.

Best of all, the waters of the Thames still ran sparkling clear, unpolluted, past Brentford—a temptation, no doubt, to Pocahontas and Matachanna to introduce little Thomas to the joys of swimming, in which Powhatan children were early initiated.

Once Pocahontas was removed from the London social whirl, she would have wanted to reclaim her little son from his aunt and other Indian nurses, to take over his care herself. Powhatan women, although they did not join the men in the hunt, were qualified to instruct their small sons in the use of the bow and arrow. Powhatan mothers played a kind of football with the little boys. Two-year-old Thomas Rolfe was too young for that; the English game of hide-and-seek was better suited to his age. His mother would have been tempted by the enchanting and novel toys for sale in London: the top, the wooden hoop; above all, the hobby-horse, the likes of which had never been seen in the wilderness! Thomas was old enough to be taught to count, as were the English children in those days, on their fingers and toes, to the tune of "This little pig went to market, this little pig stayed home. . . ." Other nursery rhymes popular in early seventeenth-century England and suitable for a two-year-old like Thomas were Three Blind Mice, Old King Cole, Ride a Cock-Horse. Jack and the Beanstalk and Little Bo-Peep were likewise children's favorites in Jacobean England. "Hush-a-bye, baby, on the tree top," dating back to Elizabethan times, would have had especial appeal for a forest-dweller like Pocahontas. Pocahontas's son—at that juncture, in all probability, bilingual, speaking Algonkian with his aunt and other Indian nursemaids, speaking English with his father—had the best of both worlds to enjoy when it came to story-telling, the verse and fables of both races (Indian tribal legends and folklore no less imaginative and poetic than English fairytales and jingles). It does not seem likely that Pocahontas, herself the product of a permissive upbringing, would have agreed to subject her child to the notoriously severe discipline then prevalent in the English nursery and schoolroom. Pocahontas had brought her sister Matachanna with her from the tidewater to be Thomas's nurse; Matachanna was retained in that capacity throughout the months of the Rolfes' visit to England, and was with them when they sailed for home.

Brentford was the site of Syon House, the ancestral home of the Percy family: Sir George Percy may very well have had some influence in the Rolfes' decision to choose that village for their residence —quite possibly some dependency, some property of the Percys made available to them in the environs of Syon House, that creamy, crenellated, machicolated, turreted pile that still stands four-square on the Syon Reach, once one of the most beautiful stretches of the Thames above London. The Lord of Syon, the Earl of Northumberland, Henry Percy—Sir George's eldest brother—was not in residence in 1616–17, still languished, for the eleventh year, in the Tower of London, a star example of Star Chamber injustice, imprisoned on merest suspicion in the Catholic Gunpowder Plot.

Given Sir George Percy's connections with the Virginia colony and Virginia Company, it would have been only natural for him to have taken an interest in the party from Virginia. It would have been unnatural, had he not sought out the Powhatan princess whom he must have remembered vividly and gratefully, from her earliest visits to James Fort.

Likewise a neighbor of Pocahontas's at Brentford during the late winter or early spring of 1617, likewise likely to have displayed a lively interest in the lady, was Thomas Hariot. That versatile genius, as a retainer of the Earl of Northumberland, occupied a house within the walls of the ancient and extensive Syon Gardens, and shuttled back and forth between the great library of Syon House and the Tower of London, purveying books to those two indefatigable researchers, those fast friends and patrons of his, the "Wizard Earl" of Northumberland and the Earl's fellow-prisoner, Sir Walter Raleigh.

It might have been Thomas Hariot, it might have been Sir George Percy, who arranged to bring together those two legendary figures, Sir Walter Raleigh and the Princess Pocahontas. If any such meeting did actually occur! The legend is one to rouse the imagination, although not a scintilla of evidence exists to substantiate it.

According to legend, Pocahontas was taken to the Tower of London to meet Sir Walter and the "Wizard Earl." Certainly Raleigh, as author of *The History of the World*, as the original patentee of the Virginia territory and prime mover in the Virginia colonization effort, would have entertained a vivid interest in seeing and conversing with this daughter of the Powhatans, this first Virginian convert to Christianity.

So, too, the Earl of Northumberland, as a man of science, a man of the Age of Exploration, could not but have responded enthusiastically to the suggestion of an interview, direct communication with this bright, English-speaking native of the recently discovered western world.

As a philologist, and compiler of an extensive Carolina Algonkian vocabulary, Hariot would have had a keen interest in engaging Pocahontas and Uttamatamakin in conversation in their native tongue in order to ascertain whether any similarity existed between the languages of the Carolina and the Virginia tribes (as, indeed, there did: both derived from the Algonkian).

If, as legend has it, a visit was arranged for Pocahontas to the illustrious prisoners in the Tower, then, beyond a shadow of a doubt, Pocahontas's husband, John Rolfe, would have been included in the party that traveled from Syon Reach to Tower Wharf.

Pocahontas's fame, generally speaking, overshadowed her husband's, but in the eyes of Raleigh and of Hariot, that "poor Gentleman her husband" (as Robert Beverley patronizingly characterized him) was, by all odds, the most interesting member of the family. Tobacco, "Divine Tobacco," the Golden Weed, the "Sovereign Remedy," was the bond that united them, was their mutual interest. They stand as the three giant figures in the history of tobacco. Where Raleigh and Hariot, between them, were responsible for popularizing (if not introducing) tobacco in England, Rolfe was the pioneer in tobacco culture in the Virginia colony.

Rolfe could have done no less than to bring a pouch of his own private stock, his home-grown Varina leaf, to the Tower to offer to those two celebrated addicts—a recommendation from two such connoisseurs as Raleigh and Hariot could make Rolfe's fortune, the fortune of the Virginia colony.

Legend (described by Muriel Rukeyser as the "accretion of history like a seeding of pearls") has it that not only Sir Walter but Sir Walter's friend, the "Wizard Earl," greeted Pocahontas in his Tower apartment, and made her the gift of a pair of earrings, made "of a peculiar white shell, set in silver," which are today exhibited—if not authenticated—by the National Park Service in the Visitor's Center at Jamestown, Virginia.

It is to be expected that Uttamatamakin accompanied the Rolfes on any visit they might have made to the Tower of London; to Raleigh, surely, this high-ranking native priest-counselor would have been an object of great interest.

To both Uttamatamakin and Pocahontas, the grim gray prison of the Tower would have come as a bewildering experience, the concept of incarceration being unknown to the Powhatans. The chief or the council of an Indian tribe held and exercised the power of life and death over the tribesmen; the death penalty was inflicted as freely as in England, and more summarily than by the due process of Anglo-Saxon law; but to confine a man as a penalty for trespass against the law was no part of the Indian approach to crime and punishment.

POCAHONTAS MAY HAVE BEEN the toast of the town, but it was her "father-counsellor" Uttamatamakin—Tomocomo—who was lionized in clerical and scientific circles. The Reverend Purchas, in both his *Pilgrimes* and his *Pilgrimage*, makes reference to frequent meetings with the Powhatan priest and tribal elder, who was consulted as a source of information on native American culture and theology. He was evidently a man of stature, a man to make himself respected in his own or any other world: "a Great Man," Beverley calls him, "esteemed" among his own people "as a very wise and understanding fellow," as Stith reports, "one of the chief of his [Powhatan's] Council, and of their Priests," one of the four high priests or "sacred persons," as Purchas explains, entitled to enter the sacred "house or temple."

If the Church of England hoped to accomplish its mission in the New World—the conversion of the heathen, the civilization of the savage—then what better opportunity to study the heathen state of mind and soul than in the person of this intelligent, articulate Powhatan hierarch? In Purchas's words,

> who fitter to be heard than a Virginian, an experienced man and counsellor . . . ? Such is *Tomocomo*, at this present in London, sent hither to observe and bring news of our King and country to his nation. With this Savage I have often conversed at my good friends Master Doctor Goldstone, where he was a frequent guest; and where I have both seen him sing and dance his diabolicall measures, and heard him discourse of his Countrey and Religion, Sir. Tho. Dales man being the Interpretour. . . .

Tomocomo agreed, on several occasions, to discourse for the benefit of these assembled prelates, scientists, and scholars upon the subjects of his native land and society, of his tribe's religious beliefs and political traditions, even to treat them to a demonstration of Powhatan ritual song and dance, although he consistently disdained to speak in his hosts' tongue or to conform to his hosts' standard of dress. Whereas Pocahontas showed herself amenable to change, her brother-in-law Tomocomo did not, he more typically Indian than she in his resistance to the white man's culture and religion. Reverend Purchas made the comparison between Pocahontas and Tomocomo, pointing to Pocahontas's "Christian sinceritie," what "shee had joyed to heare and beleeve of her beloved Saviour. . . ."

"Not such was *Tomocomo*, but a blasphemer of what he knew not, preferring his God to ours," a point of view which Purchas disparaged as "stubborn" in a pagan, but would have hailed as a sign of steadfast faith in a Christian.

Even so, not the Reverend Samuel Purchas himself, not the Bishop of London, not the Archbishops of York and Canterbury—not all the most erudite theologians, most skillful dialecticians of the topmost hierarchy of the Anglican Church in concert—could bring this half-naked, paint-streaked savage to forsake his God. Alone, unlettered, unable to make himself understood save through an interpreter, Tomocomo stood his ground in defense of his tribal tradition; confuted, at least to his own satisfaction, the premier prelates of the realm of England.

Tomocomo's God "was he which made heaven and earth," as Purchas understood the Powhatan priest's exegesis of the tribal creation myth: an eternal and perfect and benevolent deity who had revealed to the Indians their agricultural secrets ("taught them to plant so many kinds of corn"), who had foretold the coming of the white men ("had prophesied them before of our men's coming"), a concept of a Supreme Being traditional with the Powhatans (by revelation through Nature rather than through a Holy Book). The Powhatan concept of immortality was little, if any, more nebulous than that of other religions.

If Robert Beverley was correct in his theory that the Virginia Indians carefully concealed their sacred traditions—like their sacred places, shrines, and altars—from the white invader, then Tomocomo would have revealed little or nothing of the Powhatan tribal arcana to the inquiries of Dr. Goldstone, the Reverend Purchas, and other London clerics.

The confusion of seventeenth-century reportage on this score stems not only from deliberate obfuscation on the part of the Indian, but also from the fact that Indian religion lacked scripture, lacked universal dogma, lacked a formal priesthood, and for these reasons appeared amorphous to the early observers, who were inclined to generalize in describing it as anthropomorphic and polytheistic. Thomas Morton (the controversial chronicler of "Merry Mount," Massachusetts) was an exception, suggesting that though the Indians' religion was not really systematized, yet they had a concept of God and of a life after death. Colonel William Byrd II of Westover was another exception, insisting that the Indians' "religion contains three Great Articles of Natural Religion: Belief in a God, Moral Distinction between Good and Evil, Expectation of Rewards and Punishments in Another World."

Any attempt Uttamatamakin might have made to express the strong sense of harmony with nature which pervaded all Indian tradition would have been lost on Purchas and company. (The Indian never sought, as did the white man, to tame and conquer nature, but rather to live in harmony with all the elements of his universe, to maintain his delicate equilibrium in and with nature, to respect the life force in all matter, animate and inanimate. A concept which appeared a savage naïveté in the seventeenth century takes on new meaning in the twentieth, when the havoc wrought by violation of natural laws and forces has become apparent. The Indian's strong streak of mysticism —his reliance upon his own personal spiritual experience, the self-induced ecstasy of his Vision Quest—is another trait regarded with less suspicion in the modern world than in the world of the Renaissance.)

"He is very zealous in his superstition," was Purchas's contemptuous dismissal of the Powhatan high priest's exposition of his credo—a reaction typical of the European Christian vis-à-vis the pagan American (or African or Australian or Polynesian) aborigine. Uttamatamakin's lyrical fervor, the eloquence of his expression of his abiding faith in the faith of his forefathers, fell on deaf ears when he addressed Purchas and Purchas's fellow-prelates.

Despite the fact that Purchas had heard, with his own ears, Uttamatamakin's moving representation of Powhatan tribal lore and tradition, despite the fact that he had, with his own eyes, witnessed the éclat of Pocahontas's social début at the Bishop of London's reception in her honor, despite the fact that he had, with his own pen, acclaimed her as a model of the proprieties, despite all this, Purchas would take up that same pen, seven or eight years later, to describe Indians (in his *Pilgrimes*) as "having little of Humanitie but shape, ignorant of Civilitie, of Arts, of Religion. . . ."

As for Uttamatamakin, his distaste for England and the English way of life intensified with every month that passed, with every grim, gray prison he saw (he could have counted five in Southwark alone), with every lunatic asylum, every crowded wretched slum, every reeking open sewer he passed, with every polluted stream or river he crossed, with every breath of smoke-fouled air he drew into protesting lungs, with every public hanging he witnessed—a grisly monthly spectacle in London, according to one visitor from the Continent. Uttamatamakin's reflections on the English economic system and penal code may well have been unflattering as he compared them to his own: the striking contrast between the rich and poor, between the squalid tenements in the London alleys and the splendorous palaces on the Strand, must have puzzled the Indian mind: the concept of the sacredness of private property was one the Indian could never grasp or accept. There was no such crime rate in the aborigines' world as in the English, possibly for the reason that poverty and hunger were nonexistent among the Indians.

The Reverend Purchas acknowledged in print that not all the dialectics of the most formidable theologians of the Anglican hierarchy had been able to budge the Powhatan priest from his savage convictions: that stubborn fellow would "hear no persuasions to the truth," Purchas fumed, "bidding us teach the boys and girls which were brought over from thence, he being too old now to learn."

The extermination of Uttamatamakin and his kind was the only solution if England's glorious mission of bringing the gospel to the heathen was to be accomplished: such was the recommendation of one not-so-gentle man of the cloth (the Reverend Jonas Stockam writing from his Virginia parish in his *Relation* of 1621[1]): "and till their Priests and Ancients have their throats cut, there is no hope of bringing them to conversion." Uttamatamakin's suggestion to the Anglican clergy to concentrate their proselytization efforts on the "boys and girls" of his race would be adopted.

A plan to proselytize among the heathen youth in the colony was even then under way ("the most pious and noble end of this plantation," in the words of the Virginia Company). Purchas in England and Whitaker in Virginia headed the campaign to found a school and college on the James for the children of Pocahontas's tribe, a project which, at this time, awaited only the King's official sanction. That sanction would be forthcoming within months after Pocahontas's visit, and there is reason to suppose that it was her court triumph that stimulated James's interest in Virginia and the Indians. He addressed the Archbishops of York and Canterbury, soliciting the cooperation of the Church of England in collecting funds for the purchase of lands and the construction of a University and College at Henrico and a preparatory school at Charles City for the education and conversion of the children of the "barbarians" (to be taken by force from their parents if not surrendered voluntarily to the missionaries).

The question that comes to mind concerning Uttamatamakin and his increasingly hostile attitude toward the English—his angry confrontations with Purchas and the Anglican clergy—is how it ever came about that he agreed, in the first place, to subject himself to such an experience. The answer is that Uttamatamakin had undertaken the journey at Powhatan's bidding, not only to attend upon the Supreme Chieftain's daughter and watch over her, but also to reconnoiter enemy territory, to estimate the enemy's potential, to report on the population and matériel available to the invaders. Powhatan had constantly pondered the motivation for the white men's coming: the fact that they besought the Indians for corn, the fact that they gathered wood and fish to ship back as cargo whence they came, led Powhatan and his counselors to conclude that the whites' homeland lacked such resources.

Samuel Purchas would have us believe that Uttamatamakin prepared to do his census-taking in England by means of notches on a stick:

> Hee is said also to have set up with notches on a stick the numbers of men, being sent to see and signifie the truth of the multitudes reported to his Master. But his arithmetike soone failed, and wonder did no lesse amaze him at the sight of so much Corne and Trees in his comming from Plimmouth to London, the Virginians imagining that defect thereof here had brought us thither.

There is the ring of truth to the anecdote. It is twice told: Captain Smith's version parallels the Reverend Purchas's, with only the addition of the self-serving comment that Powhatan had recommended to his envoy that he seek out Captain Smith, trust in Smith alone among Englishmen:

> Comming to London, where by chance I met him, having renewed our acquaintance, where many were desirous to heare and see his behaviour, hee told me
>
>> Powhatan did bid him to finde me out, to shew him our God, the King, Queene, and Prince, I so much had told them of.
>
> Concerning God, I told him the best I could, the King I heard he had seene, and the rest hee should see when he would; he denied ever to have seene the King, till by circumstances he was satisfied he had. . . .

Was James I so deficient in majesty, in regal bearing—and so inferior in comparison, say, to Powhatan—as to leave Uttamatamakin dubious as to his identity? Not even the assurances of an old and trusted friend like Captain Smith could convince the Powhatan priest that it was truly the King of England to whom he had been presented. If, indeed, it had been the King, then the reception was unworthy of so great a sovereign, an insult to the ambassador of the great Powhatan. Uttamatamakin, according to Smith, "replyed very sadly,"

> You gave Powhatan a white Dog, which Powhatan fed as himselfe; but your King gave me nothing, and I am better than your white Dog.

Uttamatamakin was critical, resentful, touchy, eager to be on the return journey home.

NOT SO POCAHONTAS.

Not, that is, if one can trust the London gossip as it reached the ear of John Chamberlain: "She is on her return," Chamberlain wrote on January 18, 1617, "though sore against her will, if the wind would come about to send them away. . . ."

Chamberlain is trustworthy; historians from the nineteenth century on have come to trust his statements and to quote them; the foremost historians of the Stuart period depend upon Chamberlain's letters. If he was "a perfect old gossip" (as A. L. Rowse fondly describes him), he was a conscientious one, careful to get his facts right, checking every news item before relaying it to his correspondents in the shires or on the Continent. Chamberlain, happily, could gratify his passion for news by means of a wide, interesting, and strategically placed circle of friends and acquaintances including scholars, scientists, historians, diplomats, statesmen (among the latter, Sir Ralph Winwood, James I's Secretary of State, who may well have been Chamberlain's main source of news during Pocahontas's visit to England).

If we are to take Chamberlain's word for it that Pocahontas was reluctant to return to her homeland, that it was "sore against her will" to set sail for Virginia; if he had verified this report as meticulously as was his wont before passing it along to Ambassador Carleton in his bulletin of January, 1617, then we are led to suspect that Pocahontas was not only ill but distraught, that she may have become by then what sociologists characterize as a marginal person, an individual who has left one culture, one social group, for another without being able fully to enter the other, on the margin of each but a member of neither—an unhappy state.

The gulf that yawned between the woodlands American and European Renaissance man was too wide to be bridged at the age at which Pocahontas attempted it. It would be unrealistic to think that the transition she made was anything but superficial.

During her months in England, Pocahontas would have discovered that there was not only a whole, wide World (Europe, Africa, India, China!) beyond her ken, but a long, long Past as well (sixteen centuries of recorded history implicit in the term *anno domini*) of which she was equally ignorant. Impossible at her age to catch up, to make real headway in that vast corpus of knowledge (history, geography, literature, art) which was the natural heritage of European civilization.

A latecomer to that complex and necessarily bewildering European-Christian world, Pocahontas had made the transition swiftly and deftly, if superficially—mastering the English language, complying effectively with English mores and manners as with Christian ritual. Contemporary chroniclers portray her going gracefully through all the motions: kneeling and praying in her pew, bowing low to majesty at Whitehall, saluting lords and ladies in the salon, nodding, curtseying, clasping hands, scattering kisses in greeting and at farewell, as if to the manner born.

The fact that she was born in the forest primeval, the wilds of the Western Hemisphere—not only thousands of miles off, geographically, but thousands of years off, culturally—makes her achievement a truly remarkable one. If Pocahontas was intelligent enough to have accomplished even superficially so difficult a transition, she was intelligent enough to recognize her limitations. She must have teetered nervously along the thin edge of her competence; one misstep, and she would be beyond her depth, beyond her scope. Hers had to be a constant struggle to maintain a precarious balance in a strange and alien land, amidst a strange and alien society. Hers had to be a nerve-wracking existence, a well-nigh untenable position.

CHAPTER XV

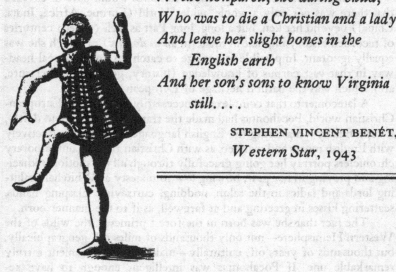

> *. . . the nonpareil, the daring child,*
> *Who was to die a Christian and a lady*
> *And leave her slight bones in the*
> *English earth*
> *And her son's sons to know Virginia*
> *still. . . .*

> STEPHEN VINCENT BENÉT,
> *Western Star*, 1943

IN A BOLD FLIGHT OF IMAGINATION, the nineteenth-century novelist John Esten Cooke (in an otherwise polite and pedestrian
novel entitled *My Lady Pokahontas*) places Pocahontas in the audience
at the Globe Theater for a performance of Shakespeare's play *The
Tempest*, wherein she recognizes herself on the stage as Miranda!
Recognizes Captain Smith as Ferdinand!

It is well within the realm of possibility that Pocahontas attended a
performance at the Globe; ladies did patronize the London theater in
the Jacobean era, and the Globe was being operated by the King's
Company in 1616–17 (not the old, original Globe which had opened
in 1599, and gone up in flames in 1613, but its replacement, which had
been completed in 1614, in Bankside, on the south bank of the Thames,
a short ride across the river by wherry from the wharves of the City).
The Tempest was in the repertoire of the King's Company and may
well have been playing that year, having had its première at the old
Globe perhaps as early as 1611.

If Pocahontas recognized herself as Miranda, if Captain Smith
recognized himself as Ferdinand, then surely John Rolfe recognized

the tempest from which the play takes its title as the "West Indian *Horocano*" that wrecked the *Sea Venture*, the flagship of the Third Supply. A fellow passenger of Rolfe's who lived to tell the tale was William Strachey; his account of the tempest and shipwreck committed to a letter (indited To A Noble Lady) enjoyed a wide circulation in manuscript form in London literary circles the following year, and is thought by some to have suggested to Shakespeare the theme for his New World drama.

If John Rolfe accompanied the Lady Pocahontas, as novelist Cooke suggests, to a performance of *The Tempest*, he would have recognized the phenomenal St. Elmo's fire that flashed along the mainmast, the Bermuda coral reefs upon which the vessel foundered, the miraculous rescue operation performed without the loss of a single life, the shores of the enchanted isle "full of noises, sounds and sweet airs"—all the veracious details supplied by eyewitness Strachey, transmuted by Shakespeare into one long haunting song of the sea, the tempest's violence succeeded by nature's sweet calm.

It was novelist Cooke's quaint conceit that Captain John Smith should count William Shakespeare as a friend, should confide to him the story of his rescue at Pocahontas's hands. (Cooke would have us believe that Shakespeare "figured" Pocahontas "in his *Miranda*, that is, *One to be wondered at*; as see where Miranda cries, 'Beseech you, father! Sir, have pity; I'll be his surety!' when *Prospero* would smite down *Ferdinand* as Powhatan would smite Smith.")

It was likewise Cooke's conceit to cast John Rolfe as the villain of the piece, a Puritan hypocrite and racist, guilt-ridden, and castigating himself for his lust for Pocahontas, winning her hand by deceit, inducing her to marry him by spreading a false report that Captain Smith was dead. Cooke places not only Pocahontas and Captain Smith in the audience at the Globe Theater for that performance of *The Tempest*, but Shakespeare himself—in complete disregard of the fact that Shakespeare had retired to Stratford by 1616, his death occurring there in November of that year.

Less fanciful, less farfetched, is the notion that Pocahontas accompanied her husband, at some time during their sojourn in England, on a visit to his family home and acres at Heacham in the county of Norfolk. This visit is a hallowed tradition of the Rolfe family, as the several volumes of *Rolfe Family Records* attest, a tradition upon which the Elwins, collateral descendants of the Rolfes, insist to this day—and a tradition with which, actually, it is difficult to take issue.

For, if John Rolfe did indeed belong to the Heacham branch of the Rolfe family, why, then, his homing instinct—after a seven years' absence—would have drawn him irresistibly back to Norfolk, to his childhood scene. And what more natural than to have taken his new wife and young son along to meet his brother Edward and Edward's family at the Rolfe homestead in Heacham village?

Whereas the identification of Edward Rolfe of Heacham as a brother to the John Rolfe of Virginia remains dubious, depending for corroboration upon the reliability of the Elwin genealogical table, the identification of another brother, Henry Rolfe, is a matter of historical record. Henry Rolfe was a prominent London merchant, a member of the Virginia Company, and in contact with John Rolfe. Henry was the brother to whom John would turn in a time of emergency, as is evident from a holograph letter of John's as well as from various Virginia Company documents.

Certainly the village of Heacham takes the story of Pocahontas's visit *au sérieux*; the parish council, in the year 1960, erected a road sign in commemoration of the occasion: a curious device embellished with a garbled version of the celebrated Van de Passe engraving, the oval of the portrait supported on one side by a prancing Norfolk hackney (in token of the region's horse-breeding renown) and, on the other, by a caracoling sea horse (in token of Norfolk's amphibious position as a maritime as well as an agricultural county; its flat, fertile fields bordering on the North Sea and the Wash).

Pocahontas is commemorated at Heacham not only by the road sign but by a memorial tablet on the wall of the north aisle of the Church of St. Mary the Virgin, where Rolfes are known to have worshipped and been entombed since the 1500s. The memorial tablet, carved in alabaster, takes the form of a bas-relief from the same Van de Passe portrait of Pocahontas (looking as cramped and uncomfortable as ever, the high, stiff, heavy Jacobean Court hat pressing on her brow, the starched lace ruff scratching her chin, the three-plumed fan grimly clutched in her right hand) and was installed in 1933 as the gift of a descendant of the Heacham Rolfes, with the Archbishop of Lynn on hand to do the honors.

Heacham lies some hundred miles to the north and east of London by road through Cambridge (believed by some to have been John Rolfe's alma mater), through Newmarket, Ely, King's Lynn—a week's journey, no less, by coach, over roads notoriously bad in seventeenth-century England.

Once past King's Lynn, the smell of the sea permeates the air—welcome and familiar to a native of the Chesapeake.

The traveler riding through the English countryside in the summer or fall of 1616 beheld the island at its verdant best, at its sunniest and brightest; he reveled in the good weather: "the finest and most seasonable weather now this whole twelve-month that ever I knew," as John Chamberlain wrote on August 24, 1617, "and as plentiful of corn, grass and all other fruits . . . that hath lightly [lately] been seen, with as timely and goodly a harvest, insomuch that all manner of grain for forty or fifty miles about London hath been carried and laid up above a fortnight since. . . . They brag what rare plums they had there, especially apricots. . . ."

Heacham Hall, the abode of the Rolfes, was modest but substantial, set within its spacious garden: the sketch that is part of family records shows the residence prior to 1945, when it was destroyed by fire. The house, at the time of Pocahontas's supposed visit, consisted of only the low, central, Elizabethan structure depicted by the artist, the rather imposing wing at the left having been added at a subsequent date.

Family memorabilia include another sketch (made at much the same period) showing an ancient, giant mulberry tree, spreading its shade over the fenced garden surrounding the house. Family legend refers to it as Pocahontas's mulberry tree, on the supposition that she planted it.

Rolfe family records point to the presence of a younger brother, Edward, whom John would have found in residence in Norfolk. He would have found his mother Dorothy (aged fifty-one) still living in the area with her second husband, an eminently respectable Dr. Robert Redmayne, chancellor of the diocese of Heacham (her first husband, father of John, Henry, and Edward, dead in 1594, entombed in the Church of St. Mary the Virgin, in the north aisle where the memorial to his Indian daughter-in-law would later be affixed).

No shred of evidence—no letter, no document in the family archives, no entry in the parish registry—has come to light to support the tradition of Pocahontas's visit to her husband's ancestral acres. And even family legend falls silent when it comes to the matter of the manner of welcome accorded by the provincial, Calvinist-oriented Norfolk Rolfes to the extraordinary bride, "the straunge wife" brought home by John. A creature from the craters of the moon could have appeared no more alien to the eyes of rustics in a remote Norfolk village than did this one from the wilds of the western world.

Eventually, to be sure, in time to come, in the lengthening perspective of the ensuing centuries, the Rolfe and Elwin genealogists would point with pride to Pocahontas's name as the supreme ornament on the branches of their family tree. But what of the immediate reaction at Heacham in 1616 or 1617 to the arrival of this outlandish in-law? Was Heacham prepared for the bizarreries of her coloring, her accent? A sophisticated capital city may have made a fuss over this Powhatan princess of John Rolfe's, but provincials take less readily to the foreigner, the stranger within their gates.

A proverb popular in the seventeenth century described England as "the Hell of Horses, the Purgatory of Servants, and the Paradise of Women."* The distaff side of life in middle-class rural England in the seventeenth century, as Pocahontas might have observed it on a visit to Heacham Hall, could not have appeared entirely paradisiacal, the proverb notwithstanding: the spinning, carding, and weaving of wool and flax was only one of a score of chores devolving upon the mistress of the country household. The life of the wife of a gentleman farmer (such as Edward Rolfe of Heacham) was no bed of roses: not only the rosebed but the kitchen-garden and herb-garden were hers to tend. She acted as apothecary, compounding and administering the herbal remedies prescribed by the pharmacopeia she consulted. Her domain included not only the pharmacy but the kitchen, the buttery, the dairy, the dove-cote and poultry-yard, the rabbitry and carp-pond. The tapestries of colored wool that warmed the walls were the handiwork of the mistress of the middle-class country house, as were the crewelwork linen curtains on the massive oak four-posters, as were the coverlets for the wooden cradles creaking on their deep rockers. The mistress of the household presided over the schoolroom as well as the nursery. Although, at that period, only the daughters of noble houses could hope to be nobly educated—permitted to share the lessons of their brothers' tutors—even the average middle-class women could read, lead home prayer, and teach the members of their households the rudiments of learning.

Theirs was a life scarcely to be considered paradisiacal even in comparison to the drudgery of the wigwam, from which Pocahontas had been spared only because of her privileged position. What comparison did she make between the two societies insofar as the women were concerned?

The notoriously harsh discipline of the seventeenth-century English nursery and schoolroom would have gone against the Indian grain, but otherwise, Pocahontas's inclination to remain in England—if Chamberlain's report to that effect is reliable—may have reflected her preference for the way of life she observed during her visit there.

---

* "The Hell of Horses, the Purgatory of Servants, and the Paradise of Women; because they ride Horses without measure, and use their Servants imperiously, and their Women obsequiously." Fitzherbert is quoted in Alice Clark's *The Working Life of Women in the 17th Century*.

She may have found difficulty in making up her mind, uncertain whether she wanted to go or to stay. She may not have known where her future—and that of her half-breed son—really lay. She may have been in the throes of an identity crisis, torn between two worlds, no longer comfortable in her own, as yet insecure in her husband's.

The final decision, apparently, rested with her husband. John Rolfe's decision, when it came to be made, was in favor of a return to the New World, to Virginia: his appointment to the prestigious post of Colonial Secretary and Recorder-General—an appointment made at a quarter court of the Virginia Company held in London in late November, 1616—clinched any argument that may have gone on in his own mind or between him and Pocahontas. His fortune seemed to await him in the west—on the broad acres, the flourishing fields of broadleaf, sweet-scented *Nicotiana tabacum* he had so industriously and ingeniously planted on the banks of the James.

Rolfe's appointment as Secretary and Recorder-General to the colony of Virginia came largely as the reward for his record of long and meritorious service to the colony: his innovative techniques in tobacco culture, his heroic gesture in marrying the native princess.

Rolfe's rise in the company ranks, however, may have owed something to the influence of increasingly powerful friends in the faction headed by Sir Edwin Sandys, one of the ablest parliamentarians of seventeenth-century England. Rolfe's *True Relation* had handsomely served the purposes of Sandys and his supporters in forcing reforms and reorganization on the party headed by Sir Thomas Smythe.

Friends of Rolfe's dominated the high command of the new expedition being readied for departure for Virginia: by action of the same quarter court to which Rolfe owed his promotion, Samuel Argall was named Deputy Governor and Admiral of Virginia, while the Vice-Admiral appointed was none other than Rolfe's bosom friend and confidant, Ralph Hamor. (If Captain John Smith's name was not to be found on the list of Virginia Company appointments to active duty in 1616, no one looked for it there; by that date, Smith and the Virginia Company were openly at odds, his lot cast with the Plymouth Company instead.)

SOMETIME IN THE LATE WINTER of 1616 or in the early spring of 1617, Captain Smith finally prepared to attend upon Pocahontas. That he was unconscionably late in paying his respects to the Powhatan princess to whom he owed his life is known because he himself acknowledges the remissness in his account of their encounter. The fact that Pocahontas felt the slight, that she reproached him for his neglect, is known because he quotes her very words to that effect.

His belated appearance at her door, he insists in his version of the story, was attributable to pressing business in connection with the Plymouth Company colonization venture, which took him repeatedly out of the capital.

Up to then, to that very day—whatever day, whatever date it was —when Smith finally appeared on the doorstep of the Rolfes at Brentford, he had been unable, to hear him tell it, to call his time his own. Just as soon, however, as the Captain had returned from his tour of the West Country, just as soon as his busy schedule permitted, he inquired as to the Lady Rebecca Rolfe's whereabouts, and "hearing shee was at Branford, with divers of my friends, I went to see her."

Smith's resort to the safety of numbers (the company of "divers of my friends") may indicate that he deliberately avoided being alone with her, fearful of a possibly painful interview *à deux*, fearful of possible recriminations on her part. Or, Smith may have reasoned, to furnish himself with companions would be a disarming gesture as far as Rolfe was concerned—reassurance to Rolfe that Smith had not come to rekindle the embers of a once-ardent liaison. Smith recognized that it was impossible for Rolfe, upon his arrival in Jamestown in 1610, not to have heard the rumors linking the names of Smith and Pocahontas, the lurid tales of the "rescue," the "adoption," the extraordinary affinity—whatever the connexus may have been. The colony, at the time of Rolfe's arrival in 1610, still buzzed with gossip about Smith's scheme to make himself ruler of Virginia via marriage to the daughter of Virginia's "Emperour."

Did Captain Smith, as the years 1616–1617 rolled around, have cause to regret not having consummated that marriage, not having seized the opportunity when it was open to him? Was Smith's inexplicable procrastination in paying his respects to Pocahontas explicable in terms of his frustrations, his regrets over opportunities lost, opportunities botched and bungled? Had Rolfe made better use of the opportunities offered to him than Smith had made of his? So it must have appeared at that juncture: where Rolfe enjoyed the fertile acres of Pocahontas's tidewater patrimony, Captain Smith—for all his prodigies of exploration, of mapmaking, of adventuring—could not lay claim to so much as a foot of land to his name in either Virginia or New England. "For," as he would write in 1624,

in neither of Those two Countries have I one foot of Land, nor the very house I builded, nor the ground I digged with my owne hands, nor even any content or satisfaction at all. . . .

A sad admission, wrenched from what would appear to be a disappointed, embittered, and lonely man. Where Rolfe enjoyed hearth and home, his wife and child beside him, Smith was alone, bereft of family, of domestic pleasures. The two colonies, New England and Virginia, had to stand him in place of the sons and daughters he might have had, in place of normal family life, in place even of normal diversions: "I call them my children, for they have beene my Wife, my Hawks, Hounds, my Cards, my Dice. . . ."

One has the impression that when Smith finally went to Brentford, he went unannounced, that Pocahontas was taken unawares, taken aback, disconcerted, even displeased at his sudden appearance on her threshold: "After a modest salutation," Smith's account continues,

> without any word, she turned about, obscured her face, as not seeming well contented; and in that humour her husband, with divers others, we all left her two or three houres, repenting my selfe to have writ she could speake English. . . .

Startled, it would seem, at the sight of this man whom she had believed dead, who had vanished from her shores seven years previously—this man to whom she had been closely bound by vows of adoption or by bonds of love or passion—her reaction to his unexpected appearance had been immediate, violent, emotional in the extreme, bordering on hysteria, robbing her of speech as of composure (a highly emotional state such as characterizes her every encounter with this man, from the first, upon the altar-stone at Werowocómoco, to the last, here at Brentford on the Thames). If Pocahontas, at Brentford, withdrew from her guests, hid her face, it was because she had lost her self-control. Several hours were required for her to regain her composure.

William Stith interpreted Pocahontas's greeting as chilly; her outburst as impassioned:

> After a cold and modest salutation, she turned from him in a passionate Manner, hid her Face, and could not be brought to speak a Word for two or three Hours. . . .

Her refusal to address Smith and his companions evidently proved embarrassing to the captain, eliciting from him the derisive comment that she had given him cause to regret having stated (in his Letter to Queen Anne) that the savage princess had achieved a perfect command of the English language. (Had he, perhaps, boasted to these friends to whom he had promised an introduction to the redskin celebrity that he had taught her English . . . among other things?)

When Pocahontas had sufficiently recovered herself to rejoin her husband, Captain Smith, and their other guests, it was to remind Smith of his obligations to her and to reproach him for his neglect of her as a stranger in his land:

> But not long after, she began to talke, and remembered mee well what courtesies shee had done: saying,

> > You did promise Powhatan what was yours should bee his, and he the like to you; you called him father being in his land a stranger, and by the same reason so must I doe you:

> which though I would have excused, I durst not allow of that title because she was a Kings daughter. . . .

Smith's excuse was lame, and Pocahontas rejected it:

> . . . with a well set countenance, she said, Were you not afraid to come into my fathers Countrie, and caused feare in him and all his people (but mee), and feare you here I should call you father. I tell you then I will, and you shall call mee childe, and so I will bee for ever and ever your Countrieman. . . .

(If there is ambiguity in this passage, the note of reproach and hurt is unmistakable.)

The next words Pocahontas spoke, as quoted by Smith, came as a wail:

> They did tell us alwaies you were dead, and I knew no other till I came to Plimoth; yet Powhatan did command Uttamatamakin to seeke you, and know the truth, because your Countriemen will lie much. . . .

(Reading between the lines of Smith's account, it is not impossible to construe Pocahontas's outcry as a reproach against Rolfe, against Dale, against the Reverend Whitaker for having deceived her in the matter of Captain Smith's death. These words of hers, as she is quoted by Smith, are open to the interpretation that she would never have married John Rolfe had she known John Smith was still alive.)

Smith's account has verisimilitude if for no other reason than that a confrontation so dramatic, a behavioral pattern so typically feminine as he here describes, seems beyond his powers of psychological invention. His account concludes with a few left-handed compliments to offset his negligence toward the woman to whom he owed so much:

> The small time I staid in London, divers Courtiers and others, my acquaintances, hath gone with mee to see her, that generally concluded, they did thinke God had a great hand in her conversion, and they have seene many English ladies worse favoured, proportioned, and behavioured. . . .

The implication is clear that it was Smith's "little booke" addressed to "the Queene" in Pocahontas's behalf that accounted for the brilliant reception accorded the Powhatan princess at Whitehall Palace:

> and as since I have heard, it pleased both the King and Queenes Majestie honourably to esteeme her . . . both publikely at the maskes and otherwise, to her great satisfaction and content, which doubtlesse she would have deserved, had she lived to arrive in Virginia.

POCAHONTAS MUST HAVE BEEN FAILING RAPIDLY, the decline in her health obvious to those about her, even as the final preparations were being made for the westward sailing. If Rolfe had hoped that the country air and quiet at Brentford would restore his wife to health after the rigors of the winter and the frenetic pace of the social season of the Court and capital, he was disappointed.

She continued, apparently, to droop and languish mysteriously. With no hint on record anywhere as to her symptoms, her illness is not open to diagnosis, except to say that it cannot have been smallpox, as has often been suggested: the symptoms readily recognizable, no smallpox patient would have been permitted to board ship to spread the dread disease among the other passengers. The likelihood, as already stated, is that Pocahontas's complaint was tuberculosis, a disease prevalent in England, at that time. There is a strong possibility that Pocahontas suffered from some virulent respiratory or pulmonary infection which, within hours after her embarkation, suddenly reached a crisis.

It may be that she had been stricken by one of the new, mysterious, malignant agues and fevers that ravaged Europe and spread from the Continent to the British Isles, from the city to the countryside, during the months following Pocahontas's arrival from the Western Hemisphere. "We have a new ague or sickness that begins to spread itself in many places," according to a letter of John Chamberlain's written toward the end of 1616,

. . . Though the season now for these fourteen months hath been such and so good as I never saw so long together, yet the sicknesses are many and dangerous and dispersed in all places, which surely must be imputed to some influence from above rather than to any natural reason within our reach, specially if it be as we hear that this malignant fever reigns as well all over France, Spain, and Italy. . . .

Lacking immunity, the Indians were exceedingly vulnerable and readily fell victim. Not only Pocahontas but also little Thomas Rolfe had been stricken in the spring of 1617. Not only mother and child but the child's nurse, as well—his aunt, Matachanna—was failing by the time the Virginia fleet made ready to sail in March.

The eminent London physician "Master Doctor Goldstone," as Purchas refers to him, would probably have been called into consultation on these cases either by the Reverend Purchas (whose parishioner he was) or by Uttamatamakin, who had paid the Doctor several visits in London.

It may have been Pocahontas's debilities—the pain and discomfort wracking her body—which made her reluctant to embark on that long and arduous journey west—if, that is, Chamberlain's gossip had any foundation in fact.

Pocahontas's husband, John Rolfe, on the other hand, was impatient to be off, to return to his greening acres on the James, his prosperous fields of broadleaf Varina, eager to assume the duties of his new post as Secretary and Recorder-General to the colony.

Whether or not Rolfe's wife still harbored any resentment for the act of kidnap perpetrated against her by Argall, now Admiral, in 1613, Rolfe himself bore no grudge, welcomed close association with his commanding officer, readily agreed to travel aboard Argall's flagship, his "good ship called the George."

Argall's flagship, the *George*, along with Vice-Admiral Hamor's *Treasurer* (the ship upon which Pocahontas had been kidnapped) and a tiny pinnace under the command of that veteran Virginia adventurer Captain Martin, were ready to start downriver as early as February. Only the fierce winds held them at their moorings.

John Chamberlain, writing on February 8, 1617, to Sir Dudley Carleton at The Hague, lamented

these south and westerly winds, that have continued so stiff and tempestuous now these three months, whereby we have yet felt no winter, unless perpetual weeping weather, extreme foul ways, and great floods may go under that name. . . .

If it was, as seems most likely, a respiratory or pulmonary infection that afflicted Pocahontas, then "the perpetual weeping weather" must have been extremely distressful to her already sensitive and irritated throat, bronchial passages, and lungs.

March came in inauspiciously.

Sometime in the second week of that month, the winds abated, and the company for Virginia embarked. The Rolfe family—John, Pocahontas, and two-year-old Thomas, along with Matachanna and Uttamatamakin—all boarded the flagship *George*, Pocahontas and her son and her sister ill, Pocahontas grievously so.

As the helmsmen guided the ships slowly downriver, the passengers' inclination was to go to the upper deck, to the Captain's Castle high over the stern, to catch the last glimpse of the London sky line with its myriad church towers and spires grazing the clouds . . . until all was suddenly lost to view as the river looped around the Isle of Dogs. Whereupon Greenwich and its noble buildings—its palace, the birthplace of the great Elizabeth—hove into sight on the other bank. Whereafter the Thames ran clearer and deeper, ran ever swifter, ever wider on its eastern course: there came the Barking Reach, Halfway Reach, Erith Reach, Long Reach (as old hands on the *George* may have pointed out to passengers), the low, marshy shoreline giving way to chalky cliffs rising tree-crowned on the Essex side . . . until, at last, some twenty-five miles down from London, Argall's ships came to the town of Gravesend.

To judge by John Chamberlain's lyrical weather bulletin of February 8, before March had turned ugly, the sights and scents of an early spring gladdened the traveler through the English countryside: "for otherwise we have all the signs and shows of a warm spring, as well in all manner of herbs and sweet flowers as in beds of roses and blossoms of apricots and peach trees." That meant the hedgerows blossomed white before the eyes of the passengers on Argall's flagship, that meant that lilac perfumed the air they breathed, that horse-chestnuts flowered pink and white, that laburnum glittered golden yellow to delight their passing.

But not for Pocahontas. Not for her "the beanflower's boon, the blackbird's tune," not for her the celebration of the rites of early English spring. She must have huddled below deck in her hammock or on her pallet, for, by the time the *George* had traveled the distance to Gravesend, Pocahontas had become so critically ill (with the onset, perhaps, of a tubercular hemorrhage or a pneumonia superimposed on her respiratory problems) as to necessitate Admiral Argall's putting her off there at the hithe, or landing-place, to seek medical assistance.

So critically ill as to necessitate Argall's delaying the entire expeditionary force, she would have been borne ashore on a litter or in the arms of Rolfe or Uttamatamakin. If Argall and Rolfe had earlier deceived themselves into thinking that Pocahontas was strong enough to undertake the transatlantic passage, that she would, once aboard, begin to show improvement, then they were far less sanguine by the time they reached the river's mouth and dropped anchor in the broad waters before Gravesend, county of Kent.

Local legend has it two ways: according to one tradition, Pocahontas was taken to the Christopher Inn, a hundred yards from the wharves; another version places her deathbed in a small cottage that once stood near the riverfront (on a street today known as Stone Street).

A drawing of Gravesend made in 1662 by Wenceslaus Hollar, a diarist-artist from Bohemia making an extensive tour of England, shows the waterfront much as it was in Pocahontas's day: the hithe, or landing-place, at dead center, the steeple of the parish church dominating the town from a rise of ground back from the river, the three-story Christopher Inn located directly behind the hithe, the one to catch the traveler's eye at disembarkation.

Another inn to which Pocahontas might well have been taken was the Flushing (recommended by the Thuringian traveler Justus Zinzerling in a guide-book published first in Lyons in 1616, and enjoying numerous editions, the last as late as 1656); the Flushing was the place to go in Gravesend if the traveler wanted to be comfortable; the host, a Belgian, "a capital fellow."

Although the seventeenth-century traveler might occasionally be devoured by vermin in his bed, even so, "the world affords not such Innes as England hath," to quote Fynes Moryson, a possibly chauvinistic Englishman, in his *Itinerary*, first published in 1617.

"Private chambers" were available, according to Moryson, to which, surely, the dying woman would have been borne, and there laid upon a bed; there, again according to Moryson, a servant would have promptly appeared to "kindle the fier"—the service being excellent: "a Man cannot more freely command at home in his owne House, than hee may doe in his Inn. . . ."

Doubtless, a summons went out at once for a doctor to attend upon Pocahontas and for a minister to bring her spiritual comfort, the services of the latter more easily available than those of the former. In an England where quacks and empirics abounded, licensed physicians—university graduates in medical science—were few and far between, at a ratio of only one to every eight thousand in population.

Doubtless, Pocahontas was purged and bled, the treatments most frequently prescribed—almost the only ones known—at the time. As for drugs available for prescription, the *Pharmocopoeia Londinensis* (to be issued by the College of Physicians in 1618) was primarily a collection of herbal concoctions little more extensive than that of the American Indian.[1] William Harvey, that very year of 1617, was lecturing in London to propound his theory of the circulation of the blood, and the Society of Apothecaries would be chartered within a matter of months, but significant advances in the modern theory of the treatment of disease would not come until later Stuart times.

When the case was desperate—as was Pocahontas's—so were the medical expedients, such as a fresh-killed pigeon or rooster to be applied as poultice to the affected part of the patient's body; *in extremis*—if the patient's pocket-book permitted—a julep of "unicorn's horn" powdered with pearl and "the bone of the Stagges heart" was prescribed.

With Pocahontas *in extremis* at Gravesend, it would have been entirely in character for Uttamatamakin to have resorted to the practice of ancient tribal healing rituals at her bedside—with or without the knowledge of her Christian husband, with or without his sanction.

No great stretch of the imagination is required to conceive of the Powhatan high priest—zealot and fanatic that Purchas's accounts have shown him to be—in contest with Rolfe, at that hour, for Pocahontas's soul.

The traditional Indian healing ceremony as practiced by the priest or shaman in almost every tribe in America was performed in a cloud of tobacco smoke, with a flurry of feathers, and to the accompaniment of chant and the clatter of rattles (deer-hooves on rawhide or pebbles in a gourd). On the theory that disease was caused by some foreign object (such as a stick or worm) which had penetrated the victim's body by chance or by witchcraft, the practice was to extract the fatal object by sucking it out through a bone tube.

Uttamatamakin's healing methods—if he was given the opportunity to exercise them—succeeded no better than those of the English. If Pocahontas was oblivious to the panoply of spring in the Kentish countryside about her, she may have been oblivious as well to the chant and wail set up by Matachanna and Uttamatamakin huddling in a corner of her sickroom.

According to John Rolfe, in a letter addressed by him to Sir Edwin Sandys from Jamestown the following June, Pocahontas nobly sought to reconcile her husband to her death, reminding him that death must come to all, "saying all men must die," and pointing to their young son, Thomas, as his father's best hope and consolation, with the words " 'tis enough that the childe liveth. . . ."

Personal courage, stoicism, and resolution in the face of death were characteristic of Pocahontas's race, as Purchas had established in his several interviews with Uttamatamakin on the subject of religion: "They hold it a disgrace to fear death," Purchas wrote of the Indians in his *Pilgrimes*. "And therefore when they must die, they do it resolutely . . . showing no sign of fear or dismaydness. . . ." (not even in the face of torture, a grisly ritual which can be construed not only as the supreme test, but the ultimate opportunity for the demonstration of valor, the purpose of the ritual deemed edifying as well as titillating).

According to John Rolfe and Admiral Argall—from whom the Reverend Purchas presumably had his account of Pocahontas's deathbed scene—she made an edifying end, assisted very likely by an Anglican divine (presumably the Reverend Nicholas Frankwell, at that date the rector of St. George's Parish Church, just up the hill from the river), summoned by Rolfe or Argall or Hamor to administer the last rites:

> At her returne towards Virginia, she came to Gravesend to her end and grave, having given great demonstration of her Christian sinceritie, as the first fruits of Virginian conversion, leaving here a godly memory, and the hopes of her resurrection, her soule aspiring to see and enjoy presently in heaven, what here shee had joyed to heare and beleeve of her beloved Saviour.

A report from Pocahontas's deathbed, addressed purportedly to the Virginia Company by Argall and Rolfe, was published in Captain Smith's *Generall Historie* in 1624, bearing the joint signatures, "Samuel Argall, John Rolfe":

> The Treasurer, Councell and Companie, having well furnished Captaine Samuel Argall, the Lady Pocahontas alias Rebecca, with her husband and others, in the good ship called the George; it pleased God at Gravesend to take this young Lady to his mercie; where shee made not more sorrow for her unexpected death, than joy to the beholders to heare and see her make so religious and godly an end.

By the end of the century, when Robert Beverley sat down to compose his *History and Present State of Virginia*, Pocahontas was already well on her way to becoming the first heroine of American history:

> Every Body paid this young Lady all imaginable Respect, and it is supposed, she wou'd have sufficiently acknowledged those

Favours, had she lived to return to her own Country, by bringing the Indians to have a kinder Disposition towards the English. But upon her Return she was unfortunately taken ill at Gravesend, and died in a few Days after, giving great Testimony all the time she lay sick, of her being a very good Christian.

By the middle of the eighteenth century, when William Stith's *History of Virginia* was published in Williamsburg, her inspiring death-bed scene was enshrined in legend:

But it pleased God, at Gravesend, to take Pocahontas to his Mercy, in about the two and twentieth Year of her Age. Her unexpected Death caused not more Sorrow and Concern in the Spectators, than her religious End gave them Joy and Surprise. For she died, agreeably to her Life, a most sincere and pious Christian.

The mission to the heathen which was the avowed motive in England's colonization of the New World would be able to point to no other such shining example of success.

The date of Pocahontas's death is established as sometime in the third week of March, as reported by John Chamberlain in a letter dated March 29, 1617, and reading,

The Virginian woman whose picture I sent you died this last week at Gravesend as she was returning homeward. . . .

The date of the interment is recorded precisely, as March 21—if, that is, the Register of Burial in the Parish of Gravesend is to be trusted. Confidence is shaken by the idiosyncrasies of the spelling of the proper names in the entry and the error in the Christian name of the husband of the deceased. The entry, still clearly discernible on the yellowed vellum page of the Burial Register, reads:

—1616—

March 21.—Rebecca Wrolfe wyffe of Thomas Wrolfe gent.
A Virginia Lady borne was buried in the Chauncel.

The chancel, that is to say, of the Parish Church of St. George's, where the funeral rites were performed; an ancient, dark medieval pile listed in the Domesday Book, it had stood there above the river at Gravesend perhaps since Saxon times (until 1727, when it was destroyed by fire).

St. George's bells, then, would have been the ones to sound Pocahontas's death knell, as to toll her passing, a custom dating from Elizabethan times, its purpose to protect the passing soul from the assault of demons, a protection for which the bereaved family paid dear, over and above the expenses of the funeral service, which themselves were high. Gravesend Parish, like every other, had its own custom in bell-ringing, a language familiar to the parishioner: in some parishes, the bells were rung downward three times for a man, twice for a woman, once for a child; in other counties, nine strokes denoted the passing of a man; six strokes, that of a woman, followed by the number of years the deceased had spent on this earth—in the case of Pocahontas, the bell-ringers would have tolled a mere twenty-one or twenty-two.

The body was decently, if hastily, prepared for burial, but there was not time enough for funerary frills, not time enough to bake the funeral meats, nor to prepare the funeral feast customary not only with the affluent upper class but with the modestly endowed middle class, as well.

No matter what wishes the bereaved husband and sister may have expressed, Admiral Argall could linger no longer than absolutely necessary; his ships tugged at anchor in the Thames; passengers and crew to the number of several hundred were making serious inroads into the ships' stores, which had been calculated on the basis of a direct, routine crossing.

Funeral services would have been arranged within hours after Pocahontas breathed her last.

It is unlikely that Rolfe would have made any concession to Uttamatamakin and Matachanna in the matter of their savage funeral customs, unlikely that he would have countenanced traditional Powhatan practices such as scattering beads among the poor in token of the passing of a princess, such as shrouding her body in doeskins and woven mats, such as depositing her jewels and personal possessions at her side, along with food and water sufficient for her journey to the other world. Not only time did not allow, but Anglican dogma would never have sanctioned Uttamatamakin's complicated and tedious processing of the corpse—a Powhatan tribal method of preservation of skeleton and skin not dissimilar to mummification—as performed on remains of the ruling elite in the tidewater.[2] Rolfe and the Church of England notwithstanding, the Powhatan high priest and his wife would have followed their ancient tribal mourning ritual: No one, nothing, could have prevented them from blackening their faces with oil and charcoal, from weeping, wailing, chanting—a barbaric uproar to affright fellow guests at the inn, to appall the townspeople.

If the dead woman was John Rolfe's wife, she was also Matachanna's sister, Uttamatamakin's sister-in-law. Clashes between red man and white, between Powhatan and Englishman, in the matter of the ceremonial of interment, were inevitable. Uttamatamakin's steadily mounting resentment against the English, in general—against Rolfe, Dale, and Argall, in particular—flared, mounted higher still, in all probability, upon the death of Pocahontas.

Admiral Argall and Vice-Admiral Hamor doubtless walked alongside their bereaved friend and fellow officer, John Rolfe, as the funeral cortège mounted the gentle rise of the hill to the Church of St. George's, whose steeple was the most prominent feature of the horizon on the south bank of the Thames at Gravesend. (Consisting of a chancel, a nave, and a north aisle, St. George's main entrance appears to have been through a porch opposite Chapel Lane.) In accordance with a custom that would remain unchanged until mid–nineteenth century, the men were seated in pews at one side of the dim, candle- and lamp-lit church, the women on the other, while the rector conducted the services prescribed in the Book of Common Prayer.

The service over, the coffin was lowered into the vault below the chancel floor: a final resting place reserved throughout the seventeenth century to rectors of Gravesend Parish and to members of the locally prominent Robinson family, now opened to Pocahontas in recognition of her rank and eminence. Whereupon the mourners dispersed, then made their way down the hill to the hithe.

When the church had emptied and the stone-masons had replaced the slab in the chancel floor, the rector took up a pen to make the proper entry in the leather-bound Parish Register of Burials, to record the funeral and interment over which he had presided on that twenty-first day of March, 1617. If the rector made errors, misspelling the family name of the deceased—Wrolfe instead of Rolfe; if he inscribed the husband's Christian name as Thomas instead of John—confusing the father's name with the son's—it was because this motley crew were not members of his flock, but transients. Seafarers, exotic strangers, they had come ashore bearing their sick, and had returned so speedily to their ships that the rector had not had time to familiarize himself with their family relations. He had shriven the dying redskinned woman without learning how to spell her name, without differentiating between the husband's name and the child's.

POCAHONTAS'S BODY was committed to an alien soil, her "slight bones" to "an English earth," the slab lowered above her head, replaced without inscription. And, as a matter of fact, once the *George* had sailed, there was no one in those Kentish parts to have recognized her name, had it been chiseled—with all its strange, outlandish syllables—upon the stone of the chancel floor. There was, in all of Kent, no relative, no friend, no neighbor to point out or tend her tomb, none to recite a prayer, to weep a tear, to drop a flower—Pocahontas's final resting place remained unidentified, unnoted, neglected, eventually forgotten with the passage of two centuries and more.

When suddenly, in the mid-nineteenth century, the story of Pocahontas captured the imagination of the young nation, when she loomed up as the premier heroine of American history, the central figure of American mythology, a frantic search began for her human remains: an unseemly disturbance in English churchyards and vaults ensued, cemeteries were ransacked, coffins exhumed and opened, skeletons rattled, ashes raked. (Mr. Pyecroft of the British Museum was photographed for the *Evening Standard* in 1923, seated on a tombstone in St. George's Churchyard, Gravesend, solemnly taking the dimensions of a human skull, one out of the many piled up beside him.)

The original, the ancient St. George's of Gravesend—the one dating from Saxon times and listed in the Domesday Book, the one in which Pocahontas presumably lay buried—was destroyed in 1727 by the fire that laid waste most of Gravesend.

Rebuilt on the same site, shortly after, the second St. George's retained no memory of the American Indian princess, save only for the three faint lines of the entry in the Burial Register, a tattered volume gathering dust in the parish archives.

In 1892, when the present chancel at St. George's was under construction, two vaults were discovered, but found to be empty. That same year, two coffins came to light under the East Window, but whatever their contents, no record was made. In 1897, when the North Aisle was added, workmen came upon a cache of charred bones and skulls; these were subsequently reinterred in the plot of the Curd family in the churchyard.

It was not until 1923 that the search for Pocahontas's last resting place began in earnest: a committee was formed, under the aegis of a native Virginian, J. Page Gaston, and with the approbation of Rolfe family heirs and descendants. The English-Speaking Union undertook to obtain an order from the British Home Office to make excavations in St. George's Churchyard, in the area of the Curd family plot. In May, 1923, a noted English anthropologist, Sir Arthur Keith, joined with Mr. W. Pyecroft of the British Museum and the Rector and Wardens of St. George's in opening the grave. If they had hoped to find the coffin of the Princess Pocahontas, they were disappointed: the spades turned up only the trash of centuries—tin cans, rubbish, animal skeletons.

When they came finally upon a heap of human bones, including seventy-five human skulls, none of the latter was identifiable by the authorities present as being Indian. The human detritus was promptly reinterred, but a great hue and cry went up from parish and press at this indiscriminate scrabbling in consecrated ground.

Rumor ran to the effect that the body of the Powhatan princess had been long ago removed by body-snatchers who, frustrated in their efforts to peddle it as a curiosity in London, transferred it to a silver coffin and reburied it in the crypt of St. John the Evangelist, in Waterloo Road, London. No trace of a silver coffin, however, was reported in 1851, when the crypt of that London church was emptied for transfer of its dead to Brookwood Cemetery. This lurid tale may have had its origin in the fact that another female American Indian was buried in the Waterloo Road Church in 1835.[8]

If the stones of the first, the medieval St. George's of Gravesend, gave no evidence of Pocahontas's passing—no slab, no tablet, no monument to mark it as her final resting-place—the second church erected on the site, the eighteenth-century structure, would end its days as a memorial to the American princess, taking on, eventually, the aspect of a shrine, a place of pilgrimage.

It barely escaped demolition in mid-twentieth century: because of the shift of population away from the old section of Gravesend, toward the suburbs south of the old town, the church was about to be abandoned by its parishioners.

Thanks to a strong tide of sentiment that rose on both sides of the Atlantic at the thought of deserting the site of burial of the seventeenth-century heroine, pounds and shillings as well as dollars and cents poured in, in time to raise a fund to preserve and maintain the former Parish Church as a nondenominational Anglo-American Chapel of Unity, dedicated to the memory of the American princess whose story is part of the folklore of both England and America, and thus represents one more of the many bonds between them.

Pocahontas's baptism constitutes the central motif of one of the chapel's two stained-glass windows; the Van de Passe Pocahontas in Court dress is the feature of the other. The Biblical character of Rebecca looms large, as might have been expected, and the flora of Rebecca Rolfe's native tidewater adorn the windows' borders—Virginia creeper, dogwood, redbud.

In 1957, the churchyard of old St. George's—the tombstones having been removed—was landscaped to form a garden. There, in 1958, a commemorative plaque was put up (unveiled by a representative of the American Embassy):

THIS
STONE COMMEMORATES
PRINCESS POCAHONTAS OR METOAKA
DAUGHTER OF
THE MIGHTY INDIAN CHIEF POWHATAN.
GENTLE AND HUMANE, SHE WAS THE FRIEND OF THE
EARLIEST STRUGGLING ENGLISH COLONISTS WHOM SHE
BOLDLY RESCUED, PROTECTED, AND HELPED.
ON HER CONVERSION TO CHRISTIANITY IN 1613,
SHE RECEIVED IN BAPTISM THE NAME REBECCA,
AND SHORTLY AFTERWARDS BECAME THE WIFE OF
THOMAS ROLFE, A SETTLER IN VIRGINIA. SHE VISITED
ENGLAND WITH HER HUSBAND IN 1616, WAS GRACIOUSLY
RECEIVED BY QUEEN ANNE WIFE OF JAMES I.
IN THE TWENTY SECOND YEAR OF HER AGE
SHE DIED AT GRAVESEND, WHILE PREPARING TO
REVISIT HER NATIVE COUNTRY, AND WAS BURIED
NEAR THIS SPOT ON MARCH 21st, 1617.

In the same Gravesend garden, in a clump of redbud trees transplanted from the tidewater, a larger-than-life bronze statue of the Powhatan princess was erected (a replica of the William Ordway Partridge sculpture that stands at Jamestown), the gift of the people of the State of Virginia to the people of Gravesend, the County of Kent, in which soil her slight bones, her red flesh, moldered, her New World dust forever mingled with the dust of the Old.

CHAPTER XVI

SEAGULL: *Come, boyes, Virginia longs till we share the rest of her maiden-head.*

SPENDALL: *Why, is she inhabited alreadie with any English?*

SEAGULL: *A whole countrie of English is there, man, bread of those that were left there in '79; they have married with the Indians, and make 'hem bring forth as beautifull faces as any we have in England, and therefore the Indians are so in love with 'hem, that all the treasure they have they lay at their feete.*

GEORGE CHAPMAN, BEN JONSON, AND JOHN MARSTON, *Eastward Hoe, 1605*

JOHN ROLFE HAD LOST and left his wife at Gravesend. Now, as the *George* continued on down the Thames past the Isle of Thanet and into the English Channel, he had cause for grave concern about his child. The two-year-old boy, Thomas, was still ailing—with no one to care for him, no one to tend and nurse him back to health. Motherless, he was now bereft of his nurse: his aunt Matachanna had survived the crisis of the disease to which Pocahontas had succumbed, but she had not yet recovered and would not regain her feet for weeks to come.

The March winds had somewhat abated by the last week of the windy month. The passage of the flagship was smooth all the way past the white cliffs of Dover, past Dungeness Point and Beachy Head, past the Isle of Wight. Passengers found the notoriously choppy Channel calm throughout their westerly passage, that week, even past Portland Bill, fearsome for its rip tide. With none but dim local lights, with only a few buoys along that treacherous coast, with the Channel tides running swift and high, a passenger felt gratitude for having an expert mariner at the helm, "for having so good a Pylott as o^r Gov^{r}no^r," as John Rolfe would express that gratitude in a letter written from Virginia, some months later. The passage of the *George* continued smooth, the waters calm all the way past Start Point and into Plymouth Sound, all the way into the port of Plymouth in the lee of its greening hills, where Argall found Hamor's *Treasurer* riding at anchor, awaiting the flagship. (A dispatch from Argall to the Virginia Company reports that the *Treasurer* had preceded the *George* out of Gravesend, "Captaine Hamar his vice-Admiral was gone before, but hee found him at Plimoth.")

The first stage of the journey, from Gravesend to Plymouth, had been smooth and swift, but by the time the *George* dropped anchor off Plymouth, John Rolfe had yielded to persuasion on the part of Admiral Argall, Vice-Admiral Hamor, and other members of the expedition that his frail and ailing two-year-old child be left in England for at least a few months' time to recover from so grave an illness.

Argall and the others had sought to convince Rolfe of the wisdom of this course even before their departure from Gravesend, but Rolfe had resisted until the ship's arrival in Plymouth, at which time he was constrained to acknowledge that there was high risk in subjecting a sick child to so long and rigorous a crossing, without proper medical attention, without a nurse's care.

For some reason that is difficult to make out—unless it was a premonition that he would never see his son again—Rolfe was profusely apologetic for this decision when he addressed his friend and patron, Sir Edwin Sandys, from Jamestown, the following June:

> I know not how I may be censured for leaving my childe behind me, nor what hazard I may incurr of yor noble love and other of my best frends. At my departure from Gravesend (notw^{t}stand-ing I was ymportuned) I hadde no such intent. But in o^r short passage to Plymouth, in smothe water, I found such feare and hazard of his health (being not fully recovered of his sicknes) and lack of attendance (for they who looked to him hadd need of nurses themselves, and indeed in all o^r passage pvd no better) that by the advise of Captaine Argall, and divers who also foresaw the

danger and knew the inconvenyence hereof pswaded me to what I did. At Plymouth I found Sir Lewes Stukely so nobly mynded toward me, that he most earnestly intreated to have the keping of him, until my Brother tooke further order. . . .

Admiral Argall's report to the Virginia Company on the matter was more succinct than that of the child's father: "Her little childe Thomas Rolfe therefore was left at Plimoth with Sir Lewis Stukely, that desired the keeping of it."

Sir Lewis, Vice-Admiral of Devonshire, had welcomed Sir Thomas Dale, Captain Argall, and the party from Virginia on their arrival at Plymouth the previous summer, and he had doubtless made the acquaintance of John Rolfe and Pocahontas. Now, Sir Lewis volunteered his services as guardian to John Rolfe's frail young son until Henry Rolfe, the London merchant, could take charge of his nephew.

Rolfe's were among the few kind words ever spoken in Stukely's behalf by a contemporary. It may be that Stukely's compassionate gesture toward the young orphan constitutes his sole good deed on record. (His betrayal of his kinsman Sir Walter Raleigh, in 1618, was to earn him the epithet of "Sir Judas" Stukely. "Thou base fellow! thou scorn and contempt of men!" was how the Earl of Nottingham reviled him to his face.) His enemies could exult in 1619 at his disgrace and downfall: charged in 1619 with clipping coins, only a royal pardon (in return for the payment of a staggering fine) could save him from the scaffold. His months of self-imposed exile on the lonely isle of Lundy—remote enough to escape public contumely—ended in 1620 in death and, as rumor had it, madness.

In the year 1617, however, when John Rolfe gratefully if regretfully confided his small son into Sir Lewis's hands, the latter was still an imposing figure, a notable of Devonshire, his admiral's uniform aglitter with gold braid.

The *George* and the *Treasurer* weighed anchor simultaneously, moved together out of Plymouth Sound, around the tip of Cornwall, into the open sea, kept together almost all the way across the Atlantic.

A record crossing, as it proved: from Lizard Point on April 11 to Point Comfort on May 25—even an ailing child might have survived it!

"Upon the 10th of Aprill wee departed from Plymouth," as Rolfe would later report to Sandys,

and the next daie lost sight of the Lyzard, having the Treasurer in oᵗ Company, wch kept with us about 3 weeks; at what tyme we lost her in foggy weather. . . .

Paying due tribute to Admiral Argall, John Rolfe took up his pen in Jamestown on June 8 obsequiously to salute Sir Edwin Sandys (the new power in the Virginia Company), to report the fleet's "speedy and prosperous passage." Except for "the thyck fogg," the "mysty weather," Rolfe's message ran, they might have "arryved in virginia in a moneth's space"!

> Wee found the Colony (God be thanked) in good estate and injoying a firmer Peace and more plenty. Howev^r in buildings, fortyficacons, and [for want] of boats much ruyned and greate want. O^r p^rsent Gov^n^r at James towne is repayring and making straight what he fyndeth decayed and crooked, to whose in-deavo^rs and noble disposicon o^r Colony hath bene, is, and wilbe much indebted. All men cheerefully labor about their grounds, their harts and hands not ceasing from worke, though many have scarce ragges to cov^r their naked bodyes. English wheate, barly, Indyan Corne, Tobacco greate plenty on the ground. Hemp and flax seed distributed to most men by the Gov^n^r and is putt into the ground: nothing neglected, wch any waies may be avayleable to advance the Colony, and to give incouragem^t to yo^rself and the rest of the Ho^ble Company. The Cattle thrive and oxen are plentyfull. The Indyans very loving, and willing to parte wth their children. . . .

If the Indians continued "very loving"—or, at least, very friendly —in their relations with the English, it was a sign that the Peace of Pocahontas would prevail even beyond her death.

If the Indians showed a willingness "to parte with their children" —to agree, that is, to send them to school with the white children at Henrico, where the new college was scheduled for construction—then the prospects for the success of that holy work appeared bright in 1617, at the date of Rolfe's report.

"My wives death is much lamented"—presumably by Powhatan and other of her relatives—as Rolfe's letter to Sandys continued,

> my childe much desyred, when it is of better strength to endure so hard a passage, whose life greately extinguisheth the sorrow of her loss, saying all must die, but tis enough that her childe liveth.

Their child, Rolfe's letter implies, would one day bring its father the comfort the dying mother had foretold, but that day was not to dawn until the lad had attained an age and stamina requisite to a rugged Atlantic crossing and frontier existence. Meanwhile, Rolfe could only hope and pray that his decision to leave the delicate little boy temporarily in England had not incurred the displeasure of his powerful friend and patron, Sir Edwin Sandys:

> I thought good to rectyfie yo^u hereof, and desyre yor self and all the Company, for those causes, to hold me excused, if in their judgem^{nt} I may be censured to have erred herein. A firme contynuance of yor favo^r and love towards me I daylie praie for. . . .

Having suffered the loss of his wife, Rolfe reminded the company, he found the renunciation of the companionship of his only child an even more painful sacrifice:

> And although greate is my loss, and much my sorrow to be deprived of so greate a comfort, and hopes I hadd to effect my zealous intencons and desyres as well in others, as in her whose soule (I doubt not) resteth in eternall happynes; yet such temperance have I learned in p'sperity, and patience in adversitie, that I will as joyfully receive evill, as good at the hand of God: and assuredly trust that Hee, who hath p'served my childe, *even as a brand snatched out of the fier*, hath further blessings in store for me, and will give me strength and courrage to undertake any religious and charitable ymplymen^t, yorself and the Ho^{ble} Company shall command me, and wch in duty I am bound to doe. . . .

Rolfe, while putting his trust in God, would look directly to Sandys and the Virginia Company for those "further blessings in store" for him:

> Now my last request at this tyme is to yo'self, whom I have found a father to me, my wife and childe, and will ev^r acknowledg it wth the best gratefullnes my hart and penn can offer, that yo^u would be pleased as yo^u have begun and ben one of ye principall instrum^{ts} herein, to contynue yo' noble favo' and furtherance even for my childe sake, being the lyving ashes of his deceased Mother, and that yo" will still be the meanes, that yo' owne free lib'ality and all others by yor pcurem^t in obtayning so liberall a stipend, may not die wth my wife, but contynue for her childes advancem^t, wch will the better inhable myself and

him hereafter to undertake and execute what may be comaunded and requyred from us. . . .[1]

Rolfe's letter, written on three sides of a folded sheet of foolscap —the fourth page left blank to form an envelope and bear the address —is signed:

At yor command,

ever ready

JO: ROLF

James Towne this 8 of June 1617

and bears a postscript:

P^tScrip^t: May yo^u please S^r as occasion shalbe offered to remember me for some place of comaund and some estate of land to be confirmed to me and my childe, wherein I have formerly found yor love and readynes, for wch I shall rest much bound unto yo^u.

JOHN ROLFE'S LETTER to Sir Edwin Sandys, written shortly after the arrival of the *George* at Old Point Comfort in May of 1617, was entrusted for transmittal to London to the captain of the first vessel to head back east from the Virginia Colony in the month of June. Along with the same captain went an official report from Admiral-Governor Argall addressed to His Majesty's Council for Virginia.

One of Argall's first official acts as governor (after taking over those duties from departing Governor George Yeardley) was to dispatch Uttamatamakin to apprise Opechancanough of the change in the colony's high command, and to invite the Pamunkey chief to come to Jamestown to accept a gift from the hand of the new chief executive.*

Uttamatamakin delivered Argall's message to the chieftain, but it was the last service the English could expect from him. The high priest had returned from England a rabid Anglophobe ("Tomakin rails ag^t Engl^d English people and particularly his best friend Tho: Dale," Argall reported).

Argall insisted, however, that he had succeeded in counteracting the hostile propaganda spread by Uttamatamakin among the con-

---

* To which Opechancanough agreed, "came to James Town recd a present with great joy," according to a letter from Argall contained in the Virginia Company papers that form part of the Ferrar Papers.

federacy leaders: "all his reports are disproved before opachank⁰ & his Great men whereupon (to the great satisfaccion of yᵉ Great men) Tomakin is disgraced. . . ."

Tomakin's report to the great men of the Powhatan Confederacy was necessarily alarming: his reconnaissance of enemy territory had revealed vast resources in both men and material at the disposition of the English. His recommendation to the chiefs and council of the Powhatan Confederacy was doubtless for a prompt and all-out offensive against the invader before the tempo of the landings and reinforcements further quickened. It was a report to strengthen the hand of the consistently militant Opechancanough.

It was Opechancanough whom Governor Argall addressed upon his arrival in June of 1617 because, by then, as Argall had been informed, the Supreme Chieftain Powhatan had withdrawn from the Peninsula to the far banks of the Potomac (to the realm of a friendly "King"), relinquishing the reins of government to his two brothers, Opechancanough and Opitchapan: "Powhatan is gone to yᵉ K. [Kingdom] of May-umps in patawamack Rivʳ & has left yᵉ Govᵐnt of his Kingdom to Opachank & his other brother," Argall reports.

This sudden abdication of power by the hereditary ruler presents history with another enigma. Samuel Purchas, in his *Pilgrimes*, suggests two possible explanations: by establishing the date of Powhatan's retreat as coincidental with the date of Pocahontas's departure for England, Purchas points to the possibility that it was an access of despair at the loss of his beloved daughter that prompted this otherwise inexplicable course of action: "Powhatan was at this time of their comming gone Southwards. . . ."

In the very same sentence, Purchas points to Powhatan's mistrust of Opechancanough as the reason for his taking refuge in the friendly kingdom of Mayumps: "for feare (as some thought) least Opachancanough his brother should joyne with the English against him."

Purchas rejects the theory that it was the burden of his years that prompted the autocrat to abdicate: "His age was not so great as some have reported, they reckoning every Spring and Autumne for distinct yeares. . . ."

And as for any fear Powhatan might have harbored of his brother, it was not fear of Opechancanough's entering into alliance with the English: Opechancanough had, from the beginning, headed the militant faction of the confederacy. Where Powhatan had advocated compromise and conciliation, Opechancanough preferred annihilation to adjustment. The conflict between the brothers on the policy to be adopted toward the invaders dated back to April 26, 1607, the day of the original

Chesapeake Bay landing, when Opechancanough had urged immediate, concerted action to wipe out the beachhead, to push the invaders back into the sea whence they had come. (The conflict between the brothers was typical of that which rent the leadership of the Indian tribes in the face of white aggression throughout the seventeenth, eighteenth, and nineteenth centuries. To the misfortune of the native inhabitants of this continent, pacifist Powhatans outnumbered militant Opechancanoughs —with only an occasional King Philip, a Pontiac, an Osceola, a Chief Joseph, a Sitting Bull, a Big Foot, a Geronimo to prove the exceptions to the rule.)

Governor Argall, reporting to London in 1617, insisted that the Peace of Pocahontas still prevailed, that Powhatan continued well disposed toward the colony: "Powhatan goes from place to place visiting his Country, taking his pleasure in good friendship with us. . . ."

Uttamatamakin, presumably upon his return, had broken the news of Pocahontas's death to her father, who, according to Argall's report, "laments his daughter's death, but [is] glad her child is living, so doth Opechancanough. Both want to see him, but desire that he may be stronger before he returns. . . ."

The interest of the Powhatan Confederacy in the half-breed grandson of Powhatan gave rise to some concern among the land-hungry colonists in the tidewater: there was a rumor current in 1618 that the domains of Powhatan would devolve upon Thomas Rolfe when the latter reached his majority. A warning communiqué on this score was duly transmitted by Argall to London, as Virginia Company records attest: "Opechankano and the Natives have given their Country to Mr Rolfe's Child and that they will reserve it from all others till he comes of yeares. . . ."

Nettled at the suggestion that the Powhatans exercised any rights over territory granted the Virginia Company by the English monarch, the Council replied by taking Argall sharply to task for his presumptiveness:

"Wee cannot imagine why you should give us warninge y^t Opachankano and the Natives have given their Country to m^r Rolfe Child and that they will reserve it from all others till he comes of yeares except as wee suppose as some do here report it to be a Devise of yo' owne to some especiall purpose for y'oselfe but whither yours or thers wee shall litle esteeme of any such conveyance.

Powhatan himself would not live to see the return of his half-white grandson. Death came to the emperor less than a year after it had laid hands on his favorite daughter. Powhatan's son-in-law, John Rolfe, reported the patriarch's death to London in *A Relation*, dated June 15, 1618:

> Powhatan died this last Aprill, yet the Indians continue in peace. Itopatin his second brother succeeds him, and both hee and Opechankanough have confirmed our former league. . . . *

Not only the tribal but the colonial hierarchy, as well, was to be subject to a transfer of power, that year of 1618: London looked with increasing disfavor on Governor Argall, who stood accused of misappropriating vast tracts of tidewater property to his own estate, of monopolizing the Indian trade to his own personal profit, of diverting the labor force intended for communal enterprises to enterprises of his own. Charges multiplied, charges of maladministration and venality, "Extortion and Oppression," "tyrannical Administration." Stoutly defended though Argall may have been by his friends—John Rolfe foremost among them—his enemies managed to bring about his recall. With Argall, Jamestown would have seen the last of the military governors. (High-handed and venal as Argall may have been, a long official inquiry in London into the charges against him produced no concrete proof of misconduct in the governancy. Within months, he was given command of one of the major vessels in a royal fleet assembled to rid the Mediterranean and Atlantic of the pirate menace.)

Argall's replacement had sailed from England in April, 1618. It was Governor De La Warre himself—along with Lady De La Warre and an imposing retinue—who boarded the large "two-hundred and fiftie tunne" vessell and headed back to Virginia to resume governorship of the colony. But contrary winds were to blow this official party off course, and the ill-fated nobleman was never to reach the Virginia shore: he succumbed, one of thirty casualties aboard ship in the course of a "sixteene weekes" crossing.

Upon receipt of the news of De La Warre's death, the Virginia Company—in the autumn of that year—appointed George Yeardley to a second term as Governor of Virginia, arranged to have him knighted within the week, and rushed him off with Instructions to be known as the Great Charter, whereby a Council of Estate was to be set

---

* Opechancanough soon wrested control from the weaker, possibly elder Opitchapan: "Powhatan died in April the same Year" (by Robert Beverley's account of the succession), "leaving his Second Brother Itopatin in Possession of his Empire, a Prince far short of the Parts of Oppechancanough, who by some was said to be his Elder Brother . . . but . . . was disinherited by him. This Oppechancanough was a cunning and a brave Prince, who soon grasp'd all the Empire to himself."

up and an assembly for Virginia to be convened (the latter, a first if puny vehicle of self-government in America).

Some warning of the imminence of his deposition must have reached Governor Argall in advance of Yeardley's arrival: boarding "a little Pinnace" dispatched "Privately" from England to fetch him, Argall decamped in April, 1619 (according to a John Rolfe report), "with all his Goods and Booty" (according to a less sympathetic William Stith).

If Argall's administration had been tyrannical, inept, and venal, that of Sir George Yeardley, his successor, was little better. The high command had proven a bad lot. (There had been "many complaints against the Governors, Captaines, and Officers in Virginia," as Captain John Smith reminds the reader of *The Generall Historie*; the military regimes had constituted "a great scandall to the generall action.")

It was to avert such abuse of power by colonial governors in the future that the Great Charter had been designed: Yeardley bore the Virginia colonists the glad news that they were henceforward to have a voice in local government, to enjoy the common law rights and privileges of their homeland, to be "restored to" what William Stith termed "their Birthright . . . all the Liberties and Privileges of English Subjects."

The name of "Master John Rolfe" appeared on the prestigious list of six comprising the first Governor's Council,[2] as his own report proudly proclaims:

> Sir George Yearly to beginne his government, added to be of his councell, Captaine Francis West, Captaine Nathaniel Powell, Master John Pory, Master John Rolfe, and Master William Wickam, and Master Samuel Mackoke, and propounded to have a general assembly with all expedition.

Of that General Assembly John Rolfe was to find himself a member, too—one of the twenty-two burgesses elected to represent the people of their communities in the enactment of legislation governing local affairs. This House of Burgesses, as it was also called, was to be composed of two burgesses from each of the colony's eleven townships or plantations along the James, and to be summoned into session once a year by the governor—the first representative legislative body to meet on American soil, the forerunner of our present system of representative government.

Upon the summons of Governor Yeardley, elections were held

and the first legislative assembly in America convened on July 30, 1619, in the church at Jamestown, remaining in session through August 4: "Sir George Yeardley (according to a Comyssion directed unto him and to the Councell of State,) caused Burgesses to be chosen in all place who mett at James City," as John Rolfe faithfully reported by letter to Sir Edwin Sandys, later in the year.

The Jamestown church into which John Rolfe and his fellow-burgesses filed—cloaked and plumed, their swords at their sides—on that warm summer morning of 1619 was a small frame structure erected in 1617 during Argall's term of office.[3] With Sir George Yeardley installed in the massive governor's chair in the chancel, with his six councilors around him, with the twenty-two burgesses seated in the "Quire of the Church," the rector of Jamestown (Rolfe's old friend, the Reverend Richard Bucke) intoned the prayer for divine guidance with which that memorable first General Assembly opened.

The session was as brief as it was significant: with the July temperatures soaring and a large number of people crowded into a small space—a mere fifty feet by twenty—one burgess succumbed to heat prostration, and the other twenty-one voted incontinently to disband on August 4, unfinished business notwithstanding.

John Rolfe was to witness and record yet another significant event in that year of 1619 although, from his point in time, its full significance was lost upon him: he takes note, in his account of the Yeardley years, of the arrival of the first cargo of slaves to be discharged on the North American shore, "About the last of August [1619] came in a dutch man of warre that sold us twenty Negars. . . ."[4]

There was significance, as well, in the first real or general "division" of land to be effected in the colony, in 1619, the year Sandys took office as Treasurer of the Virginia Company: a bonus of one hundred acres to "ancient planters" (whose arrival preceded the departure of Sir Thomas Dale in 1616), a bonus of fifty acres to colonists arriving later than 1616—a development of which John Rolfe took due note, making proper acknowledgment of the incentive inherent in personal property:

> All the ancient planters being sett free have chosen places for their dividendes according to the commission, Which giveth all greate content, for now knowing their owne landes, they strive and are prepared to build houses & to cleere their groundes ready to plant, which giveth . . . [them] great incouragement, and the greatest hope to make the Colony flourish that ever yet happened to them.

AROUND THAT SAME YEAR of 1619, Pocahontas's widower took his third wife: Jane Pierce, daughter of William Pierce of Jamestown, an Ancient like Rolfe, a large landholder and planter who had sailed and been shipwrecked with Rolfe on the flagship *Sea Venture* in 1609.

Since eligible females were in short supply and great demand in the colony, where the male population far exceeded the female, the obvious conclusion is that Jane Pierce was young, had not been earlier bespoken because she had just reached the age of nubility. If so, she was considerably younger than John Rolfe, who had been for many months a married man at the time of his departure from England, a decade earlier. A child, a girl, Elizabeth, was born of this third union of John Rolfe's, in the year 1620 or 1621 (as a Muster of 1625 indicates).

The name of Elizabeth Rolfe would fade from the memory of man; John Rolfe would go down in history as the Father of Tobacco. His extensive tobacco plantations were destined to prosper in view of the monopoly which Virginia (along with Bermuda) was soon to enjoy on the importation of that crop into the British Isles. (By 1624, only tobacco grown in English colonies—to the exclusion of the Spanish leaf—was permitted entry into England.)

Rolfe's holdings were extremely large: in company with his father-in-law, William Pierce, and "some others," Rolfe patented seventeen hundred acres on the north side of the James River near Mulberry Island. On his own, Rolfe patented four hundred acres on the south bank of the James near Hog Island.

The charge that Rolfe's prosperity stemmed, in part, from unethical practices came as a bombshell in London, in 1621, during a session of the Virginia Company's quarter court, a charge brought against Rolfe by none other than the Lady De La Warre, his former patroness, the gracious lady who had taken Pocahontas under her wing in London and had introduced her at the Court of Whitehall. Her Ladyship demanded an accounting of properties and goods entrusted into Rolfe's keeping by the late Lord De La Warre upon his precipitate return to England in ill health in 1611: "It was signified," the Virginia Company records of 1621 reveal,

> that the Ladie Lawarr desyred the Court would please to graunt
> her a Commission dyrected to Sr. Fraunces Wyatt [the new
> Governor who had succeeded Yeardley in that office in 1621],
> mr George Sandys and others to examine and certifie as well what
> goods and monny of her late husbands deceased came to the

hande of m^r Rolfe in the year 1611 and to require y^t accordinge to his promise shee may be satisfied. . . .

When no satisfaction was forthcoming, her Ladyship sought to impound a shipment of tobacco arriving in England from Virginia and presumed to be the property of Rolfe—only to discover that it was the property of Rolfe's father-in-law, William Pierce.

Whereupon John Rolfe's brother, Henry, a charter member of the Virginia Company, appeared in the court to represent his absent brother:

> it was the request of my Lady Lawarre unto this Courte that in Consideracon of her goode remayning in the hande of m^r Rolfe in Virginia shee might receave satisfaccon for ye same out of his Tobacco nowe sent home. But for so much as it is supposed the said Tobacco is none of the said Rolfe, but belonged to m^r Pierce, it was thought fitt that m^r Henry Rolfe should acquaint my Lady Lawarre of his Brothers offer (as he informes) to make her La^p: good and faithfull Account of all such goode as remayne in his hande upon her La^r: direccon to that effect.

Examination of the Virginia Company records yields no clue as to the outcome of the litigation between Lady De La Warre and John Rolfe, but Sir Edwin Sandys's confidence in his faithful friend and assiduous correspondent evidently remained unimpaired, for Rolfe's career in the colony continued to flourish. In that same year of 1621, he was appointed by the new governor, Sir Francis Wyatt, to serve— along with other prominent men of the community—on the newly created and highly select Council of State ("whose Office shall chiefly be assisting, with their Care, Advice, and Circumspection, to the said Governor").

At that juncture—at the apex of his political career and at the zenith of fortune—John Rolfe drops out of view—or, rather, off the record; at this point, documentation regarding him fails the historian.

The only document upon which John Rolfe's name subsequently appears is his "Laste Will and Testament," dated "The Tenth day of March *Anno dni* 1621" (by the Old Style, or Julian, Calendar; 1622, by the New, or Gregorian) and beginning, "I John Rolfe of James Citty in Virginia Esquire beinge sicke in body, but of perfecte minde and memory. . . ." Of the five witnesses whose signatures appear on the probate copy[5] (filed in London, May 31, 1630), two names are familiar: Temperance Yeardley (Lady Yeardley, wife of the governor) and the Reverend Richard Bucke, rector of Jamestown, the "verie good preacher" who had christened Rolfe's short-lived infant Bermuda sometime in 1609–10, who had officiated at the marriage ceremony joining Rolfe and Pocahontas (and, presumably, the recent one joining Rolfe and Jane Pierce). In the year 1622, Richard Bucke witnessed Rolfe's will (probably shrove him at the hour of his death, probably read the Church of England services at his grave).

Appointing his "deerely beloved friend and father in Lawe Lieutenant William Pyers gent" as the trustee for his "two small children of very tender age" (Thomas, aged five or six; Elizabeth, approximately one year old), John Rolfe bequeathed a four-hundred-acre tract of land on the south bank of the James, near Hog Island, "unto my sonne Thomas" ("and to the heyres of his bodye lawfully begotten"). John Rolfe's interest in the seventeen-hundred-acre parcel of land near Mulberry Island on the James, fifteen miles downstream from Jamestown, was left to his wife and daughter. His "personall estate, goodes, Chattles, Cattles and householdstuffe as god hathe Lent me" was to be equally divided between the three survivors: his wife, his son, his daughter.[6]

The date of Rolfe's death—as the cause of his death—is unknown. All that is known is that news of it had reached England prior to October 7, 1622, for on that date Henry Rolfe made inquiry of the Virginia Company regarding his brother's estate (as the company books show), while expressing some concern lest he not be reimbursed for the expenses to which he had been put—and would in the future be put—in connection with the upbringing and education of his young nephew: "Mr. Henry Rolfe," according to company records of October 7, 1622,

> in his petition desiringe the estate his Brother John Rolfe deceased, left in Virginia might be enquired out and converted to the best use for the maintenance of his Relict wife and Children and for his indempnity having brought up the Child his said Brother had by Powhatan's daughter w'ch child is yet living and in his custodie.

To which petition of Henry Rolfe's, the Virginia Company acceded, it being

> ordered that the Governor and Counsell of Virginia should cause enquiries be made what lands and goods the said John Rolfe died seized of, and in case it be found the said Rolfe made no will, then to take such order for the petitioner's indempnity, and for

the mayntenance of the said children and his relict wife as they shall find his estate will beare (his debt unto the Companie and others beinge first satisfied) and to return unto the Companie here an Account of their proceedings.

If it has been popular among Rolfe biographers to ascribe his death to a tomahawk or feathered arrow—a weapon of his late wife's people —it is because the news of Rolfe's death reached England almost simultaneously with the news of the bloody Indian uprising that came close to wiping out the infant colony established by the English in the tidewater.

The fact, however, that Rolfe's wife and child are known to have survived the surprise attack of March 22 gives rise to the supposition that John Rolfe managed—as did his friend Captain Hamor—to defend his household successfully against the redskins' assault. Either that, or the Rolfe homestead was spared on command of the Supreme Chieftain Opechancanough.

Records reveal that Rolfe's widow, Jane Pierce Rolfe, was shortly remarried (the state of widowhood necessarily brief in a colony where the dearth of eligible white brides continued for another decade) to a Captain Roger Smith—like Rolfe, an old-timer in Virginia; like Rolfe, a member of the governing élite appointed in 1621 to sit on Governor Wyatt's Council of State. In the Muster of January, 1625, the names of Captain and Mrs. Roger Smith appear, along with that of a daughter, Elizabeth, who is identified as Virginia-born, age four, a member of the Smith household.

IF JOHN ROLFE never found his way into the gallery of American heroes, it may be for the reason that, by an irony of fate, the two letters extant in his own hand—the abjectly apologetic one, cited above, indited to Sir Edwin Sandys, and the long-winded, canting address to Governor Dale, in 1613, at once a request for permission to marry Pocahontas and a denial of her sexual appeal for him, an ungallant protest that his sole motives were the good of the colony and the glory of God—show him at his sanctimonious worst, a calculating, conniving fellow, a favor-seeker, place-monger. He stands indicted by his own pen. But at his best, Rolfe is clearly in the heroic mold: an adventurous soul, a trailblazer, not only an adventurous but an enterprising man, ingenious and innovative. Not for him the staple crops of English wheat, barley, flax, and Indian corn; Rolfe experimented instead with the rare golden seeds of the golden leaf acquired from the West Indies. And of course he was also the first man in the colony to marry a red woman, to reconcile the races and bring about a peace between them, brief though it may have been.

Stephen Vincent Benét will see justice done him:

> *And few men ever crowded more life in a life*
> *Than this sober-tongued experimenter who took*
> *Shipwreck, hunger and marriages in his stride*
> *And made tobacco king of Virginia*
> *For a century and more.*
> *You may think of him as Pocahontas's husband.*
> *He was rather more than that and his seed still lives,*
> *And we would do well to fence the small plot of garden,*
> *Where, in hose and doublet, he planted the Indian weed.*

Benét's hint has been, thus far, lost on Jamestown: the ladies of the Association for the Preservation of Virginia Antiquities (who dispose of the Jamestown Foundation) have not yet seen fit to fence John Rolfe's garden plot. Nor to honor him with a statue on that historic site—as Captain Smith has been honored.

Again in contrast to Rolfe, whose grave is unknown and unmarked, Smith's name and fame are commemorated in London at the Church of St. Sepulchre-in-Newgate where he was buried (at age fifty-one) in 1631. The memorial tablet raised above his head there was destroyed in the Great Fire of 1666; the tablet, along with the church, has since been restored—the lengthy and glowing epitaph chiseled in full (all twenty-six lines beginning, "Here lies one conquered that hath conquered Kings").*

American playwright-essayist Paul Green pleads Rolfe's case as persuasively—and as vainly—as Benét. By Green's thesis,[7] the hero's laurels should be awarded to Rolfe rather than to Smith:

> It is in John Rolfe's philosophy of work that his greatness and true heroism lie, that he becomes the real hero of Jamestown. In him was represented the essential character of the English race. In him was illustrated once more the reason for England's success as a colonizing power in the world. She has been a nation of men who worked.

Granted. Rolfe is the prototype of the English empire-builder, the exemplar of the Anglo-Saxon Protestant work-ethic, and of the private-

---

* Smith's epitaph is printed as Appendix D.

enterprise system that would make America famous. Even so, it is upon Smith's head—not Rolfe's—that the hero's nimbus has settled (perhaps because Rolfe lacks a warmth, a candor, an independence, a spontaneity Smith exudes; perhaps because Smith toadies to no man; he explains, he does not apologize; he requests, he does not beseech; he personifies a rugged individualism essential to the American image of a hero).

The conjecture that John Rolfe died peacefully in his bed, rather than in a savage ambush, is based on the opening line of his last will and testament, where the testator describes himself, as of March 10, 1622 (thus within weeks or days of his death), as "beinge sicke in body"— a line that may be interpreted as more than merely a conventional rhetorical opening for such a legal instrument in the early seventeenth century.

Whether Rolfe died of natural causes in his bed or at the hands of his second wife's people, it was the year of his death that saw the end of what men had called the Peace of Pocahontas. An eight-year period of peace between white and red, between invader and indigene, it had begun with the marital union of Rolfe and Pocahontas, had not long outlasted it. The Massacre of March 22, 1622, came five years and one day after Pocahontas's interment at Gravesend.

CHAPTER XVII

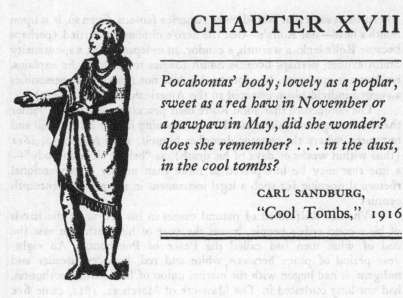

Pocahontas' body, lovely as a poplar,
sweet as a red haw in November or
a pawpaw in May, did she wonder?
does she remember? . . . in the dust,
in the cool tombs?

CARL SANDBURG,

"Cool Tombs," 1916

THE COLONY'S UTTER RELIANCE upon the Peace of Pocahontas accounted, in the opinion of Robert Beverley, for the relaxation of vigilance which had invited the catastrophe of 1622: "So great was their Security upon this Marriage," mused Beverley, that Governor Yeardley lapsed into criminal negligence:

> He let the Buildings and Forts go to Ruine; not regarding the Security of the People against the Indians . . . applying all Hands to plant Tobacco, which promised the most immediate Gain. . . . In the mean while the Indians mixing among 'em, got Experience daily in Fire-Arms, and some of 'em were instructed therein by the English themselves, and emply'd to hunt and kill wild Fowl for them.

Writing in retrospect, composing his *Generall Historie* for publication in 1624, Captain John Smith could gloat, could claim that had he been in command of the colony's defenses—an assignment repeatedly denied him by the Virginia Company Council—the disaster of March, 1622, would have been averted; he would never have condoned the laxity of discipline that prevailed during the regimes of Yeardley, Argall, and Wyatt: "It hath oft amazed me to understand," Smith snorted, that firearms should have been entrusted to the savages, that the colonists should have been allowed to disperse in settlements up and down the James, miles from the central fortifications, that the militia should have been permitted to go "rooting in the ground about Tobacco like Swine" instead of attending drill and polishing their muskets![1]

"In the mean time," Robert Beverley concluded,

> by the great Increase of People, and the long Quiet they had enjoy'd among the Indians, since the Marriage of Pocahontas . . . all Men were lull'd into a fatal security.

Not only had the colony been lulled into a false sense of security, but the wily Opechancanough offered perfidious pledges of peace, only days before the surprise attack, to the new Governor, Sir Francis Wyatt: words to the effect that "he held the peace so firme, the sky should fall or [ere] he dissolved it."

But "on the Friday morning that fatall day, being the two and twentieth of March," as Captain Smith's *Generall Historie* relates the gruesome incident, the Indians fell upon the unsuspecting and careless colonists, scattered and isolated as many were in their plantations extending some one hundred and forty miles up and down, on both sides of the James ("most plantations were placed straglingly and scatteringly, as a choice veine of rich ground invited them," by Captain Smith's indictment).

It was a concerted attack by all the tribes of the far-flung Powhatan Confederacy (an example of unified pan-tribal military effort rare in the long history of European-Indian conflict). Opechancanough had succeeded in consolidating the numerous, scattered tribes of the tidewater, where Powhatan had failed—if, indeed, he had ever tried.[2]

Opechancanough's plot was for a "general Massacre of the English, to be executed on the twenty-second of March, 1622, a little before Noon, at a Time when our Men were all at Work abroad in their Plantations, disperst and unarm'd," as Robert Beverley reported toward the end of the century when the horror was still fresh in men's memory: "This Hellish Contrivance was to take Effect upon all the several Settlements at one and the same Instant. . . ."

The plan of attack was so skilfully devised, the organization of forces so effective, the element of surprise so perfectly preserved, that the English preferred to credit the wily Spaniard with the stratagem rather than the ignorant "Salvage," although no basis for such a supposition exists. It was the work of Opechancanough, Opechancanough who patiently plotted and fearlessly carried out what even Captain Smith acknowledges to be a rather complicated tactical maneuver.

"You must remember," Captain Smith exhorts the reader of his *Generall Historie*, that

> these wilde naked natives live not in great numbers together; but dispersed, commonly in thirtie, fortie, fiftie, or sixtie in a company. Some places have two hundred, few places more, but many lesse; yet they had all warning given them one from another in all their habitations, though farre asunder, to meet at the day and houre appointed for our destruction at al our several Plantations; some directed to one place, some to another, all to be done at the time appointed, which they did accordingly.

Captain Smith's account of the Massacre (based on eyewitness accounts by returning sailors and adventurers, on news releases from the Virginia Company's London bureau) may rank as the first "Western," the earliest Wild Indian horror-story. Such was the perfidy of the Salvages,

> they came unarmed into our houses with Deere, Turkies, Fish, Fruits, and other provisions to sell us: yea in some places sat downe at breakfast with our people, whom immediately with their owne tooles they slew most barbarously, not sparing either age or sex, man woman or childe; so sudden in their execution, that few or none discerned the weapon or blow that brought them to destruction. In which manner fell that fatall morning under the bloudy and barbarous hands of that perfidious and inhumane people, three hundred forty seven men, women and children. . . .[2]

The three hundred and forty-seven casualties of the attack accounted for more than one-fourth of the colony's total population, which is estimated to have stood, at that date, at approximately twelve hundred and forty or twelve hundred and fifty.

If the casualty figure and the population figure are reliable, then the survivors on March 23 numbered some nine hundred (converging on Jamestown in response to Governor Wyatt's order to abandon the remote and indefensible plantations).

Of these nine hundred survivors of the Massacre, five hundred would be dead within the twelvemonth of malnutrition, pestilence, exposure.

Between 1606 and 1623, some five thousand immigrants took ship for Virginia; only one thousand survived at the end of that period of time. Out of the four thousand colonists transported to Virginia during the four years of Sir Edwin Sandys's administration, the net increase to the population amounted to a mere two hundred and seventy-five.

The Virginia Company was understandably reluctant to publish the figures, the shocking truth as to the desperate straits into which the colony had fallen, and the state of bankruptcy in which the company floundered.

The time had come for the Crown to intervene. A royal commission was appointed in 1623 to conduct an investigation into the affairs of the Virginia Company and the conditions in Virginia.

The recommendation of the Court of Inquiry (convened in May of 1624) was that the King should recall the several charters he had granted the Virginia Company (the first in 1606), an action tantamount to the dissolution of the joint stock company, after eighteen years of operation.

Virginia became a Crown Colony, the administration taking what would become the classic colonial form for the British Empire: a governor (and assistants) appointed by the monarch and the Privy Council, plus an assembly representative of the colonists themselves, convened at the summons of the governor to legislate the colony's local affairs.

In the tidewater, reprisal against the Indians came swift and terrible. Vengeance was done with not only alacrity but relish. Some, as Captain Smith reports, would actually find cause for satisfaction in the end result: "this massacre, which in those respects some say will be good for the Plantation, because now we have just cause to destroy them by all meanes possible. . . ." The original Virginia Company injunction, not to offend the naturals, could now be ignored and forgotten; now the colonists were free to "beat the Salvages out of the Countrey."

Overnight—the night of March 22–23, 1622—the Noble Savage had been transformed into the ignoble fiend. To exterminate and to dispossess had become the new order of the day, a method more expeditious than to civilize and Christianize, as Captain John Smith pointed out: "besides it is more easie to civilize them by conquest then faire meanes; for the one may be made at once, but their civilizing will require a long time and much industry."

Abandoned, from March 22 forward, the scruples of the earlier years, those expressed by the Reverend Robert Gray, for example, inquiring in print, "by what right or warrant we can enter into the land of these Savages, take away their rightfull inheritance . . . and plant ourselves in their places, being unwronged or unprovoked by them?"

The Indian attack of March 22 constituted the wrong and the provocation, provided the perfect pretext for extirpation of these tribes and occupation of their territories. (Some few, but very few, were willing to concede that the Indians had been justified in their aggression by previous injuries done them by the invader, by English infringement on territory over which the natives considered their sovereignty to be absolute.)

Scrapped and abandoned was the original and explicit objective of the English colonization project, "to bring the barbarous and savage people to a civill and Christian kind of government." A new and open pioneering sentiment became manifest: Edward Waterhouse, a Secretary of the Virginia Company, declared that, by their perfidy in the Massacre, the savages had actually done the company a favor!

> Because our hands which before were tied with gentlenesse and faire usage, are now set at liberty by the treacherous violence of the Savages. . . . So that we, who hitherto have had possession of no more ground than their waste, and our purchase . . . may now by a right of Warre, and law of Nations, invade the Country, and destroy them who sought to destroy us.

According to the Puritan point of view, the law cited by Edward Waterhouse was less "the law of Nations" than the law of God, less civil or natural law than divine logic. According to the logic of Christian imperialism, the colonial enterprise was a religious enterprise: God intended the savage Indians' land for the civilized Christian Englishman, who would occupy the earth, increase and multiply, who would farm the land and make it fructify, who would give it order. As John Winthrop stated it in 1629,

> the whole earth is the Lord's Garden, and he hath given it to the sons of Adam to be tilled and improved by them. Why then should we stand starving here for the places of habitation . . . and in the meantime suffer whole countries, as profitable for the use of man, to lie waste without any improvement. . . .

Why the Indians' flourishing acres of corn, peas, and beans did not constitute "any improvement," why the neat plots of tobacco, gourds, and sunflower surrounding every village of the southern and central eastern coast did not qualify as "the Lord's garden," is a point never clarified by Winthrop or any other early New England colonist. The charge that the Indian was a nomadic hunter was untrue as concerned the Atlantic seaboard tribes: these were, clearly, sedentary people, agriculturists as well as hunters and fishermen, with game preserves and fishing grounds adjacent to their cultivated fields.

Nevertheless, the seventeenth-century Puritan saw the Indian only as a beast—a creature of the Devil—blocking the course, standing athwart the path of civilization and Christianization. It was the formulation of the logic of Christian imperialism whereby the whole vast continent, from coast to coast, from Atlantic to Pacific, could be seized and appropriated, whereby the Devil's brood squatting upon its face could be exterminated, without affront to the Christian conscience.

An occasional conscience still took affront, an occasional voice still cried out, as late as 1635, as in Maryland (the voice of the anonymous author of *A Relation of Maryland*): "It is much more Prudence, and Charity, to Civilize, and make them Christians, than to kill, robbe, and hunt them from place to place, as you would doe a wolfe."

In Virginia, however, after March of 1622, prudence and charity were Christian virtues the colonists could not afford to cultivate: to kill, to rob, to hunt down the savages in the tidewater was the directive issued to Governor Wyatt, on August 1, 1622, by the Council for Virginia meeting in emergency session in London. Through the Earl of Southampton, who had succeeded Sir Edwin Sandys as treasurer, the Council for Virginia ruefully but officially renounced its original evangelical objective, its holy mission to the infidel ("the saving of whose souls we have so zealously affected"). "The Propagation of the glorious Gospel," urged upon the Virginia Company by John Donne, was no longer to be its "principal end."

Instructions from London called for "a perpetual war, without peace or truce," an organized process of extermination. The Powhatans' age-old Siouan-speaking enemies in the piedmont were to be incited to attack the tidewater (the bounty offered by the English predicated on heads rather than scalps: "by reward of beads and copper upon the bringing in of their heads"); the colonial militia was to harass the local tribes unremittingly, to raid and to ravage systematically, to extirpate or to expel the red men from the banks of the James and beyond, to "pursue and follow them" as they withdrew to distant waters of the Chesapeake. London's recommendations for a final solution of the Indian problem included

> surprising them in their habitations, intercepting them in their hunting, burning their towns, demolishing their temples, destroying their canoes, plucking up their weirs, carrying away their corn, and depriving them of whatsoever may yield them succor or relief.

Captain John Smith, in this emergency, lost no time in proposing himself as the man best qualified to rid the colony of the Indian menace. If he had been the savior of the Virginia colony in its perilous initial state, he would undertake—if granted the requisite military support—to come to the colony's rescue once again, in this new hour of crisis. One of the reasons for his publication of *The Generall Historie* in 1624 was to publicize this offer of his services to the Crown (which had, by that date, taken over from the defunct Virginia Company) "to have but fifteene hundred men to subdue againe the Salvages, fortifie the Countrey, discover the yet unknowne, and both defend and feed their Colony. . . ."

Poor Captain Smith—his proposal to the Crown met with rejection as had those previously made by him to the Virginia Company, as had that most recently made, in 1620, to the Pilgrim Fathers, who, while availing themselves of Smith's excellent maps of New England, yet passed him over in favor of Captain Miles Standish to serve as military commander of their expedition. No command post in the New World, no colonial assignment for Captain Smith was forthcoming. At age forty-four, his sailing days, exploring days, adventuring days were over. Then suddenly with the publication of his *Generall Historie* in 1624, he came into his own as a literary light. Old sea-dog that he was, old soldier of fortune, a literary career must have been the last thing in the world he had expected—success with the pen instead of the sword. His earlier works had met with no such response from the reading public, had earned him neither such financial rewards nor such national eminence as did this sixth volume.

The colonists in Virginia, in 1622, showed themselves more than ready to carry out London's instructions for a war to the death: "Wee have anticipated your desire by settinge uppon the Indyans in all places," the Council in Virginia could proudly report to the Virginia Company in London in the first month of 1623.

Shortly, by 1623–24, most of the tribes which had once made their home on the peninsula between the James and the Pamunkey had been driven off, some withdrawing toward the north banks of the Pamunkey and the York, others as far north as the Rappahannock and the Potomac. Even that was not to prove far enough; even on those far shores, the English raiders would follow and pursue, would set upon the retreating confederacy tribes, and harass them in their retreat.

As for their Supreme Chieftain, a price was on his head, a reward posted for his capture: London took the line that "if any can take Opechancanough himself, he shall have a great and singular reward from us." Several traps were laid, but the wily Pamunkey chief could not be induced to take the bait. He would live long enough to incite one more, one last desperate Indian insurrection against the occupation of the tidewater, in 1644. It can be argued that, with his greatly reduced fighting force, Opechancanough realized the hopelessness of this last attack against a better-armed and numerically superior foe, but that he and his braves deliberately chose death in battle as preferable to submission and slavery, chose physical in preference to cultural annihilation. The sole exception to the colony's rule for total annihilation of the redskins was to be made in favor of the redskin young, who were to be enslaved and converted: "we cannot but advise," the Council for Virginia instructed Governor Wyatt, "not only the sparing but the preservation, of the younger people of both sexes, whose bodies may by labor and service become profitable, and their minds not overgrown with evil customs, be reduced to civility, and afterwards to Christianity."

This attempt, like every other to use the American Indian as a slave, was doomed to failure. The Spaniards had early attempted, early abandoned the effort to impress the Caribs into service on the plantations of the West Indies; these, proving unable or unwilling to perform hard labor, were exterminated, then replaced by Negroes from West Africa, imported yearly by the thousands, beginning as early as 1518. The natives of the Western Hemisphere could not take slavery, would not endure it; in captivity, under forced labor, they languished and died. Algonkian people, Iroquois tribes, and other natives of North America preferred death to slavery, resisted every effort to convert them into a labor force. Not that their physiques were less sturdy than the Negroes'; rather, they were less malleable, more stubborn, more defiant of external authority. Freedom was the Indians' element; freedom of movement, freedom of action, freedom of speech, were their prerogatives—"the freest People in the World," as John Lawson called them in 1718 in his *History of North Carolina.* Slavery was a condition under which they apparently did not wish to live.

Opechancanough, the old Pamunkey warrior, lived long enough to see the return of his half-breed nephew. Thomas Rolfe, son of Pocahontas and John Rolfe, went to Virginia upon reaching manhood, arriving in the colony sometime in the mid-1630s, possibly as early as 1635 (at age twenty), not later than 1640 (at age twenty-five).

His return to Virginia was predictable; large property holdings awaited him there: as the bequest of his father, a four-hundred-acre plantation near Smith's Fort across the river from Jamestown; and, adjoining this, a tract three times as large which had come to him as gift of his mother's uncle, Opechancanough ("by Guifte of the Indian King," according to Surry County records).

Not only that. To Thomas Rolfe—and to the London uncle who

reared the orphan boy—it must have seemed his destiny to live in the New World, the place of origin, the homeland of his redskin mother, the land his white father had helped to explore, occupy, settle, develop, colonize. A readily comprehensible search for identity would have led the orphan straight to Virginia as soon as he reached maturity. Curiosity, interest, and sentiment all combined to impel him in that direction.

He could have expected a warm welcome from his half-sister, Elizabeth (a girl of fourteen or fifteen, in 1635, if she had survived the rigors of infancy and childhood in that pest-hole of a colony). And if Jane Pierce Rolfe Smith, Elizabeth's mother, had survived the twelve or thirteen years of famine and pestilence that had passed since the death of her first husband, she might have helped to bridge the gap of the past for this son of Rolfe's, this son who had scarcely known the father from whom he had been separated at the age of two.

Young Thomas Rolfe experienced an urge to make contact with his mother's people, too; an urge strong enough to compel him to risk public censure by fraternizing with the enemy. It was, at that time, against the law to "speak or parley" with the Powhatans: by Act of the Grand Assembly of Virginia (February 1631/32), "All trade with the Savages" had been "prohibited, as well Publique as private." Thomas was thus obliged to petition the Governor, in 1641, for permission to visit his maternal aunt and great-uncle (as old Virginia records among the Randolph MSS attest): "Thomas Rolfe petitions governor to let him go to see *Opachankeno* to whom he is allied and *Cleopatra*, his mother's sister, 17 December, 1641."

The name of Opechancanough, architect of the Massacre, was anathema throughout the colony. It was an act of courage on Thomas Rolfe's part openly to seek him out in his retreat on the Pamunkey. It was probably the aunt rather than the great-uncle whom Thomas Rolfe longed to see. *Cleopatra* must represent a garbled version, an Anglicization-Egyptianization of an exotic Powhatan proper name. One wonders whether the name was not, rather, *Matachanna*, the aunt-nurse associated with his mother in Thomas Rolfe's earliest memories, lost to him at the same hour as his mother.

When the word went out from Opechancanough, in 1641, to allow the Englishman to approach the closely guarded encampment on the Pamunkey—that it was the half-breed son of the Princess Pocahontas making his way across the peninsula from Jamestown—he may have been readily recognizable as such to the forest sentinels, possibly having inherited his mother's coppery skin tone, her high cheekbones, dark hair and eyes.

Thomas Rolfe's pilgrimage to the Pamunkey, into the heart of enemy territory in 1641, was proof that his exclusively English upbringing and education had not totally alienated him from his mother's people. Memories of early childhood were still fresh: the first words to reach his ears, the first perhaps he had spoken, were Powhatan words; the arms and the breast where the infant had sheltered were coppery, not only his mother's but his aunt's.

By 1646, however, Thomas Rolfe had resolved any conflict that might have wracked him as to his identity, as to the world and race to which he properly belonged. By October 5 of that year, by Act of the Grand Assembly of Virginia in session at Jamestown, Thomas Rolfe had been commissioned a lieutenant in the colonial militia, assigned guard duty at Fort James in defense of the colonists against the Indians, maintaining six men to assist him at that post ("in point of honor and security of the colony," according to the wording of Act II). In accepting that commission and that assignment, Lieutenant Rolfe had made his choice between two irreconcilable worlds, his father's and his mother's. (Pocahontas had not lived—as had the Aztec Malinche—to see her son take up arms to destroy her own people. Malinche's son by Cortez became a captain in the imperial armies of Spain during her lifetime.)

Thomas Rolfe's enlistment in the colonial militia was tacit admission that he had failed to span the chasm separating his parents. Whatever hope had been reposed in him as symbol of reconciliation between the two races had, at that hour, to be abandoned. The celebrated experiment in intermarriage had proved unavailing, would spur no emulation in Virginia.

When Opechancanough and his warriors—in their ever-diminishing ranks—shattered the uneasy peace in 1644, Rolfe lent his hand to what would be the rout and virtual annihilation of his mother's people.

Thomas Rolfe was to win the confidence and respect of the Anglo-Saxon community in which he had chosen to make his life—the red blood known to flow in his veins bringing no blush either to him or his descendants (whose name would be legion, predominantly Bolling). Thomas Rolfe "afterward became," as William Stith would describe him a century later, "a Person of Fortune and Distinction in this Country" (his fortune based on the rich landholdings inherited from his father and donated by his maternal great-uncle, further increased by dint of his own endeavor and enterprise).

Opechancanough, Thomas Rolfe's mother's uncle—so aged and so infirm he had to be borne into battle on a litter—was captured in 1645 and brought prisoner to Jamestown. If Thomas Rolfe encountered him there, he had no cause to blush for his ancient kinsman: "He continued brave to the last Moment of his Life," as Robert Beverley related the incident some half century later:

> Oppechancanough, by his great Age and the Fatigues of War . . . was now grown so decrepit, that he was not able to walk alone; but was carried about by his Men. . . . In this low Condition he was, when Sir William Berkeley hearing that he was at some Distance from his usual Habitation, resolved at all Adventure to seize his Person, which he happily effected. For, with a Party of Horse he made a speedy March, surprizing him in his Quarters, and brought him Prisoner to James-Town. . . . However, he could not preserve his Life above a Fortnight; For one of the Soldiers, resenting the Calamities the Colony had suffer'd by this Prince's Means, basely shot him thro' the Back, after he was made Prisoner; of which Wound he died.

Punitive expeditions were dispatched against the Pamunkey and the Chickahominy, the two largest tribes remaining, and did their work so thoroughly that the General Assembly of Virginia could report in 1646 that the Indians were "So routed and dispersed they are no longer a nation."

"After this," Beverley explains, "Sir William Berkeley made a new Peace with the Indians, which continued for a long time unviolated; insomuch, that all the Thoughts of future Injury from them were laid aside."

By the terms of Governor Berkeley's peace treaty of 1646, the line of demarcation was drawn sharp and clear between white territory and red: the remnants of the once-dominant Powhatan Confederacy were removed, restricted to an area north of the York River, all their original tribal lands in the valleys of the James and the York south of the fall-line relinquished to the English (establishing a pattern of removal and relocation which would remain constant throughout most of the nineteenth century, harbinger of the modern reservation system).

Not that the former lords of the tidewater would find security even in retreat north of the York: even there, the aggressive European newcomers worried their southern flank while inveterate native enemies raided from the north and west. Ravaged by war and imported disease, only a shadow of the once-proud confederacy survived at the end of the seventeenth century—its thirty-odd original member-tribes reduced to half a dozen, its population of approximately nine thousand diminished to approximately one thousand. Even so reduced, the Powhatans continued stubbornly to resist alien ways, would make no concession in adjustment to the alien culture—with the result that, within a hundred years after the English landings, their native culture had "simply disintegrated under the strain of constant pressure."

When, toward the end of the seventeenth and the beginning of the eighteenth century, eminent Virginia gentlemen-scholars Robert Beverley and his brother-in-law Colonel William Byrd II focused their attention on their land and its past, and sought to examine and to appraise the nature and culture of its original inhabitants in order to record such observations for posterity, they were hard put to find the few Indians and Indian communities left in Virginia upon whom to base their study. (Beverley and Byrd were the first in the colony, since the day of the Massacre, to make any attempt to understand the native inhabitants; from 1622 on, the colonists had sought only to exterminate —not to study—them.)

"The Indians of Virginia are almost wasted. . . . All which together can't raise five hundred fighting men," Beverley wrote on a note of sympathy rare among Anglo-Saxon historians vis-à-vis the Vanishing American. A man of independent spirit, of inquiring and open mind, Robert Beverley was impervious to the racial prejudices of his fellow colonists; he was favorably impressed by what he saw and learned of the red race, their handsome appearance, their simple virtues, their rapport with nature, reverence of nature, respect for natural resources, their fierce love of freedom, their propensity to share their blessings with the less fortunate: "happy, I think," he wrote,

> in their simple State of Nature, and in their enjoyment of Plenty, without the Curse of Labour. They have on several accounts reason to lament the arrival of the Europeans, by whose means they seem to have lost their Felicity, as well as their Innocence. The English have taken away a great part of their Country, and consequently made every thing less plenty amongst them.

Beverley's contact with the savage in the flesh had not prompted him to scrap the Primitivist tradition of the Noble Savage in which his mind was evidently steeped; he persisted, even up close, even at first hand, in seeing the savage life style as idyllic, "as possessing nothing, and yet enjoying all things." He even went so far—even at the risk of being denounced by his neighbors as an Indian-lover—as to suggest the assimilation of the red race by the white via intermarriage; this suggestion appeared in the first edition of his *History* (London, 1705), evidently proving so unpopular that when the revised edition appeared in London in 1722, all reference to integration of the races had been discreetly deleted. Yet it remained Beverley's firm conviction that "by this kind Method" (of intermarriage),

> the Country would have been full of People, by the Preservation of many Christians and Indians that fell in the Wars between them. Besides, there would have been a Continuance of all those Nations of Indians that are now dwindled away to nothing by their frequent Removals, or are fled to other Parts.

By the time Thomas Jefferson came, in the late eighteenth century, to list and to classify the tribes of America—their size and habitat—it was already difficult to account for more than a half dozen of the thirty-odd tribes of the original Powhatan Confederacy: they had dispersed, disintegrated—some totally extinct, some subsumed into other tribes: "Very little can now be discovered of the subsequent history of those tribes severally," Jefferson noted regretfully in 1781 in his *Notes on Virginia*:

> The Chickahominies removed about the year 1661, to Mattapony River. Their chief, with one from each of the Pamunkies and Mattaponies, attended the treaty of Albany in 1685. This seems to have been the last chapter in their history. They retained, however, their separate name so late as 1705, and were at length blended with the Pamunkies and Mattaponies, and exist at present only under their name. There remain of the Mattaponies three or four men only, and have more negro than Indian blood in them. They have lost their language, have reduced themselves, by voluntary sales, to about fifty acres of land, which lie on the river of their own name, and have from time to time, been joining the Pamunkies, from whom they are distant but ten miles. The Pamunkies are reduced to about ten or twelve men, tolerably pure from mixture with other colors. The older ones among them preserve their language in a small degree, which are the last vestiges, as far as known, of the Powhatan language.

Jefferson's notes on the Powhatan Confederacy were compiled shortly after the American Revolution, toward the close of the eighteenth century.[4]

Toward the close of the twentieth century, only a handful of so-called Powhatans are to be found in the State of Virginia, and these have ceased to function as a culturally definable entity, retaining little more than a tribal name and a sense of common origin. An odd assortment of a hundred-odd individuals calling themselves Pamunkeys and Mattaponis occupy reservations assigned them by colonial treaties later ratified by the state, and maintain some semblance of tribal organization. Several non-reservation groups—including Chickahominies, Rappahannocks, and Nansemonds—have adjusted to life in various rural communities without losing awareness of their heritage and ethnic identity. Despite the loss of all tribal tradition, all native language, these scattered groups obtained official recognition of their status as Indian tribes from the State of Virginia and, in 1923, formed an organization known as the Powhatan Confederacy. Not that this motley crew can any longer claim to be full-blooded: racially heterogeneous, showing Caucasoid and Negroid ancestry, yet they cling tenaciously to the classification of American Indian, Powhatan Confederacy—the Indian identity precious in a land where racial prejudice against dark-skinned minorities is rampant, especially precious in Virginia, whose First Families proudly trace their blood line back to the Powhatan princess Pocahontas.

The colonists of New England, even more pompously than those of Virginia, proclaimed one of their noble purposes to be to bring the gospel to the heathen, but the heathen of New England had become, by 1750, practically extinct. Even the sainted Puritans proved quick to deeds of blood. By the time the French and Indian Wars came to an end, Indian life on the Atlantic seaboard, from Maine to Virginia, had been expunged. The coastal tribes of North America bore the brunt of the first wave of invasion . . . and went under for their inability either to amalgamate with the invader or to resist him. With the presence of some twenty thousand English on the Eastern seaboard, mostly in New England, by the year 1640, in addition to the Dutch in New Amsterdam and the Swedes in New Jersey and Delaware, the doom of the Atlantic seacoast tribes was sealed. The inland tribes were to enjoy a brief respite while the French-English contest for the continent raged, while the fur trade flourished: France and England cosseted their Indian allies throughout the course of the colonial wars, and the fur traders opposed and slowed the thrust of westward settlement in that it threatened the habitat of the beaver. These were the circumstances that combined to give the aborigines of the interior a vital delay denied the peripheral tribes—time to adjust, to adapt, to accommodate to the white man's ways, and withal to preserve some degree of native cultural integrity.

IN THE ORIGINAL ENGLISH COLONY on the James, Lieutenant Thomas Rolfe—having chosen to live as a white man and English colonist, and having aided in the extermination of his mother's people—selected a wife from among his father's. His bride was Jane Poythress: the daughter, presumably, of a family by that name known to have resided in the vicinity of Charles City, a family belonging—like the Rolfes—to the planter aristocracy (one Francis Poythress is identified as a member of the House of Burgesses, in 1644, as a representative of Charles City).

The date of Thomas Rolfe's marriage to Jane Poythress is not recorded, nor is that of the birth of their only child, a daughter Jane, who is known to have been wed, early in 1675, to Colonel Robert Bolling.

Extensive Bolling family records show him to have been the first of the line in Virginia, to have come there from England in 1660 at age fourteen, early achieving success and prominence. Marrying at age twenty-nine, he took his bride, Jane Rolfe, to live at Kippax, his goodly seat on the James, below Petersburg.

Jane Rolfe Bolling, granddaughter of Pocahontas, died in 1676, at the birth—or shortly after the birth—of a son, John.

The widower, Colonel Robert Bolling, remarried, his second wife being Anne Stith (the aunt of historian William Stith), by whom Bolling had other children—the descendants of this second marriage of Colonel Bolling's to a white woman to be known as "White Bollings," in distinction to the descendants of his first marriage, who are known to this day as "Red Bollings," in token of the royal red blood bequeathed them by their progenitress Pocahontas.

Born into the landed gentry, John Bolling would have been sole heir to the large properties his mother, Jane Rolfe Bolling, had inherited from her father, Thomas Rolfe: Captain (eventually Colonel) John Bolling "settled, lived and died at 'Cobbs,' on the Appomatox, below Petersburg"—"one of the best houses in the country," as Colonel William Byrd II called it.

Like his grandfather, Thomas Rolfe, John Bolling took his seat as a member of the House of Burgesses, chosen by his neighbors to represent them at the General Assembly at the annual meeting in Jamestown. "He engaged in commerce," according to Wyndham Robertson, one of his descendants, proudly tracing that descent in a volume entitled *Pocahontas and Her Descendants* (published in 1887), "and while conducting an 'extensive and gainful trade' with his countrymen, and yet a larger one with the Indians (equally his countrymen), 'partook freely at the same time of all the pleasures of society, for which his gay and lively spirit eminently adapted him.' " Colonel William Byrd II, who was a frequent visitor at Cobbs, confirms Bolling's sociability: the two played whist, dice, and billiards together, although Byrd regarded Pocahontas's great-grandson as "a sharper" and something of a toper (a "cheerful" enough fellow, as Byrd commented, "although he talked of dying, it seemed in jest").

Colonel John Bolling, great-great-grandson of Powhatan, marrying the daughter of another prosperous and prominent colonial planter, sired a progeny sufficiently numerous to convey the imperial Powhatan bloodline to families throughout the Old Dominion, throughout the South: one son (John Bolling II) and five daughters; the eldest, Jane, married Colonel Richard Randolph, of the illustrious Randolph family, "the most distinguished in the History of the Colony and the Commonwealth of Virginia" (according to Wynne's *Colonial Records of Virginia*)—"a judgment which none will dissent from" (according to Wyndham Robertson) "on learning that Thomas Jefferson and John Marshall were of it."

"So that this Remnant of the Imperial Family of Virginia," as William Stith phrased it in mid-eighteenth century, "which long ran in a single Person" (the person of Thomas Rolfe), "is now encreased and branched out into a very numerous Progeny."

"In resumé," Wyndham Robertson, the official family genealogist, concluded his survey of the Pocahontas Stock,

> in view of all I have heard, read or known of them, I think it may be fairly said that they were more prudent than enterprising, more wasteful than liberal, more amiable than censorious, more respected than distinguished, more honest than able, more patriotic than indifferent, more conservative than radical, more pious than bigoted, and while a few fell to the depths of worthlessness, but none to crime, a few also rose to the height of genius and virtue.

(A conspectus, like the daily Horoscope column, broad enough to be applicable to one and all.*)

A long line of proud Virginians claims consanguinity or affinity with Pocahontas: Jeffersons, Lees, Randolphs, Marshalls, along with other lesser lights—to the number of two million, if the calculations of twentieth-century genealogists are accurate. Two million rather than "thousands of millions," as in the Biblical estimate. Even so, the prophecy of Pocahontas's Biblical name of Rebecca had been handsomely fulfilled: "Be thou the mother of thousands of millions, and let thy seed possess the gate of those which hate them."

---

* One prominent "Red Bolling," Edith Bolling Galt Wilson, who became the second wife of President Woodrow Wilson in a White House ceremony in 1915, traced the Bolling line to the ninth generation.

The ramifications of Pocahontas's family tree are widespread throughout the South: "When I reflect, Madame," James Branch Cabell exclaimed in wonder in his Fourteenth Letter indited "To The Lady Rebecca Rolfe, Called Pocahontas" (in his *Ladies and Gentlemen*),

> that you quitted this mortal life as lately as 1617, leaving issue only one infant son, then am I puzzled by the number of your grandchildren, in varying generations, today living. It does not seem possible that such hordes of Southerners should be descended from you as to make the Virginian who cannot boast of this honor, in at least one lineage, feel somewhat conspicuous.*

But the Powhatan princess was not to be confined within genealogical tables, nor could the First Families of Virginia exercise rights of exclusivity over her. She has escaped into legend.

* James Branch Cabell could so boast, in not one but two lineages, the names of both Cabells and Branches to be found on the "Red Bolling" family tree.

AFTERWORD

SUDDENLY, SOMEHOW, sometime in the 1800s, the figure of Pocahontas loomed up out of the yellowing pages of the first settlers' chronicles. She was rediscovered in the archives. In the deepest stratum of the archeologically rich Jamestown rubble, one came upon her traces: the original, the pristine, the primitive national heroine. There she stood, in the shadow of the forest primeval, a figure of romance, symbol of redemption, princess, paragon, a naiad-dryad of the Western World, native nymph of grove and stream, Daughter of Manitou, aboriginal Hertha/Ceres/Demeter, great Earth Mother of the Americas, who had opened up her heart and heartland to the newcomer.

Twentieth-century America, its claim to a giant share in the vast continent established beyond contest, its fear of the tomahawk finally allayed, could at last afford a pang of conscience and guilt over its relations with the red race as well as the black. It was at that hour that the Pocahontas myth surfaced in the American mind and memory.

Throughout the seventeenth, the eighteenth, and well into the nineteenth century, America had been too preoccupied with the immediate present and the future—mind, will, and sinew bent on the Here and Now, and the Hereafter—to spare a thought to the Heretofore. Not until the nineteenth century did the nation pause to catch its breath, to consider and seek out its past, its national identity.

"It has been said," says Alexander Brown, in his *The First Republic in America*, "that the history of any nation begins with myth. . . . When the age of reflection arrives and the nation begins to speculate on its origin, it has no more recollection of what happened in its infancy than a man has of what happened to him in his cradle." How much more so in America, a land without a recorded history until the arrival of Columbus in 1492: In America, above all, "having so little of it"—history—"some kind of mythological substitute had to be devised."

What more moving, more romantic genesis myth could have been devised than the one already to hand, that of the amorous redskin princess risking her life for the bold, blond Englishman?

Pocahontas was the made-to-order American heroine, the very

one to figure in a heroical, historical myth, the perfect mythic persona in the euhemeristic sense of "a greatly idealized historical character," an extraordinary being exhibiting a "cynosural, charismatic potency . . . exciting and transfixing attention, interest, wonder, awe," as Henry A. Murray analyzes the elements of myth in *Myth and Myth-making*.

To characterize Pocahontas as the heroine of the first, the original American myth is to be obliged to define the word *myth* in the special anthropological/psychological sense of the word used here: not in the negative, pejorative Oxford English Dictionary sense of "a wholly fictitious story," but in the positive sense of "purportedly true," "more or less actual/imaginary," a story based on fundamental truths, "a story of importance to human beings because of its relevance to their origins, survival, development, happiness or glory." The historical myth is not necessarily false, although its "truth" cannot always be established on historical reality: if not based on historical reality, it is nonetheless a historical force. Myth, by the Jungian definition, is a psychic reality no less real than physical reality. "Myth is always poetry," according to Johan Huizinga: "Working with images and the aid of imagination, myth tells the story of things that were supposed to have happened in ancient times. . . . It may succeed in expressing relationships which could never be described in a rational way."[1] To the ears of Henry Thoreau, myth or "fable" spoke "that universal language" which is able "to satisfy the imagination ere it addresses the understanding."

Myth may also be defined as exposition, narrative: the stories and parables, for example, in the Bible and in Indian sacred lore. The word *mythos*, as Aristotle uses it, translates, simply, as "plot": "a dramatic representation of profound human longing, of our deepest instinctual life"—often in the sense of wishful thinking, the "if only" or "might have been" motif: "if only" all American savages had been as amenable to civilization as Pocahontas, then "there might have been" no necessity for the civilizers to exterminate them in the process. ("Our dearest myth," Leslie Fiedler calls it, "this vision of love and reconciliation between the races whose actual history is oppression and hate."[2]) The Pocahontas legend, from this point of view, presents a model for emulation, what the anthropologists call an "exemplar" or "educational" myth.

However the Pocahontas myth is categorized—whether "historical," "heroical," "educational"—it remains a live, a vital mythical representation (to Virginians, a sacred one!), "peculiarly and mysteriously attractive to the senses and imagination . . . the focus of rapt attention, excitement, wonder, thought and talk," according to Murray, retaining the power—across the centuries—to inspire "receptors with artistic gifts to reproduce it in its original form or in variant forms and thus, through chains of transmission, to propagate it down the generations. One measure of the value of a myth, then, is the quality of the imaginative symbolism and of the works of art which it inspires."

Works of art inspired by the Pocahontas myth have proliferated with the passage of time, with almost every category of the arts involved in the mythicization. Long ages have passed since Pocahontas left "her slight bones in the English earth,"[3] but she takes shape, again and again, in clay, in bronze, in marble. Oil and watercolor and the lithographer's stone preserve her form and features, so familiar to us as to defy dust: a bronze nude (done by David McFall, Royal Academy) reclines serenely amid the swirl of traffic in London's Red Lion Square; a larger-than-life bronze statue stands on a low natural rock base at the Jamestown Churchyard gate (fully clothed, to be sure), hands outstretched in greeting to the adoring tourist throngs; a replica of the Jamestown statue stands on the bank of the Thames at Gravesend's Chapel of Unity, her overseas shrine. A large canvas (titled *The Baptism of Pocahontas*) commissioned by order of Congress in 1840 hangs in the Rotunda of the Capitol, one of the few so to honor a national heroine. And the famous Pocahontas portrait is a treasure—despite its obscure provenance—of Washington's National Portrait Gallery. The Pocahontas legend served as inspiration to a raft of low-camp nineteenth-century artists; the highlights of her life pass in kaleidoscopic review in color and black-and-white, in woodcuts, etchings, lithographs: Pocahontas to the rescue of John Smith, Pocahontas at the baptismal font, Pocahontas and John Rolfe at the marriage-altar.

Not for her that "cortical tomb" (of which Murray speaks) "where memories decompose and perish": Pocahontas emerges as the heroine of poetry, drama, fiction, as the subject of biography, essay, monograph. A vast literature has grown up around the Pocahontas legend.

Although, oddly enough, for almost two hundred years after her death, she had been consigned to limbo, her name cropping up only occasionally in some obscure history of the epic period of the Virginia Colony.

It remained for a roving and romantically inclined young Englishman, shortly after the American Revolution, to revive and celebrate her memory. On a tour of the newly independent states, John Davis stumbled onto the trail of Pocahontas in the Old Dominion: a chance encounter with a fascinating young Indian maiden at Occoquan fired his imagination—she "appeared" to him "such another object as the mind imagines *Pocahontas* to have been." Davis not only deserves the credit for rescuing Pocahontas's name from oblivion, he demands it: her story, by his claim, had been "reserved" for his pen, and thus became his personal literary property.[4]

Not so, in actual fact: Davis's pen had not been the first to romanticize Pocahontas; an Englishwoman, Mrs. Unca Eliza Winkfield, had beaten him into print with *The Female American*, published in London in 1767, a short novel about Pocahontas (her name changed to Unca and Captain Smith's to Winkfield, in honor of the authoress!). Mrs. Winkfield's work found an audience, the English edition followed by two American editions (1790 and 1814), but it was undoubtedly John Davis's Pocahontas Quartet that brought about the revival of interest in her story on both sides of the Atlantic, at the dawn of the nineteenth century.

There is little there, unfortunately, to recommend it, in the way of literature. Regrettably, none of the century's major talents was attracted to the theme. Herman Melville touches upon it, but only in passing, only on a note of mockery, putting the following lines in the mouth of one of the most scoundrelly and hypocritical of the characters in *The Confidence Man*, in a chapter entitled "The Metaphysics of Indian-hating":

> Indians I have always heard to be one of the finest of primitive races, possessed of many heroic virtues. Some noble women, too. When I think of *Pocahontas*, I am ready to love Indians.

Thoreau, obsessed as he was by Indians, never got around to the full treatment of the subject he had intended. (It was his contention that the Indian must be the subject of the new American mythology, the Indian at the moment of confrontation with the white invader.) James Fenimore Cooper specialized in Mohicans, to the neglect of Powhatans. Henry Wadsworth Longfellow had his highly successful Indian fling with *Hiawatha*. Walt Whitman avoided the big names of American mythology (an exception to the rule was made in favor of Columbus), although he did evoke a nameless, voluptuous Indian maiden as a symbol of the lure of the West:

> I saw the marriage of the trapper in the open air in the far west, the bride was a red girl. . . . She had long eyelashes, her head was bare, her coarse straight locks descended upon her voluptuous limbs and reach'd to her feet.

Pocahontas was overlooked by Hawthorne, overlooked by Poe.

If she suffered neglect at the hands of the literary great of nineteenth-century America, she became the dramatist's delight.

Grease-paint Pocahontases overran the stages of America throughout the first half of the nineteenth century, despite the basic defect inherent in the story line: with the highlight of the dramatic action—the execution/rescue scene—coming in Act One, all else was anticlimax.

A German, Johann Wilhelm Rose, was the first to discern the possibilities of the Pocahontas story as a dramatic theme, but his play written in 1784 was little known, and the great Pocahontas theatrical vogue may be said to date from 1808 with James Nelson Barker's *The Indian Princess; or, La Belle Sauvage*, "An Operatic Melo-Drame in Three Acts," which enjoyed gala premières in Philadelphia (of which city the author had once been Mayor), Baltimore, and New York prior to a cross-country tour; with a London production to follow, Barker was the first American playwright to be so honored in "the mother country."

A rash of redskin dramas broke out in the wake of Barker's: at least forty plays written (if not all produced) between the years 1830–1850—a last-minute rush to glorify the Noble Savage on the stage ere he was exterminated on the Plains.

When the curtain rose, in Philadelphia in 1827, on a drama entitled *Pocahontas; or, The Settlers of Virginia*, "A National Drama in Three Acts," its success was assured by the name of Washington on the playbill: George Washington Custis, the author, was the son of Martha, stepson of George (and father of Mrs. Robert E. Lee). A penchant for the theater and for Pocahontas ran in the family: Custis's wife's daughter, Charlotte Barnes Connor, not only wrote but starred in *The Forest Princess* in 1848—an example of nineteenth-century theater at its worst, a pageant rather than a play. The heroine's last lines are declaimed in heroic verse from her deathbed, her gaze and index finger pointing heavenward:

> *I hear my father—Husband, fare thee well.*
> *We part—but we shall meet—above!*

As she breathes her last, she is vouchsafed a vision of the glorious future in store for her native land; the curtain falls on a *tableau vivant* featuring George Washington, Columbia, Old Glory, and the American Eagle.

In 1837, Pocahontas was cast in the role of—of all things!—an avant-garde aboriginal feminist, the curious conceit of playwright Robert Dale Owen, a radical social reformer and advocate of women's rights, including birth control.

By midcentury, Indian plays had become (to quote James Rees) "a perfect nuisance," and the time was ripe for parody, such as *Po-ca-hon-tas; or, The Gentle Savage* ("An Original Aboriginal Erratic Operatic Semi-Civilized and Demi-Savage Extravaganza") from the pen of English playwright-actor James Brougham, which had its opening at Wallach's Theater in New York on Christmas Eve of 1855. With Scene One as "The Palace of Weramocomoco," the play opens with "A Grand March of the Tuscarora [sic] Court," the "Opening Chorus to the Air of 'King of Cannibal Islands,'" the "King's Song to the Air of 'Widow Machree.'" Pocahontas, billed as an "Alumna of the Jamestown Finishing School," makes her entrance with a "Heigho" and the boast that "This is the greatest story of them all!" Brougham's redskins speak American slang instead of the measured prose of Cooper's *Leatherstocking Tales*. Powhatan, played by the author, is a punster: "These arrows make me quiver!"

Welland Hendrick's *Pocahontas*, produced in Chicago in 1886, went Brougham one better: a frankly "Burlesque Operetta in Two Acts" with a Cast of Characters (including "LO, The Poor Indian") headed by "Pocahontas, A Poetic Brunette," "John Rolfe, A Seventeenth Century Dude," "Captain John Smith, An Uncommon Man with a Common Name," and Smith's servant, "Mahogany," played in black-face, strumming a banjo and serenading Pocahontas to the tune of "Polly-wolly-doodle" (the faint suggestion of a "black-and-tan" romance ere Captain Smith took over the wooing); "A Chorus of Braves, Brave of Course" sing (to the tune of "The Torpedo and the Whale"):

> *Now you see it is no myth*
> *Pocahontas saved John Smith*
> *The brave raised his ax-oh!*
> *She kept off the whacks-oh!*

But the greenrooms of America had still not seen the last of the Powhatan princess. Playwright Edwin O. Ropp added Hiawatha, Minnehaha, and Geronimo, for good measure, to the cast of his *Pocahontas*, although he was in dead earnest about his play, dedicating it to "The Jamestown Exposition of 1907" (and to "Those Who Construct the Panama Canal"). In 1957, on the occasion of the 350th anniversary of the planting of Jamestown, a "Symphonic Outdoor Drama" entitled

The Founders, and featuring Pocahontas in a prominent role, was composed by Paul Green for performance at Williamsburg.

In Effie Koogle's "Historical Play" entitled *Royalty in Old Virginia* (1908), Pocahontas addresses the hero as "Paleface Smith," and he addresses her as "My little girl." Rolfe exclaims to Smith,

> *It's love at first sight, sir!*
> *Won't she be a handsome little wife, sir?*

At the finale, as the clergyman blesses the happy, mixed-blood pair, "Six Colonial Men, Six Colonial Ladies" make their entrance ("to any familiar marching tune," according to the stage directions); "Twelve Negro Slaves, Six Boys and Six Girls" come on, "cake-walking"! To be followed onstage by "Six Bow-Bearers, Six Indian Maids with tom-toms or tambourines," emitting "war-whoops"!

Philip Moeller was poking fun, in 1918, in his *Pokey; Or, The Beautiful Legend of the Amorous Indian*, but war whoops would resound at least once more in the American theater, as late as the fourth decade of the twentieth century: in Virgil Geddes's *Pocahontas and the Elders*, described as "A Folkpiece in Four Acts" and published in 1933, Pocahontas dashes to the rescue of Captain Smith, exclaiming, "Let the white man live!" to which "the warriors" assent with "grunts." And when John Rolfe finds their little son Thomas "unmanageable," a First Gentleman reminds him, "He's part savage, you know," whereupon Rolfe concedes that "Yesterday he spat on the flag."

If the Pocahontas dramatic theme finally wore thin, the gush of Pocahontas verse continued unabated, generation after generation; like the drama, mostly mawkish, mostly drivel. The muse is frequently invoked ("Descend, my Muse, from Heaven's bright sphere, descend!"), but fails to improve the quality of the poetry ("Simple child of nature—lovely heroine," "Purer than she to live never given").[5] The Pocahontas of nineteenth-century poets is a conventional romantic heroine, losing almost every trace of her Indian identity along with her suntan ("browner than European dames, but whiter, far, than other natives are," to quote the Pilgrim suitor of a New England Pocahontas in Joseph Croswell's 1802 rhymed play, *A New World Planted*).

George P. Morris, a minor poet with an enthusiastic contemporary following, who had made a career of apostrophizing ("Woodman, Spare That Tree" and "Hail, Columbia" among his *oeuvres*), in 1842 apostrophized Pocahontas, "the heroic maid":

> *Above his head in air,*
> *The Savage war-club swung:*

> *The frantic girl, in wild despair*
> *Her arms about him flung.*
> *Then shook the warriors out of the shade*
> *Like leaves an aspen limb,*
> *Subdued by the heroic maid*
> *Who breathed a prayer for him!*
> *"Unbind him!" gasp'd the chief;*
> *"It is your King's decree!"*
> *He kissed away the tears of grief,*
> *And set the captive free!*
> *'Tis ever thus, when in life's storm*
> *Hope's star to man grows dim,*
> *An angel kneels, in woman's form,*
> *And breathes a prayer for him.*

Even such a first-rate novelist as William Makepeace Thackeray slipped into cliché in his "Pocahontas" ballad (attributed to the pen of a character in *The Virginians*):

> *From the throng, with sudden start,*
> *See there springs an Indian maid.*
> *Quick she stands before the knight,*
> *"Loose the chain, unbind the ring,*
> *I am daughter of the king,*
> *And I claim the Indian right!"*
>
> *Dauntlessly aside she flings*
> *Lifted axe and thirsty knife;*
> *Fondly to his heart she clings,*
> *And her bosom guards his life!*
>
> *In the woods of Powhatan,*
> *Still 'tis told by Indian fires,*
> *How a daughter of their sires*
> *Saved the captive Englishman.*

Thackeray should have known better: there were no more "Indian fires" burning "in the woods of Powhatan," no more Powhatans to be seen on the banks of the James, and few on the York or the Pamunkey by the end of the seventeenth century, certainly none by the mid-1800s, when Thackeray toured America.

Lydia Huntley Sigourney ("The Sweet Singer of Hartford") knew better; she knew that "The Council Fires are quench'd." Her poem "Pocahontas" saluted the vanishing Powhatans, "Forgotten race, farewell!"; commiserated their fate, "I would you were not from your fathers' soil/Tracked like the dun wolf"; hailed the immortal heroine of the tribe, "But thou, O forest-princess, true of heart / It is not meet thy name should moulder in the grave"—not if Mrs. Sigourney could prevent it, inditing her nineteen-page poem to Pocahontas in 1841 ("A sweet, wild girl with eye of earnest ray / And olive cheek, at each emotion glowing").

Singers more or less mellifluous than Mrs. Sigourney continued to hail "the simple child of nature,"[6] "the forest maid" whose "modest shade"[7] broods over the hills and streams of Virginia. Card-files marked "Pocahontas" run over at the Library of Congress, the New York Public Library, the Virginia State Library. Nathalia Crane manages to avoid the stereotype by turning her *Pocahontas* into an anticommunist battle-hymn: seeing America in 1930 as defenseless through disarmament, and Washington in peril of being taken over by the Soviets, the poet summons up the shade of the daughter of imperial Powhatan ("Brave as Godiva, sweeter than Elaine") to lead "the red against the red," to "Be our Queen":

> *If we must have an empire, let it be*
> *With an empress from the family tree.*
> . . . .
> *If Pocahontas can be found as said,*
> *I also pledge the red against the red . . .*

Pocahontas was, from the beginning, limned as a noble character in the schoolroom, in the textbook. Samuel P. Goodrich of Hartford, author and publisher of the popular "Peter Parley" editions (dedicated to the "Instruction and Amusement of Children") came out in 1829 with his *Stories of Captain John Smith, of Virginia.* Although the doughty Captain was featured in the title, Pocahontas came off best in the text:

> What a worthy girl was this! She was a savage, but her deed was noble! She (unlike Smith) had never been taught to love her enemies; but she shewed a benevolent disposition. . . . The name of Pocahontas, and her generous deed, ought to be remembered, and will be remembered while America lasts.

Mattie Owen McDavid, addressing her *Princess Pocahontas* to a youthful audience, in a 1907 publication, apologized for so much as mentioning the Captain's name: "It is a pity," she wrote in the Preface,

> that one must bring John Smith into the story of Pocahontas, at all, with all due respect to that courageous gentleman, for it detracts from Pocahontas's loyalty to and romance with her own beloved husband, John Rolfe.

Children's books, textbooks, tracts, treatises, magazine articles, newspaper feature-stories, the Pocahontas bibliography swells with every year that rolls around: master's theses, dissertations, published and unpublished, privately printed; scholarly monographs (Philip Young's "The Mother of Us All: Pocahontas Reconsidered," for the *Kenyon Review*, 1962; Jay B. Hubbell's "The Smith-Pocahontas Story in Literature," for *Virginia Magazine of History and Biography*, 1957). The reader's choice is wide when it comes to essayists: everyone from James Branch Cabell (*Ladies and Gentlemen; Let Me Lie*) to William H. "Alfalfa Bill" Murray, Governor of Oklahoma (*Pocahontas and Pushmataha*). In the genre of the short story, there is John Erskine's "Variation XIII" in his *Young Love*—Pocahontas treated as flippantly by the author as was Helen of Troy. Academicians and politicians, ethnohistorians and amateurs and professionals, all have tried their hand at establishing the moral, deciphering the message conveyed in the Pocahontas myth; all in vain. As of 1976, revelation is not yet.

Both Mary Wall's *Daughter of Virginia Dare* (1908) and Christopher Ward's *The Saga of Cap'n John Smith* (1928) attempted to explain the Christian virtues exemplified by the pagan, savage, American aboriginal maid by furnishing her with Anglo-Christian antecedents: without a trace of levity, Mary Wall makes Pocahontas the daughter of none other than Virginia Dare, "the first Christian borne in Virginia," the first child of Anglo-Saxon heritage to be born in America. Virginia Dare was born on Roanoke Island on August 18, 1587, the child of Ananias Dare (an armigerous gentleman and assistant to the Governor) and Eleanor Dare, daughter of Governor John White, the distinguished artist who had accompanied the earlier expedition to the Carolina Banks in 1585–86. White, taking ship to England on a mission for his colony, was delayed from returning to it until 1590, when he found Roanoke Island deserted, without a sign of life. Where were the one hundred and seventeen men, women, and children—including his daughter and granddaughter—whom he had left there, three years earlier?

According to Mary Wall's ingenious solution, Indians attacked the island, sparing only Eleanor Dare and baby Virginia (only "the squaw and the papoose"). Tied to a tree, the babe in her arms, Eleanor manages to carve the initials C.R.O. on the bark. Chief Winganoa raises his tomahawk and crushes her skull. He directs it, next, upon the head of the squawling infant when—of all things!—the crying stops, and tiny (fair-haired, blue-eyed) Virginia Dare holds out her arms to him. And is thereby saved! Her new name will be Water-Lily of the Catawbas. Later, when Powhatan raids the Carolina Banks and defeats Winganoa, he claims Water-Lily (née Virginia Dare) as his bride. Although "no entreaties or commands could win a smile from her," she grimly bore him a daughter . . . and died. The Supreme Chieftain of the tidewater looked upon the new-born babe, and issued the command: "Call her *Pocahontas!*"

The Powhatan princess, thus, was no savage, after all, no savage at heart or in mind and soul—a half-savage, at worst, brought up by savages. It is the spirit of Virginia Dare that imbues her daughter Pocahontas, that responds so eagerly to the call of Christianity, the call of civilized society. The call is actually a recall! The inexplicable is thereby explained, although Mary Wall must dexterously juggle dates to bring it off: Virginia Dare, with a recorded birth date of 1587, must have been highly precocious to bear a child in 1595 (at age eight!), as must have been the case to account for Pocahontas having reached an estimated eighteen years of age in 1613.

Christopher Ward, tongue firmly in cheek, gives Pocahontas Queen Elizabeth as mother, Powhatan as father—not an Indian at all, but English-born, born Earl of Upper Tooting! (Pocahontas's handkerchief, embroidered with a lion, a unicorn, and the initial E, provides the clue to her identity.)

Despite an occasional brash burlesque or gentle parody, the tone of the Pocahontas literature prior to the twentieth century was generally reverent; no slur on the reputation of the national heroine was to be tolerated: a literary vendetta was declared in the South against the Honorable Waddy Thompson, Ambassador to Mexico, when his published *Recollections* were found to contain an odious comparison between the Aztec Malinche (Hernando Cortez's "*chère amie* and interpreter") and the Algonkian Pocahontas (*chère amie* and interpreter to John Smith), the latter suffering in comparison to the former ("whose great qualities throw into the shade our own Pocahontas"). It was heresy. A pamphlet published in Washington in 1847 and entitled "The Memory of Pocahontas Vindicated . . . by A Kentuckian" demanded a public retraction ("Pocahontas possessed what the other did not . . . 'a good name' "!).

Southern chauvinism aside, Pocahontas's title to premier American

Indian heroine was not undisputed: Sacajawea, the "savior" of the Lewis and Clark expedition of 1803–5, has been sentimentalized, mythicized, memorialized across the Mountain West where a snowy Oregon peak, a pass, and a river (not to mention motels and cafés) still bear her name. If not the savior, as in the view of numerous historians, Sacajawea—in her role of guide and interpreter—contributed significantly to that important transcontinental mission: it was her intercession with hostile chieftains that assured the party a safe passage and a supply of horses for transportation to the far Pacific. As heroic a character as the Lewis and Clark Journals make her out, still Sacajawea was a matron, twice-married and gravid with child when she joined the explorers in Missouri, a far less romantic figure than that of "the tender virgin," the high-born Princess Pocahontas, racing to the rescue of the English captain, warding off the blows of the battle-axes at risk of her life.

Priscilla Alden fared better literarily than Pocahontas, finding her Longfellow early on (1858) to memorialize her with his *Courtship of Miles Standish*, whereas Pocahontas had to wait until the twentieth century to be sung by poets and novelists of distinction and elevated by them to full mythical stature: by Carl Sandburg (in "Cool Tombs"), by Vachel Lindsay (in "Our Mother Pocahontas"), by Hart Crane (in *The Bridge*), by Stephen Vincent Benét (in his posthumously published epic poem, *Western Star*), by David Garnett in his novel *Pocahontas* (his considerable fictional talent strait-jacketed in historical fact).

Sandburg was among the first, in 1916, in his "Cool Tombs," to hymn Pocahontas's beauty (that "uncommon beauty" listed by Murray as one of the attributes that distinguish the mythical hero or heroine):

> *Pocahontas' body, lovely as a poplar, sweet as a red haw in November or a pawpaw in May, did she wonder? does she remember? ... in the dust, in the cool tombs?*

And Vachel Lindsay who answered Yes, who picked up Sandburg's refrain and elaborated on the theme, to show us "Our Mother Pocahontas,"

> *Who laughed among the winds and played*
> *In excellence of savage pride,*
> *Wooing the forest, open-eyed,*
> *In the springtime,*
> *In Virginia,*

Our Mother, Pocahontas.
Her skin was rosy copper-red.
And high she held her beauteous head.
Her step was like a rustling leaf:
Her heart a nest, untouch'd of grief.
She dreamed of sons like Powhatan,
And through her blood the lightning ran,
Love cries with the birds she sung,
Birdlike,
In the grape-vine swung . . .

If Vachel Lindsay saw Pocahontas as the great American Earth Mother, Native Earth goddess ("Because we are her fields of corn"), so Hart Crane saw her, too ("bride immortal in the maize!") in *The Bridge, a Myth of America*: "Powhatan's daughter or Pocahontas, is the mythological nature-symbol chosen to represent the physical body of the continent, or the soil . . . whose first possessor was the Indian. . . ."

Crane's notes—almost as long as the poem itself—tell us that he envisioned Pocahontas as "the natural body of American fertility"; that he would depict her as the land lying before Columbus, "like a woman ripe, waiting to be taken." And so he did, in Part II of *The Bridge*, under the title, "Powhatan's Daughter": All those making the westward trek across the continent—pioneers, hobos, even "Pullman breakfasters"—all "have touched her, knowing her without name,"

They know a body under the wide rain;
. . . .
They lurk across her, knowing her yonder breast
Snow-silvered, sumac-stained, or smoky blue—

The poet himself recalls "O Nights that brought me to her body bare," has heard trains "Wail into distances I knew were hers." He describes her as a bloom upon the land ("And winds across the llano grass resume / Her hair's warm sibilance. Her breasts are fanned / O stream by slope and vineyard—into bloom!"); he describes her as a bride (although "virgin to the last of men"), as a pioneer mother, as the ultimate fertility symbol of the continent, "our native clay . . . red, eternal flesh of Pocahontas."

Endless significance is to be read into the Pocahontas legend: the psychological explication of its mythic vitality would be that it is adolescent love glorified and romanticized to the *n*th degree—the classic theme of adolescent love, with its characteristically destructive bent.

(Pocahontas, unlike Juliet, survives to find a mature love, but it is in the grip of her first, fragile, adolescent love that she has so vividly manifested her defiance of parental authority, has so dramatically shattered and destroyed the paternal bond.)

The survival of the Pocahontas legend into the atomic age and the age of outer space is evidence of its validity, its vitality. Take Ogden Nash who, as late as 1939, found the Pocahontas figure good for a laugh:

> But along came Pocahontas and she called off her father's
>   savage minions,
> Because she was one of the most prominent Virginians,
> And her eyes went flash flash,
> And she said, Scat, you po' red trash,
> And she begged Captain John Smith's pardon,
> And she took him for a walk in the gyarden,
> And she said, Ah reckon ah sho' would have felt bad
>   if anything had happened to you-all,
> And she told him about her great-uncle Hiawatha and
>   her cousin Sittin' Bull and her kissin' cousin King
>   Philip, and I don't know who-all,
> And he said you'd better not marry me, you'd better
>   marry John Rolfe,
> So he bade her farewell and went back to England,
>   which adjoins Scotland, where they invented golf.[8]

As late as 1960, the wittiest, wickedest, most outré version of the Pocahontas story ever to be told came off the press in John Barth's *The Sot-Weed Factor*.

Barth, with his exhaustively and impeccably researched, his hilariously funny novel, has dared to improvise—brilliantly if bawdily—on the solemn theme, to travesty the heroine's final vicissitude. In all the three hundred and fifty and more years that have rolled by since Captain Smith made good his escape from the executioners at Werowocómoco, Barth is the first to come up with a wholly original *éclaircissement*: he would have us believe that he discovered the long-lost manuscript of Captain Smith's *Secret Historie* (slyly suggested by Barth to have been "the original draft of the author's well-known *Generall Historie*") and also Sir Henry Burlingame's *Privie Journall*, containing the hitherto untold tale of what really happened at Werowocómoco. In the so-called *Privie Journall*, we learn for the first time the true meaning of the name "Pocahontas": not "Bright Stream Between Two

Hills,"[9] not "Frisky," but, "The smalle one, *or*: she of the small-nesse and impenetrabilitie." What it came down to was that Smith's fate hung not by a thread, but by a hymen! By the terms of the ancient tribal custom (à la Barth), Smith might go free, and claim the chieftain's daughter as his bride, if he proved man enough to take her—a feat no suitor, no brave had yet been able to accomplish before him. If, how-ever, he failed—if he could not relieve Pocahontas of her perdurable maidenhead—then Powhatan's "Dearling" was doomed to perpetual virginity and he, Smith, to the block, the war-club, the bludgeon!

"The carnall joust was set for sunup," "in the publick square," and thither Smith was led (waddling, spraddling, walking awkwardly) "as if loath to keep his leggs together," into the midst of a "hollowing & howling" multitude, into the presence of Powhatan.

And, "before him [Powhatan], upon a manner of altar stone, lay Pocahontas, stript & trust with thongs of hyde for the heethenish rites."*

Now, "For all his boasting," Smith was (Barth claims) "but pass-ing well equipt for Venereal exercise." How then to account for that "weapon of the Gods" that stood revealed at the moment of truth? How to explain "that mysterie, whereby he had so increas'd him selfe"? It was a "trick which Captain John Smith had employed to win the day in Virginia"—a trick done not with mirrors but with eggplants, an aubergine dildo! He had recourse to "the Devils subtile arts" in prepara-tion of that "devilish brewe" (a concoction of aubergine, floure, herbes, and spyces): the "product of his magick," erect—"in verie sooth a frightful engine"!

At sight of which,

A mightie sownd went up from the populace; the Lieutenants, that had doubtlesse been the Princesses former suitors, dropt to there knees as in prayer; the Emperour started up in his high seate, dismay'd by the fate about to befall his daughter; and as for that same Pocahontas, she did swoone dead away.

Straight leapt my Captain to his work . . . did what none had done before! And so inordinatelie withal, that anon the Emperour begg'd for an end to the tryall, lest his daughter depart from this life.

Anon the Emperor declared the Captain "victorious"; anon "feasted him after their best barbarous manner"; anon "express'd his

---

* "This vile manner of presenting maidens for betrothal" was not—as Barth well knew!—"in common use among the Salvage nations."

intent to marrie his daughter" to the Captain, "inasmuch as no Salvage in his trybe c^d match his virilitie"—an offer the Captain respectfully "declyn'd." At which rebuff, the Emperor "wax'd wroth"—so wroth that only Smith's offer to share his magic formula (his "egg-plant trick") with the aging chieftain won him his liberty and a safe-conduct back to Jamestown!

As for Smith's "savior," "the guardian angel" of the colony, she is not far behind the prodigious Captain:

> As for the Princesse, she still lingers at the gate, all wystfullie, and sends him, by her attendants, woven basketts of great dry'd egg-plants. . . .*

The list of Pocahontas titles lengthens with every passing year. *Daughter of Eve*, a novel by Noel B. Gerson, was a book-club selection in 1958. Philip L. Barbour's meticulously researched study of *Pocahontas and Her World* was published in 1970, preceded in 1969 by another biography bearing the colophon of a Midwestern university press. *First Lady of America*, "a romanticized biography" of Pocahontas, found a Virginia publisher in 1973, while a historical novel, *Powhatan's Daughter*, appeared on the 1974 list of a major New York publishing house.

An old tale, endlessly retold, reexamined, reinterpreted; every generation producing a new poet, new biographer, new audience, with new insights, new perspectives; with new disciplines such as anthropology, archeology, ethno- and psycho-history presently brought to bear upon the few hard facts on record.

Transcending history, Pocahontas has passed into American folklore. The dates of her birth and death may be hazy, the entire panorama of her life obscure, seen through a glass darkly, but her name is forever familiar to our ear; no American child fails to recognize it. Her name and her image are inextricably associated with our national origins; her legend, a part of our genesis myth, a magic and moving symbol of our beginnings on this continent. The bare bones of recorded history, the fragmentary biographical data have been irradiated by imagination, and thus transmuted, have become tradition.

The *tableau vivant* at the altar-stone—the death-defying embrace, white man and red woman aswoon with love and terror—seems fixed,

---

* In Virginia, the consternation at publication date of *The Sot-Weed Factor* was considerable. The Richmond *News-Leader* book review was headlined, "Novelist Libels Pocahontas Story," the reviewer going so far as to claim that—in view of the heroine's extensive and illustrious issue—the libel might be "actionable."

frozen in time, indelibly imprinted on the mind's eye, reminding us that at least once in our history, there existed the possibility of interracial accommodation. For that one fleeting moment—with the bloodthirsty blades arrested in midair—came a flicker of hope that on this continent, at least, there would be no cause to mourn man's inhumanity to man.

APPENDICES

APPENDICES

APPENDIX A

Captain John Smith, from the Generall Historie
(The Third Booke), London, 1624

At last they brought him to Meronocomoco where was Powhatan their Emperor. Here more than two hundred of those grim Courtiers stood wondering at him, as he had beene a monster; till Powhatan and his trayne had put themselues in their greatest braueries. Before a fire vpon a seat like a bedsted, he sat couered with a great robe, made of Rarowcun skinnes, and all the tayles hanging by. On either hand did sit a young wench of 16 or 18 yeares, and along on each side the house, two rowes of men, and behind them as many women, with all their heads and shoulders painted red: many of their heads bedecked with the white downe of Birds; but every one with something: and a great chayne of white beads about their necks.

At his entrance before the King, all the people gaue a great shout. The Queene of Appamatuck was appointed to bring him water to wash his hands, and another brought him a bunch of feathers, in stead of a Towell to dry them: hauing feasted him after their best barbarous manner they could, a long consultation was held but the conclusion was, two great stones were brought before Powhatan: then as many as could layd hands on him, dragged him to them, and thereon laid his head, and being ready with their clubs, to beate out his braines, Pocahontas the Kings dearest daughter, when no intreaty could preuaile, got his head in her armes, and laid her owne vpon his to saue him from death: whereat the Emperour was contented he should liue to make him hatchets, and her bells, beads, and copper: for they thought him aswell of all occupations as themselues. For the King himselfe will make his owne robes, shooes, bowes, arrowes, pots; plant, hunt, or doe any thing so well as the rest.

> *They say he bore a pleasant shew,*
> *But sure his heart was sad.*
> *For who can pleasant be, and rest,*
> *That liues in feare and dread:*

And having life suspected, doth
It still suspected lead.

Two dayes after, Powhatan having disguised himselfe in the most fearefullest manner he could, caused Captain Smith to be brought forth to a great house in the woods, and there vpon a mat by the fire to be left alone. Not long after from behinde a mat that divided the house, was made the most dolefullest noyse he ever heard; then Powhatan more like a devill then a man, with some two hundred more as blacke as himselfe, came vnto him and told him now they were friends, and presently he should goe to Iames towne, to send him two great gunnes, and a gryndstone, for which he would giue him the Country of Capahowosick, and for ever esteeme him as his sonne Nantaquoud.

So to Iames towne with 12 guides Powhatan sent him. That night they quartered in the woods, he still expecting (as he had done all this long time of his imprisonment) every houre to be put to one death or other: for all their feasting. But almightie God (by his divine providence) had mollified the hearts of those sterne Barbarians with compassion. The next morning betimes they came to the Fort, where Smith having vsed the Salvages with what kindnesse he could, he shewed Rawhunt, Powhatans trusty servant, two demi-Culverings and a millstone to carry Powhatan: they found them somewhat too heavie; but when they did see him discharge them, being loaded with stones, among the boughs of a great tree loaded with Isickles, the yce and branches came so tumbling downe, that the poore Salvages ran away halfe dead with feare. But at last we regained some conference with them, and gaue them such toyes; and sent to Powhatan, his women, and children such presents, as gaue them in generall full content.

APPENDIX B

Captain John Smith, from A True Relation
London, 1608

Arriving at [Werowocómoco] their Emperour proudly lying upon a Bedstead a foote high, vpon tenne or twelue Mattes, richly hung with manie Chaynes of great Pearles about his necke, and couered with a great Couering of Rahaughcums. At [his] heade sat a woman, at his feete another; on each side sitting vppon a Matte vppon the ground, were raunged his chiefe men on each side the fire, tenne in a ranke, and behinde them as many yong women, each [with] a great Chaine of white Beades ouer their shoulders, their heades painted in redde: and [Powhatan] with such a graue and Maiesticall countenance, as draue me into admiration to see such state in a naked Saluage.

Hee kindly welcomed me with good wordes, and great Platters of sundrie Victuals, assuring mee his friendship, and my libertie within foure days. Hee much delighted in Opechan Comoughs relation of what I had described to him, and oft examined me vpon the same.

Hee asked mee the cause of our coming.

I tolde him being in fight with the Spaniards our enemie, beeing ouerpowred, neare put to retreat, and by extreame weather put to this shore: where landing at Chesipiack, the people shot [at] vs, but at Kequoughtan they kindly vsed vs: we by signes demaunded fresh water, they described vs vp the Riuer was all fresh water: at Paspahegh also they kindly vsed vs: our Pinn[a]sse being leak[i]e, we were inforced to stay to mend her, till Captaine Newport my father came to conduct vs away.

He demaunded why we went further with our Boate. I tolde him, in that I would haue occasion to talke of the backe Sea, that on the other side the maine, where was salt water. My father [i.e., Newport] had a childe slaine, whiche wee supposed Monocan his enemie [had done]: whose death we intended to reuenge.

After good deliberation, hee bagan to describe [to] mee the Countreys beyond the Falles, with many of the rest; confirming what not onely Opechancanoyes, and an Indian which had beene prisoner to Pewhatan had before tolde mee: but some called it fiue dayes, some sixe, some eight, where the sayde water dashed amongest many stones and rockes, each storm; which caused oft tymes the heade of the Riuer to bee brackish. . . .

I requited his discourse (seeing what pride hee had in his great and spacious Dominions, seeing that all hee knewe were vnder his Territories) in describing to him, the territories of Europe, which was subiect to our great King whose subiect I was, the innumerable multitude of his ships, I gaue him to vnderstand the noyse of Trumpets, and terrible manner of fighting [that] were vnder captain Newport my father: whom I intituled the Meworames, which they call the King of all the waters. At his greatnesse, he admired: and not a little feared.

He desired mee [i.e., the English] to forsake Paspahegh [i.e., James-town], and to liue with him vpon his Riuer, a Countrie called Capa Howasicke. Hee promised to giue me Corne, Venison, or what I wanted to feed vs: Hatchets and Copper wee should make him, and none should disturbe vs.

This request I promised to performe: and thus, hauing with all the kindnes hee could deuise, sought to content me, hee sent me home, with 4. men: one that vsually carried my Gowne and Knapsacke after me, two other loded with bread, and one to accompanie me.

APPENDIX C

Letter from John Rolfe to Governor Thomas Dale

When your leisure shall best serve you to pvse theise lynes, I trust in God the begynninge will not strike you into a greater admiracon, then the ende will gyve you good Content. It is a matter of noe small moment, Concerninge myne owne pticular, wch heare I impart vnto you, and wch toucheth me soe nearely as the tendernes of my Salvacon. Howebeit I freely subiect myselfe to yor grave & mature Iudgement, deliberacon, approbacon, and determynacon, assuringe my selfe of yor zealous admonicons & godly Comforts; either pswadinge me to desist, or encouraginge me to psist herein wth a religious feare, & godly Care. ffor wth (from the very instant that this beganne to roote it selfe wthin the secrett bosome of my hart) my dailye & earnest prayers have byn, still are, and over shalbe powred foorth wth a sincere & godly zeale to be directed, ayded and governed in all my thoughts, woords, and deeds, to the glory of God, and for my eternall Consolacon^e to psever wherein I never had more neede, nor (till nowe) coulde ever ymagyne to have byn moved wth the lyke occasion^e But (my Case standinge as it doth) what better wordly refuge can I heere seeke, then to shelter my selfe vnder the safety of yor favourable pteccon? and didd not my Cause pceede from an vnspotted & vndefiled Conscience) I shoulde not dare to offer to your view & approved Iudgement these passions of my

troubled Soule, soe full of feare and tremblinge is hipocrisie & dissimu-
lacon. But knoweinge myne owne innocency, & godly fervor in the
whole prosecucon hereof, I doubt not of yor beninge acceptance and
Clement construction. As for malitious depravors, & turbulent Spiritts,
to whome nothinge is tastefull, but what pleaseth there vnsavory pal-
ate, I passe not for them° beinge well assured (by the often tryall
and provinge my selfe in my holiest meditacons and prayers) that I
ame called herevnto by the spirit of God° and it shalbe sufficient for
me to be protected by yor selfe in all vertuous & pious endeavors. And
for my more happy proceedinge herein my daily oblacons shalbe ever
addressed to bringe to passe soe good effects that yor selfe and all the
worlde maye truely saye, this is ye woorke of God and merveilous
in our eyes.

But to avoide teadious preambles, and to come more neare the matter. ffirst suffer me wth yor patience to sweepe & make cleane the waye
wherein I walke from all suspicons and doubte wch maye lye covered
therein, and faithfully to reveale vnto you what shoulde move me
therevnto.

Lett therefore this my well advised ptestacon, wch here I make
betweene God and my owne Conscience be a sufficient wyttnes, at the
dreadfull day of Iudgement (when the secretts of all mens harts shalbe
opened) to condemne me herin yf my chiefe intent & purpose be not
to stryve with all my power of boddy and mynde in the vndertakinge
of soe waighty a matter (noe waye leade soe farr foorth as mans weak-
nes may pmytt, wth thevnbridled desire of Carnall affection) for the
good of the Plantacon, the honor of or Countrye, for the glorye of
God, for myne owne salvacon, and for the Cnvertinge to the true
knowledge of God and Iesus Christ an vnbeleivinge Creature, namely
Pohahuntas° To whome my hart and best thoughts are and have byn a
longe tyme soe intangled & inthralled in soe intricate a Laborinth that
I was even awearied to vnwynde my selfe thereout. But Almighty
God whoe never faileth his that truely invocate his holy name, hathe
opened the Gate and ledd my be the hande, that I might playnely see
and discerne the safest pathes wherein to treade.

To you therefore (most noble Sr) the Patron and ffather of vs in
this Countrye, doe I vtter the effects of my longe Contynued affection
(wch haue made a mighty warre in my medytacons) and here I doe
truely relate to what issue this dangerous Combatt is come vnto°
wherein I have not onely examyned, but throughly tryed & pared
my thoughts even to the Quicke. before I coulde fynde and fitt wholesome and apt applicacons to Cure soe dangerous an vlcer. I never failed
to offer my dailye and faithfull prayers to God for hys sacred and holye

assistance, I forgatt not to sett before myne eyes the frailtie of man-kynde, his prones to ill, his indulgency of wicked thoughts wth many other impfections, wherein man is daylie insnared, and often tymes overthrowen, and them Compared wth my present estate.

Woe am I ignorant of the heavy displeasure wch Almighty God Conceyved against the Sonnes of Leuie and Israell for marrienge of straunge wyves, nor of the inconvenyences wch maye thereby arrise, wih other the lyke good mocons° wch made me looke aboute warely and with circuspection, into the grounde and principall agitacons wch thus shoulde provoke me to be in love wth one, whose education hath byn rude, her manners barbarous, her generacon Cursed, and soe dis-crepant in all nutriture from my selfe, that often tymes with feare and tremblinge I haue ended my pryvate Controversie wth this, Surely theise are wicked instigations hatched by him whoe seeketh and delighteth in mans distruction. And soe wth fervent prayers to be ever preserved from such diabolicall assaults I have taken some rest. Thus when I haue thought, I have onteyned my peace and Quyetnes⁰ be-holde, an other, but more gratious temptacon hath made breaches into my holiest and strongest meditacons⁰ with which I have byn putt to a newe tryall, in the stricter manner then the former. ffor (besides the many passions and sufferings wch I have daylie, howerly, yea in my sleepe endured even awakeinge me to astonishment, taxinge me with remissnes and Carelessnes refusinge and neglectinge to pforme, the duety of a good Christian, pullinge me by the eare, and cryene why doest not thowe endeavour to make her a Christian; and these haue happened to my greater wonder, even when shee hath byn farthest sepated from me, wch in Comon reason (were it not an vndoubted woorke of god) might breede a forgettfullnes of a farre more woorthy Creature) besides this I saye, the holy Spiritt of God hath often de-maunded of me, why I was Created? if not for transitory pleasures and worldly vanyties, but to labour in the Lords vyneyard there to sowe and plant, to nourishe and encrease the ffruyts thereof, daylie addinge wth the good husband of the Gospell somewhat to the Tallent⁰ that in the ende the ffruyts may be reaped to the Comfort of Laborer in this lyfe, and in the worlde to come, And yf this, as vndoubtedly, This is the service Iesus Christ requyreth of his best servants And woe to him that hath theise Instruments of pietye offered and putt into his hands, and willfully dispise to woorke wth them. Lykewyse addinge heerevnto her greate apparance of love to me, her desyre to be taught and instructed in the knowledge of God⁰ her Capablenes of vnderstand-ing her aptnes and willingnes to receyve any good impression, and also the spirituall besides her owne incytements stirringe me vpp herevnto. What shoulde I doe? shall I be of soe an vntoward a dis-

posicon to refuse to leade the blynde into the right waye? shall I be
soe vnnaturall not to gyve breade to the hungry, or soe vncharitable
not to Cover the naked? shall I dispise to actuate theise pious duetyes
of a Christian? shall the base feare of displeasinge the worlde overpower
and wthholde me from revealinge to man theise spiritual woorkes of
the Lorde, wch in my medytacons and my prayers I have daylie made
knowne vnto him. God forbidd[e] I assuredly trust he hath thus dealt
wth me for my eternall felicitye, for his glory, and I hope soe to be
guyded by his heavenly grace, That in the ende by my faithfull paynes and Christianlyke labour I shall attayne to that blessed
promise pronounced by the holye Prophett Daniell to the righteous,
that bringe many to the true knowledge of God, namely, that they shall
shine lyke the Starres for ever and ever. A sweeter comfort cannott
be to a true Christian nor a greater encouragement for him to labour
all the dayes of his lyfe in the pformance thereof, nor a greater gayne
of Consolacon to be desired at the hower of death, and at the daye of
Iudgement. Agayne for the lawfullnes of marriage. I hope I doe not
farre erre from the meaninge of the holy Apostle, That the vnbeleivinge
husband is sanctified by the beleivinge wyefe, and the vnbeleivinge
wiefe by the beleivinge husband &c. vppon wch place Mr. Calvin in
his Institucons lib. 4. cap. 16[e] Sect[e] 6[e] sayeth, Even as the Children
of the Iewes were called a holy seede, becawse beinge made heires
of the same Covenant wch the Lorde made wth Abraham, they were
different from the Children of the vngodly[e] ffor the same reason even
yett also the Children of Christians are accompted holye, yea although
they be the yssue but of oen parent faithfull, and (as the Prophett
wytnesseth) they differ frome the vncleane seede of Idolatry. And
thus wth my readinge and conference wth honest and religious psones
have I receaved noe small incouragement, besides serena mea con-
scientia, pure from the fylth of impuritye quoe est instar muri ahenei.
If I shoulde sett downe at lardge the pturbacons and godly motions
wch have stroue wthin me in this my godly Conflict. I shoulde but
make a tedious and vnnecessary volume, but I doubt not these shalbe
sufficient both to Certifie you of my true intent, in dischardginge my
duety to God, and to your selfe. To whose gratious providence I
humbly submytt my selfe for his Glorye, your honor our Countryes
good, the benefitt of this Plantacon, and for the Convertinge an ir-
regenerate to regeneracon, which I beesech God to graunte for his
deare sonne Christ Iesus sake.

Nowe if the vulgar sorte, whoe square all mens actions by the
bare rule of theire owne filthines, shall taxe or taunt me in this my
godly labor, Lett them knowe tis not my hungrye appetite to gorge
my selfe with incontinencye, Sure (if I woulde and were soe sensually

inclyned) I might satisfie suche desire, though not wthout a seared Conscience, yet with Christians more pleasinge to the eye and lesse fearefull in the offence vnlawfully Comytted. Nor am I in soe desperate estate that I regarde not what becometh of me, nor am I out of hope but one daye to see my Countrye nor soe voyde of ffriends, nor meane in Birth but there to obtayne a matche to my greate content[e] nor have I ignorantly passed over my hoapes there, or regardlessly seeke to loose the love of my ffriends by takinge this Course. I knowe them all & have not rashely overslipped any. But shall it please God thus to dispose of me (which I earnestly desire to fulfill my ends afore sett downe) I will hartely accept it as a godly taxe appointed me, And I will never cease (god assistinge me) vntill I have accomplished and brought to pfection soe holy a woorke, in wch I will daylie praye God to blesse me to myne and her eternall happines. And thus desireinge noe longer to lyve to enioye the blessings of God, then this my Resolucon doe tende to suche godly endes as are by me before declared, not doubtinge of your gracious acceptance, I take my leave beseechinge Almighty God to rayne downe vppon you such plentiude of his heavenly graces as your harte can wishe and desire. Ans doe I reste

At yor Commaund most willinge
to be desposed.

Jo Rolfe.

APPENDIX D

Smith Epitaph, London

To the living memory of his deceased friend
Captain John Smith,
sometime Governour of Virginia,
and Admiral of New England,
who departed this life the 21st of June 1631.

ACCORDAMUS VINCERE EST VIVERE

Here lyes one conquered that hath conquered Kings.
Subdu'd large Territories, and done things
Which to the World impossible would seem,
But that the Truth is held in more esteem.
Shall I report his former Service done
In honour of his God and Christendom?
How that he did divide from Pagans three
Their Heads and Lives, Types of his Chivalry.
For which great Service in that Climate done,
Brave Sigismundus, King of Hungarion,
Did give him as a Coat of Armes to wear
These Conquered Heads got by his Sword and Spear.
Or shall I tell of his Adventures since
Done in Virginia, that large Continent?
How that he subdu'd Kings unto his Yoke,
And made those Heathen flee, as Wind doth Smoke:
And made their land, being of so large a Station,
An Habitation for our Christian Nation,
Where God is glorify'd, their Wants supply'd;
Which else, for Necessaries must have dy'd.
But what avails his Conquests, now he lyes
Interr'd in Earth, a Prey to Worms and Flyes?
O! May his Soul in sweet Elysium sleep,
Until the Keeper that all Souls doth keep,
Return to Judgment; and that after thence,
With Angels he may have his Recompence.

NOTES,
BIBLIOGRAPHY,
AND INDEX

NOTES

IN MOST INSTANCES, quotations are identified within the text; many of the contemporaries speak for themselves, in their letters, diaries, journals, reports, travel narratives, histories, sermons, or tracts; further information on the source of such citations will be found in the Bibliography, among the Primary Printed Sources. Captain John Smith speaks for himself in no less than nine published works; John Rolfe does so in his *True Relation*, in his two letters to Sir Edwin Sandys, and in his famous letter of intentions addressed to Sir Thomas Dale, as also in his last will and testament. Quotations from Captain Gabriel Archer, Henry Spelman, and Lord De La Warre are from their respective *Relations*, published in the form of pamphlets or as segments of other travel narratives and histories. Other quotations from Lord De La Warre derive from a letter addressed by him to the Earl of Salisbury. When Sir George Percy is quoted, the source is either his *Trewe Relacyon* or his *Observations*, as published at various times by various editors. Captain John Ratcliffe is cited in his letter to the Earl of Salisbury which was published in John Smith's *Travels and Works*, edited by Arber. Quotations from Sir Samuel Argall derive from a letter which appeared in print in *Purchas His Pilgrimes*; quotations from William Strachey derive from either his *Historie of Travell into Virginia Britania* or from his *True Repertory of the Wracke* (published in *Purchas His Pilgrimes*). Quotations from Edward Maria Wingfield and from Ralph Hamor are from their respective *Discourses*; the former was published in Arber's edition of Smith's *Travels and Works*, the latter originally appeared in pamphlet form in London in 1615. From the *Records of the Virginia Company* of London come letters and instructions from the officers of that company. The words of William Symonds and of William Crashaw are taken from their sermons; those of the Reverend Alexander Whitaker, from his *Good Newes from Virginia* and from a letter to Crashaw. Citations from William Stith, Robert Beverley, and William Byrd are from their histories and, in the case of Byrd, from his diaries; those from Richard Hakluyt and Samuel Purchas are from their published works. Citations from John Chamberlain are from his letters, from a collection of his correspondence published in the last decade; those from Thomas Hariot are from his *Briefe and True Report*; those from John White, from his *Journal*.

Prologue

1. Papal Bull of 1493; Treaty of Tordesillas, 1494.
2. Thinking he had come upon Cipango or Cathay, somewhere along the coast of Asia, Columbus misnamed the Caribbean Islands the "Indies"; the West Indies they would remain.
3. English state papers, E. P. Chayney, "International Law Under Queen Elizabeth," *Eng. Hist. Review*, 1905; A. L. Rowse, *The Elizabethans and America*.
4. "The absurdity of gaining possession of a continent by sailing along its coastline was so obvious that some writers facetiously suggested that Europe would have to be conceded to any Indian prince who happened to send a ship to 'discover it.'" Wilcomb E. Washburn, *Dispossessing the Indians*.
5. The Plymouth Company's colony in Maine was planted in an area designated as "North Virginia," defined by the Crown Patent as extending between parallels of 34° and 45° north latitude, from Cape Fear, N. C., roughly speaking, to New Brunswick (not yet so named).
6. "It is a shameful and unblessed thing to take the scum of people and wicked men to be the people with whom you plant. . . ."
7. Louis B. Wright, as quoted by Virginius Dabney in *Jamestown Before the Mayflower*.

Chapter I

1. D. H. Lawrence's phrase.
2. Actually, two Virginia Colonies were specified in the Royal Charter: one, "North Virginia," to occupy the area between the parallels of 38° and 45° north latitude, from the mouth of the yet-to-be discovered Potomac River to the border of the yet-to-be named New Brunswick; the second colony, "South Virginia," to occupy the area between the parallels of 34° and 41° north latitude, from Cape Fear, N.C., to New York Bay, roughly speaking. The overlapping belt—34° to 38°—the territory comprising present-day Pennsylvania, New Jersey, Delaware, Maryland—was open to plantation by either North or South Virginia colonists, subject to certain restrictions.
3. "False orthography" and "broken English" were "small faultes in souldiers," as one of Smith's companions-in-arms would state in the Introduction to the *Map of Virginia*; military men, unable "to write learnedly, onlie strive to speake truely, and be understood without an Interpreter."

Chapter II

1. The Algonquin tribe, as distinguished from the Algonkian-speaking peoples, was a small Canadian tribe, among the first of the Indians to ally themselves with the French. Their name was later used to designate other, cognate tribes in the region; dispersed by the Iroquois in the seventeenth century, the Algonquin tribesmen took refuge in Quebec and Ontario, and having been assimilated by the whites, the tribe is, to all intents and purposes, extinct.
2. Each of the five major linguistic stocks has numerous dialects and variations; it is estimated that over five hundred different Indian tongues were spoken on this continent. Among Algonkian-speaking tribes, according to Alden T. Vaughan in his *New England Frontier*, "local dialect differences were as pronounced as are national distinctions within the Romance languages."
3. It was Pope Paul III, in 1537, in his *Bulla Veritas Ipsa*, who declared that "The above mentioned Indians and all other nations (Gentiles) who in the future will come to the knowledge of Christianity, although they live without the faith of the Church, can

freely and lawfully enjoy and live their freedom and their possessions, and they should not be reduced into slavery." (*Dictionnaire de Théologie Catholique*, Tome Vème, Ière Partie)

4. Algonkian-speaking tribes of the Northeast Woodlands were the first Indians to be encountered by the invading whites, the first casualties of English colonization. The Indians of early American song and story are Algonkian-speaking: Longfellow's Hiawatha (an Ojibway culture-hero) as well as Cooper's Uncas—the Mohicans of which he was "The Last"—were natives of the region between the Hudson River and Narragansett Bay. (The name Narragansett is of Algonkian origin, and a reminder that without these Algonkian place names—Connecticut, Massachusetts, Allegheny, Chesapeake, Illinois—the map of the eastern states would be unrecognizable.)

5. By 1655, there was not one Arawak out of 60,000 left alive on the island of Jamaica; the population of Hispaniola was reduced from 300,000 to 100,000; the Bahamas were to be totally depopulated.

6. Strachey is the only contemporary to give her clan name as Amonute, all others giving it in some form of Matoax or Matoaka. Strachey, in interpreting the name Pocahontas as "Little-wanton," is apparently using the word "wanton" not in the usual sense of licentious or abandoned, but in the other, less commonly used meaning of "a playful or frolicsome child or animal," as the Webster's Unabridged Dictionary gives it, much in the same sense as the Chippewan adjective, "playful, sportive, frolicsome," etc. (the Chippewan language being a form of Algonkian still in use today). The Middle English word was *wantowen*, from *wan* (lacking) + *towen* (the past participle of the Old English verb *tee*, to discipline, train), thus literally, lacking in discipline or training, undisciplined, untrained.

7. Little is known, specifically, of Pocahontas's childhood and girlhood, but there is a great store of general knowledge on the subjects of child care, religious and domestic training, and upbringing as practiced by American Indians. There is some knowledge on these scores regarding the Northeast Woodland tribes, much more regarding the Plains Indians and the western tribes. Whereas tribal traditions varied widely across the continent, still the similarities were more pronounced than the diversities.

8. Thomas Hariot, *A Briefe and True Report of the New Found Land of Virginia*.

9. Robert Beverley, *The History and Present State of Virginia*, London, 1705.

10. William Strachey, *Historie of Travell into Virginia Britania*.

11. Colonel William Byrd II, *Journey to the Dividing Line*.

12. Some of the sturgeon were as long as "seven foote," according to Captain Gabriel Archer's *A Relatyon of the Discovery of Our River*.

13. The river ritual included "strewing tobacco on the water or the land, honouring the Sunne as their god," as Percy relates.

14. The Occaneechi Path, for example, leading from the banks of the James to the trading town of the Occaneechi Indians, then southwest through the Carolinas into Georgia, was taken up by the white traders and settlers; in time, it developed into a turnpike; and finally into the roadbed of the Southern Railway. The Great Indian War Path and its branches later served white settlers who moved into Virginia from the north and opened up all the valley section of Virginia, spreading through the southwestern part into Kentucky, Tennessee, and West Virginia.

15. *Wampum*, another Algonkian word for another form of currency, was introduced into Virginia from the north in the early seventeenth century: very small cylindrical beads polished and strung together in strands, belts, or sashes. Wampum was made from the white and purple nacre of the thick clam shell (Venus mercenaria), the rarer purple having twice the value of the white. Roanoke beads were the cause of "as much dissention among the Salvages," as Anas Todkill drew the parallel, "as gold and silver among Christians. . . ."

16. The Northeast Woodlands tribes practiced tattooing and scarification—but not body mutilation, as did the tribes of Meso-America, notably the Maya, who practiced cranial deformation and dental mutilation, and induced crossed eyes.

17. M. L. T. Astrov, *The Winged Serpent.*

18. Ibid.

Chapter III

1. The slash-and-burn technique has been used in forest areas all over the world: the tree is slashed, girdled; fire is applied at the base to kill the roots. When the tree dies and falls, it is burned. In the tidewater, the custom was that the clearing wrought by this method was planted in the following year. It was one of the few agricultural duties to devolve upon the men of the tribe.

2. Sassafras, regarded as a specific medicine in the cure of syphilis, was gathered as a commodity for export back to England.

3. This gentleman's name is spelled "Dru Pickhouse" in the list of First Planters published in 1612 in Smith's *Map of Virginia.* Not only is seventeenth-century orthography idiosyncratic (Thomas Gower's name appears elsewhere in the text as Gore; Gosnold varies as Gosnoll; Studley is spelled sometimes Stoodie); the list is, furthermore, incomplete, including only some sixty-seven names out of the complement of one hundred or more.

4. When the Council discovered that "the common store of oyle, vinigar, sack, and aquavite" was all spent "saveing twoe Gallons of each," and that the sack barrel had been "Boonged upp," "reserved for the Communion table," tempers flared. "But, Lord, how they then longed for to supp up that little remnant," Wingfield commented spitefully, "for they had nowe emptied all their owne bottles, and all other that they could smell out. . . ."

Chapter IV

1. "The rivers . . . covered with swans, geese, duckes and cranes" provided Smith with his pretext when the Indians inquired the purpose of his trip upriver.

2. Smith could have read Hariot's *Briefe and True Report of the New Found Land of Virginia,* published in London in 1588, reprinted in Amsterdam by Theodore De Bry in 1590—a landmark in the history of English natural sciences. Or Smith may have had the account direct from Hariot's mouth, prior to Smith's departure for the New World.

3. There was some truth to the reports of cannibalism in the New World, since Verrazano was eaten alive—before his brother's eyes—by ferocious Caribs on what was probably the island of Guadaloupe.

4. Edward Arber, nineteenth-century editor of Smith's works, establishes the date as January 5, 1608.

5. Historians cannot agree, from the descriptions by Smith and other seventeenth-century travelers, whether Werowocómoco was located on the Pamunkey River, as Smith noted, or farther downstream, below the point where the Pamunkey flows into the York. Purtan Bay, on the York, just below West Point, fulfills Smith's specifications on many points, and may be what Smith described as the site of Werowocómoco, although no archeological findings have yet confirmed that site.

6. Since there are no pictures of seventeenth-century Virginia Algonkian towns and dwellings, one must turn to John White's drawings of the North Carolina Algonkian communities of the late sixteenth century. Fortunately, there was a great similarity between the two, according to contemporary witnesses.

7. "Uppon a Bedstead a foote high, upon tenne or twelve Mattes," to quote from Smith's account of this interview in his *True Relation* of 1608. Excerpts from this account as well his *Generall*

Historie of 1624 have been used in this compilation.

8. When Captain Smith mentions "some six weeks" spent "fatting amongst those Salvage Courtiers," it is another example of his memory lapses: he spent only four weeks, not six, among the Pamunkeys and Powhatans in the winter of 1607–8.

9. Authorship of the *True Relation* was orignally attributed to "A Gentleman of the Collony"; later, to "Th. Watson, Gent. . . . one of said collony"; finally, in 1615, there appeared the notice: "Written by Captain Smith, Coronell of the said Collony, to a worshipfull friend of his in England."

10. In line with Adams's anti-Southern bias are his lines in *The Education* about the "cotton planters" from whom, in his judgment, "one could learn nothing but bad temper, bad manners, poker and treason."

11. Eight more guides in this 1624 version than in the account of 1608.

12. Wingfield's *Discourse* gives the date of Smith's return as January 8.

13. "Good Master Hunt our Preacher" aroused a special sympathy among the men: he had "lost all his Library, and all he had but the cloathes on his backe: yet none never heard him repine at the losse." His name appeared on a casualty list in the summer of 1608.

14. Publishing in Frankfurt, de Bry made engravings of twenty-three John White drawings and forty-three copperplates of sketches by the French artist, Jacques Le Moyne, artist for the 1564 Florida expedition under Laudonnière. DeBry's works were issued in four languages—Latin, German, English, and French. His first volume, on Virginia, appeared in 1590; the second, on Florida, in 1591.

15. Smith elsewhere describes *pocones* as "a small roote that groweth in the mountains . . . which being dryed and beate in powder . . . turneth red." The oil was usually bear oil, usually rancid, used to keep off the vermin that infested the Indians' dwellings.

16. Robert Beverley, speaking of the Virginia Indian women as he knew them at the close of the seventeenth century, observed that he "never heard of Child any of them had before Marriage, and the Indians themselves disown any such custom."

Chapter V

1. William Strachey, *Historie of Travell into Virginia Britania.* Strachey was a member of a London green-room coterie that included Marlowe, Ben Jonson, and probably Shakespeare. On his use of the descriptive *wanton*, see Note 6, Chapter II.

2. John Smith's *Accidence for Young Seamen; Or, Their Pathway to Experience*, published in 1626, furnishes further information on the status of ship's boys: "But the Boyes, the Boteswaine is to see every Munday at the chist to say their Compasse; which done, they are to have a quarter of a can [presumably of beer] and a basket of bread." The ship's boys shared in the profits of the voyage to the extent of "a single share" compared to the sailor's "two or one and a halfe" shares.

3. In *A True Discourse of the Present State of Virginia* (London, 1615), Ralph Hamor notes of a Powhatan maiden he encountered that she was "not full 12 yeares olde and therefore not marrigeable."

4. Further confusion may well have emanated from the language barrier: the Powhatan vocabulary lacked specific words for numerals between ten and twenty; above ten, counting was by tens. Thus it would have been impossible to state Pocahontas's age precisely.

5. Dogs were the only animals domesticated by the North American Indians prior to 1492.

6. With Martin's departure, Smith inherited the services of Martin's batman, Anas Todkill, whose name appears as one of the chroniclers of *The Generall Historie.*

7. Likewise by courtesy of Captain Nelson, Smith sent a letter and a sketch map to his friend Henry Hudson, an English navigator and pilot in the service of the Dutch East India Company, information put to use by Hudson in his discovery in 1609 of the Bay and River that would bear his name.

8. "The Easterne Shore" is another place name of Smith's that stuck, one of the few that did.

9. Sending an expedition into the wilderness so ill equipped as to lack fishing nets and lines is another example of the colony's organizational ineptitude.

10. Smith's recovery was made with "the helpe of a precious oile, Doctour Russel applyed."

11. Some small brass crosses were also affixed to tree trunks, although none has ever been turned up, despite diligent research in that area.

12. Mistress Forrest was apparently the wife of Thomas Forrest, whose name is listed among the "Gentlemen" of the Second Supply. The maid's name of Burras is probably a variation of the name Burroughs.

13. Most of the musical instruments used by the Indians were percussive; foremost among them was the drum, with its repetitive, insistent, hypnotic thud, probably the first of all musical instruments to come to the hand of man. The two types most commonly in use by the Indians were the double-headed drum and the water-drum, the latter made by lashing a deerskin over the top of an earthen pot half-filled with water. Some drums were held in the hand and beaten with a short stick, others were large round drums that rested on the ground or were suspended from sticks, or supported by the chanters. Drums were audible across great distances and were used for transmitting signals or messages. The drums of the early seventeenth century (thus of the Powhatan tribes) were made of a wooden platter covered with a tightly drawn skin. Beverley remarks of the Virginia Indians, as he knew them in the late seventeenth century, "Their musical instruments are chiefly drums and rattles:

Their drums are made of a skin stretched over an earthen pot half full of water." The rattle may have been as ancient an instrument as the drum: the Indians made them of gourds, pumpkins, or turtle-shells, filled with stones or pebbles; the stroke was firm and strong, with the emphasis on the first note, as is the Indian way. There were some few wind instruments in use: the crude bone or wooden flute, the eagle-bone whistle, and the giant conch-shell, which gave off an eerie hoot. The flageolet, precursor of the modern flute, was another of the old instruments. It was found not only in Virginia but over much of the Southeast. Smith describes the flute in use by Powhatans in 1607: "For their musicke they use a thicke cane, on which they pipe as on a recorder"; and Percy speaks of "a flute made of a reed."

Twentieth-century music composition has prepared the modern ear for the lack of rhythm and melody that characterized Indian music, distressing the ear of the listener in earlier centuries. Even to the modern ear, however, there is a monotony in Indian music, the same few notes repeated endlessly without dramatic variation. The songs are sometimes recitative; otherwise, words are generally few, songs often consisting mainly of nonsense syllables.

14. Other early travelers in Virginia said that the masks on the painted posts represented gods.

15. Smith's *Map of Virginia* (1612) carried the first account of the entertainment offered him and his party at Werowocómoco in October, 1608; the account carried in his *Generall Historie* (1624) differs very little from the earlier version.

16. Ribaldries came naturally to the Indian women's tongues. William Strachey reports on "their *errotica* [sic] *carmina*, or amorous dittyes in their language, some numerous and some not, which they will sing tunable ynough." And William Clark (in *The Journals of Lewis and Clark*) makes reference to the women's ribaldry, "as almost too general to be called obscene." Robert Beverley commented on the freedom

"they [the Indian women] take in conversation," although his main criticism was for "the uncharitable Christians" who interpret it as "Criminal, upon no other ground, than the guilt of their own Consciences."

17. The roasting ears were what the English insisted on calling "green." Fortunately for agricultural history, Robert Beverley made note of the dates for planting and harvesting of the four varieties of corn on his tidewater plantation toward the close of the seventeenth century. There were four varieties of corn growing in that region when he wrote: two early and two late crops. The small corn of the popcorn variety grew only three or four feet high and was the earliest to ripen, yielding two crops in a season. The second variety was the flint or hominy corn with its large, smooth, multicolored grains—yellow, red, blue, and white. The third variety, dent or flour corn, was known as "she corn." In Virginia, the planting began in April and continued until the middle of June, but the major planting came in May. The April planting was harvested in August; the May crop, in September; the June planting was ready for harvesting in October.

18. Whereas throughout the seventeenth and eighteenth centuries, the Indians stood condemned by the Puritans for sexual permissiveness, it became the fashion in the 1920s—beginning with William Carlos Williams's In the American Grain—to exalt the Indians' sensual élan and to repudiate the repressive Puritan ethic.

Among the Iroquois, sex was used in a surprisingly sophisticated therapeutic sense, on the theory that frustration of desire was the root of all evil. Basing their diagnosis on the patient's dream, the Huron priests—in treatment of certain psychosomatic disorders—prescribed ritual gratification of sexual desires (such as the Huron Andacwandat feast, the culmination of which was a mating of the men with girls).

A similar therapeutic use of sex is implied by David Garnett in his novel Pocahontas, where he suggests that the woman's role as torturer was a calculated one, to the purpose of sexual stimulation, the ensuing orgy serving as catharsis for the passions aroused by the torture.

19. Subsequently, and perhaps not surprisingly, both young Collier and Edward Brinton agreed to stay with the Indians—Brinton as fowler to Powhatan, Collier as interpreter at Warraskoyak.

20. Shakespeare, through Prospero, voiced the Anglo-Saxon horror of miscegenation. Hariot made a point of the continence of the English on the Raleigh expedition to the Carolinas: "They noted also we had no women, nor cared for any of theirs. . . ." The English were more reticent than the Latins (the French, Spanish, Italians) on the subject of interracial sex. The Spaniards' lurid and complex relations with aboriginal women in South and Central America and the Caribbean created the mishmash of mestizos, castizos, and the innumerable other degrees of mixed blood that have become the pattern of the southern half of the Western Hemisphere. The French, in the seventeenth century, tried but failed to promote intermarriage in Canada.

Captain Smith, in accordance with Virginia Company policy, was generally evasive about interracial sexual relations. Only an occasional hint escapes him, as that of a sojourn in a Pamunkey village —the succinct notation, "This day we spent in trading, dancing, much mirth." Since it is unlikely that the Englishmen danced with each other or with the Indian men, the inference must be that fraternization did take place between white colonists and red tribeswomen, and proved so agreeable as to be continued through the next day: "the afternoon was spent in playing, dauncing, and delight." Puritan New England, of course, sternly censured and harshly punished interracial sexual offenses or indiscretions. A familiar story in the annals of early Massachusetts is that of Thomas Morton, who was arrested by Captain Miles Standish, stocked, and finally shipped back to England, his goods confiscated, his house "burnt downe to the ground" as the scene of revelry with Indian women who had been invited there "for dancing and frisking togither . . . and worse practices. . . ." If intermarriage was not specifically proscribed by the New England Colony's legal code, it was clearly discouraged: from the date of the founding of the colony in 1620 until as late as the year 1676, the records show no marriage between white and red.

Chapter VI

1. The ship had to sail down the James, through the Chesapeake, and up the York-Pamunkey to reach Werowocómoco. By overland trail, it was a matter of only fifteen miles or so.

2. Archeologists have not yet abandoned hope of turning up that copper crown in the debris of Virginia excavations.

3. The Indians showed an aversion to kneeling. The suppliant posture did not come naturally to them; to their view, it was one of the least attractive elements in the Christian ritual.

4. Tradition has it that the American Indian mantle at Oxford is the one given by Powhatan to Captain Newport at the time of Powhatan's coronation. Measuring 7'8" x 4'11", it is made of four pieces of tanned buckskin embroidered in shell beads in a design depicting the standing figure of a man flanked by two strange beasts; roundels of shell arranged in rough symmetry decorate the edges and fill the space between. This mantle came to the Ashmolean as one item of a collection that had belonged to John Tradescant, a world traveler (like his friend Captain John Smith) as well as a collector of books and curiosities.

The so-called Powhatan Mantle has been positively identified as a Virginia Indian artifact dating from the early seventeenth century. Another item listed in the Tradescant catalogue as "a Matchcoat of Virginia made of raccoon-skins" is missing from the collection at the Ashmolean, but may just as well have been the mantle given by Powhatan to Newport.

5. Smith's *Relation* was expanded and published in 1612 under the title *A Map of Virginia*. . . . The sketch map was so accurate and so detailed that the engraving made by William Hole in 1612 would be borrowed to illustrate every major geographical work for the rest of the seventeenth century, would be reprinted as late as 1873 in a work dealing with a Maryland-Virginia boundary problem. Hole, possibly England's premier engraver at that time, used two illustrations to decorate Smith's *Map of Virginia*: one of Powhatan, seated in state; one of a Susquehannock warrior.

6. The gentle Reverend Hunt had died, as noted, in the late spring or early summer of 1608.

7. Captain Smith describes his force as consisting of "Eight men" in the 1612 *Map of Virginia*; the force has increased to "eighteene" by 1624 in his *Generall Historie*.

8. Robert Beverley wrote that, as late as the late 1600s, the hunters in Virginia "carry their great Dogs out with them, because Wolves, Bears, Panthers, Wild-Cats, and all other Beasts of Prey, are abroad in the night."

9. The matchlock musket, which preceded the flintlock and the wheel-lock, was a clumsy weapon to handle: the loading procedure was complicated, and a lighted cord or match was required to set off the charge.

10. "Counting coup" as it came to be called in the jargon of the Plains Indians, was a public recital of such exploits, an enumeration of the "coups" made by the warrior in battle. Erich Fromm, in his *Anatomy of Human Destructiveness*, minimizes the American Indian's instincts for destruction of other cultures, clears him of the intent to destroy or enslave, interpreting war-party raids as "expressions of adventurousness and the wish to have trophies and be admired" rather than "socially lethal" (the latter being anthropologist Ruth Benedict's term).

11. Only the *Generall Historie* mentions Pocahontas as the agent of Wiffin's delivery; the *True Relation* contains no reference to her in connection with Wiffin's mission.

12. Smith showed a charity for which he was criticized in some quarters: "Those temporizing proceedings to some may seeme too charitable," he wrote, "to others not pleasing that we washed not the ground with their blouds, nor shewed such strange inventions in mangling, murdering, ransacking, and destroying as did the Spanyards."

13. As Thomas Carlton makes clear in his Complimentary Verses printed in the Introduction to Smith's *Description of New England*, Smith eschewed profanity, neither drank nor smoked nor gambled, lending credibility to the theory that Smith was a Puritan.

14. The Reverend Alexander Whitaker, *Good Newes from Virginia*, London, 1613.

15. The rats were not indigenous to the New World, but imported from the Old, skittering ashore over the mooring cables from the English ships. The other livestock had thrived: "Of three sowes in eighteene moneths increased 60 and od Pigges." Results with poultry had been equally successful: "And neere 500 chickings brought up. . . ."

16. Those "thirtie or fortie" gentlemen who pitched in of their own free will and accord "would doe more in a day then 100 of the rest that must be prest to it by compulsion; but twentie good workemen had been better then them all"! It was skilled craftsmen of which the colony stood in need, as Smith well recognized.

17. Nine and a half weeks was fast compared to the eighteen and more required in the first crossing to Virginia by the *Susan Constant* in 1606–7. The new route tested by Argall encouraged belief that the crossing could be made, under ideal weather and sea conditions, in as few as seven weeks.

18. The Third Supply, consisting of seven major ships and two pinnaces (one of which turned back early) represented the largest expedition to be mounted for America until 1630, when the mass migrations to Massachusetts began.

19. Robert Johnson was Deputy-Treasurer of the Virginia Company.

20. In addition to the seven major vessels of the Third Supply, the fleet included several small pinnaces: one had turned back early in the voyage; another, separated from the rest in the storm, finally reached Jamestown in October.

21. The little *Unity* had more than her share of grief: "In the *Unity* were borne two children at Sea, but both died." There were one hundred women among the passengers in the Third Supply.

Chapter VII

1. In another chapter of his *Generall Historie*, Captain Smith made further reference to Pocahontas's neglect of the colony after he left: "and though she had beene many times a preserver of him [Smith] and the whole Colonie, yet" (until 1613) "she was never seene at James towne since his departure" in 1609—a period of four years over which she shunned Jamestown.

2. "Now whether shee was better roasted, boyled or carbonad'd, I know not," the anonymous humorist of the *Generall Historie* report continues, "but of such a dish as powdered wife I never heard of. . . ." President Percy's account of the cannibalism at Jamestown during the Starving Time lacks the grisly humor of the other reporter.

3. Sir Walter Raleigh had been, as usual, overly optimistic in 1602 when he declared, "I shall yet live to see in Virginia an English nation."

4. With Spain as sole adversary, the ever more powerful Indian nations might have found a way to defend the Atlantic coastline against invasion.

5. Sermons were preached from London pulpits and tracts rushed into print by the Virginia Company to cele-

brate the providential act: "If ever the hand of God appeared in action of man, it was heere most evident," according to William Crashaw, the eminent London divine, "for when man had forsaken this businesse, God tooke it in hand." "The finger of God hath been the onely true worker heere," the Reverend Alexander Whitaker recognized as he and his fellow passengers aboard the *Patience* and the *Deliverance* followed the *De La Warre* back to Jamestown.

6. Sir Thomas Gates was named Lieutenant-General; Sir George Sommers, Admiral; Christopher Newport, Vice-Admiral; Sir George Percy, Captain of James Fort.

7. Lord De La Warre was one of the few high-ranking noblemen to go in person to the New World; most confined themselves to financial investments in the colonial enterprise.

8. The "town" of London "was filled with ill reports" about the Virginia colony, according to John Chamberlain, premier letter-writer and newsmonger of the Jacobean age, in a letter dated July 9, 1612. No need for the Spanish Ambassador to "expostulate about our plantation in Virginia," Chamberlain informed his most eminent correspondent, Sir Dudley Carleton, English Ambassador to The Hague, "seeing it is to be feared that that action will fall to the ground of itself. . . . Two or three of the last ships that came thence bring nothing but discomfort. . . . Sir Thomas Gates and Sir Thomas Dale are quite out of heart. . . ." According to the eighteenth-century Virginia historian William Stith, it was "unjust Scandal" whereby Virginia, "one of the finest Countries in British America," acquired its bad name, "of being a mere Hell upon Earth, another *Siberia*."

9. Although the Virginia Company made no objection to the declaration of martial law in the colony, Stith, in his *History of the First Discovery and Settlement of Virginia* (1747), would see it as a violation of the British Constitution, of the English legal code upon which the colony was founded.

10. "All these extreme and cruel tortures he used and inflicted upon them to terrify the rest for [from?] attempting the like," in the words of Sir George Percy.

11. Powhatan is quoted by Captain Hamor, in his *True Discourse*, as saying that this youngest daughter had been "sold" for "two bushels of Rawrenoke"— Roanoke, a medium of exchange like the better known wampum, likewise a shell bead.

12. "Every man doth his best to show his dexteritie, for by their excelling in those qualities, they get their wives," according to Captain Smith's *Map of Virginia*. Smith was often paraphrased, even plagiarized, by Strachey.

13. Earlier the rector of Henrico on the upper James, William Stith was, at the time of his death in 1757, the President of William and Mary College at Williamsburg. His *History of the First Discovery and Settlement of Virginia* was published first in Williamsburg in 1747.

14. "Many of them doubtless perished in the State-house at Jamestown, and other Accidents," Stith said of the documents already missing when he wrote; "others were mangled by Moths and Worms." Others fell prey to "the Flames and Injuries of Time." Sir John Randolph, to whose papers Stith had access, was his uncle.

15. Smith was not one to kiss and tell. If he had loved and left these ladies, he intended no slur on their honor or their virtue: "Yet my comfort is," he wrote in The Epistle Dedicatory of *The Generall Historie*,

that heretofore honorable and vertuous Ladies, and comparable but amongst themselves, have offred me rescue and protection in my greatest dangers: even in forraine parts, I have felt reliefe from that sex. The beauteous Lady Tragabigzanda, when I was a slave to the Turkes, did all she could to secure me. When I overcame the Bashaw of Nalbrits in Tartaria, the charitable Lady Callamata supplied my necessities. In the utmost of many extremities, that blessed Pocahontas, the great Kings daughter of Virginia, oft saved my life. When I escaped the crueltie of Pirats and most furious stormes, a long time alone in a small Boat at Sea, and driven ashore in France, the good Lady Madam Chanoyes, bountifully assisted me.

16. Captain Smith, without family as without home, died in the house of a friend and patron, Sir Samuel Saltonstall, whose family name is well known in American colonial history.

17. The lines are quoted from *The Generall Historie.* Spelman's own narrative, *The Relation of Virginea,* omits any mention of Pocahontas in relation to his escape: "I shifted for myself and gott to the Patomeckes cuntry. With this Kinge Patomecke I lived a year and more at a towne of his called Pasatanzie, untill such time as an worthy gentleman named Capt: Argal arrived." The Captain "gave the Kinge" some "copper" as ransom: "Thus was I sett at libertye and brought into England."

Chapter VIII

1. Stith seems to be in error on this point: Japazaws (Iapassus) was a petty werowance in comparison to his brother, the great chief of the tribe.

2. Argall's "65. leagues," the equivalent of ninety-five statute miles, is a quite accurate computation of the distance from the head of the river at Washington to the Bay of Chesapeake.

3. "Old Jew" was a derogatory term in common use at that epoch, but the association of Jew and Indian was also common at the time. The Indians' being one of the Lost Tribes of Israel was the only possible explanation for the presence of members of the human race on the American continent—an article of faith among the Mormons to this day.

4. Hamor's lengthier account in the *True Discourse* makes the point that Powhatan did not act entirely on his own, autocrat though he was, but that he consulted his council of elders and priests: "He could not without long advise & delibertion with his Councell, resolve upon anything. . . ."

5. One wonders how Pocahontas reconciled Dale's benevolence to her with his brutality to her people, her own kin: his raid, for example, on the town of Appomatock, five miles from Henrico, over which her aunt Opossunoquonuske had ruled until Dale ravaged and appropriated it for the colony in 1611.

6. Pocahontas would have remembered Collier well; he had been, as Captain Smith's page, a witness to the harvest festival in which Pocahontas (presumably) led the thirty dancers. Having survived the perils of the first frightful fifteen years—to become "one of the ancientest Planters" and "Governor of a Towne" —Collier met his death in 1622, while making the rounds of the watch, not by an Indian arrow but by an English musket accidentally discharged.

7. The foreign diplomatic corps in London got wind of the encouraging developments in Virginia as soon as—but no sooner than—John Chamberlain, private citizen though he was. Antonio Foscarini reported to the Doge and to the Senate in Venice on August 9 (O.S. Calendar, July 31), 1613, "A ship has arrived here from Virginia which has caused universal rejoicing by the news of success. It appears that the soldiers of the colony have inflicted a great defeat upon the King of Poitan, and have taken prisoner one of his daughters by reason of which he has offered friendship, peace and the knowledge of some rich gold mines. This he has already done, and vessels are being prepared to strengthen the colonists with new blood" (Calendar of State Papers, Venetian XIII 22 No. 42, London).

8. In time, Jamestown came to be considered primarily a port. It served as seat of government of the colony until 1698, when the Assembly voted to

remove to Middle Plantation which was to become Williamsburg, re-named for King William III.

9. Robert Johnson, in his *Newes from Virginia* in 1612, found Henrico far superior to the port of Jamestown, "a place of high ground, strong and defensible by nature, a good air, wholesome and clear, unlike the marshy seat at Jamestown, with fresh and plenty of water springs, much fair and open grounds from woods, and wood enough at hand."

Henrico was already in ruins when historian William Stith came upon it, little more than a century later: "The Ruins of this Town are still plainly to be traced and distinguished upon the Land of the late Col. William Randolph, of Tuckahoe, just without the Entrance into Farrar's Island. It lay from River to River, upon a Plain of high Land, with very steep and inaccessible Banks. . . . there may still be seen upon the River Bank within the Island, the Ruins of a great Ditch, now overgrown with large and stately Trees. . . ."

10. Whitaker had his Master of Arts degree as well as his Bachelor of Arts from Cambridge. Reverend Crashaw, in the Epistle Dedicatory written for Whitaker's *Good Newes from Virginia*, says that unlike most who went west at this period, Whitaker was neither "in debt nor disgrace . . . rich in possession, and more in possibilitie; of himselfe without any perswasion (but God's and his own heart) did voluntarily leave his warme nest. . . ."

11. The Reverend Whitaker, for his day and time, was astonishingly broadminded in his view of the savages; he even attributed to the Virginia Indians the glimmerings of the light of civilized nature: "they are a very understanding generation, quicke of apprehension, suddaine in their dispatches, subtile in their dealings, exquisite in their inventions, and industrious in their labour."

12. During the antebellum years in Virginia, such "catechetical sessions" were held as frequently on Sunday afternoons as the needs of the parish children—black as well as white—might require.

13. It was "only the displeased Okeus" who had to be "sacryficed unto," thus a dichotomy, a clearcut theological theory of good and evil which should have been readily recognizable to the Christian Strachey.

14. John G. Chapman's oil painting of the Baptism of Pocahontas, commissioned by order of Congress for the Rotunda of the Capitol, shows her in white robes kneeling beside the ornate font, on the steps below the white-robed Anglican minister officiating at the ceremony (whether the Reverend Bucke at Jamestown or the Reverend Whitaker at Henrico). The lordly mail-clad figure with baton in hand would be Governor Dale, who presides over the function. A descriptive pamphlet published in 1840 identifies the numerous figures in the scene: John Rolfe, fiancé of the celebrated Indian convert, stands immediately behind her, and grouped behind him are to be discerned Sir George Percy, Captain Argall, Henry Spelman, and Richard Wiffin. Pocahontas's brother, Nantequas, is in attendance, as is a sister of Pocahontas's, with a child in her arms.

The pamphlet describes Pocahontas's garb as "a snowy mantle of swans' skins falling from her shoulders tipped with a gay plumage that still may be be seen among the thickets of Jamestown." The Indian convert is "both in mind and person one of the choicest models the hand of nature ever formed. To the timidity of a spotless virgin she joined a sagacity of mind, firmness of spirit and an adventurous daring. She deserves the dignity of a historical character. Though a simple Indian maid, her life and actions are closely associated with events which in their consequences have assumed a magnitude that fully entitles her to be placed among those who exercised an extensive influence in the destinies of states and the course of human events. She was therefore deemed fit subject for a National Picture painted by order of Congress to commemorate the history and actions of our ancestors."

Chapter IX

1. Secretary William Strachey is listed in Alexander Brown's *First Republic* as a fourth witness to the christening of Bermuda Rolfe.

2. *Nicotiana rustica* was not a natural growth of North America, north of Mexico, but probably came—like corn—to the coastal tribes of North America from Mexico and Central America (Yucatán and Tabasco), where it had been for centuries a part of the agricultural economy. By the time the white men reached these shores, it was growing in North America, east and immediately west of the Mississippi River, and in lower eastern Canada. West of the Mississippi, other species of *Nicotiana* were found in a wild state or under cultivation. The Indians along the eastern seaboard added such substances as dogwood bark, sumac leaves, pungent herbs, and oils as binder to their blend of tobacco (for which the Algonkian term was *kinnickinnick*, "that which is mixed"), the formula for this blended tobacco varying from tribe to tribe.

3. Linnaeus estimated over 40,000 tobacco seeds to the pod, 300,000 to 400,000 seeds to the ounce, the surface of the earth insufficient to contain all the plants if all the seeds were to mature at once. Robert Harcourt, in his *Relation of a Voyage to Guiana*, 1613, held that tobacco would "bring as great a benefit and profit to the undertakers as ever the Spaniards gained by the best and richest silver-mine in all their Indies."

4. Taking the Scriptures as an absolute rule of life, the Puritans wished to remodel the laws of England upon the code delivered by Moses to the Israelites.

5. Philip Young, "The Mother of Us All: Pocahontas Reconsidered," *Kenyon Review* XXIV, 1962.

Chapter X

1. Beverley may have been in error, too, in placing the baptism after the marriage ceremony: "Pocahontas, who upon the Marriage, was Christen'd, and call'd Rebecka. . . ."

2. The piedmont tribes, Monacans along the upper James and Manahoacs along the upper Rappahannock, have long been designated as Siouan-speaking, although recent study casts doubt on this identification of their language group. By the time the fur trade in the west became important, the piedmont tribes no longer held sway there.

3. A little later, tobacco would become a monoculture in Maryland and Carolina, as well, although to a lesser degree than in Virginia.

4. Alexander Brown, in *The First Republic in America*, thus quotes an unidentified seventeenth-century writer. There is more to the tradition: By widespread Algonkian legend, corn and beans and tobacco had a common origin, gifts of the clean-limbed Daughter of Manitou (the Algonkian name for the Great Spirit): a party of hunters surprising her in slumber in a remote valley, watched awe-struck as she opened her eyes and directed them by signs to return the following summer. Upon their return to the valley, they found corn sprouting where the reclining goddess's right hand had touched the earth, beans growing in the soil touched by her other hand, and tobacco burgeoning on the spot where her bare buttocks had rested.

5. It was not until later that Virginia tobacco growers developed the practice of planting in specially prepared seedbeds, later transplanting the seedlings to the field.

6. Botanists recognize six varieties each of *N. rustica* and *N. tabacum*, although some consider those of *N. tabacum* to be subspecies rather than varieties.

7. Like "Pepper dust" was Jacques Cartier's description of a pipe he smoked during an expedition to Canada in 1535–36. The native *N. rustica* had a higher nicotine content than the imported species.

Chapter XI

1. Although most of the early houses at Jamestown and Henrico were timber-framed, there were part-brick structures there as early as 1611; buildings called "half-and-half"—the downstairs brick, the upstairs timber-framed—were common, a medieval English type of construction. President Wingfield mentions "ould Short, the bricklayer" as a member of the colony as early as 1607.

2. Rolfe, in addressing his report to the attention of The King's Most Sacred Ma'tie, would not forget to include a direct, personal appeal to the Crown to reduce the tobacco tax on the several thousand pounds of Virginia leaf being exported annually from Virginia to England.

3. The open platform or "lattice-work head" in the forepeak or prow of the vessel was used by women as well as men, no doubt, since no other facility was available. Sanitation fell to "The Lyer" whose "onely" task in the words of Captain Smith, was to make lavish use of lye "to keepe cleane the beake head and chaines," the chains being those of the pumps which ran from keelson to spar deck to bring up the foul bilge-water that accumulated in the bowels of the ship. What happened was that such slops (food waste as well as human) as did not go overboard, as instructed, went into the ballast (the deposit of sand, stone, and shingle that filled whatever hold space was not taken up by cargo). The pumps could never succeed in pumping up all the bilge-water that accumulated in the course of a long voyage. Such "pestilential funkes," such "foul stinkes" were emitted after weeks at sea that the only recourse was to "rummage the ship"—to heave overboard all the polluted ballast, to scrape out the holds, to spray with vinegar, and reload with fresh stone.

4. By Tomakin's reckoning, the *Treasurer*'s eastbound time of forty to fifty days was lengthened into eighty or a hundred, since he construed day and night as two separate units of time. Or so

the Reverend Samuel Purchas would quote him: "reckoning each night (when hee expected they should have anchored by the shoare) another day. . . ."

Chapter XII

1. The fabrics available for court costumes were sumptuous: cloth of gold, silver tissue, silk grosgrain, gold and silver chambletts, tuff-taffetas, tinseled taffetas, china silk, naples silk, genoa velvets, "branched saints."

2. The oval band in which both painting and engraving are set contains the inscription: "MATOAKA ALS REBECCA FILIA POTENTISS. PRINC. POWHATANI IMP. VIRGINI"; the age appears below: "Aetatis suae 21. A° 1616."

The caption beneath the engraving bears the words: "Matoaka als Rebecka daughter to the mighty Prince Powhatan Emperour of Attanoughkomouck als virginia converted and baptized in the Christian faith, and wife to the worthy Mr Joh. Rolff." Whereas the engraving gives her husband's name correctly, as it should be, "Mr Joh. Rolff," the legend on the painting contains a glaring error: the subject is described as "Wife to the Worthy Mr Tho. Rolff." Curiously enough, the same error would be repeated in her burial notice. The artist for the engraving did a poor job in the spacing of the words in the inscription in the oval band, but the artist working in oils made a point of correcting that spacing.

Chapter XIII

1. The few Powhatans from among Pocahontas's entourage who managed to survive continued to cost the company money for years to come: "At a Preparative Court" in June, 1621, a motion was made "that some course might be taken that the two Indian maydes might be disposed of to free the

Company of the weeklie charge that they are att for the keeping of them." At a Quarter Court held later that month, relief was sought: "Itt beinge referred to this Courte to dyrect some course for the dispose of two Indian maydes havinge byne a longe time verie chargeable to ye Company itt is now ordered that they shall be furnished and sent to the Summer Ilands whyther they were willinge to goe . . . towards their preferm't in marriage with such as shall accept of them," to the end that "after they were converted and had children, they might be sent to their Countrey and kindred to civilize them." And so it came to pass, according to Captain Smith's *Generall Historie* (1632 edition): "the mariage of one of the Virginia maides was consummated [in Bermuda] with a husband fit for her, attended with more than one hundred guests, and all the dainties for their dinner could be provided. . . ."

2. King James expressed the wish that it would be said of him that he found London made of sticks and left it made of bricks. A few principal thoroughfares, such as Cheapside, were paved with broad, flat stones; other important streets were paved with cobble; beginning in 1614, broad freestones were being used for paving. Moccasined feet may or may not have winced on cobble; barefoot most of the year, the sole of the Indian's foot became so heavily callused as to be impervious to pain.

3. Similar instances of Indian composure in the face of white power display are to be found in nineteenth-century accounts of Indian chiefs being brought from the Plains or far West to Washington expressly to be impressed by the Great White Father in his great White House, who gazed upon the wonders of the capital with the same imperturbability manifested by Uttamatamakin and Pocahontas in London.

4. When flames destroyed the Banqueting House in 1619, Inigo Jones was immediately commissioned by King James to design and supervise construction of a replacement, using the same site and dimensions, this time in stone, a masterpiece of Palladian design, the sole structure of the whole royal complex to have survived the fire of 1698, sole relic of Whitehall standing today.

5. Thomas West, third Baron De La Warre, and his wife, Cecilia, had seven children, five being daughters.

Chapter XIV

1. Master Stockam's *Relation* is printed in Liber 4 of Smith's *Generall Historie.*

Chapter XV

1. There were at least fifty-nine herbal preparations in use by the American Indians, including *coca*, base of cocaine and novacaine; *curare*, a muscle relaxant; *cinchona* bark, source of quinine; *cascara sagrada*, a laxative; *datura*, a pain reliever; and *ephedra*, a nasal remedy—an important legacy to modern medicine from the American aborigine.

2. ". . . the corp(s)es being lapped in skins and mats with their jewels," according to Captain John Smith's description of an "ordinary burial" among the Powhatans. The mummified body of a chieftain or priest was placed in a secret, holy place or temple under guard of priests, but the body of the ordinary tribesman was laid upon a scaffold out of reach of animals to dry, the bones later to be reburied in ossuaries.

3. When Representative Hamilton Fish Jr. announced, as he is quoted by Associated Press on April 23, 1975, that he had "introduced legislation to authorize the Secretary of the Interior to arrange the removal of the remains of Pocahontas from England to the United States," the conclusion must be that either the legislation was introduced without sufficient research on the matter of her remains and last resting place, or that

new information pertaining thereto has recently come to light. The New York Republican Congressman is further quoted as advocating that "American Indians should be recognized and honored as extensively as possible during this bicentennial anniversary observance." To this purpose, the measure he introduced "calls for the building of a memorial at the U. S. burial site of the Indian woman. . . ." The decision as to "where the remains of Pocahontas should be buried in this country" is one Representative Fish would leave to the American Indians.

Congressman G. William White-hurst, introducing a similar resolution on the eve of the Bicentennial celebration, proposed that the Indian princess's burial site be located on the Pamunkey Reservation in her native Tidewater: "It would be a real fine gesture if her bones could be returned to the banks of the James, where she roamed as a little Indian girl," he is quoted as saying by *The New York Times* (November 5, 1975). As a professor of history at Norfolk's Old Dominion College, the Congressman should have known better, should have been aware of the fact that the soil of Gravesend Churchyard had been thoroughly and vainly sifted in 1923 in that very endeavor. The Reverend Colin Pilgrim, Vicar of Gravesend's St. George's Church, in a United Press interview in November, 1975, gently reminds the two Congressmen that "There have been many attempts to find her bones. . . . No one has ever succeeded."

Chapter XVI

1. Virginia Company records give no indication as to whether the stipend paid by the Company to Pocahontas during her lifetime was continued to her widower and child and, if so, whether it was paid to John Rolfe or to Henry Rolfe, in London, in compensation for expenses incurred in the care and education of his nephew. This letter from John Rolfe to Sir Edwin Sandys came to light toward the turn of this century among Virginia Company papers included in the papers of John Ferrar, who was Sir Edwin's deputy throughout the latter's regime as treasurer of the company. The Ferrar papers came as a gift to Magdalene College, Cambridge, from a descendant of Ferrar's.

2. Rolfe's appointment by Yeardley to the Governor's Council partially compensated for his having been displaced from the post of Secretary and Recorder-General to make way for Yeardley's cousin, John Pory.

3. The church in which the first Assembly met was the third to be erected at Jamestown. The first had been the "cruck" church built in 1607; the second, the small timber-framed church built in 1610, in which Rolfe and Pocahontas had been married. The bell-tower and foundations still to be seen in Jamestown today are the remains of the fifth church built there, the Brick Church of 1647.

4. Rolfe, in his more expansive account by letter to Sir Edwin Sandys, establishes the fact that the black freight from the West Indies was acquired by trade rather than outright purchase: "About the latter end of August, a Dutch man of Warr of the burden of a 160 tunes arrived at Point-Comfort, the Commando^{rs} name was Capt. Jope. . . . He brought not anything but 20 and odd Negroes, wch the Governo^r and Cape Marchant bought for victualle (whereof he was in great need as he p^{r}tended) at the best and easyest rate they could." Susan Kingsbury, *Records of the Virginia Company*, vol. III.

5. The original copy of the will has disappeared.

6. The name of his father-in-law was spelled variously, in other contemporary records, as Pierce, Perce, Peirce, Pyers. The seventeen-hundred-acre parcel of land near Mulberry Island was actually left in trust, with his wife Jane owning a life interest, and the remainder interest passing to his daughter Elizabeth.

7. Paul Green, in his essay collection *Dramatic Heritage*, published in 1953, propounded the theory that America

should follow the example of the Greeks, "to dramatize and re-dramatize our heroes —the pioneer figures, the explorers, the statesmen, the builders."

Chapter XVII

1. "But it hath oft amazed me," to quote Smith's paragraph from Book Four of *The Generall Historie*, "to understand how strangely the Salvages hath beene taught the use of our armes, and imploied in hunting and fowling with our fowling peeces; and our men rooting in the ground about Tobacco like Swine. Besides, that the Salvages that doe little but continually exercise their bow and arrowes, should dwell and lie so familiarly amongst our men that practised little but the Spade; being so farre asunder, and in such small parties dispersed, and neither Fort, exercise of armes used, Ordnances mounted, Courts of Guard, nor any preparation or provision to prevent a forraine enemy, much more the Salvages, howsoever. . . ."

2. "No person who encountered Opechancanough," according to James Branch Cabell in his *Ladies and Gentlemen*, "seems ever to have forgotten, while life lasted, that dark statesman who was so far in advance of his era that, as early as 1622, he foresaw the necessity of restricting immigration into this country."

3. The victims of the Massacre of 1622 fell, Captain Smith continues, "mostly by their owne weapons; and not being content with their lives, they [the savages] fell again upon the dead bodies, making as well as they could a fresh murder, defacing, dragging, and mangling their dead carkases into many peeces, and carrying some parts away in derision, with base and brutish triumph." The death toll of the massacre is thought by some historians to have exceeded three hundred and forty-seven. The Virginia Company of London suppressed as much of the bad news as they could, minimized the death toll.

4. Jefferson, like his fellow Virginians Robert Beverley and William Byrd, was pro-Indian in sentiment. While Jefferson accepted the legality of the seizure of Indian lands by the European settlers, he lamented the injustice of the act. Jefferson's *Notes on the State of Virginia* manifest his tremendous interest in the Indians of North America and his desire that they should be studied closely, and express his concern lest Indians become extinct before their languages had been studied. John Adams, Benjamin Franklin, and George Washington, as well as Jefferson, encouraged the collection of Indian word lists as part of an international project in comparative linguistics, but it is Jefferson from whom our science of Indian linguistics primarily descends. It was Jefferson who encouraged Americans to pursue systematically the facts concerning the Indians, Jefferson who, in 1803, suggested the categories of information to be searched out by Lewis and Clark in their exploration of the western country: "The extent and limits of their possessions; Their relation with other tribes or nations; Their Language, traditions and monuments; Their ordinary occupations in agriculture, fishing, hunting, war, etc.; Their food, clothing, and domestic accomadations," to name only a few of Jefferson's directives to the expeditionary force.

Afterword

1. Johan Huizinga, *Homo Ludens*, 1950.

2. Leslie A. Fiedler, *The Return of the Vanishing American*, 1968 (p. 105).

3. Stephen Vincent Benét, *Western Star*, 1943.

4. John Davis wrote several books based on his tour: *The Farmer of New Jersey*, 1800; *Travels of Four Years and a Half in the United States of America*, 1803; *Captain Smith and the Princess Pocahontas*, 1805; *The First Settlers of Virginia*, 1805.

5. William W. Waldron, *Pocahontas, Princess of Virginia*, 1841, in Two Cantos.

6. William W. Waldron, *Pocahontas, Princess of Virginia*, 1841.

7. Philip A. Bruce, *Pocahontas and Other Sonnets*, 1912.

8. Ogden Nash, *I'm a Stranger Here Myself*, 1939.

9. "Bright Stream Between Two Hills" is the translation suggested by Marguerite Stuart Quarles in her pamphlet *Pocahontas*, published in 1939 by the Association for the Preservation of Virginia Antiquities. Among linguists, there is little or no support for that translation.

BIBLIOGRAPHY

Primary Printed Sources

[Archer, Gabriel.] A letter of M. Gabriel Archer, touching the voyage of the fleet of ships, which arrived at Virginia, without Sir Tho. Gates, and Sir George Summers, 1609. In: *Purchas His Pilgrimes*. Reprinted in: John Smith, *Travels and Works*, ed. Edward Arber.

———. Capt. Newport's discoveries, Virginia, May [1607]. A relatyon of the discovery of our river, from James forte into the maine. American Antiquarian Society, *Transactions and Collections*, 4, 1860. The "relatyon" itself is reprinted in Smith's *Travels*.

Argall, Sir Samuel. A letter touching his voyage to Virginia, and actions there, written to Nicholas Hawes, June, 1613. In: *Purchas His Pilgrimes*.

———. The voiage from James Towne to seeke the ile of Bermuda, and missing the same, his putting over toward Sagadahoc and Cape Cod, and so back againe to James Towne, begun the nineteenth of June, 1610. In: *Purchas His Pilgrimes*.

Barbour, Philip L., ed. *The Jamestown Voyages under the First Charter, 1606—1609*. Cambridge, England, 1969.

Beverley, Robert. *The History and Present State of Virginia*. London, 1705, 1722.

Biddle, Nicholas, ed. *The Journals of the Expedition under the Command of Captains Lewis and Clark*. New York, 1962.

Brown, Alexander. *The Genesis of the United States*. Boston, 1890.

Byrd, William. *The Secret Diary of William Byrd of Westover, 1709–1712*, eds. L. B. Wright and Marion Tinling. Richmond, 1941.

———. *William Byrd's Histories of the Dividing Line Betwixt Virginia and North Carolina*, ed. William K. Boyd. Raleigh, N.C., 1929.

Chamberlain, John. *The Chamberlain Letters*, ed. Elizabeth Thomson. London, 1966.

Crashaw, William. *A Sermon Preached in London Before the Right Honourable Lord La Warre, Lord Governour and Captaine Generall of Virginea, and Others of His Majesties Counsell for That Kingdome, and the Rest of the Adventurers in That Plantation . . . Febr. 21, 1609.* London, 1610.

Dale, Sir Thomas. A letter of Sir Thomas Dale . . . from James Towne in Virginia, June 18, 1614. In: *Purchas His Pilgrimes.*

De La Warre, Thomas West, 3rd Lord. *The Relation of the Right Honourable the Lord De La Warre.* London, 1611. Reprinted New York (1868?), London, 1858. In: Tyler, *Narratives of Early Virginia;* Brown, *Genesis of the United States.*

———. Lorde De la Warr to the right honourable . . . the Earl of Salisbury, 1610. In: Brown, *Genesis of the United States.*

Fuller, Thomas. *The Worthies of England.* London, 1662.

Godwin, Francis. *The Man in the Moone.* Reprint, Hereford *Times,* 1959.

Hakluyt, Richard. *The Principal Navigations Voyages Traffiques & Discoveries of the English Nation.* London, 1598–1600. Reprinted Glasgow, 1903–05.

Hamor, Raphe [Ralph]. *A True Discourse of the Present Estate of Virginia . . . till 1614. . . .* London, 1615. Reprinted Richmond, 1957.

Hariot, Thomas. *A Briefe and True Report of the New Found Land of Virginia, 1588.* De Bry ed., 1590, with engravings of John White drawings. Numerous reprints. In: *The New World,* ed. Stefan Lorant, New York, 1946.

James I, King. *A Counter-Blaste to Tobacco.* London, 1604. Reprinted Edinburgh, 1885.

Jefferson, Thomas. *Notes on the State of Virginia.* The Works of Thomas Jefferson, ed. P. L. Ford, 12 vols. New York & London, 1892–99.

Kingsbury, Susan Myra, ed. *The Records of the Virginia Company of London.* Washington, D.C., 1906–35.

Lawson, John. *History of North Carolina.* London, 1714. Reprinted Richmond, ed. Frances L. Harriss, 1937, 1952, 1960.

Lorant, Stephen, ed. *The New World.* New York, 1946.

Moryson, Fynes. *An Itinerary* (first published 1617). Glasgow, 1908.

Percy, George. "Observations Gathered Out of a Discourse of the Plantation of the Southerne Colonie in Virginia by the English, 1606." In: *Purchas His Pilgrimes.* Reprinted in John Smith, *Travels and Works,* ed. Edward Arber.

———. " 'A Trewe Relacyon.' Virginia from 1609–1612," *Tyler's Quarterly,* 3, 1922.

Purchas, Samuel. *Purchas His Pilgrimage . . .* London, 1613.

———. *Hakluytus Posthumus, or Purchas His Pilgrimes.* London, 1624. Reprinted Glasgow, 4 vols. 1905–07.

Quinn, David Beers, ed. *The Roanoke Voyages. 1584–1590*. Cambridge, England, 1955.

Ratcliffe, John. Captain John Ratcliffe Alias Sickelmore. Letter to the Earl of Salisbury, 4 October, 1609. In: John Smith, *Travels and Works*, ed. Edward Arber.

Rolfe, John. Letter to Sir Thomas Dale, appended to Ralph Hamor's *True Discourse*.

————. *A True Relation of the State of Virginia Lefte by Sir Thomas Dale, Knight, in May Last, 1616*. From original manuscript, eds. J. C. Wylie, F. L. Berkeley, Jr., and John M. Jennings. New Haven, 1951.

————. "Letter of John Rolfe [to Edwin Sandys, 8 June], 1617." *Virginia Magazine of History and Biography*, X, 1902.

————."The Will of John Rolfe." *Virginia Magazine of History and Biography*, LVIII, 1950.

Smith, John:

1608. *A True Relation of Such Occurrences and Accidents of Noate as Hath Hapned in Virginia since the First Planting of That Collony . . .*

1612. *A Map of Virginia. With a Description of the Countrey, the Commodities, People, Government and Religion.*

1616. *A Description of New England; or, The Observations, and Discoveries, of Captain John Smith.*

1620. *New Englands Trials.*

1622. *New Englands Trials.* (This edition, 12 pages longer than that of 1620, carries the account into 1622.)

1624. *The Generall History of Virginia, New England, and the Summer Isles . . .*

1626 *An Accidence [for the Sea], or the Pathway to Experience.*

1627. *A Sea-Grammar, with the Plaine Exposition of Smiths Accidence For Young Sea-Men, Enlarged.*

1630. *The True Travels, Adventures, and Observations of Captaine John Smith, in Europe, Asia, Affrica, and America, from Anno Domini 1593 to 1629.*

1631. *Advertisements for the Unexperienced Planters of New England, or Any Where. Or, The Path-way to Experience to Erect a Plantation.*

————. *The Last Will and Testament of Captain John Smith* (1631); with some additional memoranda relating to him (by Charles Deane). Cambridge, Mass., 1867.

PRINCIPAL MODERN EDITIONS OF SMITH'S WORKS:

Works, ed. Edward Arber. The English Scholar's Library, No. 16, Birmingham, 1884.

The Generall Historie of Virginia, New England & the Summer Isles. Together with The True Travels, Adventures and Observations, and a Sea Grammar. 2 vols. Glasgow, 1907.

Travels and Works, ed. Edward Arber. A New Edition, with a Biographical and Critical Introduction by A. G. Bradley, Edinburgh, 1910.

Spelman, Henry. *Relation of Virginea, 1609.* London, 1872. Reprinted in: John Smith. *Travels and Works* (1910 edition), ed. Edward Arber.

Stith, William. *History of the First Discovery and Settlement of Virginia.* Williamsburg, 1747. Reprinted Chapel Hill, N.C., 1912.

Strachey, William. A true repertory of the wracke, and redemption of Sir Thomas Gates, Knight; upon, and from the ilands of the Bermudas; his coming to Virginia, and the estate of that colonie then, and after, under the government of the Lord La Warr, July 15, 1610. In: *Purchas His Pilgrimes.*

————. *The Historie of Travell into Virginia Britania.* 1612. London, eds. Louis B. Wright and Virginia Freund, 1953.

————, ed. *For thé Colony in Virginea Britannia. Lawes Divine, Morall and Martial.* London, 1612.

Symonds, William. *A Sermon Preached at White-Chappel, in the Presence of Many Honourable and Worshipfull, the Adventurers and Planters for Virginia, April 25, 1609.* London, 1609.

Thompson, David. *David Thompson's Narrative, 1784–1812.* Toronto, 1962.

Tyler, Lyon G., ed. *Narratives of Early Virginia, 1606–1625.* New York, 1907.

Weldon, Sir Anthony. *The Court and Character of King James.* London, 1650.

Whitaker, Alexander., *Good Newes from Virginia.* London, 1613. Reprinted New York, 1936.

White, John. Journal, In: *The New World*, ed. Stefan Lorant. New York, 1946.

Wingfield, Edward Maria. *A Discourse of Virginia.* In: John Smith, *Travels and Works,* ed. Edward Arber.

Zinzerling, Justus. Description of England circa 1610 ("Itineris Anglici brevissima delineatio") in guide-book entitled *Itinerarium Galliae . . .* first published at Lyons, 1616, under name of Jodocus Sincerus.

Secondary Works: Books and Articles

The following abbreviations will be found in the entries listed below:

VAC—A series of 23 booklets edited by E. G. Swem, published by The Virginia 350th Anniversary Celebration Corporation, Williamsburg, 1957.

17thC—*17th Century America, Essays in Colonial History,* ed. James Morton Smith. Chapel Hill, N.C., 1959.

VMHB—*Virginia Magazine of History and Biography.*

Abbot, William W. *A Virginia Chronology, 1585–1783.* VAC.

Adams, Henry. "Captaine John Smith." *North American Review,* 104, January, 1867. Reprinted in *The Great Secession Winter of 1860–1861 and Other Essays.* New York, 1958.

Adamson, J. H., and Folland, H. F. *The Shepherd of the Ocean: An Account of Sir Walter Raleigh and His Times.* Boston, 1969.

Akrigg, G. P. V. *Jacobean Pageant.* Cambridge, Mass., 1963.

Ames, Susie M. *Reading, Writing and Arithmetic in Virginia, 1607–1699.* VAC.

Apperson, G. L. *Social History of Smoking.* London, 1914.

Arents, George. "The Seed from Which Virginia Grew." *William & Mary Quarterly* (ser. 2), 19 (1939).

Astrov, M. L. T., ed. *The Winged Serpent, An Anthology of American Indian Prose and Poetry.* New York, 1946.

Babbitt, Irving. *Rousseau and Romanticism.* Boston and New York, 1919.

Barbour, Philip L. *The Three Worlds of Captain John Smith.* Boston, 1964.

———. *Pocahontas and Her World.* Boston, 1970.

Barth, John. *The Sot-Weed Factor.* New York, 1960.

Bemiss, Samuel M. *The Three Charters of the Virginia Company of London.* VAC.

BIBLIOGRAPHY

Benét, Stephen Vincent. *Western Star*. New York, 1943.

Besant, Walter. *London in the Time of the Stuarts*. London, 1903.

Bloomfield, Leonard. *Linguistic Structures of Native America*. New York, 1963.

Boorstin, Daniel J. *The Americans, The Colonial Experience*. New York, 1958.

Bradley, E. T. *Life of Lady Arabella Stuart*. London, 1889.

Bradley, Rose M. *The English Housewife in the 17th and 18th Centuries*. London, 1912.

Brandon, William. *The American Heritage Book of Indians*. New York, 1961.

Brinton, Daniel G. *The Lenape and Their Legends*. Philadelphia, 1885.

Brooks, Jerome E. *Tobacco: Its History Illustrated by the Books, Manuscripts and Engravings in the Library of George Arents Jr*; Bibliographic Notes by Jerome E. Brooks. New York, 1937–1952.

———. *The Mighty Leaf*. Boston, 1952.

Bruce, P. A. *Economic History of Virginia in the Seventeenth Century*. 2 vols. New York, 1896.

———. *Institutional History of Virginia in the Seventeenth Century*. 2 vols. New York, 1910.

Brydon, George MacLaren. *Religious Life of Virginia in the Seventeenth Century*. VAC.

Bushnell, David I., Jr. "Virginia—From Early Records." *American Anthropologist* (new series), 9, 1907.

———. "The Virginia Indians." *American Anthropologist* (new series), 9, 1907.

———. "John White—The First English Artist to Visit America, 1585." VMHB, XXXV, 1927.

Cabell, James Branch. *Ladies and Gentlemen*. New York, 1934.

———. *Let Me Lie*. New York, 1947.

Campbell, Mildred. "Social Origins of Some Early Americans." 17thC.

Carrier, Lyman. *Agriculture in Virginia, 1607–1699*. VAC.

Charlton, John. *The Banqueting House*. London, 1964.

Clark, Alice. *The Working Life of Women in the 17th Century*. New York, 1920.

Cleaveland, Rev. George J. "The Rev. Alexander Whitaker, M. A." *The Virginia Churchman*, LXVI, June, 1957.

Cooke, John Esten. *My Lady Pokahontas*. Boston and New York, 1885.

Cooper, Charles S., and Percival, W. W. *Trees and Shrubs of the British Isles, Native and Acclimatized*. 2 vols. London and New York, 1909.

Crane, Hart. *The Bridge*. New York, 1930.

Craven, Wesley Frank. *The Virginia Company of London, 1606–1624*. VAC.

Croswell, Joseph. *A New World Planted*. Boston, 1802.

Dabney, Virginius. "Jamestown Before the Mayflower." *New York Times Magazine*, 1957.

Davies, Godfrey. *The Early Stuarts, 1603–1660*. Oxford, 1937.

Davis, John. *Travels of Four Years and a Half in the United States of America*. London and New York, 1803.

———. *Captain Smith and Princess Pocahontas*. Philadelphia, 1805.

Deloria, Vine, Jr. *Custer Died for Your Sins, An Indian Manifesto*. New York, 1969.

Dockstader, Frederick J. *Indian Art in Middle America*. New York, 1964.

Dodge, Richard I. *Our Wild Indians*. Hartford, 1883.

Dunn, Richard S. "Seventeenth-century English Historians of America." 17thC.

Eastman, Charles A. *The Soul of the Indian*. Boston and New York, 1911.

Eliade, Mircea. *Mythes, Rêves et Mystères*. Paris, 1957.

Erikson, Erik H. *Childhood and Society*. New York, 1950.

Erlanger, Philippe. *The Age of Courts and Kings, 1558–1715*. London, 1967.

Erskine, John. *Young Love*. New York, 1936.

Evans, Cerinda W. *Some Notes on Shipbuilding and Shipping in Colonial Virginia*. VAC.

Farb, Peter, *Man's Rise to Civilization as Shown by the Indians of North America* . . . New York, 1968.

Farrar, Emmie F. *Old Virginia Houses along the James*. New York, 1957.

Feder, Norman. *American Indian Art*. New York, 1971.

BIBLIOGRAPHY

Fenton, William N. *Songs from the Iroquois Longhouse: Program Notes for an Album of American Indian Music from the Eastern Woodlands. . . .* (from records in the Archives of American Folk Song, the Library of Congress). Pub. No. 3691. A Smithsonian Institution publication. Washington, D. C., 1942.

Fiedler, Leslie A. *The Return of the Vanishing American.* New York, 1968.

Ford, C. S., and Black, F. A. *Patterns of Sexual Behaviour.* New York. 1968.

Foreman, Carolyn T. *Indians Abroad.* Norman, Okla., 1943.

Forman, Henry Chandler. *Virginia Architecture in the Seventeenth Century.* VAC.

Fromm, Erich. *The Anatomy of Human Destructiveness.* New York, 1973.

Garnett, David.. *Pocahontas.* London, 1933.

Garrett, George. *Death of the Fox.* New York, 1971.

Godfrey, Elizabeth. *Home Life under the Stuarts, 1603–1649.* New York, 1903.

Goodwin, Mary F. "Virginia Ever Missionary." *The Virginia Churchman,* LXVI, June, 1957.

Green, Paul. *Dramatic Heritage.* New York, 1953.

———. *The Founders.* New York, 1957.

Grett-James, Norman G. *The Growth of Stuart London.* London, 1935.

Gunther, A. E. *A Guide to Heacham, Its History and Architecture.* Norfolk, England, 1963.

———. *The Rolfe Family Records.* Vols. I and III in one volume, Heacham, Norfolk, and London, 1962.

Gunther, R. T. and A. *The Rolfe Family Records.* Vol. II, Heacham, London, Aylesbury, 1914.

Haberland, Wolfgang. *The Art of North America.* New York, 1964.

Handlin, Oscar. "The Significance of the Seventeenth Century." 17thC.

Harris, John; Orgel, Stephen; and Strong, Roy. *The King's Arcadia: Inigo Jones and the Stuart Court.* London, 1973.

Hatch, Charles E. *The First Seventeen Years, Virginia, 1607–1624.* VAC.

Herndon, Melvin. *Tobacco in Colonial Virginia.* VAC.

Hubbell, Jay B. "The Smith-Pocahontas Story in Literature." VMBH, LXV, 1957.

Hudson, J. Paul. *A Pictorial Booklet on Early Jamestown Commodities and Industries.* VAC.

Hughes, Thomas P. *Medicine in Virginia, 1607–1699.* VAC.

Huizinga, Johan. *Homo Ludens.* Boston, 1955.

Hunt, David. *Parents and Children in History.* New York, 1970.

Jacobs, Wilbur R. *Dispossessing the American Indian.* New York, 1972.

Jennings, John Melville. "A Biographical Sketch" [of John Rolfe]. In: *A True Relation of the State of Virginia Lefte by Sir Thomas Dale, Knight, in May Last, 1616.* From original manuscript in the library of Henry C. Taylor, Esq. Edited by J. C. Wylie, F. L. Berkeley, Jr., and John M. Jennings. New Haven, Conn., 1951.

Jester, Annie Lash. *Domestic Life in Virginia in the Seventeenth Century.* VAC.

Josephy, Alvin M. *The Indian Heritage of America.* New York, 1968.

Jung, C. G. *Memories, Dreams, Reflections.* New York, 1961.

Kent's Encyclopedia of London. London, 1937, 1970.

La Farge, Oliver. *The Changing Indian.* Norman, Okla., 1942.

Lahontan, Louis Armande de Lom d'Arce. *New Voyages to North America,* ed. Reuben G. Thwaites. 2 vols. Chicago, 1905.

Lawrence, D. H. *Studies in Classic American Literature.* New York, 1961.

Lennard, Reginald, ed. *Englishmen at Rest and Play: Some Phases of English Leisure, 1558–1714.* Oxford, 1931.

Lévi-Strauss, Claude. *La Pensée Sauvage.* Paris, 1962.

Lewis, Clifford, M. S. J., and Loomie, Albert, S. J. *The Spanish Jesuit Mission in Virginia, 1570–1572.* Chapel Hill, N.C., 1953.

Lindsay, Vachel. "Our Mother, Pocahontas," from *The Chinese Nightingale and Other Poems.* New York, 1917.

Lossing, Benson, J. *Description of Marriage of Pocahontas* (Key to Henry Brueckner portrait, John McRae engraving). London, 1887.

Lurie, Nancy Oestreich. *Indian Cultural Adjustment to European Civilization.* VAC.

Marambaud, Pierre. *William Byrd of Westover, 1674–1744.* Charlottesville, 1971.

Marriott, Alice, and Rachlin, Carol K., eds. *American Indian Mythology.* New York, 1968.

McCary, Ben C. *Indians in Seventeenth Century Virginia.* VAC.

———. *John Smith's Map of Virginia.* VAC.

———, and Pierce, Roy B. *Bibliography of the Virginia Indians.* Special Publication No. 1. Archaeological Society of Virginia, 1969.

McElwee, William. *The Wisest Fool in Christendom.* London, 1958.

Meade, Bishop William. *Old Churches, Ministers and Families of Virginia.* Philadelphia, 1861.

Meagher, J. C. *The Method and Meaning of Jonson's Masques.* South Bend, Ind., 1966.

Miles, Charles. *Indian and Eskimo Artifacts of North America.* Chicago, 1963.

Miller, Perry. *Errand into the Wilderness.* Cambridge, Mass., 1956.

———. "Religion and Society in Early Literature: The Religious Impulse in the Founding of Virginia." *William and Mary Quarterly* 5, 1948.

Mook, Maurice A. "The Anthropological Position of the Indian Tribes in Tidewater Virginia." *William and Mary Quarterly* 2, No. 1, 1943.

Mooney, James. "The Powhatan Confederacy, Past and Present." *American Anthropologist* (new series), 9, 1907.

Moore, Virginia. "Pocahontas in London." *Hollins Critic,* February, 1968.

Morison, Samuel E. "The Plymouth Colony and Virginia." *Virginia Magazine,* 62, 1954.

———. *The European Discovery of America, The Northern Voyages, A.D. 500–1600.* New York, 1971.

Murray, Henry A. *Myth and Mythmaking.* New York, 1960.

Nash, Ogden. *I'm a Stranger Here Myself.* Boston, 1939.

Neill, Edward D. *History of the Virginia Company of London.* Albany, N.Y., 1869.

Nichols, John. *The Progresses, Processions, and Magnificent Festivities of King James the First.* 4 vols. London, 1828.

Noel Hume, Ivor. "Digging Up Jamestown." *American Heritage,* XIV, April, 1963.

Notestein, Wallace. *The English People on the Eve of Colonization, 1603–1630.* New York, 1954.

————. *Four Worthies: John Chamberlain, Anne Clifford, John Taylor, Oliver Heywood.* London, 1956.

O'Meara, Walter. *Daughters of the Country.* New York, 1968.

Orchard, William C. *The Technique of Porcupine Quill Decoration among the Indians of North America.* New York (Museum of the American Indian, Heye Foundation), 1971.

Orgel, Stephen. *The Jonsonian Masque.* Cambridge, England, 1965.

————, and Strong, Roy. *Inigo Jones, The Theatre of the Stuart Court.* 2 vols., London, 1973.

Pearce, Roy Harvey. *The Savages of America.* Baltimore, 1953, 1965.

Quarles, Marguerite Stuart. *Pocahontas.* Richmond, 1939.

Quinn, David Beers. *England and the Discovery of America, 1481–1620.* New York, 1974.

Reyher, Paul. *Les Masques Anglais.* Paris, 1909.

Reynolds, Myra. *The Learned Lady in England, 1650–1760.* Boston, 1920.

Robertson, Wyndham. *Pocahontas, Alias Matoaka, and Her Descendants.* Richmond, 1887.

Robinson, W. Stitt, Jr., *Mother Earth: Land Grants in Virginia, 1607–1699.* VAC.

Rooth, A. G. "Creation Myths of North American Indians." *Anthropos,* 52, 1957.

Rouse, Park, Jr. *Tidewater Virginia.* New York, 1958.

————, and McCary, Ben C. *Virginia Indians Before and After Jamestown.* Jamestown Foundation.

Rowell, M. K. "Pamunkey Indian Games and Amusements." *Journal of American Folklore,* 56, 1943.

Rowse, A. L. *The Elizabethans and America.* London, 1959.

————. *The Elizabethan Renaissance.* New York, 1971.

Rukeyser, Muriel. *The Traces of Thomas Hariot.* New York, 1970–71.

Sandburg, Carl. "Cool Tombs," from *Cornhuskers.* New York, 1918.

Sanders, R. "William Strachey, The Virginia Colony and Shakespeare." VMHB, LVII, 1949.

Sebeok, Thomas, A., ed. *Current Trends in Linguistics.* The Hague and Paris, 1973.

Severin, Timothy. *The Golden Antilles.* New York, 1970.

Sheppard, William L. *The Princess Pocahontas*. Richmond, 1907.

Shirley, John W. "George Percy at Jamestown, 1607–1612." *Virginia Magazine*, 57, 1947.

Siebert, Frank T., Jr. "Resurrecting Virginia Algonquian from the Dead: The Reconstituted and Historical Phonology of Powhatan." In *Studies in Southeastern Indian Languages*, ed. James M. Crawford. Athens, Ga., 1975.

Sigourney, Mrs. L. H. *Pocahontas and Other Poems*. New York, 1841.

Speck, Frank G. *Chapters on the Ethnology of the Powhatan Tribes of Virginia*. Museum of the American Indian, Heye Foundation. Indian Notes and Monographs, 5, no. 3. New York, 1928.

Steiner, Stan. *The New Indians*. New York, 1969.

Sullivan, Mary. *Court Masques of James I*. New York, 1913.

Summerson, John. *Inigo Jones*. London, 1966.

Sumner, W. G. *Folkways*. Boston, 1906.

Swem, E. G. *Bibliography of Virginia*. 3 vols., Richmond, 1916–19.

———. *Virginia Historical Index*. Roanoke, 1934–36.

———, and Jennings, John M., with collaboration of James A. Servies. *A Selected Bibliography of Virginia, 1607–1699*. Jamestown Foundation.

Tillyard, E. M. W. *The Elizabethan World Picture*. New York, n. d.

Turner, Frederick Jackson. *The Frontier in American History*. New York, 1950.

Underhill, Ruth Murray. *Red Man's America*. Chicago and London, 1953, 1971.

———. *Red Man's Religion*. Chicago and London, 1965, 1972.

Vaughan, Alden T. *New England Frontier, 1620–1675*. Boston, 1965.

Vogel, Virgil J. *This Country Was Ours*. New York, 1972.

Wall, Mary. *Daughter of Virginia Dare*. New York and Washington, D.C., 1908.

Wallace, Anthony F. C. *The Death and Rebirth of the Seneca*. New York, 1970.

Washburn, Wilcomb E. *The Moral and Legal Justifications for Dispossessing the Indians*. VAC.

Waters, Frank. *Book of the Hopi*. New York, 1963.

Wertenbaker, Thomas J. *Patrician and Plebeian in Virginia*. Charlottesville, 1910.

————. *Virginia under the Stuarts*. Princeton, 1914.

————. *The Planters of Colonial Virginia*. Princeton, 1922.

————. *The Government of Virginia in the Seventeenth Century*. VAC.

Wharton, James. *The Bounty of the Chesapeake*. VAC.

Williams, William Carlos. *In the American Grain*. New York, 1939.

Wilson, Violet A. *Society Women of Shakespeare's Time*. London, 1924.

Woodward, Grace. *Pocahontas*. Norman, Okla., 1963.

Wright, Louis B. "Ancestors and Descendants of John Rolfe." VMBH, XXI, 1913.

————. "The 'Gentleman's' Library in Early Virginia." *Huntington Library Quarterly*, I, 1937.

————. *Middle Class Culture in Elizabethan England*. Ithaca, N.Y., 1963.

Young, Philip. "The Mother of Us All: Pocahontas Reconsidered." *Kenyon Review*, XXIV, 1962.

INDEX

A Coniurer.   Their

Their   triumph about him

Their

How they take him prisoner in the Oaze 1609

C: Smith bindeth a salvage to his arme, fighteth with the King of Pamaunkee and all his company, and slew 9 of them.

Mountaynes forest

OULD

VIR   GI
NI
A

Masons bushe   L:D: Lenox rocks
Wildens Oake
Mangoack Rich
Stuard
Cawrwock
Pananaiei
Anadates
Nuffoc   Secota
Setuog
Cotan   Ceals Harbor
Paspanip
Daverfle
Abigails Iles   Rom.
Den Hygon
Salvage Ile   Box   P. Vaughan
Gordens Ile   Ile
Greenevi
Abbo

C: Smith takes the King of Paspahegh prisoner. Aº 1609.

Graven and extracted out of ÿ generall

Idoll   A Preist

C.Smith taketh the King of Pamavnkee prisoner 1608

A description of part of the adventures of Cap: Smith in Virginia.

The Country wee now call Virginia begiuneth at Cape Henry distant from Roanoack 60 miles, where was S.r Walter Raleigh's plantation: and because the people differ very little from them of Powhatan in any thing, I have inserted those figures in this place because of the conveniency.

Ramushonoq
L. Salvage Rocke
Beauchamps playne
Ohanoack
Chawanok flu:
Alice
Catoking   Smith
Maraton   seig:
Mascoming   Segars grove
Chepanu   Chisapeack
riots Ile   Townrows end   Adams Sound
Pasquenock   Wildmaids roade   C. Henry
P. Bacon   Barkly
Arundells Ile

Vincere est viuere

w England, and Somer Iles: by Robert Vaughan.

Printed by James Reeve

King Powhatan comands C. Smith to be slayne, his daughter Pokahontas beggs his life his thankfullness and how he subiected 39 of their kings read: idoli:

CPSIA information can be obtained
at www.ICGtesting.com
Printed in the USA
LVHW041646151221
706294LV00012B/1400

9 780306 806995